Second Track / Citizens' Diplomacy

Praise for

Second Track / Citizens' Diplomacy

"Despite hopes that the 21st century would be the age of maturity and peace, events since September 11, 2001 indicate that many political leaders and non-state actors have been seduced by the power of violence. This book is an excellent antidote to those who think that force is the best or only way of dealing with complex intractable conflicts. It is an excellent guide to the theoretical underpinnings, development and practical uses of Track II diplomacy. These Track II initiatives play critical roles in the management and transformation of complex conflicts. The book provides scholars and practitioners with a rich resource of theoretical and practical examples of ways in which civil society actors can play more central roles in the delicate art of peacebuilding all around the world. I strongly recommend it to anyone seeking more enlightened paths to peace than those currently being pursued in the Middle East and elsewhere."
—**Kevin P. Clements,**
Secretary General, International Alert

"This book makes evident the growing contributions and the potentiality for even greater contributions of non-official exchanges in overcoming destructive conflicts in the contemporary world. The authors are distinguished practitioners and analysts doing significant work in this vital field." —**Louis Kriesberg,**
Syracuse University

"I find this book a valuable resource for those of us teaching, researching and/or working to transform conflicts both in and outside the Western world. It offers powerful conceptual and theoretical frameworks for conflict analysis, as well as an abundance of practical, proven tools for empowering people to deal with complex, protracted conflicts. The authors, an impressive array featuring a welcome mix of top academic scholarship and hands-on experience, incite us to share the challenge of thinking about conflict management within and across different cultural settings." —**Gabrielle Gueron,**
Universidad Central de Venezuela

"In recent years conflicts, especially in the developing world, have resulted in untold suffering of innocent civilians. Teaching and research in conflict analysis, management and prevention is especially needed. This book is a very useful addition to the field, for scholars and practitioners alike. It provides a firm foundation in the theories of conflict resolution, as well as practical approaches to peacemaking and peacebuilding. The contributions are from both scholars and professionals with practical experience, and the book should be a 'must read' for anybody who wants to gain insight into the field or who is interested in its applications to real life situations. I would strongly recommend the book to anyone interested in conflict management." —**Lebohang K. Moleko,**
Ambassador and Permanent Representative of
Lesotho to the United Nations

Second Track / Citizens' Diplomacy

Concepts and Techniques for Conflict Transformation

EDITED BY

JOHN DAVIES
AND
EDWARD (EDY) KAUFMAN

ROWMAN & LITTLEFIELD PUBLISHERS, INC.
Lanham • Boulder • New York • Oxford

ROWMAN & LITTLEFIELD PUBLISHERS, INC.

Published in the United States of America
by Rowman & Littlefield Publishers, Inc.
A Member of the Rowman & Littlefield Publishing Group
4501 Forbes Boulevard, Suite 200, Lanham, Maryland 20706
www.rowmanlittlefield.com

P.O. Box 317, Oxford OX2 9RU, United Kingdom

Copyright © 2002 by Rowman & Littlefield Publishers, Inc.
First paperback edition 2003

British Library Cataloguing in Publication Information Available

The hardback edition of this book was previously cataloged by the Library of Congress as
follows:

Library of Congress Cataloging-in-Publication Data

Second track / citizens' diplomacy : concepts and techniques for conflict transformation /
edited by John Davies and Edward Kaufman
    p. cm.
  Includes bibliographical references and index.
  ISBN 0-8476-9551-4 (alk. paper)
  ISBN 0-8476-9552-2 (pbk. alk. paper)
    1. Pacific settlement of international disputes. 2. Conflict management. 3. Ethnic
conflict. 4. World politics—1989- I. Davies, John, 1948- II. Kaufman, Edy.

JZ6010 .S43 2002
327.1'7—dc21

2001057860

Printed in the United States of America

♻™ The paper used in this publication meets the minimum requirements of American
National Standard for Information Sciences—Permanence of Paper for Printed Library
Materials, ANSI/NISO Z39.48-1992.

Dedication

This book is dedicated to the memory of Edward Azar, who inspired several of the contributors to this volume—as teacher, colleague, and friend—to work in the field of conflict management and peacebuilding. As founder of the Center for International Development and Conflict Management (CIDCM) at the University of Maryland, his commitment to systematic analysis of the causes, dynamics, and management of protracted societal conflicts, and to bringing unofficial representatives of the parties together for constructive dialogue through his "problem-solving forums," was at that time a pioneer's work. Ed dedicated CIDCM to addressing the "needs of nations" through empirical research, theory building, and the practice of second track diplomacy. His recognition of the importance of non-state identity groups, the non-negotiability of human needs, and elucidation particularly of intangible needs for identity and respect, were critical contributions to the understanding of the roots of complex societal conflicts. Many of us have found in his writings and passionate discussions a primary source and inspiration for ideas later expanded and put into practice, as reflected in the pages of this book. His untimely departure a decade ago left a great vacuum at College Park and in the field at large. Let this joint effort be a tribute to his great wisdom, humanity, and deep understanding of the "other" in societal conflict.

Contents

Acknowledgments

The inspiration for this volume came initially at a seminar held in Ed Azar's honor at the University of Maryland's Center for International Development and Conflict Management in 1993, in which several of the current contributors participated. The idea gained momentum as the Center's Partners in Conflict Project has continued to grow, with projects in the Middle East, former Soviet countries, Latin America, South East Asia, and Africa. More recently, the availability of the Center's Certificate Programs in Second and Multi-Track Diplomacy in Washington, D.C. and College Park has led to a demand from professionals, students, and intending practitioners for a text that would provide a balanced introduction to the field, practical guidance in how to put the concepts into practice, and reflect the diversity of opinion among leading scholars and practitioners on issues of current concern.

We are grateful for the support and encouragement of our colleagues at the Center and the University's Department of Government and Politics, including particularly Ernest Wilson, Jonathan Wilkenfeld, and Joe Oppenheimer; and that of our spouses Vicki Davies and Lisa Kaufman who have both put in many hours working with us through the intricate details of translating ideas and drafts into easily readable and properly formatted text. Equally we are indebted to our students and partners around the world who inspire and expand our perspectives on conflict transformation at least as much as we can contribute to theirs. Robert Haddad was instrumental in bringing together the original seminar and proposing an initial concept for the book. Several students and interns have provided critical support as editing staff, including Victor Assal, Matthew Bowker, Philip Brenner, Lusine Dadayan, Tom Davies, Jason Fink, Julia Hancock, Steven Maloney, Reham Nasr, Jennifer Nitkowski, Claudia Sauerborn, and Sarah Vins.

Our deepest gratitude is of course for inspired contributions from the chapter authors, who remain solely responsible with us for the viewpoints expressed and for any errors of form or substance that may have slipped through the editing process.

Second Track / Citizens' Diplomacy: An Overview

John Davies and Edy Kaufman

Since just after the end of the Cold War, the number of states experiencing serious conflict has dropped by almost half.[1] The same drop is apparent if we take into account intensity of conflict, including deaths, dislocations and damage, or if we consider only ethnic or only nationalist conflicts (Gurr and Davies, this volume, figures 2.1 and 2.2). Why hasn't anyone noticed? One answer is that we did not see the drop we expected immediately after the fall of the Berlin Wall in 1989 (not surprisingly, given the instability of transitional regimes—see Gurr and Davies, this volume), and stopped looking. Another is that we tend to focus on current crises, and on the most protracted and deeply entrenched conflicts, while peacemaking efforts, conflict settlements and peace building are overlooked as less newsworthy.

Even so, just those wars still ongoing (often after decades, as in Sudan, Afghanistan or Sri Lanka) are responsible for several millions killed—an estimated 80 percent of them civilians—with roughly 100,000 more deaths per year and over 25 million refugees and other displaced people. Such conflicts impose devastating losses in quality of life, stunt development, destroy the natural and social environment, entrench dependency and remove hope, creating a breeding ground for terrorism, crime and disease, which impact the security of all states and peoples in the international system (see Azar, this volume). These conflicts represent an enormous challenge to our collective capacity for conflict management and sustained development. Yet the successes of the last decade offer an opportunity. To the degree that we can understand the dynamics motivating these conflicts and the strategies through which they can be settled and transformed into sustainable processes of structural reform and social development, perhaps we can contribute to extending the post-Cold War turnaround and to strengthening international consensus on democratic norms for managing conflict based on respect for human needs and minority rights. This is the challenge addressed by the authors in this volume, in the framework of second track, or citizens', diplomacy.

Almost all recent wars involve complex, often protracted conflicts with a nonstate community (usually ethnic or nationalist) as at least one of the parties. Even where two states are involved, as with India and Pakistan, the role of nonstate communities, such as Kashmiri Muslims, is typically pivotal. These ethnic or communal identity groups, mobilized around shared culture, race, religion, language, etc., are not clearly recognized or protected in our state-centric international system. Where there is a perceived imbalance in the distribution of economic, political and social resources (social injustice) that coincides with identity-group boundaries, there is the potential for violent and protracted conflict that will further devastate the communities involved.

These conflicts may be directed toward improved access or distributive justice, or toward greater autonomy or independence; either way, they cannot adequately be managed through a system of diplomacy designed almost entirely to serve the interests of states. When people's sense of self is invested in communities that are seen to be marginalized or threatened by the state (or by rival groups controlling or favored by the state), the issues tend to be emotionally charged and the legitimacy of the other party called into question, precluding collaborative diplomatic work to manage or resolve the conflict constructively. In our increasingly interlinked world, outside parties are called to support one side or the other, often causing the conflict to spill over into neighboring states and new issues, adding to the complexity and intractability of the conflict, as currently in Central Africa and Central Asia.

"Second track" diplomacy has developed in response to the profound challenge that these complex conflicts present to all those working to build a sustainable and just peace. Second track, or "citizens'" diplomacy may be broadly defined as the bringing together of professionals, opinion leaders or other currently or potentially influential individuals from communities in conflict, without official representative status, to work together to understand better the dynamics underlying the conflict and how its transformation from violence (or potential violence) to a collaborative process of peace building and sustainable development might be promoted. It complements "first track" or official diplomacy, opening up opportunities for communication, cross-cultural understanding and joint efforts to explore how the needs of the parties might be addressed when official dialogue is blocked or constrained. It can inject new insights and ideas into the official process, help to humanize the "enemy," reduce tensions and misunderstanding, build capacity in civil society, promote reconciliation and build public support and political will for peacemaking and long-term structural development that will address the needs of all parties.

Equally important, by engaging civil society the second track process can provide a powerful model for the evolution of a democratic political culture. Since wars now impact civilians more than formal militaries, it is fitting that citizen diplomacy empowers those most impacted to participate in the search for peace. It facilitates the emergence of strong normative support for nonviolent conflict management and respect for the needs and human rights of diverse interest groups. In this way, it helps to erase the gap between process and outcome, since the most significant outcome of successful peacemaking, along with short-term relief from violence and oppression, is the long-term emergence of norms and corresponding structures which institutionalize the constructive processes for conflict management at the core of democracy. In contrast, attempts to impose democracy by force set up a contradiction, providing a model that tends to undermine the desired outcome, as currently in Kosovo and parts of Bosnia.

Pioneered from the 1960s by Herbert Kelman, Edward Azar, John McDonald, John Burton, Johan Galtung, Joseph Montville, Harold Saunders and others (see Fisher, this volume), second track diplomacy is increasingly recognized as an essential component in a multilayered diplomatic process aimed at transforming the contentious power dynamics of complex, protracted conflict into processes of constructive engagement and joint problem solving. It promotes an expansion of social capital as needed to move from the logic of mutual hostility and imposed solutions (zero- or negative-sum outcomes) to the integrative logic of peace building as a process of collaboratively addressing human needs, leading to zero- or positive-sum outcomes that encourage buy-in by all parties and development of a self-sustaining democratic culture.

Citizens' diplomacy embraces a positive concept of peace that is more than the mere absence of war; it recognizes that sustainable peace requires social and economic justice, participatory political processes, and environmentally and economically sustainable development supported by appropriate, long-term, endogenously driven structural reforms. A dynamic and just peace implies not only the absence of war but also the systematic reduction of structural violence and militarism that degrades the quality of life and respect for human needs and rights. The field aims, therefore, not merely to contain or manage violent conflict but to prevent or resolve it through addressing its root causes, transforming violent or contentious relations into sustainable working partnerships dealing constructively with those root causes. There is no effort to resolve or eliminate conflict as such, since social conflict (the perceived incompatibility of the interests or aspirations of two groups) is an inevitable feature of social relationships. When properly managed, it can be a powerful motivator for constructive adaptation, reform and development, which is the lifeblood of sustainable peace. Conflict "management," in this constructive sense, is often used interchangeably with conflict "resolution" or "transformation." They convey different emphases in a common attempt to minimize violence and build a sustainable, just peace. Our preference for the term "transformation" is to highlight the shift in perceptions and attitudes which often takes place among those engaged in citizens' diplomacy, empowering them to build working relationships across community lines and actively take responsibility for moving the peace process forward.

This book aims to illuminate the way in which the field of second track diplomacy and interactive conflict transformation (Fisher, this volume) not only seeks to bridge the divide between conflicting parties, between process and outcome, and between justice and peace but also to assist in bridging other critical divides that complicate and often retard the process of conflict transformation. These include the divisions between government and civil society, between elites and grassroots levels within communities, and between different cultural worldviews and assumptions about how to manage conflict and change. We will consider each of these below and also consider the need to help bridge one more gap: that between the conceptual rigor of social science and the pragmatic, applied orientation of practice in the field.

First Track and Second Track Diplomacy

Interest in second track diplomacy has grown with the awareness of the extent to which all states and communities on the planet are profoundly interdependent. Cross-border flows of information, people, goods, money, entertainment, weapons, drugs, pollution and disease link our quality of life ever more closely with those of other peoples and cultures. Interstate and intercommunal relations are multidimensional, involving all sectors of society. They are no longer peripheral matters to be left to diplomatic specialists, particularly when those specialists are trained in a model of interstate relations that focuses almost entirely on state interests rather than those of substate or transstate communities.

First track diplomacy is tied to the interests of states as the primary unit of the international system and the ultimate legitimate vehicle of coercive power, with no formal standing given to other identity groups or private citizens. Ambassador John McDonald (Diamond and McDonald, 1996; McDonald, this volume) describes the culture of the first track diplomatic system as formal and bureaucratic, male dominated, rewarding loyalty, conformity and low-risk behavior in its practitioners. It is oriented toward the application of power to manage short-term crises and to compete against other states for economic and political advantage, with relatively little investment of time and resources in long-term or collaborative international planning. Habits of official secrecy and elitism, internal rivalry, fear that dialogue or negotiation may be perceived as weakness, and frequently inadequate training in conflict-management skills all tend to promote insularity and limit effectiveness in peacemaking and long-term peace building. The role of international organizations (IOs) such as the United Nations (UN) is seen as subsidiary to that of the state; international access to prevent or ameliorate internal wars is proscribed unless by government invitation, even when the government represents only one party to the conflict or is in a state of collapse. The Genocide Convention and a small number of treaty provisions are beginning to modify such absolutist notions of state sovereignty, but the failure to respond to the 1994 Rwanda genocide is a reminder of the continuing strength of state-centric norms.

Nevertheless, the first track diplomatic system has the legitimacy and resources necessary for completing the peacemaking process. A peace agreement must ultimately be negotiated, approved and implemented at the official level. Second track diplomacy is not an alternative but a complementary system that takes advantage of resources and opportunities unavailable at the official level. It can create or build momentum for peace by engaging a broader spectrum of civil society, as needed also to translate any official agreement into a sustainable reality. In contrast to the power politics involved in official diplomacy and predominant in protracted violent conflicts, second track facilitators draw on integrative methods of dispute resolution, emphasizing the joint responsibility of the parties for approaching their problems in a way that respects the interests, needs and values of all. These "interest-based" approaches have been referred to as "alternative" or "appropriate" dispute resolution (ADR), as they provide an alternative to both the power-based and rights-based (judicial) adversarial approaches that dominate first track processes; they can be found in, or adapted to work well in, most cultures. The role of the third party in second track diplomacy is not to impose a settlement but to facilitate movement from an unbalanced state of dependence, or oppression, or from a hostile stalemate, to recognition of interdependence and shared responsibility for addressing needs in an integrative and sustainable manner. It may include dealing with deeper psychological issues, such as mourning, victimhood and forgiveness, that must be addressed before reconciliation between communities in conflict can occur.

Unofficial, facilitated face-to-face dialogue, free of institutional policy constraints, can allow communication, understanding, rehumanization of the enemy, relationship building, and reframing of the conflict as a shared problem to be solved rather than a battle to be won or lost. The approach tends to be transformational, moving from exclusive and competitive power politics to inclusive processes of mutual empowerment dealing with human, social and environmental concerns. It recognizes nonstate identity groups, along with states, as having the power to facilitate satisfaction of human needs. It emphasizes the distinct importance of ongoing relationships between peoples, relationships that are irreducible to strategic policies and crisis-oriented intergovernmental relations.[2]

Second track diplomacy embraces a broad range of practitioners from many fields, including former first track officials, social scientists, psychologists, mediators, lawyers and peace activists. As the concepts, values and practices of the field of conflict transformation mature into a coherent disciplinary framework with its own graduate training and research programs, a professional core of practitioners and scholar-practitioners is beginning to emerge. The multilateralism and broader democratic consensus developing after the Cold War has also allowed many more opportunities for second track involvement and successes, increasing the visibility and legitimacy of the field.

At the same time, it is helpful to place this professional core of second track diplomacy in a larger context. McDonald (this volume) now suggests recognizing not just two but nine tracks, reflecting the idea that all parts of the community, including government, nongovernment organizations (NGOs), business, education, media, religious and funding organizations, as well as activists and other private citizens, all must be involved in the larger enterprise of peace building to make a peace agreement effective and lasting. In this larger view, a core of second track professionals (based mainly in NGOs and university research centers) not only facilitates integrative dialogue and problem solving but also provides a leading and coordinating function for a range of more specialized activities. For example, at the University of Maryland's Center for International Development and Conflict Management (CIDCM), we have helped international businesses find ways of investing in local communities in ways that will reduce the risks of violence and instability that may threaten their own activities in the area; we have developed educational partnerships providing support for collaborative research, exchanges and curriculum development in conflict management and peace building; and we have brought together journalists from opposing parties engaged in protracted violent conflict to look at the evidence for their role in polarizing and inflaming the conflict, and to help them find ways of presenting both sides of the picture through mutual consultation and even joint publications or newsletters.[3]

A key function of second track diplomacy—along with addressing the "horizontal" divisions between parties across multiple sectors, as above—is to address the "vertical" divisions within each community, rooted in the absence of responsive and coordinated relations among top central government or military leaders and middle-level or informal grassroots opinion leaders (see Lederach, 1999). Second track processes will typically engage middle-level, civil society leaders, including academics and NGO professionals, traditional ethnic or religious leaders, national level women's group leaders, or humanitarian and other sectoral leaders from the different communities. New insights or options for moving the peace process forward will then be communicated with top-level leaders (typically ministers or their representatives, and equivalent senior leaders in nonstate communities), and efforts will be made to engage them in dialogue with their own civil society representatives to consider how they might help each other in moving toward settlement or resolution of the conflict, or long-term peace building. Commonly, neither level of leadership recognizes the extent of its interdependence with the other, except perhaps in a crisis situation, when there is no time to build a relationship based on trust (rather than instrumentalist manipulation).

The same is true with grassroots leaders (such as local officials or traditional "influentials," leaders of indigenous NGOs or local women's groups, local guerilla or refugee camp leaders). They tend to be isolated from the other levels and must at some stage be included in vertical dialogue to ensure that ideas and initiatives emerging at each level adequately address the concerns that dominate thinking at other levels. An inability to communicate vertically and to act collaboratively may be exploited by militants on the other side and will certainly undercut community capacity for managing the conflict or building a lasting peace. Therefore, promotion of dialogue across all three levels should be a fundamental part of second track diplomatic efforts.

Bridging Cultural Divides

Typically, separate identity groups locked in complex, protracted conflicts have distinct cultural traditions and perspectives, through which they perceive not only the nature of the conflict and the issues in dispute but also the processes through which conflicts may be appropriately managed or resolved. Often, third-party facilitators, mediators or trainers in conflict management skills will come from yet another (usually Western) culture, with its own assumptions regarding conflicts and how to deal with them. This entails not just a simple issue of translation, or repackaging the same ideas about conflict in different words: culture represents the accumulated, shared knowledge and experience of a people through which meaning is created, situations are perceived and interpreted, and actions are decided on. Conflict, either as a general concept or a specific occurrence, can best be understood as a socially constructed reality, inseparable from the cultural frameworks in which it has emerged (see Lederach, 1995).

The implication for second track facilitators or trainers working cross-culturally is that they will need to develop skills in putting aside their own cultural preconceptions and focusing not so much on prescriptive delivery of expert knowledge as on eliciting from the parties their perceptions of the conflict and of the process through which it might be addressed (Lederach, 1995). This is better done by working with cofacilitators or cotrainers from the communities involved, with whom it has been possible to develop a culturally appropriate framework in advance. However, this does not imply that outside experience is irrelevant: the fact that outside third parties or trainers have been invited in means there is a sense that local capacity for managing conflict may be insufficient, or that a common process acceptable to both/all parties has been elusive, leading the parties to look for ways of enhancing capacity or consensus through exposure to others with experience elsewhere.

As Moore and Woodrow point out in this volume, it can be just as dangerous to romanticize cultures as primally unique and sacred realities that can only be understood or approached in their own terms. Cultures are neither monolithic nor static; they are isolated neither from each other nor from the basic needs, intelligence and environmental features that are common to all human beings. Cultures are living entities and as such are constantly developing and adapting, motivated in large part by the pressure to manage conflict in sustainable ways. Just as integrative approaches to conflict management look for outcomes that address the needs of both parties, Moore and Woodrow point to the value of first looking to identify or develop a process which is comfortable and accessible to both parties, thus advancing shared norms (and hence cultures) of constructive conflict management, rather than compromising or forcing one or both parties into interactions which leave them feeling at a disadvantage.

Davies (chapter 6) examines normative patterns of social reasoning that have been found across many cultures, corresponding to basic strategic options for managing conflict that are understandable to members of any culture if appropriately contextualized. Conflict management processes elicited from one culture need not be difficult to interpret, evaluate, or interface with equivalent or complementary processes from another culture, allowing collaborative work toward identifying, advancing or constructing approaches that work well for both cultures. These findings point to the possibilities for building greater cross-cultural consensus on normative goals and methods for conflict management—including conflict transformation, prevention and related development work—as rooted in the shared dynamics of human intelligence, rather than being imposed through the dominance of any one culture or political/institutional system. For this to happen, the number of practitioners and scholars engaged in research and applied work in conflict management and second track diplomacy, drawing and building on their own (particularly non-Western) cultural frameworks, will need to grow substantially.

Social Science and Professional Practice

While much has been written on interactive conflict resolution and collaborative problem-solving methods, the emphasis has been more on theory or on applications in Western institutional and/or business settings. Relatively little is available to guide prospective practitioners in the application of these methods to the management of complex, protracted violent conflicts across cultural boundaries. The purpose of this volume is to explain the theory, development and current practice of second track diplomacy for such complex conflicts in a manner that will be broadly accessible to both practitioners and students, including those from communities in conflict, for whom it is intended as a resource from which they can draw in beginning their own applied work and teaching programs.

In addition to explaining the theoretical bases for conflict dynamics and management derived from social science research, some chapters draw directly from research findings to illustrate recent insights in the field. However, our intent in this volume is not to focus on the research as such, as this has been done elsewhere, drawing on large-*n* analyses, time-series event-data analyses, laboratory and game-theory work, and case studies of specific conflicts and management initiatives to identify key factors driving or ameliorating conflict. Rather, we are concerned to draw out what can be of immediate use to both beginning and experienced practitioners.

One aspect of research with which all practitioners should be familiar is the evaluation of their own projects. Evaluation presents a dilemma in that research protocols consume scarce time and resources and may be resisted as a distraction from the serious business of peacemaking. Nor is it easy to demonstrate success in preventing violence, given the uniqueness and complexity of each case, or to quantify the transformations that take place in attitudes or relationships. Yet systematic evaluation is increasingly demanded by funders anxious to invest in activities that have demonstrable value in promoting and sustaining peace. Further, it can yield insights which will allow practitioners to learn more systematically from their own as well as others' successes and failures. Field research by practitioners cannot introduce observation protocols or controls that may compromise the effectiveness of their activities or the well-being of participants. Second track dialogue is almost always done in private, in order to encourage honesty and flexibility in exploring new perspectives or options for resolving the issues in dispute, away from pressures of a polarized public or constituency, and to ensure the safety of participants who otherwise might be targeted by militants who would interpret any dialogue as betrayal. Therefore, discussions normally cannot be observed by nonparticipants or recorded in ways that risk compromising the ground rule of confidentiality. Nor can practitioners be held to rigid protocols for their work—or to objectives set at the beginning of a project—for the sake of research precision, when changing circumstances indicate that either methods or objectives should be revised to make best use of opportunities to promote larger goals of peace building.

"Action research," on the other hand, integrates research and evaluation into the work itself in ways that support rather than constrain it (see Rothman and Friedman, this volume). Objectives and methods may change, but this should be done explicitly through consultation with the parties at each stage of the project; participants themselves should be asked to give feedback at regular intervals, and practitioners (facilitators) also should be willing to evaluate constructively their own and each other's performance and to adjust their approaches to incorporate lessons learned in the short as well as long term. Funders or sponsors can often be involved at certain points in the process: where participants have developed proposals or action plans that they are willing to present, doing so can focus and energize both their work and the longer-term commitment of the funders. Similarly, presentations by participants to policy makers or other interested audiences may make sense in the context of project activities, eliciting feedback that can be used to adjust the objectives and approach. Some participants may be willing to take on the role of coordinating feedback, either alone or in rotation, to ensure adequate evaluation and adjustment of the dialogue process at each stage, as well as of generating material needed for periodic reports to funders. Action-research procedures can thus integratively address the needs of both research and practice, both funders and participants, embedding a model for integrative conflict management in the process of promoting it.

Whereas professional associations have emerged in many countries for those working in dispute resolution in commercial, court-referred and local community conflict cases, there is no equivalent forum for practitioners and scholar-practitioners working internationally on complex intercommunal conflicts. There is a need to foster educational, associational and regulatory support for those working in and developing the field. This will help to consolidate an emerging transcultural profession with its own knowledge base, commitment to human welfare, and ethical standards that will attract the more secure funding and institutional support needed for the field to play its part more fully in addressing complex conflicts (see Fisher, this volume).

The book is intended as a contribution to the professionalization of the field of second track diplomacy, drawing together diverse perspectives from several of its leading scholars and practitioners to provide a coherent conceptual framework supported by research, and a clarification of available applied methodologies and appropriate professional standards. Professional standards require not just adequate preparation and training but also transparency, integrity, self-awareness, long-term commitment (to goals, projects, partners), respect for other cultures, openness to partnership with other professionals, continuous learning and personal transformation, supporting and empowering others, adaptability in integrating knowledge from different cultures and continuous evaluation of one's work (see McDonald, Strimling, this volume).

Section I of this book explores the dynamics of complex social conflicts and the processes through which they may be managed constructively, drawing together recent social science theory and research. For these issues, Ed Azar (chapter 1) provides a rich theoretical framework that has helped to shape the field, showing the inadequacy of simple power-oriented theories for understanding or responding to deep-rooted, identity-driven, protracted communal conflicts. He argues the value of second track problem-solving forums for addressing human needs and promoting the structural development needed for peace.

Ted Gurr and John Davies (chapter 2) provide a more detailed model of the motivational, mobilization and opportunity factors driving these conflicts, with results of recent empirical testing. They also report recent trends showing marked shifts in the actors and strategies involved in conflict intervention since the Cold War, and radically improved outcomes from these efforts, with most settlements since 1950 occurring just in the last decade. They examine nonviolent alternatives for promoting communal interests and provide guidelines for assessing the potential for second track conflict-transformation initiatives for specific conflict situations.

Ambassador John McDonald (chapter 3) writes from the perspective of a long-term practitioner, illustrating both the systemic causes of complex conflicts and the ways in which multi-track diplomacy has helped to transform them. He emphasizes the personal nature of the commitment needed to engage in this work and the principles which must be upheld in practice. Ron Fisher (chapter 4) maps the evolution of the field of "interactive conflict resolution," placing the work of several of the contributors to this volume in larger historical context, and reviews some critical challenges to the field which remain to be addressed.

Section II of the book offers more detailed analysis and guidance on applied processes of conflict transformation and peacebuilding. Herbert Kelman (chapter 5), writing from the perspective of the scholar-practitioner, goes more deeply into the mechanics of conducting interactive problem-solving workshops, discussing practical lessons from long experience with the Middle East conflict, and drawing out the social-psychological dynamics involved in the workshop process. John Davies (chapter 6) reconciles several competing conceptual models of conflict management processes (power-rights-interests, dependence-independence-interdependence, autocracy-transitional-democracy), identifying seven distinct strategies or perspectives that represent different normative paradigms of social reasoning found (with varying popularity) in most cultures, though always uniquely operationalized and expressed in each different context. He emphasizes their complementarity and the need to help build communities' capacities to manage conflict by developing a more complex repertoire of these strategic options as required for a sustainable democratic peace.

Chris Moore and Peter Woodrow (chapter 7) focus on assessment and management of the cultural dimensions of conflict-resolution processes such as negotiation and second track dialogue. Careful assessment can lead to integrative agreement on new processes for conflict resolution that work for both cultures (figure 7.4), making integrative outcomes also more likely (compare figure 6.1). Eileen Borris (chapter 8) addresses the crucial processes of community and national reconciliation, drawing on experience and research on the postapartheid transition in South Africa to explore how the needs for truth and justice can be satisfied in a way that also promotes forgiveness, healing and reconciliation as needed for a sustainable and just peace.

In section III, Edy Kaufman (chapters 9 and 10) presents a richly detailed manual for conducting Innovative Problem Solving Workshops (IPSWs), an evolving methodology with which we have had good results in "Partners in Conflict" projects in the Caucasus, Latin America and the Middle East, as well as in academic and professional training programs in the United States. and elsewhere. The purpose is not to prescribe but to present, with a level of hands-on guidance that we have not otherwise seen in the literature, one model for citizens' diplomacy that exemplifies the principles discussed in this volume, and which can be freely adapted to a range of cultural contexts in collaboration with indigenous partners, for training and/or second track dialogue. IPSW builds on Azar's theoretical framework (chapter 1) and Rothman's (1997c) models, emphasizing a reflective reframing process to allow participants to move from adversarial stalemate to integrative problem solving and partnerships for action.

Finally, section IV directly addresses the practical issues involved in training or skills-building initiatives and in evaluation of conflict-resolution projects. Andrea Strimling (chapter 11) provides a guide for organizers, funders and evaluators of conflict-transformation training programs, organized around key questions and principles of planning, implementation and evaluation. Jay Rothman and Victor Friedman (chapter 12) introduce the process of "action evaluation," a methodology integrated into conflict-resolution processes which helps project organizers, facilitators, participants, and funders interactively define and adapt their shared goals as a project evolves and to monitor and assess progress toward those goals.

The book draws on the experience and insights of leading first- and second-generation citizen-diplomats and scholar-practitioners, working in all parts of the world through NGOs, universities and government or IO agencies, based in developing and developed countries, each bringing a slightly different flavor or perspective to the conflict-transformation process. In this way we hope to convey the richness and diversity of the field as well as its coherence and its adaptability to the needs of different cultures and conflict situations. It is intended for use as a practical resource by practitioners and scholars, trainers and trainees, professionals working in the public (government and IO) and private sectors (NGOs, academics, foundations, businesses, media) in any of the overlapping fields of multi-track diplomacy, foreign affairs, conflict prevention and transformation, peace building, peacekeeping, development and human-itarian aid. It should also be of interest to the general reader, tapping into principles that are applicable for transforming conflict at every level, from the interstate to the interpersonal.

We hope that this volume will help to empower those who aspire to build peace in their own communities of concern, helping to move us all beyond a century of turmoil to one where strengthening democratic norms of mutual respect and accommodation allow us to imagine and create a better world.

Notes

1. From a peak of fifty-one states (with at least 500,000 population) in 1991 to twenty-six states in 2000 (Gurr, Marshall, and Khosla, 2000).

2. See Diamond and McDonald (1996) for a fuller systemic analysis of the first, second and "higher" diplomatic tracks.

3. Search for Common Ground (SFCG) has been particularly effective in working with media-related peacebuilding projects in many countries, including developing popular children's programs, soap operas and musical events coorganized and produced by professionals from opposing communities, modeling integrative approaches to managing conflicts at every level of community life (see www.SFCG.org).

I
Conflict Dynamics and the Evolution of Second Track Diplomacy

1
Protracted Social Conflicts and Second Track Diplomacy

Edward Azar

Editors' Note

This chapter was compiled by the editors from Ed Azar's latest work (primarily unpublished: e.g., Azar, 1988). It elucidates key concepts that have contributed to the formative stages of an emerging interdisciplinary field (see Fisher, this volume) and still belong at its cutting edge. Drawing from political science, sociology, anthropology and psychology, Azar was able to reconceptualize the most troublesome and recalcitrant type of social conflicts and to clarify new avenues for their management and resolution. Because his seminal work shaped not only our approach to second track diplomacy at the University of Maryland's Center for International Development and Conflict Management but also the broader field, we offer this new summary as a useful way to frame the contributions that follow.

In his conceptualization of *protracted social conflict*, Azar emphasized the role of human needs—and particularly the need for acceptance or recognition of identity—as the primary motivating factors in such conflicts. Human needs are universal and nonnegotiable, in contrast to the more specific interests or aspirations which derive from them. Any settlement that seeks to suppress human needs or trade them off for other interests not addressing those needs will not be sustainable. It is the progressive effort to satisfy human needs that sustains *development* (broadly defined to include political and human development as well as economic), which in turn sustains peace. Given the inadequacy of normal diplomatic processes for addressing protracted social conflict, which typically involves nonstate actors whose autonomy is not guaranteed in the state system, Azar argued that second track diplomacy is critical to their management, and he sought to demonstrate that facilitating forums for collaborative problem solving could lead to structural development supported by development diplomacy.

Protracted Social Conflict (PSC)

Conflict is an inseparable part of social relations. Perception of mutually incompatible goals among communities with limited coordinating or mediating mechanisms gives birth to conflict, which if not understood and addressed becomes entrenched and violent. We use the term "community" as a generic reference to politicized groups whose members share ethnic, religious, linguistic or other cultural identity characteristics. Most countries are not homogeneous; and in multicommunal societies, protracted conflicts are likely to arise unless pluralism is adopted and access to needed resources is extended to all.

Protracted social or intercommunal conflicts are breeders of crises and armed struggles as well as continued structural violence and underdevelopment. They have evolved as a result of factors such as colonial legacies of "divide and rule," communal rivalries, the impact of economic migrants and escapees from man-made or natural disasters, and unmet expectations for satisfaction of basic needs for security, communal recognition, and distributive justice.

The main characteristics of PSCs, as identified through a systematic analysis of our Conflict and Peace Data Bank (Azar, 1980) and fifty cases of PSC since 1946, are:

- Protracted hostility and insecurity characterized by periods of armed violence and crises with no clear cycle of genesis, maturity, reduction and termination;
- Fluctuation in the intensity and frequency of interactions, oscillating between overt and covert patterns of conflict, while hostile attitudes continue;
- Absence of a distinct termination point, where war has become the status quo and the threat of peace may mean crisis (Cohen and Azar, 1981); and
- Conflict spillover in terms of both actors and issues, so that the conflict is no longer intrastate or one-dimensional but regional and multicausal, with blurring of the internal and external boundaries of the conflict.

Perspectives on PSC

My understanding of the nature and dynamics of PSCs has evolved through three different periods or intellectual orientations toward the subject:

The Behavioral Interactions Perspective

In this early period, influenced by the dominant realist paradigm, I focused mostly on the quantitative, analytical side of conflict behavior, emphasizing the dynamics of escalation and deescalation, the measurement of violence and of mechanisms for its reduction. The realist international relations research agenda was then focused on conflict behavior (power maximization, arms races, containment, balance of power, etc.), as a function of the anarchical nature of the international system, while peace building and the positive management of social change were not taken seriously. Toward the end of this phase, through my collaborative work on Middle East peace building with scholars like Herbert Kelman, Stephen Cohen and others, I became interested in the social-psychological content and ecological context of conflict events.

The Structuralist Perspective

I became sensitized to the negative impact of certain social structures and deformities in political and economic development, in matters of conflict, reconciliation and peace building. I came to understand "development" as the process by which a community organizes itself in coping with change in its physical and social environment. Organization, in turn, refers to the structure of interdependencies between the economic, political, technological and ideational/valuative systems which constitute the community. I began to study the linkages between physical quality of life, conflict spirals and victimization, overlooked in state-centered realist thinking. Studies on poverty, nutrition and the like helped me learn about the relationships between economic and social-structural factors and overt violence. Johan Galtung's (1969) concept of covert or "structural" violence was particularly helpful in this regard. However, while the structuralist perspective effectively pointed out that rank inequality and disequilibrium at domestic and international levels were necessary (not sufficient) conditions for the rise of PSCs, it was unable to account for process-level dynamics of PSCs. Economic reductionism (class analysis) and holistic determinism (dependency and world system theory) further weakened the approach. In this context, the pluralist paradigm emerged as a theoretical alternative.

The Pluralist Orientation

Linking peace with development was a shift toward a better understanding of the management of conflict. The presence of armed conflict in so many parts of the world appeared to be linked to ethnic identity, minorities and the differential integration and development of societies. I observed that in some parts of the world, the state retards, rather than enhances, development and the movement from war to peace. The smaller communities (religious sects, ethnic groups, linguistic groups, etc.) tend to be more relevant to identity and more responsive to human needs than are centralized national governments. By positing individuals and communal groups as important units of analysis, the pluralist paradigm allowed a more dynamic and realistic grasp of PSCs. PSCs are initiated by individuals and their associations, not by the state, state system or world system. In recognizing the value of the realist approach in understanding some PSCs, and the usefulness of structural analysis in elucidating the roots and ecology of PSCs, the PSC perspective attempts to synthesize, rather than falsify, the realist and structuralist paradigms within the pluralist framework.

Genesis of PSC

The key propositions of the PSC perspective have been formulated to allow continued empirical testing and refinement. The genesis of PSCs may be understood in terms of five clusters of variables or preconditions: human needs, communal context, governance and the role of the state, environmental factors, and international linkages.

Human needs are the primary motivating factor in both development and conflict dynamics. Individuals strive to fulfill their basic human needs (such as security, access and acceptance—see next section) through the formation of communal identity groups. These needs are seldom evenly or justly met. Complaints of deprivation are expressed collectively rather than individually, and failure of the state to meet collective demands creates a niche for PSC.

Communal context refers to the multicommunal composition of states that are vulnerable to PSCs, and the necessity of understanding communities (and individuals) along with states as primary participants in international relations and conflict dynamics. Multicommunal societies arise from the legacy of "divide and rule" in the colonial era as well as from historical patterns of intercommunal rivalry. Both the division of communal groups between states and the incorporation of distinct communal groups into one state can retard the nation-building process, fragment the social fabric, and breed tension.

The role of the state or governing authority, as the regulator of social, political, and economic interactions, is a critical intervening factor in satisfaction of human needs. States prone to PSC tend to be parochial, fragile and authoritarian, lacking in competence, fairness, resources and policy capacity. Political authority tends to be monopolized by a dominant group or coalition of groups using the state to maximize their own interests at others' expense. Modes of governance are distorted to block access by other groups, leading to crises of legitimacy.

Environmental factors may further constrain policy capacity in dealing with communal tensions. They include depletion of natural resources and degradation of the environment through unsound development policies; rapid population growth and demographic imbalance (urban explosion and youth bulge) from rapid changes in health care, technology and mobility; and rising expectations and pressures for change arising from exposure to mass media and global comparisons.

International linkage patterns may exacerbate the role of weak states in deprivation of human needs in two ways. The first is economic dependency, which may arise through a coalition of international capital with local economic and political elites to facilitate exploitation of existing national resources or the evolution of newly introduced single-crop economies. Dependency not only weakens state autonomy but (as in Guatemala during the Cold War) often marginalizes the access and security needs of citizens by distorting the development of political and economic systems to sustain the power of the elite coalition. The second is political and military "cliency" relationships with strong states. In a cliency relationship, the patron provides protection for the client state in return for the latter's loyalty and obedience. This involves some sacrifice of autonomy and induces the client state to pursue both domestic and foreign policies disjoined from, or contradictory to, the needs of its own public (as in Lebanon since the 1950s: Azar et al., 1984).

PSC Dynamics

The dynamics through which these preconditions are transformed into manifest violent conflict are determined by communal actions and strategies, state actions and strategies and the built-in properties of conflict.

Communal Actions and Strategies

When organizational and communication systems break down in an environment of mutual distrust between groups, a PSC can begin to escalate. Even a trivial event (e.g., an insult to an individual with strong communal ties) may become a turning point at which individual victimization is collectively recognized. Collective recognition of individual grievances or incompatible communal goals naturally leads to collective protest, which is usually met by some degree of repression or suppression. Leaders of victimized groups draw their constituents' attention to a broad range of issues involving communal security, access, or acceptance needs (e.g., selective poverty and political inequality). The spillover of the trigger event into multiple issues increases the momentum for organizing and mobilizing resources, as groups attempt to formulate more diverse strategies (secessionist movement, armed struggle, etc.). When the state is more powerful and favors coercion over accommodation, groups often seek external military and economic assistance, often from kin in neighboring countries. Support from neighbors may involve regional hegemonic or other designs, manipulating communal tensions to destabilize and subvert the regime, so that communal conflicts spill over into regional ones.

State Actions and Strategies

A PSC can be averted if the state improves satisfaction of communal needs at an early stage. But accommodation strategies are seldom employed, not only because of the political and economic costs but also because of prevailing "winner take all" norms where any accommodation is perceived as a sign of defeat. The state (or the communal actor monopolizing state authority) usually employs coercive repression and co-optation designed to fragment or divert the opposition. This invites equally militant responses from communal contestants, and if co-optation fails, further coercion leads to a spiral of violent clashes. The state may seek to contain the conflict by severing groups' ties to external sources of support, and seek out its own; if dependency or cliency relationships exist, external powers may intervene, amplifying and protracting the conflict.

Built-In Mechanisms of Conflict

Once violence erupts, the cost of human life escalates the conflict into a spiral of acts and hostile communications that throw apart the parties even further, as "conflict begets conflict" (Gurr, 1970). In conflicts associated with communal identity, the worst motivations are attributed to opposing parties and are not open to falsification, leading to reciprocal negative images which perpetuate antagonisms and solidify PSCs. Political solutions become unavailable, being evaluated only in terms of relative power gains. Hostility gains velocity as the deepening deprivation of basic needs leads to stereotyping, tunnel vision, separation, bolstering and polarization along communal lines.

PSC Outcomes

The outcome of PSCs is negative sum. There are no winners or losers, for all parties are victimized. There is no clear end-point, each outcome being the possible cause of another conflict spiral. PSCs carry devastating physical, psychological, economic and political costs, as we have seen in Sudan, Sri Lanka and El Salvador.

Physical security deteriorates, with not only a tragic loss of human life but also destruction of physical and social infrastructure, as economic retrenchment to support excessive military expenditure leads to discarding of welfare and development programs. A vicious cycle of underdevelopment and poverty is institutionalized, depriving all groups of human needs and economic well-being.

Institutions become paralyzed and deformed, rendering government ineffectual, blocking satisfaction of access needs, and hardening communal cleavages so that nation building becomes impossible.

Even worse is the psychological disorientation of those trapped in a PSC situation, absorbed into a violent war culture where hostile mindsets are ossified, leading to high levels of frustration and depression. PSCs reinforce pessimism, demoralize leaders, and build a sense of paralysis that afflicts the collective conscience of the population. A siege mentality develops, inhibiting constructive negotiation for conflict management, severing meaningful communication among parties, and eliminating any chance for satisfaction of acceptance needs. In the long term, unmet needs lead to dysfunctional cognitive and behavioral patterns that are not easily remedied.

Fear of marginalization, which is at the root of PSCs, leads to alliances of convenience with external actors, encouraging *dependency* rather than reliance on domestic or communal abilities and resources. As external actors are drawn into the complexity of PSC, communities lose their access to decision-making institutions, entrenching them in cycles of dependency, conflict and despair.

Before considering how such complex conflicts might be managed, it will be useful to take a closer look at the basic human needs motivating the participants.

Human Needs

There are relatively enduring human needs that must be fulfilled for individuals to grow and develop. Individuals strive to satisfy these human developmental needs through the formation of identity groups. A community is an identity group, constructed around common experiences, values and norms. Human needs may be grouped into three constellations: security, access and acceptance.

The most basic needs are those of physical survival and well-being. Survival and well-being are contingent upon the satisfaction of infrastructural needs for basic physical resources (food, clothing, energy, water), safety, and productive capability. In reality, the deprivation of such security needs per se does not give rise to conflicts, since the means of satisfying such needs is a function of access to the superstructure of society.

Access to, or effective participation in, the social institutions in which allocation and exchange takes place is essential for fair and just distribution of resources and opportunities needed for security, and may thus also be counted as a human need. This includes participation in the political system, access to the market, engagement in the authority structure and decision-making machinery, and access to institutions which can act as honest brokers in allowing redress without retribution or discrimination on a communal basis. Deprivation of human needs may be exacerbated by unbalanced development strategies distorting equitable allocation of both resources and access. The ability of disadvantaged groups to correct such matters will in turn be influenced by their perceived level of acceptance and inclusion.

Acceptance or recognition of identity is a social-psychological or metastructural need essential to the psychological well-being of individuals and groups. Group identity is manifested in terms of values, norms, ideas and customs, often linked with more ascriptive factors, such as class, race, language or religion. When there is a refusal to accept or recognize the identity of a group, relative deprivation of physical needs and denial of access creates covariance among the victimized and facilitates the distinctive group dynamics of PSC. Satisfaction of acceptance needs, unlike those that depend on the distribution of scarce material and positional values, involves exchange of social goods. Social goods can increase in supply with consumption: groups who are accepted are more likely to accept others in turn.

The satisfaction of needs for communal security, fair governance by ruling elites, and acceptance and recognition of cultural diversity are all fundamental to state building. The deprivation of security cannot be understood without reference to equitable access to the institutions of government, tolerance and acceptance of the right to be different from the "other." Deprivation of one form of developmental need usually leads to problems in other areas. Therefore, it is important to elucidate the complex relationship among these needs if we are to understand the causes of any protracted social conflict.

Needs can thus be tangible or intangible, and the combination of both tends to make PSCs intractable. Whereas it may be difficult to identify deep-rooted psychological needs, material needs tend to be more explicit. Intercommunal conflict is driven not only by hostility and distrust but also by political and economic impoverishment or gross exploitation of communities on the basis of their collective identities and historical misfortunes. Economic development is a key component of conflict management, and like other components, it must be explored jointly by all the parties. A development strategy cannot be imposed from the outside: it must harmonize with the broader process of societal development and reflect intercommunal effort and consensus.

In the conflict management process, a clear distinction should be made between interests that can be negotiated, mediated, subjected to judicial determination or bargained over, and these ontological needs and related values that cannot be compromised, traded or repressed as mere interests.

Track Two Diplomacy

We have advanced the use of the term conflict "management" rather than "resolution" because of our understanding that conflict is an inseparable part of social interactions among two or more parties. The more familiar approaches to conflict management can be grouped into two clusters (see Davies, this volume). Bureaucratic managers, on the one hand, aim at gaining control over events either by co-opting conflicting parties with material rewards or by punishing them through force or repression. They seek to contain behavioral (but not structural) violence and to arrest conflict spillover. On the other hand, legal-formalists aim to transform the conflict situation through judicial settlements, arbitration, mediation, conciliation, legal awards and direct bargaining. Both approaches are top-down and preoccupied with settlement or containment of overt conflicts, in which outcomes are "win-lose" or some zero-sum compromise in which several parties are to some degree losers.

Neither approach is adequate for the management of PSCs. Settlements or control strategies that do not address the deeper structural roots underlying the crisis tend to be nullified when unattended grievances held by isolated or victimized communal groups transform them into "spoilers." Moreover, the intractable and entangled nature of PSC struggles over communal needs reduces the efficacy of third-party interventions: there are no "quick-fix" solutions to these problems.

An alternative approach for PSCs is to combine short-term efforts to arrest or contain impending crises with long-term designs to transform the entire conflict system by addressing its structural roots. It emphasizes an "underdog" rather than the conventional "top-dog" orientation, singling out the alienated and victimized groups in conflict as major parties for consultation and negotiation, so that all involved parties are engaged. It embraces not only settlement but also prevention, avoidance and resolution of conflict as potentially appropriate goals. It suggests problem-solving workshops to facilitate breakthroughs and promote self-sustaining structural development. These efforts can be supported by development diplomacy to alleviate external barriers to prevention or termination. It thus involves, as a necessary supplement to official diplomacy, the nonofficial, subnational and analytical problem-solving orientations which constitute track-two diplomacy (Montville, 1987).

"Track two" refers to processes that parallel and eventually link up with track-one (official) diplomacy. The participation of individuals in their personal capacities, and yet with access and potential to influence decision makers, is a useful supplement to the work of professional diplomats and political leadership, while also facilitating discussion at the grassroots level. Ultimately, all nonofficial processes are aimed (at least in part) at influencing official opinion, even though the link may at first seem very remote.

A growing number of experiments in alternative forms of diplomacy have been undertaken in recent years. Terms used to describe nontraditional diplomatic processes include citizenship diplomacy, supplemental diplomacy, prenegotiations, walks in the woods, face-to-face diplomacy, problem-solving workshops and back-channel diplomacy. In order to avoid confusion when talking about initiatives and processes which in practice may be quite dissimilar, it is important that clear distinctions between different practices be established on the basis of goals, structure and procedure.

For example, a "walk in the woods" between individual negotiators will enable them to explore options free from the large teams of negotiators present at official negotiations. Of course, agreements reached in this way may not be ultimately acceptable to the highest decision makers. To avoid this problem, "face-to-face" diplomacy attempts to facilitate the official process by bringing together individuals with real decision-making power.

Another approach involves the use of third parties. The idea behind the traditional use of third-party mediation is to induce warring factions or states to meet together, usually by offering mediation services. This approach is most useful in cases where parties to a dispute have ceased communicating with each other. This may occur when one or both parties is or are reluctant to suffer the negative political consequences associated with meeting with the "enemy." In highly conflictive situations between parties of dissimilar military strength, the stronger party may be reluctant to grant "legitimacy" to the weaker by agreeing to negotiate with it. It is not uncommon that a government derives positive political capital by publicly refusing to negotiate with an adversary, even though the policy may be detrimental in the long run. It is possible in this case to "save face" (i.e., avoid the appearance of capitulation or legitimizing the opponent), while at the same time opening a useful channel of communication, by agreeing to deal with a respected third party. Thus, legitimacy is granted not to the opponent but to the mediator, and little or no political capital is risked in what, given the volatility of such situations, may turn out to be a failed venture. However, traditional third-party mediation preserves the bargaining or negotiating framework within a power-politics environment, and third parties may bring their own agendas, influencing the outcome in several different ways. Mediators may inhibit frankness by placing a premium on concluding agreements rather than searching for options and nonbinding outcomes, so that a profound analysis of the sources of conflict is not achieved.

A third class of nontraditional diplomacy involves the use of "independent" or private third parties (such as academics, clerics, retired diplomats) who bypass official channels in an attempt to open clogged channels of communication or to propose, discuss or explore alternative solutions to a dispute. This type of effort, which has been called "citizenship diplomacy" or "problem-solving workshops," can be useful for initiating contact between parties or for bringing to light possible new solutions. Its effectiveness is limited, however, as long as it does not induce the parties to educate themselves, explore, and recognize the underlying needs (as opposed to immediate interests) motivating the conflict.

The Problem-Solving Approach

The use of the term "problem solving" is intended to convey that conflict is not a contest to be won but rather a shared problem to be solved. Interactive or collaborative problem-solving workshops involve informal and unofficial face-to-face encounters in neutral settings. Key to these efforts is facilitation by a group of social scientists or other professionals knowledgeable about group process and conflict theory.

This approach goes beyond simple "process-promoting" techniques for achieving greater trust at the interpersonal level, whose primary aims are to influence the conflict in the long term and to work to improve relationships at the grassroots level. Problem-solving workshops, on the other hand, attempt to influence leaders and representatives of the parties to a conflict in the near or medium term, through working with surrogates and "influentials" to address practical conflict issues.

Problem-solving workshops permit parties to sort out their grievances and hear one another in a nonbargaining setting. They allow exploratory discussions with a panel of third-party facilitators who invite participants, selected as credible representatives of the parties, to be open and frank about their needs and interests. While they possess no authority, facilitators are responsible for creating a climate of constructive dialogue where goodwill can prevail over cynical attitudes and for ensuring that participants do not turn prematurely to negotiation or bargaining.

The immediate goals of the workshop are to assess interactively what is at issue in a PSC situation and to differentiate needs-issues from interests-issues.

Facilitators act as honest brokers to enable each side to appreciate and address the basic grievances and needs of the other. There is a tendency for afflicted groups to center their attention on their own concerns. Thus, it can be extremely difficult for one group to recognize that a competing group may also have been fundamentally wronged. Once the grievances and needs of the different communities have been identified (e.g., fears of marginalization or assimilation, need for recognition), and once each group can acknowledge the legitimate needs and aspirations of the others, a constructive process of accommodation can begin, and the groundwork for future negotiation can be established. An analytical assessment of the causes and nature of the conflict can help participants to define structural and institutional options. Breakthroughs occur when participants identify problems to be solved, co-explore new ideas and opportunities to reduce violence and hostility, and plan for further joint activities and workshops.

While conventional third-party mediation might be able to establish a cease-fire between conflicting parties, it often does so without addressing the underlying causes of the conflict. Innovative proposals for political solutions are rare, as parties to PSC tend to become closed-minded and tend to perceive proposed resolutions as mechanisms for gaining relative power and control. Therefore, it becomes essential to analyze, as part of the facilitated workshop process, the perceptions and cognitive processes generated through experience of conflictual interactions, such as premature closure, misattribution of motives, stereotyping, tunnel vision, bolstering and polarization. Only when these phenomena are recognized is it likely that the parties will trust each other, work together in good faith, and uphold understandings that may be reached.

From my own experimentation with this approach (in workshops focusing on Lebanon, Sri Lanka, Falklands/Malvinas, Israel/Palestine and other conflicts) I have developed a model suited for addressing PSCs called "problem-solving forums" (Azar, Davies and Shahbazi, 1990). The framework is designed to establish a prenegotiation stage to encourage analytical breakthroughs by the disputants themselves. The approach is comprehensive, including successive forums as well as pre- and postforum phases. A workshop should not be a one-time event: in most cases, breakthroughs tend to happen after several workshops have been held. For example, in our Lebanon forums in 1984, participants from warring Moslem and Christian communities were surprised to discover that they shared a common value in Lebanon as an integral, independent state. In a subsequent forum, they were able to agree on a declaration of twenty-two principles defining a shared vision for Lebanon. These principles were used to draft a National Covenant Document that was incorporated into the 1989 Taif Accords, thus making a significant contribution toward the peace process.

In the preforum phase, serious attention is given to the choice of the forum environment, preparation of the setting and logistics, criteria for and selection of participants, and a clear definition of the role of facilitators. The forum process is not designed to resolve differences, tensions or hostilities within each party; if these are too great, the forum process will not function effectively. Therefore, a thorough intracommunal needs analysis is essential to engage representatives of each party in a separate dialogue where their differences may be addressed in advance of the workshop.

The postforum phase requires a follow-up agenda, including further analysis and communication with decision makers, leading ultimately to negotiations and other appropriate official actions to manage the dispute and promote self-sustaining structural development. At this stage, there is a risk that those who reach agreement or even make contact with the adversary may be alienated from their constituents unless they are able to convince the group that its interests have not been betrayed. This is known as the "reentry" problem. Third parties can help by preparing participants for this and by remaining engaged throughout this phase.

The problem-solving approach is predicated on the belief that violent and prejudicial, or peaceful and cooperative, thinking and behavior are learned phenomena, and that what is learned can also be modified. Problems of communication in conflict situations obscure common interests and potentials for mutual benefit. Thus, the conditions for adaptive learning and conflict management will be enhanced if the parties are able to talk and approach conflict not as something to be won but as something to be resolved. This analytical framework allows the parties to explore their perceptions of the conflict and its roots, to discover that they are pursuing similar or potentially compatible goals through adversarial tactics. The "win-lose," zero-sum environment of traditional diplomacy can be transformed into one of "win-win," in which the possibilities for cooperation and mutual progress are maximized. An outcome beneficial to both parties may be found, for example, by cutting relative losses or by inventing new formulas for "expanding the pie" by going beyond deterministic perceptions of finite resources to include other benefits such as potentially abundant social goods—recognition, cooperation, safety, etc.—which may not originally have been perceived as significant. When no clear solution to an issue is found, the problem can simply be flagged and left open for future collaborative work.

Practitioners (facilitators) have a duty to the participants who invest trust in them, as well as to the process itself. The effectiveness of the process depends on the care, honesty and integrity of the individuals and organizations involved. If a participant's trust is betrayed, for example, by a failure to maintain the private, confidential nature of a forum, the political stature and even the lives of participants may be threatened.

We must be alert to screen out potential participants who may be searching for opportunities to score personal and intragroup gains through intelligence gathering or grandstanding, or who might betray the confidential nature of the process by publicizing the event. The perception that a problem-solving work-shop may be suitable prey for exploitation should be minimized by adherence to clear guidelines for selection and by requiring advance commitments to guidelines on confidentiality and respect. On the other hand, it is important to ensure inclusion of representatives from each primary group affected, providing they are willing to deal with the deeper dynamics underlying the crisis. We must be aware that settlements between conflicting sides are nullified when isolated or victimized communal groups become spoilers, and attempts at settlement or control of a crisis that do not tackle the underlying dynamics will be temporarily successful at best.

Facilitation

A key assumption is that only representatives of the parties can identify and address the substantive issues required to manage and resolve their conflict. However, their interactions in problem-solving workshops can be facilitated by a panel of experts who possess personal integrity and professional competence. The members of the panel are nonofficial and may be drawn from social science and/or other professional fields. Acting as a team, the panel should be able to operate in a nonthreatening, depoliticized and open-minded manner.

The expertise of the facilitators is a significant element for the success of a problem-solving forum. Facilitators evaluate or recruit credible representatives of the parties, formulate and get consensus on the ground rules, create a climate of constructive dialogue, ensure that participants do not turn prematurely to negotiation and bargaining, bring the participants to see each other's grievances, and assess interactively what is at issue, separating nonnegotiable needs from negotiable interests. This requires the ability to distinguish for the participants defensive, conflict-related cognitive habits such as premature closure, misattribution, stereotyping, tunnel vision, bolstering and polarization as they arise in the forum. Facilitation of constructive communication can then allow the parties to arrive at consensus over contending interests and to plan for further joint activities, eventually without the need for external intervention.

The training of professional facilitators had not been developed when we started to experiment with our approach, so I have advocated the creation of permanent, private third parties with the skills needed to pursue track-two diplomacy, or the training of individuals in already existing organizations such as the International Red Cross.

However, in our experience, participants expect facilitators to come to the workshop with a sophisticated understanding of their specific problems. If they are not established experts on the region or country concerned, they should learn the issues at stake, including not only the historical record but also the nuances of relations within and between the parties. Preparatory learning should include a systematic and thorough identification, tracking and analysis of the specific conflict, including its genesis, dynamics, consequences, and possible management strategies. We are convinced that the ability to inspire trust is closely related to the respect that participants feel for the facilitators' level of knowledge. Participants do not respect facilitators who display ignorance about important issues and facts or those whose intense involvement with the dispute leads them to support any specific position.

A balance might be achieved that would benefit from both the professionalism guaranteed by a permanent body and the particular insights into a conflict that knowledgeable experts provide. Panels could be composed of both "conflict-specific" experts and experts in conflict management via the forum model. The best way to guarantee serious, professional and dedicated facilitation is through rigorous analysis, by the community of practitioners and students, of the proper goals and methods of track-two diplomacy and the dissemination of their findings.

Given the nature of the enterprise and high sensitivity toward third parties, it is imperative that facilitators guarantee neutrality. Of course, each facilitator will come to a forum with her or his own intellectual, professional, ideological and personal baggage. Individual perceptions, even those of trained facilitators, are influenced by their experiences. This is unavoidable, but not necessarily problematic, unless facilitators' baggage impairs participants' ability to arrive at solutions or to make analytical progress. When effectively managed, facilitators' opinions may even be seen by participants as evidence that the facilitators have a good grasp of the issues at stake.

In PSCs, parties become adept at psychological warfare and make great efforts to enlist the support of outside powers, or those perceived as associated with them. Facilitators who are sensitive to this danger and who work well as a self-monitoring team can avoid this problem. We believe that practitioners should not be reluctant to abandon the process if the conditions necessary for success are not met, even if this means the loss of a great investment of time, money and effort. If it is susceptible to being taken hostage, private diplomacy will degenerate into just another form or tool of power.

At this stage, almost all practitioners of alternative-diplomacy processes come from Western political and economic traditions. We must strive to be aware of our own perspectives and keep our inclinations in check. This can be accomplished in part by making an effort to train individuals from non-Western societies and to include them in the facilitating process. We must also ensure that it is the participants who identify the needs, issues, and options for managing their own conflict.

Finally, a key aspect of the process is the peer chemistry of the facilitators. Given the intense environment of forums, facilitators must be capable of working well with one another, which requires, above all, the ability to communicate effectively in a group. This is a question both of training and personality. Much effort must go into figuring out the best mix, and into continuing analytical and empirical efforts to understand the preparations and process required for an effective routing of problems into shared solutions.

Structural Development and Development Diplomacy

Facilitation of problem-solving dialogue is only a beginning. Effective management of conflicts needs to go beyond problem solving. Breakthroughs from the forum process must be carried over into the management of PSC situations and prevention of their recurrence. These goals imply satisfaction of needs, but societies experiencing PSC tend to be characterized by poverty, inequality, authoritarian-repressive regimes, and acute problems of population growth amidst resource scarcity, all interacting in a vicious circle. Initiatives are needed to help ruling elites realize that uncorrected communal grievances can fester into destabilizing revolts that threaten not only their positions but the entire social and economic fabric of the country.

To respond to these grievances and satisfy communal needs, structural development is essential. This may include reducing structural inequalities (political, economic and social), altering development strategies to focus on correcting regional, sectoral and communal imbalances, and progressive reforms in sociopolitical structures to redistribute power through sharing and devolution while promoting institution and consensus building among groups.

This endogenous development process should be supported on both domestic and international levels by development diplomacy—i.e., assistance designed to reduce levels of structural deprivation in developing countries, to the long-term benefit of all parties. Such interventionist diplomacy should be based on a careful analysis of the idiosyncratic features of the PSC and its linkages to specific sociopolitical relations and economic policies. In order to reduce structural inequalities and related institutional deformities that act as barriers to sustained development, development diplomacy needs to focus on building responsive domestic institutions.

Internationally, development diplomacy should address global systemic sources of domestic structural deformities. It should promote multilateral initiatives to reduce the dependency and cliency that exacerbate communal imbalances and distort domestic institutions. External development assistance should be directed away from fragmentary deployment of military-economic aid and toward innovative and comprehensive long-term policy packages that enhance authentic and self-sustaining economic development and political reform which respond to the needs and aspirations of all groups. Individuals and communities need to believe that their participation is assured and that it makes a difference: it is the sense of involvement that facilitates conflict management and stability.

Development strategies should aim not merely for economic growth but also for a more balanced distribution of benefits to address the basic human needs of deprived people. Development diplomacy can leverage the current short-term emphasis on meeting immediate needs through emergency relief by placing it in the context of planning for long-term, comprehensive structural reform efforts.

Concluding Remarks

The classical understanding of conflicts is one of zero-sum outcomes, of winners and losers. But protracted social conflicts result in negative-sum outcomes, because of their inherent behavioral properties. There are no winners: all parties to these conflicts tend to be victimized in the process. Outcomes (military victories, negotiated agreements, etc.), insofar as they do not begin to satisfy basic human needs, contain latent conflicts which cause further cycles of manifest conflict, often spilling over into new issues and actors.

In sum, the management of protracted social conflict cannot be understood without addressing the issues of economic development and communal pluralism. The long-term approach conducive to conflict management requires severing the causal chains between underdevelopment and structural inequalities, and between communal imbalance and institutional paralysis. Peace, as a sustainable end-process rather than a means of gaining influence or strategic benefits, requires balanced economic and political development.

Identity-driven conflicts cannot be resolved without grasping them at the level of both tangible and intangible developmental needs. Only working together can parties to a conflict determine the substantive ideas required to address their needs and thus to manage and resolve their conflict. Helping party representatives understand each other helps them realize that not all required resources are finite, that they can find ways for authorities to expand the pie to meet needs. In a needs framework, the notion of legitimacy is central: the degree to which authorities are valued by their electorates reflects the degree to which official structures and policies facilitate the pursuit and satisfaction of human needs. The processes of facilitation, structural development and development diplomacy represent a gradual, collective, and comprehensive approach to the management of PSC, as opposed to temporary strategic containment or partial legal settlement.

The problem-solving forums at Maryland have been useful, and we will continue to improve them in the years to come. As a field, conflict management is in the early stages of its development, but we cannot wait for increased theoretical sophistication before we attempt to contribute to peace-building efforts. We must research our approach at the same time as we apply it.

Taking a broad view, we find two competing images of politics. For many, "real" politics is about power acquisition and engaging in conflict over scarce goods and values. Within this framework, conflict is thought to be inevitable at all levels of human interaction, from the interpersonal to the international. However, there is an alternative view, to which we have been sensitized through protracted social conflicts, positing that politics is about collective security, community building and prosperity. As we see it, the goals of politics are the promotion of cooperation, the management of conflict, the pursuit of socioeconomic development, and the facilitation of peaceful interactions at all levels.

2
Dynamics and Management of Ethnopolitical Conflicts

Ted Robert Gurr and John Davies

This chapter provides, first, a brief review of factors which motivate or increase the risk of ethnopolitical conflicts; second, a look at recent trends in such conflicts, their management and outcomes; third, a consideration of nonviolent strategies as alternatives to war, and emerging norms for accommodating these conflicts; and finally, a framework for conflict assessment, as a basis for identifying possibilities for conflict prevention or management.

We define ethnopolitical conflicts as those involving, as a primary party, at least one nonstate group with distinct cultural, ethnic, or religious traits. It is a broad definition that includes nationalist conflicts aimed at greater autonomy or independence, as well as other forms of conflict aimed at improving or defending economic or political access, or promoting or defending cultural identity as reflected in the use of language, religion or other distinctive traditions (see also Azar, this volume, and McDonald, this volume). Two necessary conditions for social conflict are distinct collective identities and a perception by group members that their respective aspirations probably cannot be simultaneously achieved. These identities may be political or economic rather than ethnic or cultural. However conflict in turn strengthens separate identities, allowing greater opportunity for distinct cultures to develop (as between North and South Korea); hence protracted social conflicts tend to acquire an ethnopolitical character even when it was missing initially.

Risk Factors for Ethnopolitical Violence

The Minorities at Risk Project (Gurr, 2000a) has identified 275 politicized ethnic groups that are or have been subject to discriminatory or invidious treatment by other groups because of their cultural, ethnic, or religious traits, or which are mobilized for political action to promote or defend their common interests. Some have been victimized by past discrimination and repressive state policies that in two dozen cases reached genocidal proportions. More than thirty were engaged in armed conflicts at the turn of the millennium. Others, like Québeçois separatists and indigenous activists in Australia and the Americas, are using conventional political means to pursue collective ends.

The theory and data of the Minorities Project provide a means for systematically identifying groups at high risk of future armed conflict. Risk models are developed along the lines used by medical researchers to assess the risks that individuals will suffer from heart disease. Risk factors are measured and used to assess each group's probability of new or escalating conflict in the next few years, for use preferably in conjunction with assessments by locally based observers and assessment of dynamic factors which may accelerate or inhibit escalation of an unstable situation into high-intensity conflict (Davies, Harff and Speca, 1998; Harff and Gurr, 1998). The model includes five key factors, each with several indicators, which have been tested and found useful in predicting rebellion (see especially Gurr and Marshall, 2000). Of these factors, the first two (group incentives and salience of group identity) together provide the motivational dynamics driving conflict, while the other three (group capacity and opportunity factors) are mediating variables codetermining whether a conflict becomes violent.

1: Group Incentives for Collective Action. The greater the disadvantages imposed on a people and the greater their sense of injustice, the easier it is for group leaders to convince them that they have something to gain from armed conflict. Opposition to new discriminatory policies such as cultural restrictions, anger about state repression, and hopes for redress of such past wrongs as loss of collective autonomy, therefore, are among the precursors of sustained political action by ethnopolitical groups.

- *Lost autonomy* is correlated with future rebellion.
- *Government repression* is one of the strongest leading indicators of rebellion. Any inhibiting effect that repression might have on ethnopolitical action is more than offset in the longer term by the mutually reinforcing spiral of attack and counterattack.
- *Increased political restrictions* is a leading indicator of rebellion, probably for the same reason as repression. Other forms of disadvantage also serve as incentives but are listed below under factor two because of their relevance to group identity.

2: Salience of Group Identity. The more important group identity is for people with a shared culture, the more likely they are to define their interests in ethnocultural terms, and the easier it is for leaders to mobilize them. Collective identity is most important for people who experience discrimination and have recently been involved in conflict.

- *Persistent protest during the previous decade* falls within the range of normal politics but has a strong leading relationship with future rebellion, persistence implying lack of adequate accommodation.
- *Economic and political discrimination* (relative deprivation) is an important predictor of rebellion (see also Dudley and Miller, 1998).
- *Cultural restrictions,* as a significant risk factor for protest, contribute indirectly to risk of rebellion.
- *Intensity of past conflicts* with the state or rival groups is a strong indicator of future armed conflict, particularly if persisting in the last decade.
- *Extent of cultural differentials* in relation to other groups is assumed to facilitate discrimination and mobilization.

3: Group Capacity for Collective Action. Identity and shared grievances alone are not sufficient for joint action: they need organizational expression.

- *Territorial concentration* is a precondition for most ethnorebellions. It is one of the strongest risk indicators in the rebellion model.
- *Group organization,* reflecting the cohesion and authentic leadership needed for sustained political action, is also one of the strong risk indicators in the model.
- *Reduced support for conventional ethnopolitical organizations,* other things being equal, increases the likelihood of future rebellion. Conventional organizations tend to favor nonviolent strategies; their failure to gain support in conflict situations points to an opening for violent alternatives.

4: Domestic Opportunity Factors for Collective Action. Group leaders make strategic decisions about when to initiate or escalate political action in the context of changing political environments that shape the chances of success. Many factors affect the opportunities for successful rebellion. Among them:

- *Autocratic or mixed polities* are significantly more likely than democratic ones to experience ethnopolitical violence. The presence of democratic norms and institutions favors reliance on protest rather than rebellion.
- *Regime transitions:* Ethnic protest and, sometimes, rebellion increase during the first five years after an abrupt change in political regime, particularly for transitions toward democracy.
- *Weak states with limited resources* are less able to accommodate ethnic and other sectoral interests and are also more vulnerable to violent challenges following any further drop in living standards (as measured by GDP per capita, infant mortality, etc.; see also State Failure Task Force, 1999).
- *History of government repression* rather than engagement or accommodation in response to challenges is an indicator for rebellion (see factor one above).

5: International Opportunity Factors for Collective Action. Direct international factors include diplomatic, material, and military assistance from kindred groups, sympathetic states, and international organizations. More diffuse factors include the effects of armed conflicts being fought in adjoining countries. Their spillovers—arms, refugees, militants looking for safe havens—may give ethnic contenders incentives and opportunities to press their claims. They also contribute to a general climate of insecurity that can provoke preemptive action.

- *Support from kindred groups:* Ethnopolitical groups that get support from kindred in neighboring states are significantly more likely to rebel. Regional or global networks of kindred or coreligionists have a similar effect.
- *Lack of international political support:* Whereas bilateral support for ethnopolitical groups (from kindred or states) increases the risks of violent conflict, sustained engagement by international organizations reduced the risks of future rebellion in the 1990s (see next section).
- *Lack of international economic engagement* (i.e., lack of trade openness, and of the rule of law required for it) similarly increases the risk of violent conflict or state failure (State Failure Task Force, 1999).
- *Spillover effects of regional conflicts:* Protest is significantly less likely and rebellion is more likely in countries in "bad neighborhoods" (such as currently in Central Africa and Central Asia).

Retrospective testing using just the six strongest of these indicators from data available to 1995 (not including the prior existence of persistent armed conflict—since we already know existing conflicts tend to persist) correctly identified which of 275 at-risk minorities would be engaged in armed conflict in 1997 and 1998 75 percent of the time (or 88 percent including correct predictions of nonwar: Gurr and Marshall, 2000). Addition of dynamic event-data models can improve accuracy even further for shorter projections (about 80 percent accuracy for wars six months in advance: Harff with Surko and Unger, 2001). Combining evaluations by locally based experts with model-based assessments should also enhance accuracy without sacrificing the reliability, transparency and intercomparability of model-based assessments (see last section below).

Trends in Conflict and Conflict Management Outcomes

The conventional view is that violent conflict within states surged upward at the end of the Cold War and continued to increase during the 1990s. Certainly given the prevalence of many of the above factors in this period, such as transitional regimes and weak states, this would seem reasonable. It is not supported by the evidence, however, and leads to unjustified pessimism about the prospects for management of internal wars.

Globally, the frequency and magnitude of armed conflicts, weighted for destructiveness and human costs (deaths and dislocations), increased throughout the Cold War, with only a slight upward surge in the early 1990s, but then from 1992 onward fell off sharply, by almost half (figure 2.1 is adapted from Gurr, Marshall, and Khosla, 2000). The same is true if we look only at number of armed conflicts, or the number or proportion of states with armed conflicts, or all internal conflicts, or at ethnopolitical conflicts only.

Figure 2.1 Global Trends in Violent Conflict 1946-1999

Total Magnitude of Armed Conflict

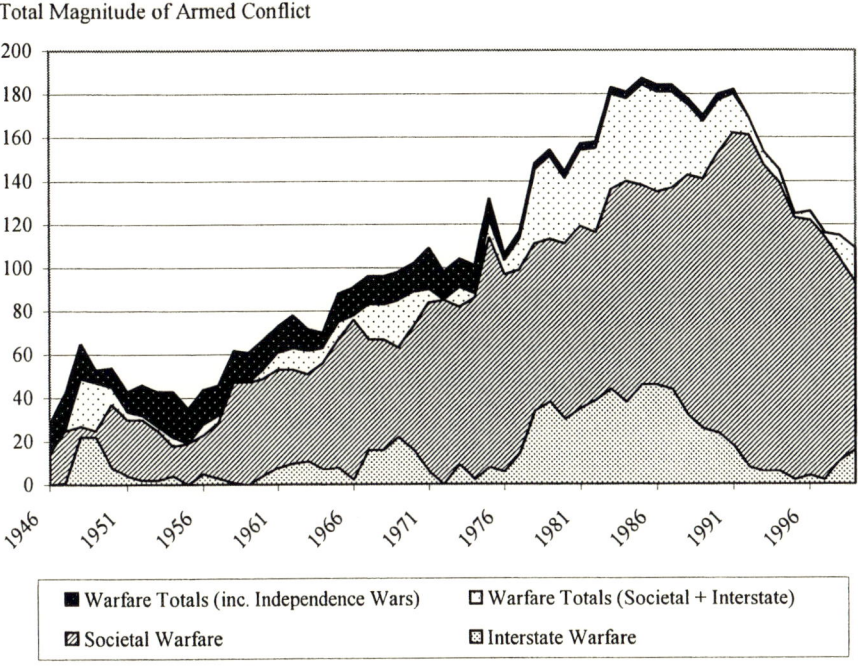

Warfare Totals (inc. Independence Wars) □ Warfare Totals (Societal + Interstate)
🖾 Societal Warfare   🖾 Interstate Warfare

We can sharpen our understanding of the global trends by examining one particular type of conflict, wars of self-determination. These are separatist wars like those of Kosovo, Aceh, and southern Sudan. These are among the most deadly and protracted of all wars within states. Spillovers from them have posed the greatest regional security threats of the post-Cold War era. The Minorities at Risk Project has tracked these and other ethnopolitical conflicts from the 1950s onward. Figure 2.2 (adapted from Gurr, Marshall and Khosla, 2000) represents the trends in ethnonational wars and their outcomes over the last half-century.

Figure 2.2 Trends in Armed Conflicts for Self-Determination 1956-2000

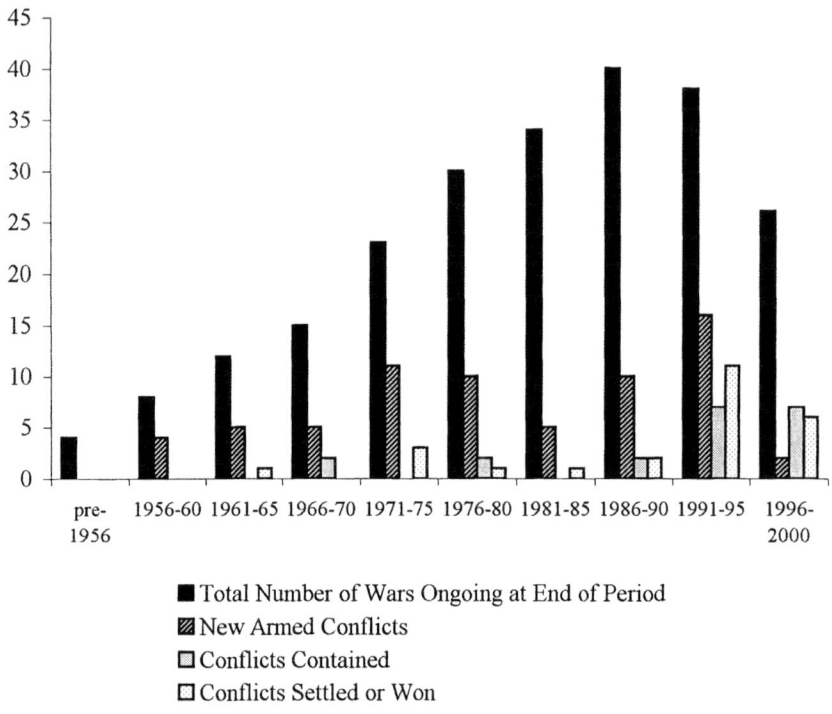

■ Total Number of Wars Ongoing at End of Period
▨ New Armed Conflicts
☐ Conflicts Contained
☐ Conflicts Settled or Won

During the 1990s, sixteen separatist wars were settled by negotiated agreements, and ten others were checked by cease-fires and ongoing negotiations. Half of all war terminations now involve negotiated settlements, in contrast to an estimated fifteen percent during the Cold War. Fewer separatist wars were being fought in 2000 than at any time since the early 1970s; fewer new wars were starting in the last years of the century than at any time during the Cold War; and the magnitudes data in figure 2.1 indicate that conflicts since the end of the Cold War have been no more intense and deadly on average than those of earlier decades (see also Ayers, 2000).

In the face of this evidence, why do so many observers remain convinced that the world is being overwhelmed by a tidal wave of ethnic conflicts? The answer is selective attention. Because they are preoccupied with immediate crises, most policy makers and journalists find it difficult to see the larger trends. Another part of the explanation is that observers tend to fixate on the most persistent conflicts, like those between Palestinians and Israelis, and between the north and south in Sudan—conflicts that have lasted for decades.

A third factor is that conflict prevention, peacemaking efforts and settlements of ethnic conflicts are seen as less newsworthy than warfare itself.

The more destructive phases of the war in Chechnya, for example, have attracted intense media attention and international criticism. In contrast, there is virtually no recognition that between 1994 and the present the Russian Federation has peacefully negotiated power-sharing agreements with Tatarstan, Bashkiria, and some forty other regions in the federation.

This is a critical issue for prospects of maintaining momentum for peacemaking. In the post-Cold War environment, where democracies now outnumber autocracies by more than two to one (reversing the ratio in 1978, when autocracies were predominant; Gurr, Marshall, and Khosla, 2000), there has been a marked increase in local, regional and international efforts to contain and settle wars of self-determination. Two-thirds of all terminations of separatist wars in the last half-century have occurred since 1990. The most common outcome (such as in South Africa, Mali, Niger, Nicaragua, and for India's Mizos and Moldova's Gagauz) has been a settlement between government and group representatives that acknowledges collective rights and gives institutional means for pursuing collective interests within states. This may involve better access to central government decision making, a level of regional autonomy, or elements of both. Few separatist wars lead to recognized independence.

Such wars are easier to settle in their early years and when there is strong international engagement. In contrast to high levels of intervention in wars within the postcommunist states in the 1990s, for example, recent settlements or containments of Asian and African separatist wars have involved little international support for mediation or peacekeeping and have resisted containment on average more than twice as long (seven years as compared to three; Gurr, Marshall, and Khosla, 2000).

In addition to the overall increase in international engagement, our analysis of Minorities at Risk data in the 1990s indicates a slight but significant shift in the forms of external support provided to politically active minorities. Whereas in 1990 to 1993, 42 percent of all instances of external material support provided to groups was military/strategic, this dropped to 35 percent in 1997 to 1998. At the same time, nonmilitary economic support increased from 26 percent to 33 percent, and support in providing access to external communication and dialogue increased from 13 percent to 16 percent. These figures provide evidence of a shift to more constructive international engagement, the effect of which is to improve the likelihood that conflicts can be settled without violence, by addressing group needs and promoting constructive dialogue.[1]

The same data also show a shift in the types of organization providing external support to politically active minorities, symbolic as well as material, at least to the extent reflected in the public sources relied on for the Minorities at Risk data. In 1990 to 1993, 34 percent were bilateral, from single states to specific groups, reminiscent of Cold War-style patron-client relations, while 16 percent each came from international organizations (IOs) and nongovernment organizations (NGOs), 15 percent from multiple states, and 7 percent from diasporas or kindred groups. In contrast, during 1997-1998, only 29 percent came from a single state, while other foreign governments contributed 24 percent and NGOs 17 percent, with IOs at 14 percent and diasporas and kindred groups still 7 percent.[2] These figures suggest a trend toward broader international engagement, particularly by smaller states and nongovernment organizations, which fits with the parallel trend from military to more economic and process-oriented support.

Overall, these findings provide evidence that the end of the Cold War has freed up political energies and material resources that have been made available for institutional reform and the constructive management of conflicts. They also emphasize the potential value of multi-track approaches to managing conflict, such as those explored in other chapters in this volume.

Nonviolent Strategies for Managing Ethnopolitical Conflicts

The media-driven preoccupation with ethnic violence in the Balkans, the Middle East, Central Africa and other regions with high-intensity conflicts obscures the fact that most of the gains made by minorities during the latter half of the twentieth century have been achieved by peaceful means.[3] Ethnonationalists and minority-rights activists can successfully pursue their collective objectives through conventional politics and nonviolent protest. Violent strategies are usually chosen only after other means have been tried and found wanting.

For example, during the early 1990s, Tatarstan challenged the integrity of the Russian Federation by declaring itself an independent state. Radical nationalists mobilized supporters for a self-determination campaign that began with mass demonstrations. What followed was not ethnic war but protracted negotiations between Russian and Tatar officials that culminated, in 1994, in a power- and revenue-sharing treaty that gave Tatarstan virtual independence and preempted open rebellion.

Similarly, in 1999, after decades of political activism by and on behalf of Canada's indigenous peoples, the Canadian government gave self-government to the newly created, resource-rich territory of Nunavut, which occupies 20 percent of the country's land and is home to 22,000 Inuits. No violence or even civil disobedience contributed to this outcome. Also in 1999, the German government passed legislation making it much easier for two million legal Turkish residents, most of whom have long resented their and their children's second-class status, to gain German citizenship. German and Turkish activists have pushed for such reforms for many years, but the only acts of violence that accompanied the conflict were neo-Nazi attacks on the Turks.

More than one-third of the 275 groups monitored by the Minorities at Risk Project in 1998 engaged in no overt (i.e., reported) political activism. Like Inuits in Canada and Turks in Germany, these peoples relied on conventional politics to pursue group objectives. Another 40 percent used less conventional means— such as symbolic opposition, movement building, and mass demonstrations— which are the classic techniques of nonviolent struggle. At the other end of the spectrum, one-fifth of the groups were in open rebellion, but, for the most part, their violence was limited to terrorism and small-scale guerrilla actions. Only twenty-one groups were fighting medium- to large-scale guerrilla or civil wars, like the KLA in Kosovo and militant Hutus in Burundi (Gurr, 2000a).

Leaders of movements for minority rights and national self-determination make choices about how best to pursue the interests of their peoples. Nonviolence is one kind of choice: it is a bundle of nonconventional, hence dramatic, strategies and tactics midway between electoral and interest group politics and organized violence. Nonviolence is, in some respects, a misnomer. Movement leaders like Mohandas Gandhi and Martin Luther King accept, sometimes solicit, violent retaliation, because as victims they will be better able to gain sympathetic support from bystanders. Leaders may also encourage observers to fear that if nonviolent claims for justice go unmet, violence will follow. Small doses of deniable violence can strengthen the hands of leaders of nonviolent movements.

The specific strategies of nonviolence are varied. A key strategy for most contemporary nonviolent movements is a public assembly of large numbers of demonstrators or marchers, showing officials and opponents that many people support a cause and, not incidentally, signaling their capacity for disruption. Gandhi's *satyagraha* movement for Indian independence, shaped by a distinctive ideology of nonviolent resistance to injustice, added to the repertoire. The success of civil rights activists in the American South provided another widely emulated strategy.

The tactics of nonviolent movements of the late twentieth century were distinct in at least three important ways from the politically inspired marches, protests and strikes common in Europe and North American cities over the last two centuries. First, their reliance on explicitly nonviolent resistance and disavowal of violence gives protesters a moral advantage. Second, because the tactics of nonviolent movements were creatively disruptive of public order and economic activity, authorities were compelled to respond to disorder in ways that almost invariably placed them at a moral and political disadvantage vis-à-vis the protesters. Third, they effectively used the news media to project their messages and images far beyond the immediate sites of confrontation. Whereas the primary audience for nineteenth-century demonstrators and strikers was public officials and employers who could redress their grievances, a principal audience of nonviolent activists has been a distant but potentially sympathetic public composed of people who might enlisted as allies and agents of reform (see also Sharp and McCarthy, 1997; Ackerman and Kruegler, 1994).

Leaders must assess the potential costs and gains of different strategies of collective action, and others must choose to follow or defect, depending on whether they are convinced the leaders have chosen wisely. Ethnic warfare is invariably costly, and its outcomes are highly uncertain, which is probably the most important reason why less than a tenth of minorities that were politically active in the late 1990s fought large-scale rebellions.

Decisions to rebel are seldom taken unless a significant segment of an aggrieved group gives up on other strategies. Most of the fifty-two new violent uprisings that began in the twelve years up to 1998—all but a half-dozen—proved to be outgrowths of longer-term conflicts. In the typical (median) case, a decade elapsed between the emergence of protest movements, or a previous violent episode, and the outbreak of new rebellions. Public policies during these intervening years are mostly inconsistent and expedient, often mixing limited and partly implemented reforms with repression. The implications for understanding why movement leaders choose the strategies they do are pretty clear. Usually activists choose rebellion only after experimenting with nonviolent strategies and finding that they do not work very well (Gurr, 2000a).

If rebellion is the last resort of those seeking minority rights and self-determination, does that imply that conventional politics is their first resort? Sometimes yes, but minorities often are closed out of conventional politics. Dominant groups in multiethnic societies and empires have preconceptions about who belongs to the political community and who does not. Few nineteenth-century southerners, even after the Civil War, thought that African Americans were legitimate participants in the political process. Until the early 1960s, aborigines in Australia were legally defined as wards of the state; they had neither citizenship nor the right to vote. Until the late 1980s, Russian communists paid lip service to the political rights of non-Russian peoples but made sure that Russian Communist Party members vetted decisions by titular leaders of the non-Russian republics.

If the political rules of the game exclude or marginalize ethnic and national minorities, engaging in conventional politics constitutes a poor strategic choice. Advocates of minority rights may be left standing outside the chambers of government, petitions in hand, hoping that someone will take up their cause. At this point strategies of active nonviolence may be seen as the only viable alternative to passive resignation or bloody rebellion and repression. The repertoire of accessible strategies that leaders can draw on and adapt has grown with the information revolution. So it was that "freedom rides," modeled on the voter registration drives of the U.S. civil rights movement, were organized in Australia by aborigines and their white student allies in an effort to desegregate private clubs and call attention to discrimination. Acehnese students and other democratic reform activists in Indonesia have established nonviolent action networks which adapt and create new tactics of disruptive nonviolent struggle.

The ideas and examples of successful nonviolent movements travel, particularly in democracies where they are most likely to reshape the political landscape, since governments are expected to be responsive to organized groups with a grievance, and elected leaders are susceptible to political pressures. Doctrines of individual and collective rights have also been codified in the national laws and international covenants at least of the Western democracies, though only since the mid- to late twentieth century. During the Cold War international human rights doctrine focused mainly on individual rights. The principles that ethnic minorities have collective rights to protect their culture and to pursue local and regional autonomy were not widely accepted in most Western countries until the early 1990s (see Preece, 1997).

More broadly, even without such laws in place, nonviolent political movements can affect the thinking of elites and potential allies in the broader public by highlighting current norms about what means of governance are acceptable or unacceptable. With the *satyagraha* campaign for Indian independence, for example, Gandhi sought to capitalize on the British sense of fair play. The movement's success in doing so was demonstrated when India's British viceroy told Gandhi: "You have reduced me to helplessness. . . . How can we lay hands on you without being villains?"[4]

The campaign led to a gradual shift in British thinking toward acceptance of the basic rightness or justice of Indians' demand for independence. What began in India in the 1930s and spread throughout the British political establishment during the 1940s and 1950s was the principle that colonized people had the right to self-governance. This norm shift followed from acceptance of the twin democratic principles that people should have the right to political participation and that leaders should be responsive to popular demands. Once a country's elite accepts these principles, there is no intrinsic or logical barrier to applying them in dealing with all those they rule. Thus, suffrage expanded in European democracies during the last two centuries from upper to lower classes, from men to women, from majorities to minorities, and, ultimately, to subjugated peoples. Social movements have been the engines driving much of this norm shifting. Thanks to the agitation of subordinate groups, what had been unthinkable became not only thinkable but obvious (see Finnemore and Sikkink, 1998).

The goal of nonviolent activism should be not only to attain at least some of the movement's goals but to do so in a way that encourages a buy-in by the elite, a stable "win-win" outcome that has positive payoffs for both parties. Public officials dealing with calls for social change will usually be aiming to maintain the state, stay in office, and secure public order, which are not necessarily incompatible outcomes. They do not like to be "reduced to helplessness" by minority and ethnonational challengers. Their most basic choices involve whether to rely mainly on strategies of repression or accommodation, and if they choose the latter, what specific accommodations to make. Within the realm of the expedient and the acceptable, officials look for cues about what has worked either to defuse other movements or to respond to them in ways that incorporate antagonists in a nondisruptive way into the political system. Each ethnopolitical conflict resembles a very serious game of moves and countermoves chosen from each side's repertoire. Over time, it becomes clear to most players that some sets of interdependent choices are more likely to have win-win outcomes. When efforts are made to coordinate these choices, we can think of them as scenarios for accommodating ethnic conflict.

More concretely, three types of ethnopolitical movements have lent themselves to win-win resolutions in the past forty years. The U.S. civil rights movement exemplifies the first kind: the demand by disadvantaged minorities for greater political and economic rights and benefits. The U.S. scenario for accommodation of such demands has been an individualistic one, emphasizing the legal and political incorporation of African American individuals into the political and economic system across local, state, and federal systems, and educational and economic opportunities have been opened up for those with the personal skills to take advantage of them. The Canadian federal government, alternatively, has pioneered multiculturalism as a solution to a similar problem. This strategy treats non-Anglo Canadian individuals as members of cultural collectivities and gives each group some of the political and economic means to maintain its separate collective existence. A similar strategy seems to be working so far, after thirty years of violent conflict, in Northern Ireland.

The specific policies of incorporation vary widely across countries, but all are designed to respond to minority interests and to avert the threat of disruptive collective action by giving minorities a stake in the system. One can question just how "equal" minorities become with the adoption of these policies, but it is undeniable that the targeted groups think they have made relative gains, that collective action by minorities is at a low ebb in Western democracies, and that most public officials are committed to maintaining the policies that contributed to these outcomes.

The strategies of demanding and granting minority rights have traveled widely. Guarantees for minority rights are incorporated into the constitutions of virtually all the postcommunist states and also in the new democracies established in Asia and Southern Africa during the last fifteen years. Practice lags behind constitutional precepts, but the general pattern, documented in analyses of the data on group discrimination in the Minorities at Risk study, is a slow but steady global improvement in the political and cultural status of politically active minorities during the 1990s (Gurr 2000a, chapter 4).

Nationalist struggles by ethnic minorities represent the second type of ethnopolitical struggle that has increasingly been resolved peacefully. Demands for separate statehood by conquered people are nothing new. When they emerged during the 1960s among Basques, Bretons, Catalans, Corsicans, Scots and Québeçois in established Western democracies, however, political leaders were shocked. The most ardent regional nationalists sought independence, like that won by colonial Africans and Asians, but generally were outnumbered by moderates who proved willing to settle with reformers at the center who offered packages of regional autonomy, cultural rights, and reallocation of development resources. For most ethnonationalists in Western societies, the attainment of autonomy within existing states by peaceful means is more attractive than the quixotic pursuit of complete independence through armed struggle. For government officials, devolution of central authority within an otherwise strong state is less costly than fighting a protracted conflict. If substate autonomy fails to satisfy the nationalists, most democratic leaders—like those in Prague in 1993 and Ottawa today—seem to prefer divorce to war. The negotiated settlement of ethnonational conflicts has thus become increasingly common throughout the world. Wars of independence in Western and postcommunist states in the twenty-first century seem out of time and place, a vestige of the past that is being superceded by newer strategies of accommodation and negotiated devolution of power.[5]

The third wave of conflicts that has reconfigured ethnopolitics emerged out of indigenous claims for cultural recognition and land rights. The contemporary indigenous rights movement originated in North America in the late 1960s and by the 1980s had gone global. Indigenous people do not usually seek to establish independent states as ethnonationalists do. Instead, they want the physical and political space in which to protect and re-create their distinctive ways of life. The U.S. and Australian federal governments were innovators in devising positive, low-cost responses to indigenous claims such as self-determination for tribal governments in the United States and recognition of traditional land rights (including subsoil mineral rights) in Australia. Officials responsible for what used to be called "native policy" in English-speaking democratic countries watched and learned from one another's innovations. Indigenous activists learned from and taught lessons to each other. Since the 1970s, activists have held periodic international meetings, also attended by officials, out of which have emerged a common doctrine of indigenous rights, an evolving list of best practices for making demands, and transnational networks of alliances with environmental and other activists. Road blockades and demonstrations have been used by members of First Nations in Canada to contain logging operations, by Sami in northern Scandinavia to resist construction of dams, and by Aborigines in Western Australia to stall mineral exploration. The similarity of the issues and tactics illustrates vividly the modularity of indigenous activism at the end of the twentieth century (see Wilmer, 1993).

Most governments in the Americas, and some in East, South and Southeast Asian countries, have accepted the basic principles of indigenous rights and have taken legal and practical steps to implement them. Open confrontations still recur between indigenous activists and government agents, as in Chiapas and Ecuador, but the general pattern is one of grudging cooperation in implementing a common agenda.

Nonviolent politics is not a sovereign remedy for all disadvantaged minorities and hopeful ethnonationalists. In some countries and situations, nonviolent ethnic movements are very likely to fail. In Milošević's Serbia there was little respect for minority rights and no accommodation with national minorities, though nonviolent mass action by Slav opposition did lead to his ouster after several minority wars. In Iran, the Baha'is' doctrine of political passivity has not protected them from persecution by Islamists. Indeed, throughout much of the Islamic world, the rights of non-Muslims and members of "heretical" sects are restricted by religious doctrine and public policy. In Turkey, the Kemalist doctrine of secular nationalism justifies the government's exclusion of Islamist parties and Kurdish nationalist parties alike from what is in principle a democratic political system. The Beijing government has adamantly opposed accommodation with Tibetan, Uighur, and Mongol "splittists," the Chinese epithet for regional peoples who want greater autonomy or independence. Nonviolence has so far been a nonstarter for warring Hutus and Tutsis in Central Africa. The irony of genocide in Rwanda and ongoing ethnic warfare in Burundi is that both followed the failure of attempts, promoted by international actors, at democratization and accommodation of ethnic rivalries (see Davies, this volume, regarding issues in promoting democratic transition).

Nonviolent movements in the last half-century have proved very effective for advancing the rights of minorities and ethnonationalists in democratic societies. They added greatly to the repertoires of collective action in democracies, old and new, and they have evolved hand in hand with strategies of public response that rely on incorporation and accommodation. It is also true that successful management of ethnic conflict requires parties on both sides to make compromises. As Gandhi recognized, political movements "can't have everything at one stroke"—indeed, they may never achieve everything. Moreover, accommodation in plural societies may prompt opposition from people in the majority who resent policies designed to guarantee minorities "unfair advantages." Some disillusionment with the compromising outcomes of ethnic conflict is inevitable and adds to the potential for the organization of new ethnopolitical movements. Chances are, though, that future ethnic activists will rely on the nonviolent strategies that proved effective in the recent past.

Assessing Conflicts for Potential Preventive or Management Initiatives

In the previous section, we discussed the options open to parties engaged in conflict to pursue their goals either through normal politics or through nonviolent direct action, without resorting to war. In this final section, we look at the options open for unofficial (second track) conflict management professionals who may wish to evaluate the prospects for constructive engagement in a specific conflict. As noted earlier, more NGO professionals (including university-based scholar-practitioners) are becoming involved in ethnopolitical conflicts, more of this involvement is directed toward promoting communication and providing economic support to at-risk groups, and more international involvement is associated with earlier cessation of hostilities.

It is critical that such interventions be carefully planned, in close consultation with representatives of the parties and with potential funders. If official representatives are not involved, relevant authorities should also be informed, if possible, and their assent or tolerance assured for any dialogue or other conflict management activities.

An important first step in promoting such consultations is a conflict assessment. This goes beyond the model-based risk assessments discussed above but can benefit greatly from them as an aid to identifying the key factors driving the conflict and how they might be addressed. Conventionally, preconflict preventive diplomacy is distinguished from peacemaking initiatives during conflict (typically focused more on short-term conflict containment) and from longer-term postconflict peacebuilding. With protracted ethnopolitical conflicts, however, given the fluctuating levels of violence (see Azar, this volume), these distinctions may become blurred. An initiative aimed at preventing a renewal or escalation of violence may require attention both to short-term containment and confidence building, and to long-term structural reforms addressing the needs and grievances of the parties. In any case, appropriate engagement requires careful prior assessment.

A conflict assessment should address three broad elements, following a structure such as that suggested below for potential second track initiatives:

1. Assessment of the current dynamics and larger context of the conflict, a necessary precondition to evaluating the appropriateness or feasibility of a conflict prevention or transformation initiative.
2. Analysis of alternative future scenarios, showing plausible long-term outcomes of the conflict, and considering possible actions or interventions that might increase the likelihood of a preferred outcome.
3. Planning for any proposed initiative, such as bringing together unofficial representatives of the conflicting parties (second track diplomacy).

1. Conflict Dynamics, Context and Feasibility of Second Track Initiatives
a) What is the conflict about? Place the issues in historical and regional context, considering relevant motivating, mobilization and opportunity factors as reviewed above.
b) What stage is the conflict in now? Examples (from mid-2001) include: conventional politics (e.g., Canadian Québeçois), unstable or militant politics (e.g., Tibetans in China), low-level or escalating hostilities (e.g., Kurds in Turkey, Albanians in Macedonia), war (e.g., Tamils in Sri Lanka), talk-fight or stalemate (e.g., Southerners in Sudan), deescalating or largely contained hostilities (e.g., Armenians in Nagorno-Karabakh), contested settlement (e.g., Serbs and Croats in Bosnia), settlement (e.g., Tuaregs in Mali and Niger), and reconciliation (e.g., El Salvador). Accordingly, the need may be prevention, crisis management, conflict mitigation or containment, termination, conflict transformation or resolution, or long-term peacebuilding.
c) Who are the parties involved, including states, minority groups, key leaders, organizations, factions, alliances, spoilers, and regional or international stakeholders? How are they affected, what are their sources of relative power and legitimacy, and what are their agendas or demands (positions)?
d) Identify the needs and interests of each party motivating these positions and perceptions. Distinguish negotiable interests from nonnegotiable human needs (Azar, this volume), and primary from secondary or derivative interests. Which are shared, which complementary, and which conflicting?
e) What are the main parties' perceptions of each other, and what information and communication channels are available between or among them? What cultural contrasts are involved? (See Moore and Woodrow, this volume.) To what extent do the groups need each other to achieve their goals?
f) What previous attempts to settle the conflict have been or are being made, by whom and with what results? Reasons for failure or limited success?

g) To what extent are the groups willing to talk with each other? At what level (officials, informal leaders or grassroots)? What factors are pushing them to talk? What is inhibiting them? Under what conditions and at what level might they be willing to talk?

2. Alternative Future Scenarios and Options for Preferred Outcomes

a) What are the plausible alternative future scenarios, or long-term outcomes, for the conflict as a whole? Note the assumptions on which each is built, going beyond simplistic war/no-war dichotomies. Further exploration and comparison of such scenarios may be a useful way to bring the parties into an integrative dialogue focusing on common futures rather than past injustices, as happened in South Africa in the transition from apartheid rule in 1991-1992 (see, e.g., Kahane, 1998).

b) Of these scenarios, which is the preferred outcome considering the interests of all parties? In contrast, for each of the main parties identify its likely best alternative to negotiating an agreement ("BATNA"; Fisher and Ury, 1991), and discuss which scenario(s) they would likely lead to. BATNAs provide a comparison point to evaluate what would be needed to motivate each party to improve on their BATNAs through negotiated settlement.

c) What are some specific integrative options for conflict prevention, containment, transformation or peacebuilding (sustainable development) that might increase the likelihood of a preferred outcome for both (all) parties? Explain how each addresses key interests/needs of the main parties, who might implement it, and whether it represents a short-term response (e.g., threat containment, confidence building), medium-term strategy (e.g., structure for a peace process) or long-term objective (e.g., appropriate new institutions of inclusive democratic governance, power sharing, autonomy).[6]

d) Which of these options, or what action steps to promote such options, might be undertaken by nonofficial actors from the conflicting communities?

3. Planning for a Proposed Second Track Initiative

a) What are your organization's (and funders') goals in the initiative, and what representatives of the parties have expressed interest in your assistance?

b) What are some possible points for initiating dialogue—natural links, bridges, common activities, contacts between the groups—and what issue(s) might they be willing to discuss? Who might be able to convene a dialogue, who might be acceptable to the parties as facilitators, and who would be both willing and credible or influential representatives in such talks? (Specify individuals, organizations or categories.)

c) What steps are needed to prepare the ground for a suitable dialogue among appropriate unofficial representatives of the parties? How will they be selected and agreed to? What predialogue caucusing within each party may be required to ensure agreement on an agenda?

d) What processes do you propose for facilitating movement by the participants in the dialogue toward better communication and willingness to cooperate in seeking common ground?

e) What framework do you propose for facilitating longer-term constructive engagement by participants and other key actors in building on their initial meetings? (A multi-year commitment is usually needed for participants in protracted conflicts to have the confidence needed to engage seriously in such activities.) How will the process link into or promote an official peace process or otherwise facilitate constructive official engagement and/or broaden grassroots support?

f) How will the initiative be evaluated throughout (see e.g., Rothman and Friedman, this volume), and what support is needed to make it happen?

This suggested framework for conflict assessment should, of course, be adapted as needed, adding or omitting material according to the specific objectives and resources of those involved. The second and third sections (future scenarios and planned initiatives), for example, may be brief in the early stages of planning but will need to be filled out in collaboration with representatives of the parties before and during second track dialogue processes. If, as is often the case, there is a need also for related capacity building for conflict management, this will add another dimension to project planning, discussed in Andrea Strimling's chapter in this volume.

Notes

1. Each minority is coded for each period for types of external support it receives from governments, international organizations, NGOs, and diaspora and exile organizations. These percentages are based on the total number of instances of support recorded for the two- and three-year periods in the Minorities at Risk data set. Figures for 1994-1996 are generally intermediate between the other two periods. For example, in 1994-1996, 41 percent of external material support was military/strategic, while 29 percent was economic and 16 percent provided access to communication and dialogue. Data prior to 1990 are not available in equivalent format and detail.

2. Figures for 1994-1996 are again generally intermediate between the other two periods. For example, in 1994-1996, 31 percent of external support was from a single foreign government, 20 percent from other governments, and 17 percent from NGOs.

3. Most of the material for this section is drawn from Gurr (2000b).

4. The quotes about Gandhi's movement are from Peter Ackerman's *A Force More Powerful: A Century of Nonviolent Conflict* (Santa Monica Pictures 1999).

5. The status of all ethnonational conflicts at the end of 2000 is assessed in Gurr, Marshall, and Khosla 2000. For a discussion of the emerging international doctrine and practice of "managed ethnic heterogeneity," see Gurr (2000a, chapter 7).

6. Among many useful sources discussing integrative options and peace processes are: The European Center for Conflict Prevention, 1999; Harris and Reilly, 1998; and multiple issues of *Accord: An International Review of Peace Initiatives* (London).

3
The Need for Multi-Track Diplomacy

John W. McDonald

Ethnic Violence—Three Theories

Why is there so much ethnic violence today? I have three theories to explain the unexpected explosion of ethnic violence in recent decades.

The Empire Theory

At the beginning of the twentieth century the world was dominated by ten great empires. Today there are none. In less than a hundred years all ten have collapsed. At the end of World War I, the Ottoman Empire, which had been around for over five hundred years, disappeared. So did the German and Austro-Hungarian Empires. At the end of World War II the Japanese Empire collapsed in defeat. During the course of the next twenty-five years the British, French, Dutch, Belgian, and Portuguese Empires expired. In 1991, the last of these ten great empires, the Soviet Union, collapsed in three months' time.

Why is this important to us? Those ten empires all ruled by force and fear, controlling the peoples within their domains. They kept the lid on ethnic conflict within their own realms. Today there is no intergovernmental structure or international force to keep the lid on these internal conflicts, and they are flourishing.

Over a hundred new nations have emerged out of those collapsed empires. In 1945, every nation except Switzerland signed the United Nations (UN) Charter. There were fifty-one signatories. There are now 185 member states in the UN, and almost all the new states have their own newly created ethnic minorities. National sovereignty is a fresh concept to the new states, and they cherish it, resisting both internal challenges and outside interference.

Nonnegotiable Issues

Over the centuries these empires, and many of their successor states, have stimulated violence by ignoring three fundamental human rights issues, which are at the core of a people's identity and which I consider to be nonnegotiable.

In October 1989, John Marks (Search For Common Ground), Ray Shonholtz (Partners For Democratic Change), and I (Iowa Peace Institute) were invited to Moscow by the Soviet Academy of Sciences to bring conflict resolution to the Soviet Empire. This was a dramatic challenge for us. Shortly after we arrived, we realized that not only was the theory of conflict resolution unknown, there was not even a word in the Russian language for it. The Russians had never needed one, because they had always ruled by power and force. Our first task was to come up with a word which would describe what we were talking about. With the help of interpreters we succeeded, and now "conflictology" (*konfliktologiia*) is part of the Russian lexicon.

During our visit, we were invited to meet with five members of the Supreme Soviet, the new parliament that had just been elected in the first free election in seventy years. After our introductions, one of them turned to me and asked if I would solve the Azerbaijan-Armenian conflict for them. I laughed and said, "I can't do that. Our field is a relatively new one but we don't have a magic wand." I added that they could not solve the conflict either, because they were a part of the problem. The Soviet government had created the problem in the first place and no one trusted people from Moscow who might try to intervene. They would have to find a neutral third party to take on the task of peacemaking.

By this time I had their attention and went on to say that we estimated there were about seventy ethnic conflicts bubbling below the surface of their empire. The Soviet government had created these conflicts by ignoring three fundamental, nonnegotiable issues dealing with a people's identity.

The first is *language*. I pointed out that the Soviet government had frequently denied an ethnic group the right to speak, read, or write its own language, as a means of controlling the group. This control mechanism does not work, because a people will kill for the right to speak their language. It is at the heart of their ethnicity, their identity.

I gave two examples. When the Japanese invaded Korea in 1910, they denied Korea the right to speak, read, or write Korean. Japanese was the only language allowed. This rule lasted until 1945, when their empire collapsed. Many Koreans today have still not forgiven the Japanese. The second example was Turkey. The 1922 constitution did not allow the Kurdish people to speak, read, or write their language. Some 30 percent of the population of Turkey is Kurdish. I said I believed that 95 percent of the violence in Turkey could be resolved if the law were reversed and Kurdish identity recognized.

I told the parliamentarians that they could change these restrictions in their empire by a stroke of the pen. They could reduce the potential for violence dramatically if they would allow all groups under their control to speak whatever language they wished.

The second nonnegotiable issue is *religion*. History has shown that people will kill and die for the right to practice their own religion. For seventy years the Soviet Empire was an atheist empire. It banned all religious practices in the name of the state. By the time of our meeting in 1989, the government was beginning to recognize the error and had started to change. I urged that the process be expedited to prevent more violence.

The third nonnegotiable issue is *culture*. The Soviets had denied ethnic groups their identity by trying to destroy their cultures. Soviet officials would deny a people the right to produce its own literature or poetry. They would take away its music, its dance, and the beautiful clothes the people wore for special occasions, and would not allow ceremonies of birth, death and marriage. All of these things impact on a people's cultural identity, and a people will kill to maintain that identity. When the denial of language, religion, and culture takes place simultaneously, violence is guaranteed.

The common thread linking these three issues is that they are all man-made—all imposed by the state. This means that they can all be changed. Of course, there are other long-term reasons for violence in the world, such as poverty, destruction of natural resources, etc., but these cannot be changed overnight. If language, religion and culture were universally allowed to be free of state control, the world would be a far more peaceful place.

Structure and Governance

The world is not designed or structured to cope with the kind of violence it is facing today. There has been a paradigm shift in the nature of conflict over the past decades. The symbolic date of that shift, for me, is that of the fall of the Berlin Wall, November 1989. Governments have refused to acknowledge this shift and so have not changed their historical approach to conflict.

Between 1989 and 1993, there were eighty-two conflicts in which more than a thousand people were killed per year. Only three of those conflicts were "wars" in the legal sense of invasion of one state by another, like the Iraq-Kuwait war. The world is structured to cope with this kind of war. The UN Charter and the UN Security Council were specifically designed to cope with such wars, and since the end of the Cold War, the Security Council has proven to be an effective instrument to deal with this kind of violence.

What about the other seventy-nine conflicts? They took place within the boundaries of single states. National sovereignty precluded intergovernmental organizations like the UN from entering a state wracked by internal conflict, unless specifically invited by its government. For example, in Algeria, many thousands of civilians have been murdered over the past several years. In early 1998, the European Union became concerned about this conflict, but it took weeks of negotiations before a small group of senior officials were allowed into the country, even for a few days, to hold ineffective talks with the government.

In 1999, there were no "wars," but there were twenty-four intrastate ethnic conflicts. Most of the violence is directed toward civilians, women and children, yet the world seems unable to move. We are not structured to cope with this kind of internal ethnic violence.

No government or intergovernmental organization anticipated this dramatic shift from war to intrastate conflict. Few institutional changes are taking place, nationally or internationally, because the problem is not officially recognized. Because the principle of national sovereignty is still supreme, it will take another twenty years before some sort of intergovernmental mechanism is put in place. Chapter 7 of the UN Charter would be the best place to start, but the Security Council still has a long way to go—witness its total inaction in the 1994 Rwandan genocide.

What can be done to fill the vacuum? Where are the peace builders? I believe that nongovernmental organizations (NGOs), private citizens practicing second- or multi-track diplomacy, are presently filling at least a small part of that vacuum. They are certainly the hope for the future.

Track-Two Diplomacy—Three Stories

Joe Montville, a close colleague and fellow diplomat, coined the term "track-two diplomacy" in the winter 1981-82 issue of *Foreign Policy*. I produced the first book using that term in the title in 1987 (McDonald and Bendahmane, 1987). The book was based on a symposium I organized in 1985 at the State Department's Center for the Study of Foreign Affairs, part of the Foreign Service Institute, toward the end of my forty years as a U.S. diplomat. My fellow diplomats scoffed, as many still do, at the thought that private citizens could play an effective role in any aspect of foreign affairs. I flatly disagreed with them and brought together nine experienced private citizens who had demonstrated great skill in track-two diplomacy and asked them to tell their stories. Publication of the book was delayed for eighteen months because it was seen as a threat to the State Department's mandate. The book was seen as a revolutionary document then, and in some circles it is still so considered. The following stories illustrate the power of track-two diplomacy.

Terrorism

In early 1989, John Marks, private citizen, decided to take on the two super-powers and try to get them to work together in the very delicate area of antiterrorism. The United States and the Soviet Union were at opposite poles on this subject. The United States, in effect, blamed the Soviets for every terrorist act that had taken place anywhere over the past forty years. The Soviets denied ever having been involved in any terrorist act. Of course, they refused to talk to each other.

John Marks gathered together ten U.S. private citizens who were experts in various aspects of anti-terrorism and brought them to Moscow, where they met for a week with ten Soviet experts, allegedly in their private capacity. The group had a difficult time at first, because neither side trusted the other. However, toward the end of the week there was a breakthrough. The Soviets stated that in the previous four years, seventy Soviet citizens had been murdered in nonwar zones, and the government needed help. Some constructive discussions then took place, and it was decided to meet again six months later, at the RAND Corporation in Santa Monica, California, to continue the talks.

The Santa Monica participants, still ten from each side, were more closely connected to track one. A former head and a retired deputy head of the CIA were on the U.S. team. The Soviets brought in two just-retired three-star generals from the KGB. This group picked up where the earlier meeting had left off. At the end of their week together they had agreed, in writing, to twenty specific areas of joint cooperation. All twenty participants signed the document and agreed to inform their respective governments of the constructive progress made.

On July 31, 1991, at a summit meeting in Moscow, Mikhail Gorbachev and George H. W. Bush announced that they had agreed to work together on the issue of terrorism and had signed a document that contained twenty recommendations for joint action. In two years, one private American citizen had made history, in a most sensitive area of foreign affairs. This is track two at its best.

The PLO

During the four years of the Carter presidency, Dr. Landrum Bolling, former president of Earlham College, journalist, Quaker and Middle East expert, met with Yasser Arafat, head of the PLO, for several days at a time, three or four times a year, to talk about the Middle East peace process. Landrum got to know Arafat very well and was able to pass Arafat's views to his track one connections in the United States. I believe those informal, track-two conversations went a long way toward bringing about the reversal of U.S. policy toward the PLO, in the last year of the Reagan administration, when the State Department was allowed for the first time to begin to talk and negotiate with Arafat.

In contrast, during those same Carter years, Andrew Young, U.S. ambassador to the UN and a close friend of the president, had a cup of coffee at the UN in New York with a member of the PLO delegation to the UN. Young was fired the next day for breaking the rules in talking to the PLO. This is a classic example of the rigidity of track one and flexibility of track two.

Northern Ireland

In 1985, the Anglo-Irish Agreement was signed by the governments of Ireland and Great Britain. Joe Montville and I were at the Center for the Study of Foreign Affairs at the time and decided to hold a one-day seminar on the treaty, bringing experts together from around the country. I focused on the fact that the treaty talked about the need for a bill of rights for Northern Ireland. I was fascinated by this, since neither country had its own bill of rights.

Over the years I kept lookout for any progress that might be made on a bill of rights, but saw nothing in the press. In 1989, as president of the Iowa Peace Institute, I was attending a conference in London and asked friends in the Foreign Office what, if anything, was going on with regard to this issue. Nothing was happening. I asked why language about a bill of rights had been included in a formal treaty if no action was being taken. After some hesitation there was an acknowledgment that the language had been put in the treaty for public relations purposes; no action was planned.

I was annoyed and disappointed. I contacted several friends from Belfast and learned that there was great interest by all parties in a bill of rights. Joe Montville and I hosted a meeting in Boston in January 1990, which consisted of six Americans and two men from Belfast, one Catholic and one Protestant. They were both private citizens who wanted to help build peace in their troubled land. At the end of our three days together, it was agreed that if the two from Belfast would draft their own bill of rights and check it out with the various political leaders in Northern Ireland to see if there was support for the idea, the Iowa Peace Institute would host a quiet consultation to discuss the draft and bring together international experts to critique it.

It took the two men a year to produce an excellent first draft. Then it took us a year to raise the money and organize the meeting. In December 1991, fifteen private citizens met to discuss this draft. Eight came from Northern Ireland: the two drafters, a professor, and five politicians, one from each of the five interested political parties. Seven were international experts: a justice of the Supreme Court of Canada, who had drafted the Bill of Rights of Canada; a New Zealand professor who was familiar with the New Zealand Bill of Rights; and several human rights and U.S. Bill of Rights experts from the United States.

There was tension at first among the eight from Northern Ireland, but they all had a specific task to work on, which they agreed was sorely needed, so there were no extraneous political exchanges. By the end of the week, a strong text had been developed, building on the first draft. Something else happened during this week: the eight men were beginning to get to know each other as human beings. We had set up a hospitality suite in the hotel that was open day and night, where the men could relax after the day's events. Twice, my wife and I dropped in at midnight and saw all eight sitting around together, coats off, shoes off, talking to each other like normal people. By the end of their time in Iowa the eight had bonded and trusted each other.

In late 1992, a conference was called by the British and Irish governments to discuss the conflict. At this six-week session an ad-hoc committee on a bill of rights was created. The text developed in Iowa was used as the basic document for discussion, and three of the five political leaders who were in Iowa were on the committee. At the end of the conference the two governments told the press they believed in a bill of rights for Northern Ireland and would see that such a document was approved. The April 10, 1998, Draft Peace Agreement for Northern Ireland includes the basic text which came out of Iowa.

A small, Iowa-based NGO was able to play a role in this peace process by focusing on one issue which was critical to the participants from Northern Ireland. By stimulating their involvement and having them draft their own bill of rights, by bringing them together with experts in the field and by recognizing the power of the various political parties involved, we were able to facilitate a process that eventually fit into the larger whole—citizen diplomacy at work.

Multi-Track Diplomacy

I launched the phrase "multi-track diplomacy" in a chapter in Kriesberg and Thorson's (1991) book. My chapter expanded track two by adding three more tracks to the process. Track five was the media, track four dealt with citizen-to-citizen exchange programs, and track three urged private-sector business involvement in peace processes. I envisaged a vertical hierarchy with tracks five, four, three and two designed to change the thinking of track one.

Later in 1991, Dr. Louise Diamond and I coauthored a book called *Multi-Track Diplomacy: A Systems Approach to Peace* (see Diamond and McDonald, 1996) which added four more tracks: education and training, peace activism, religion, and funding. Dr. Diamond recommended putting the nine tracks in a circle, so that all could be seen as equal participants in a larger system, rather than an all-powerful track one. All parts of the community had to be involved in peacebuilding if a peace agreement was to be effective and lasting.

In May 1992, Dr. Diamond and I formally launched our Institute for Multi-Track Diplomacy as a not-for-profit NGO based in downtown Washington, D.C. The institute is practice oriented and applies the theories we have developed on the ground in conflicted countries.

Peacebuilding

We break peacebuilding into three categories:

Political Peacebuilding

The Dayton Accords on Bosnia was a breakthrough document in political peacebuilding. Track one finally got together under U.S. leadership, and after arduous negotiations were able to end the conflict in Bosnia and start the long political process of rebuilding a political system so that a nation-state could begin to emerge. Only track one can carry out such tasks. Governments can do an excellent job when they have the political will needed to take action.

Economic Peacebuilding

Track one plays the essential role here as well. The World Bank, the International Monetary Fund (IMF), the UN Development Program, UNHCR and other UN and state aid agencies are invited into a country like Bosnia to help rebuild infrastructure destroyed by years of war. This need is recognized in the Dayton Accords and track one institutions can do an excellent job here as well, once the decision has been taken to act.

Social Peacebuilding

This area is not mentioned in the Dayton Accords. When I talk to most governments about it, they have great difficulty in acknowledging the need for it. Social peacebuilding is not about working with material things; it is about working with the people, working with the heart. It is about addressing the hate, anger, fear, lies, trauma and loss a people has experienced during years of devastating war. It is about trying to ensure that community leaders have the skills and support, at the community level, to stop the violence from spreading when allied troops eventually withdraw from Bosnia and violence breaks out shortly thereafter, as it usually does. Their goal must be to prevent the cycle of violence from re-creating itself. That is the goal of social peacebuilding, and that is what multi-track diplomacy is all about. That is how we define the role of the Institute for Multi-Track Diplomacy.

Operating Principles

We do not have one model that we apply to every situation. Each conflict is different and we respond to those differences in our approach. However, we do have twelve basic principles that we follow, which are fundamental to the way we work with conflicted societies (Notter and Diamond, 1996).

1. *Invitation.* We do not impose ourselves on any conflict. We are always invited by a party to the conflict. If we decide to accept the invitation (we turn down more than we accept), we go to the site of the conflict and listen, sometimes for two or three weeks. We listen to as many sides of the conflict as possible and ask the participants what their needs are. Are we in a position, as a small, not-for-profit organization, to meet any of the needs identified?
2. *Long-Term Commitment.* Once we decide we can be of assistance, we make a long-term commitment. This is a personal, professional and institutional commitment of at least five years. We talk about this commitment; we tell people that we are not there for a weekend training, or for a month. We know that conflict-habituated systems take a long time to develop and

cannot be resolved quickly. In effect, we are there as long as the participants want us there.

3. *Relationship.* We believe that our success as peacebuilders is directly related to the quality of the relationships that we establish with the people and institutions we work with. The way we build a relationship with track one is to say, very clearly, that we are not in their country to try to solve the political issues that are part of the conflict. That is clearly their responsibility, and we don't want them to misinterpret our presence. We tell them that we are totally transparent and invite them to participate in our training of community leaders if they are interested. We don't want to be seen as a threat by track one.

4. *Trust.* Trust is critical to our success; we cannot make progress without it. Relationships must be built slowly, based on mutual trust. Announcing our five-year commitment is an important part of building trust. Just showing up every few months is another way to let people know that you care about them and want to help them. We also say we have no hidden agenda, that our sole goal is peacebuilding. This takes more time for people to accept, but once accepted, it is an important part of building trust. We also honor the participants by acknowledging that they are the risk takers. We respect their courage.

5. *Engagement.* We let people know that we are engaged and caring partners. We are interactive and fully present with our local participants, sharing in the projects and developing deeply human relationships. We are concerned about what happens to them. We do not charge for our services, so that money does not get in the way of our engagement. We do not advertise our trainings, allowing information about them to spread by word of mouth. We have found this is less threatening to participants and allows them to decide if they really want to become risk takers. You have to be a risk taker to be a peacebuilder.

6. *Partnership.* We believe in the concept of partnership, both among professionals in the field of conflict transformation and in working with our local partners in the conflict situation. We recognize that we do not have all the skills or answers in this difficult arena, so we create coalitions to bring together the best talent available to work in a particular conflict. We also seek out local partners who can help us learn about the conflict. We recognize that women are usually the best peacebuilders, and we make an effort to bring them in as local partners.

7. *Synthesis of Wisdom.* Western conflict-resolution principles and practices are culture-bound and may not be as effective in other cultures, so we seek out indigenous wisdom, learn from it and then try to weave the two together. We acknowledge skills and traditions used by the local people, often for centuries, and offer our skills as a supplement to their practices. We talk about the fact that we are a learning community and encourage all

participants to learn from each other. We believe in sharing and synthesizing wisdom, wherever it occurs.

8. *Multiple Technologies.* We bring together a number of different methodologies, activities, and techniques, recognizing that each situation is unique. We recognize that different talents are needed at different stages of interaction with participants. This can mean that we bring in different trainers at different stages of the transformative change process. At the beginning, one learns basic skills of listening, rephrasing and putting oneself in the shoes of another. At another level, one can learn how to open one's heart to the enemy and begin to build trust. This requires different talents on the part of a trainer, or it might mean a different trainer. We adapt to the needs of the participants.

9. *Action Research.* We believe that our work is on the cutting edge of this new field of conflict resolution, and so we want to continue to learn from our practical work in the field. We then want to apply what we have learned to the next conflict situation. This is action research. Action research also includes the idea of evaluation. We build into our projects, from the beginning, evaluation techniques in order to test if what we are doing is effective and responds to the needs of the participants. Evaluation is an important element of our work.

10. *Responsibility.* Our work is to assist parties in conflict to address their own problems. We cannot and do not promise to solve their problems for them. We can facilitate, train, teach participants to become trainers, and build local capacities and institutions, but ultimately the responsibility for dealing with the conflict is theirs. Solutions imposed from the outside rarely work. We are there to help and to support. We are also sensitive to the need to help participants with their reentry process. When one has been working and training with the enemy, how does one explain what has happened when one returns to the home, work place, or local coffeehouse? We take responsibility for helping in these areas, but application of these new skills is the responsibility of the participant.

11. *Empowerment.* We seek to achieve conflict transformation in our partners and that requires local empowerment. This is critical to what we are about, and it can take a variety of forms. We try to tailor our interaction with each of our participants individually, so that the goal of empowerment can eventually be achieved by all with whom we work.

12. *Transformation.* This last principle is probably the most important. It is central to our mission. We are interested in trying to change a participant's view of "the enemy," to bring him to look at history, at values, at fear, at anger, at the perception of the other. To me, transformation means learning how to work and live together, in the same community, without violence, fear and strife. Wherever that occurs, anywhere in the world, it means transformation has taken place, and there is a little more peace in the world because of it.

Practice

We have projects in Cyprus, Israel, Palestine, Bosnia, Liberia, Tanzania, Kenya, India, Pakistan, and with the government-in-exile of Tibet. We raise money to carry out our work and have received financial support from a number of U.S. foundations, three governments and several international organizations. We are a membership organization, with over a thousand dues-paying members, and send our quarterly newsletter to over 5,000 people in eighty-five countries. We were founded in May 1992 and are incorporated as a not-for-profit organization in Washington, D.C. Our annual budget is about half a million dollars. We have six paid staff, five or six unpaid interns and work with some twenty trainers from around the world under short-term contracts.

Let me briefly examine our work in Cyprus, our first and ongoing project.

Cyprus is a beautiful island in the eastern Mediterranean. Its history goes back some 8,000 years. In 1960, the island became independent from the British Empire. At the end of 1963, intercommunal violence broke out, and the UN Security Council sent in a UN peacekeeping force in 1964. In 1974, there was more violence, and Turkey sent in 30,000 troops. Both the UN and the Turkish forces are still there. All Turkish Moslems now live in the North and all Greek Christians in the South. A "green line" divides the island and the capital city, Nicosia, and access to the "other" side is extremely limited. A whole generation has grown up hating the other side, having never met anyone from there.

Louise Diamond was invited into the conflict and in 1991 spent three weeks on Cyprus listening to both sides. We decided we could help and that this would be our first project. We made a five-year commitment and began raising funds for our work. Early in the process we called on senior officials in the North and South, at the UN and at the U.S. State Department. We said to all of them that we were not interested in solving the political issues; that was their business. We wanted to work with community leaders and help them to develop their conflict-resolution skills so that when a peace treaty was signed and all the troops withdrew, the people we had trained could help to keep the peace and prevent the cycle of violence from starting up again. Nobody stopped us.

Louise made seven trips to the island in the next fifteen months. Each time, she strengthened relationships, built trust, did training in the North and South, thanks to the support of the UN, and finally, brought six persons from each side together on the Green Line. They had the skills, they trusted her, and they bonded. They formed a steering committee to help us manage the project.

We then partnered with the Conflict Management Group at Harvard, and Louise and Diana Chigas became codirectors of the Cyprus Consortium. They have now trained thousands of Cypriots, from all parts of our multi-track system, and also a number of trainers who are carrying their new skills across the island. In 1997, we brought forty high school students to the United States for a summer camp, for training in conflict-resolution skills. We have been told that we started a social movement on the island! Our work continues.

Let me conclude with a story that will give you an idea about what I meant when I said we work with the heart. Louise and I put on a half-day training session in the Turkish North in 1992. Since we do not advertise our workshops, we were pleased that thirty-five people had gathered and that 40 percent were women. All "tracks" were represented except funders. We always sit in a circle, and as I opened the session I asked that each person give his or her first name and say why he or she had decided to be with us that day. Halfway around the circle a man in his mid-forties said his name and then said:

> I have hated the Greek Cypriots all my life, because they killed both of my parents. I went on with my life, however, became a medical doctor, got married and have a 4-year-old son. I came to this workshop because of what happened three nights ago in my home. I went in to kiss my son good night and found, lying next to him in bed, a toy wooden rifle. I asked my boy why he had that rifle in bed with him and he said, "To kill the Greek Cypriots when they come after me." I herewith forgive the Greek Cypriots for killing my parents. I am here to learn some new skills so that I can help my son to have a different life than I have had.

Conclusion

I have described my theories as to why we have so much ethnic violence in the world and expressed my concern that this type of violence will continue to expand because we, as a world, are not structured to cope with ethnic conflict. My hope is that more skilled nongovernmental organizations will enter the peacebuilding field and fill the vacuums currently left by governmental inaction.

4
Historical Mapping of the Field of Interactive Conflict Resolution

Ronald J. Fisher

The field of interactive conflict resolution (ICR) is approximately thirty-five years old, although the term itself was not introduced until the early 1990s (Fisher, 1993). The label is used to capture small-group, problem-solving methods for analyzing and contributing to the resolution of protracted intercommunal and international conflicts which have escalated to violent interaction and apparent intractability. The approach brings together unofficial yet influential representatives of identity groups or states engaged in destructive conflict for informal and flexible discussions in a neutral setting designed and facilitated by a team of impartial social scientist-practitioners. On a broad scale, ICR can be conceived of as face-to-face activities between members of conflicting parties that engage them in communication, dialogue, analysis, training, or reconciliation with the intention of increasing mutual understanding and trust. However, the core of the method represented most strongly in its history focuses on conflict analysis and problem-solving discussions directed toward creating greater understanding of the conflict and collaborative actions to deescalate and resolve it (Fisher, 1997).

ICR assumes that the keys to the resolution of conflict lie in the parties themselves and that face-to-face interaction between representatives, whether in dialogue, analysis or negotiation, are ultimately required to increase mutual awareness and build cooperative relationships and agreements. ICR also takes a social psychological stance in assuming that subjective aspects of conflict, such as misperceptions, hostile attitudes, and miscommunication, have to be improved and that relationship issues, such as mistrust, adversarial orientations and frustrated basic needs, must be addressed in order to move toward true resolution or transformation of the conflict. This is not to deny the importance of objective or substantive issues, such as scarce resources or power imbalances, but to assert that methods which deal only with objective aspects are not likely to produce mutually satisfactory and enduring outcomes. Thus, the usual objectives of ICR interventions, including improved attitudes, greater under-standing, increased trust and a more cooperative orientation, are quite comple-mentary to those of traditional methods of conflict management which emphasize agreements on substantive issues. In this way, proponents of ICR see it as having unique potential as a prenegotiation method and more broadly as an avenue to peacebuilding in divided societies.

ICR further assumes that in highly escalated and protracted conflict between identity groups, the involvement of an impartial and trusted third party is necessary to induce effective communication and creative problem solving. The role of the third party is primarily facilitative and diagnostic, rather than directive or prescriptive; it can perhaps be best seen as a form of professional consultation (Fisher, 1972, 1990). The demands of this role require that the team or panel of scholar-practitioners have moderate to considerable knowledge about the conflict and the parties in question, knowledge and expertise in conflict analysis, and human relations skills in interpersonal and cross-cultural communication and small-group processes. All this is necessary so that the participants can be assisted to engage in an in-depth (and in some ways threatening) analysis of their conflict and in productive confrontation on the issues and the interests, values and needs which underlie them.

Participants in ICR interventions have varied from citizen members of their respective states or groups, to influential individuals from particular sectors of their society (politics, business, education, etc.), to high-level, unofficial representatives who report back to their leaderships. Probably the most common participants are influential opinion leaders who carry weight in their societies and "have the ear" of the political decision makers or at least important political constituencies. The identity and influence of the participants is a primary determinant of the potential effects which any interactive experience may have on policy making and the ultimate resolution of the conflict. This is because the method assumes that individual changes in attitudes or realizations about the conflict or ideas for deescalation have to be transferred back to the political arena to have any impact on the conflict. Thus, the more influential the participants and the more direct their connection to policy making, the greater the probability that ICR interventions, in a complex field of multiple causes, can have discernible positive effects on the process of conflict resolution.

This chapter will provide a brief overview of the history of ICR over the past three decades. An attempt will be made to ascertain the main streams of development which have been associated with leading scholar-practitioners and identified to some extent with different disciplines and professions. Linkages among individuals and streams will be provided, and important contributions to theory and practice will be charted (see figure 4.1). After the review of historical developments, the conclusion will identify some of the significant issues and challenges which currently face the field.

Figure 4.1 Evolution of the Field

Field	Social Psychology	International Relations	Unofficial Diplomacy	Psychiatry
1960	Blake et al 1964 Intergroup Conflict Walton 1969 Interpersonal Peacemaking	Burton 1965 Malaysia Burton 1966 Cyprus Burton 1969 Controlled Communication		Wedge 1970 Dominican Rep.
1970	Doob et al 1969 The Horn[1] Doob 1970 Fermeda Doob 1971 N. Ireland Doob 1974 Cyprus Fisher 1972 Consultation Fisher 1976 TPC Model Fisher 1976 India-Pakistan Kelman & Cohen 1971 Israeli-Palestinian Kelman 1972 Problem-Solving Workshop Kelman & Cohen 1976 Problem Solving Cohen & Azar 1979 Egypt-Israel	De Reuck 1974 Controlled Communication	Berman & Johnson 1977 Unofficial Diplomats	Volkan et al 1979-1984 Israelis, Egyptians, Palestinians

Figure 4.1—Continued

Field	Social Psychology	International Relations	Unofficial Diplomacy	Psychiatry
1980	Doob 1981 Pursuit of Peace · Fisher 1983 TPC Review · Kelman & Cohen 1986 Interactional Problem Solving · Doob 1985 Cyprus · Kelman 1986 Interactive Problem Solving · Doob 1987 Adieu	Mitchell 1981 Peacemaking · Azar & Burton 1983 U.K.-Argentina · Azar & Burton 1986 · Azar 1984 Lebanon · International Conflict Resolution · Azar 1985 Sri Lanka · Burton 1987 Deep-rooted Conflict	Dartmouth Conference Task Force 1981 US-USSR (Stewart, 1987) · McDonald & Bendahmane 1987 Track-Two Diplomacy	Montville 1987 Track-Two Diplomacy
1990	Fisher 1990 Conflict Resolution · Rouhana & Kelman 1994 Continuing Workshop · Doob 1993 Interventions · Fisher 1990 1991 1993 Cyprus · Fisher 1997 Interactive Conflict Resolution · Kelman 1995 Contributions	Burton 1990 Conflict Series · Azar 1990 Protracted Social Conflict · Rothman 1992 Prenegotiation · Mitchell & Banks 1996 Handbook · Rothman 1997c Identity-Based Conflict	Chufrin & Saunders 1993 Public Peace Process · McDonald 1991 Beyond Track Two · Saunders & Slim 1993 Tajikistan · Diamond & McDonald 1996 Multi-Track Diplomacy · Saunders 1998	Volkan et al. 1991 Unofficial Diplomacy · Volkan & Harris 1992 The Baltics · CSMHI 1995 Continuing Workshops

Streams of ICR History

The Genesis of Interactive Conflict Resolution

The creation of small-group, interactive methods of conflict resolution in the mid-1960s is generally attributed to John Burton and his colleagues at University College, London (Burton, 1969), although the work of Robert Blake and Jane Mouton on intergroup problem solving in organizational settings also had seminal effects (Blake, Shepard and Mouton, 1964). Burton was an Australian diplomat turned academic who challenged traditional, realist approaches to international relations and sought to supplant them with a pluralistic, systems-orientated perspective (Burton, 1965; Banks, 1984). One implication of this "world society paradigm" is that violent conflict, rather than being inevitable and amenable only to power strategies, is actually a problem that is open to diagnosis and resolution involving integrative solutions.

Challenges from realists led Burton and his London group to select a case in which to intervene in order to demonstrate the utility of their thinking. Drawing on his diplomatic contacts, Burton invited representatives from Malaysia, Indonesia and Singapore, which were engaged in an escalating conflict that had resisted diplomatic attempts at management and mediation. With some confusion and differences among the third-party team, but also with expertise in conflict analysis and small-group problem solving, Burton and his colleagues engaged the delegates in five days of intense discussion in December 1965, followed by briefer sessions over the next six months. The parties were invited to describe the basis of the conflict from their perspectives, and the ensuing open discussion allowed the third-party panel to bring in concepts and interpretations for analysis and to draw comparisons with other cases. According to de Reuck (1974), the workshop was successful in correcting mutual misperceptions, redefining the conflict, reassessing the costs of it, and developing options for movement toward resolution. After the initial session, the representatives returned home, and diplomatic contact was restored. Following the series of discussions, a framework was established for resolution that was ultimately incorporated into the 1966 Manila Peace Agreement. Burton (1994) maintains that the London group had discovered a process of facilitated mutual analysis that led to new realizations conducive to conflict resolution.

In the wake of their perceived success, Burton and his colleagues established their Centre for Conflict Analysis and looked for other destructive conflicts to address. They found their next opportunity on the Mediterranean island of Cyprus, where UN mediation had failed to repair the escalating schism between the Greek and Turkish Cypriots that followed independence in 1960 and constitutional breakdown in 1963. Burton invited high-level representatives to a five-day workshop in London in October 1966. After initial adversarial presentations, the panel was able to induce analysis, and the parties developed fresh insights and considered directions by which they might return to negotiations, which they ultimately did (Mitchell, 1966, 1981). This second positive outcome confirmed for the Burton group that it had discovered an important new tool for addressing international conflict.

Burton (1969) initially termed his approach "controlled communication," to capture the role of the third party in building a nonthreatening atmosphere in which the high-level representatives of the adversaries can examine their perceptions of the conflict and each other prior to exploring avenues for resolving it. The term "problem solving" entered after the Cyprus workshop, to distinguish the work from that of diplomatic negotiations and to stress the search for cooperative solutions (de Reuck, 1974). In the late 1960s, members of the London Centre explored the possibilities for intervening in a number of protracted conflicts, but nothing materialized. In the early 1970s, Burton spearheaded an initiative in Northern Ireland which resulted in two workshops before the British administration withdrew support (Fisher, 1997). In 1978, the Centre was relocated to the University of Kent in Canterbury, with Burton and A. J. R. (John) Groom as the primary faculty members. In the early 1980s, Burton moved to the United States, where he collaborated with Edward Azar in a series of interventions (see below) before heading up the Center (now Institute) for Conflict Analysis and Resolution at George Mason University. Groom became director of the Center, which continues to foster research on international conflict resolution and has had some involvements in problem-solving workshops over the years. Burton continued to develop his theory of practice, producing a *Handbook* for problem solving in 1987, and a four-volume set on conflict resolution in 1990, in collaboration with Frank Dukes, which placed particular emphasis on needs theory for explaining "deeply rooted conflict." Thus, his contributions to ICR include both the creation of the basic method and the theoretical underpinnings that give the supporting rationale for its appropriateness and effectiveness. Two other founding members of the Center, Christopher Mitchell and Michael Banks, have recently articulated the problem-solving methodology in a concise yet comprehensive handbook covering all phases of the process (Mitchell and Banks, 1996).

Human Relations Contributions and Controversies

Also in the 1960s, but independent of Burton's work, American social psychologist Leonard Doob looked for ways to bring social scientific knowledge and methods to bear on the disturbing problems of intergroup and international conflict. A visit to Somalia in 1965 led Doob and a group of colleagues at Yale to consider how human relations training methods, then popular in the United States, might be applied to the conflict in the Horn of Africa involving Somalia, Ethiopia and Kenya. Years of planning punctuated by numerous delays finally brought together a mixed group of "influentials" for a two-week workshop in 1969 which used sensitivity training supplemented by other interactive exercises to increase understanding and improve attitudes (Doob, 1970). The rationale, different from Burton's, was that through learning about themselves and their relations with others, the participants could enter into more genuine interaction and possibly create innovative solutions to the conflict. Indeed, the two mixed sensitivity training groups did produce proposals to end the conflict, but the total workshop could not agree and ended with frustration and differing evaluations.

Undeterred, the Yale group next applied Tavistock training, in a 1971 workshop with Protestant and Catholic community leaders from Belfast, Northern Ireland, producing a variety of positive and negative effects (Doob and Foltz, 1973). Unfortunately, an acrimonious conflict ensued between the organizers/trainers and two local associates over the goals and outcomes of the intervention, resulting in a legacy of controversy (Alevy et al., 1974; Boehringer et al., 1974; Doob and Foltz, 1974, 1975). Doob also invested considerable energy in addressing the Cyprus conflict, organizing a 1974 workshop which was aborted by the Athens-inspired coup and Turkish invasion (Doob, 1974). In 1985, he was able to organize a series of meetings with "influentials" from the two communities, but the intervention was terminated when the Turkish-Cypriot administration withdrew its approval (Doob, 1987). Doob has also made important contributions to ICR's theory of practice, discussing the components involved in unofficial efforts (Doob, 1975), building a model of the underlying elements and processes of war and peace (Doob, 1981), and providing a broad analysis of intervention in human affairs (Doob, 1993).

Interactive Problem Solving

Herbert Kelman, an American social psychologist at Harvard University, was a member of the third-party panel at Burton's 1966 Cyprus workshop and came away convinced that this new method was a way of applying social psychology to international conflict (Kelman, 1998). In collaboration with Canadian social psychologist Stephen Cohen, he developed a prototype workshop, based in part on a comparison of the Burton and Doob approaches, for application to the Israeli-Palestinian conflict (Kelman, 1972; Cohen et al., 1977). Following the approach of "interactional [now interactive] problem solving," the workshop begins with separate preworkshop sessions with each side to build familiarity within the national team and understanding for the third party. The joint interaction begins with each side expressing its views of the conflict and its underlying concerns—i.e., fears and needs—and through facilitation and analysis provided by the third party moves toward discussing the overall shape of a solution as well as resistances and constraints and how to overcome these (Kelman, 1979; Kelman and Cohen, 1986; Kelman, this volume). Following the initial work with Kelman, Cohen collaborated with Edward Azar on the Israeli-Egyptian peace process (see below) and then shifted his attention to the official diplomatic process, where he has served as third party for contacts between Egyptian, Israeli and Palestinian representatives.

Kelman and a succession of colleagues and graduate students have now completed over fifty workshops involving increasingly influential Israelis and

Palestinians and contributing to the political discourse within and between the two societies and to the peace process in general (Kelman, 1986, 1995). After years of single workshops, Kelman and his colleagues developed a continuing workshop in which the same participants met regularly for several sessions (Rouhana and Kelman, 1994), and next a joint working group that held continuing sessions with interim work on difficult political issues related to the final-status negotiations (Kelman, 1995). In total, the contribution of Herbert Kelman serves as a compelling demonstration of how the carefully articulated work of scholar-practitioners can contribute to the process of conflict resolution.

Third-Party Consultation

My own work in ICR began with the creation of a generic model of "third party consultation" (TPC; Fisher, 1972, 1976) based largely on the contributions of Richard Walton in interpersonal peacemaking (Walton, 1969), Robert Blake, Jane Mouton, and their colleagues in intergroup problem solving in organizational settings (Blake, Shepard and Mouton, 1964), and John Burton at the international level (Burton, 1969). Following applications of the model to intergroup conflicts in community settings, which demonstrated positive effects on attitudes (Fisher and White 1976), I organized a series of problem-solving sessions bringing together "pre-influentials" from India and Pakistan (Fisher, 1980). This study was distinguished by a systematic process analysis of the meetings, which supported ICR as a form of small-group problem solving, and also documented the implementation of the third-party functions and tactics as specified in the model (Fisher, 1997). A comprehensive review of TPC interventions in organizational, community and international settings generally supported the validity of the model for guiding practice but called for more rigorous research to document processes and outcomes (Fisher, 1983).

In the 1990s, under the auspices of the now-defunct Canadian Institute for International Peace and Security, I was able to initiate a series of conflict-analysis workshops on the Cyprus conflict (Fisher, 1991, 1992, 1994a). These sessions brought together influential Greek and Turkish Cypriots to discuss the sources and nature of the conflict, the underlying fears and needs of each side, and the qualities of a renewed relationship that would be part of the resolution. The second workshop, held near London, England, resulted in plans for a number of peacebuilding initiatives, some of which came to fruition, including cross-line meetings of business leaders and a series of bicommunal art exhibits. Two subsequent workshops held on the island focused on the central role of education in the conflict, both in terms of helping to maintain the conflict through nationalist influence and the potential contributions of education to peacebuilding. The Cyprus initiative serves to illustrate the utility of the model of third-party consultation in planning and implementing ICR interventions (Fisher, 1997). It also demonstrates how ICR is a form of consultation, one that goes through the usual phases of consultation and carries the professional and ethical requirements of intervening in someone else's system (Fisher, in press).

Protracted Social Conflicts and Problem-Solving Forums

Edward Azar was a Lebanese-American political scientist whose early career was distinguished by his contributions to the quantitative study of international relations, specifically on how conflict episodes are reflected in interstate interactions (e.g., Azar, 1970). His tracking of conflicts over time indicated that since the Second World War, most conflicts were ethnic rather than strategic, were occurring in the Third world, and were being exacerbated by the involvement of the United States, the Soviet Union and their allies. This finding led Azar to decry the "superpower bias" in international relations and to acknowledge that most of the world's states are small, destitute entities that are highly vulnerable to intergroup cleavages and negative international influences (Azar, 1983). His analysis of the world situation led Azar to coin the term "protracted social conflict" to denote the most violent and apparently intractable conflicts between communal groups that are struggling to satisfy their basic needs within the same political framework (Azar, this volume).

In the 1970s, Azar was involved in numerous conferences on the Middle East conflict and served as a member of the third-party team in one of Kelman and Cohen's early Israeli-Palestinian workshops. This led to a period of collaboration with Cohen involving various action-research activities to analyze and address the Middle East conflict. This work included a problem-solving workshop in 1979 which brought together Israeli and Egyptian "influentials" to consider issues arising from the Camp David Accords and to find ways of building a peaceful, enduring relationship between the two societies. The resulting analysis identified the major issues facing the peace process, such as acceptance and security, which needed to be addressed if there was to be a lasting resolution (Cohen and Azar, 1981).

Moving away from the predominant strategic analysis in international relations, Azar and his colleagues focused on the social structural properties of protracted social conflict (PSC) at the local level. PSCs were initially seen as hostile interactions between groups over long periods of time with sporadic outbreaks of violence. They were considered to be extremely difficult to resolve, because they are linked to social and national identities (Azar, Jureidini and McLaurin, 1978). A major aspect of PSCs is struggle for recognition and acceptance, and this explains both their incredible capacity to absorb resources and their resistance to traditional methods of settlement or termination. Although PSCs involve deep-seated racial, ethnic or religious hatreds, ethnicity is not the sole causative factor (Azar and Farah, 1981). Structural inequalities and differences in political power crossed with opposing group identities lie at the heart of the problem. That is, when certain groups or coalitions have access to power and resources and deny other groups access to these benefits, the seeds for PSCs are sown. This analysis led Azar to consider the linkages between intractable conflict and international development, and to identify such factors as resource maldistribution, population dynamics, and ineffective development projects within a postcolonial context (Azar, 1983). Thus, he was drawn to the needs-analysis postulated by Burton and others and came to see PSCs as due to denial of basic human needs—for security, identity and effective participation—that determine developmental requirements (Azar, 1985). Following this line of analysis, Azar (1990, this volume) developed a comprehensive and systematic model of the sources and processes of PSCs that is a laudable blend of psychological, sociological, economic and political factors.

The immediate implication of Azar's PSC model is that traditional methods of conflict management will not work (Azar and Moon, 1986). What is required is a combination of short-term interventions, particularly problem-solving workshops, to initiate breakthroughs, leading to long-term efforts to promote structural development by addressing the basic needs of the contending groups. In the mid 1980s, Azar teamed up with John Burton to launch the Center for International Development and Conflict Management at the University of Maryland, where he articulated his method of "problem-solving forums" to address PSCs (Azar, 1990). There followed a series of problem-solving forums focusing on three of the world's most difficult conflicts.

Three forums addressed the conflict between the United Kingdom and Argentina over ownership of the Falklands/Malvinas Islands, which after lengthy negotiations had led to war in 1982. "Influentials" from the two countries analyzed the conflict and searched for directions toward resolution, with particular attention to balancing the need for self-determination with concerns about sovereignty. A set of principles was developed that eventually served as a basis for official negotiations, which unfortunately were unsuccessful in ending the dispute (Little and Mitchell, 1989). The Lebanese conflict served as the focus of two forums which brought together representatives from the various political and religious groups. These meetings produced a set of principles for a united Lebanon, and a resulting network of participants and others used these to draft a National Covenant Document that was integrated into the 1989 Taif Accords, thus making an important contribution to the peace process. One forum was held on the conflict in Sri Lanka, resulting in a commitment to develop tension-reduction measures. This forum was followed by two briefer seminars of a more academic nature.

Edward Azar challenged the field of international relations to shift its focus from the power politics of the Cold War to the destructive conflicts gripping the Third World (and now Eastern Europe and the nations of the former Soviet Union). He challenged the field of conflict resolution to realize that conflict and development are intertwined in both theory and practice. He articulated how the methods of conflict resolution should go hand in hand with structural development to analyze intergroup cleavages, reduce inequities and address the basic needs of all groups and individuals. His legacy for the practice of interactive conflict resolution is thus a rich and powerful one (Fisher, 1997).

The ARIA Framework

One of Azar's former students, Jay Rothman, has extended the problem-solving approach to provide a systematic model of prenegotiation and a broad framework for understanding and addressing identity-based conflicts. His model of prenegotiation is a process-oriented and prescriptive one, which defines the stages of (1) framing, wherein the parties develop shared definitions of the conflict and develop the will to negotiate; (2) inventing, wherein the parties create cooperative strategies for addressing the central issues and build confidence in the negotiation process; and (3) structuring, wherein the parties make joint decisions about setting the formal table and build a momentum of negotiation. Rothman has used this model in planning and implementing a variety of prenegotiation and conflict-resolution training workshops focusing on the Israeli-Palestinian conflict, including the status of Jerusalem (Rothman, 1991, 1992).

Rothman's ARIA framework (Antagonism, Resonance, Invention, Action) provides a structured process for addressing identity-based conflicts: ongoing struggles between groups that are relatively impervious to resolution because people's identities as expressed by their group affiliations are threatened or frustrated. These conflicts are different from interest-based conflicts, which are primarily about competition for tangible resources. Identity-based conflicts are deeply rooted in underlying human needs, particularly those for safety, dignity, recognition, control, efficacy and purpose, and therefore they cannot be addressed with methods, such as negotiation, that are appropriate to interest-based conflicts. In fact, Rothman contends that identity-based conflicts are exacerbated by the application of traditional methods of conflict management. What is required is creative engagement wherein all parties express their essential concerns and hear those of the other sides, thus building a base for reconciliation and cooperative action.

The ARIA framework provides a road map for the parties to bring forward their motives and values with third-party facilitation, to understand their deeper needs, and to search for and implement cooperative ways out of the conflict. The first step of "Antagonism" involves adversarial framing, in which the *what* of the conflict is expressed in terms of the resources at stake and the opposing solutions that the parties are proposing. The second stage, "Resonance," moves the parties into reflexive reframing that focuses on the *why* and *who* of the conflict—that is, the identity needs of the two groups. The third stage, "Invention," then engages the parties in the *how* of resolving the conflict through integrative solutions that address both sets of needs. The final step, "Action," consolidates the work of the three previous stages through agenda setting that lays out how to implement the joint solutions. Once the analysis, reframing and creation required by the ARIA process are complete, the parties are in a good position to move into conventional negotiation and problem solving on concrete agreements to address the many differences between them. In applying his model to organizational, community and international settings, Rothman (1997c) contends that even people who hate each other can be brought together through the ARIA process, not necessarily as friends but as partners who appreciate and respond to each other's identity needs.

Unofficial, Track-Two, and Multi-Track Diplomacy

A number of individuals have sought to inform and complement official diplomacy with concepts and approaches from the emerging field of conflict resolution. Prominent among these pioneers was Bryant Wedge, a psychiatrist who saw psychological elements as a major source of unpredictability and danger in conflict between peoples and states. Following his successful involvement as an intermediary in a mid-1960s crisis in the Dominican Republic involving the United States, Wedge (1970) developed a model of "third party intercession" that defines five stages, in which an intermediary induces dialogue, defines interests, establishes contact, facilitates the development of cooperative programs and terminates the intervention once official negotiation is established. Wedge, as a founder of the Center (now Institute) for Conflict Analysis and Resolution at George Mason University, and of the National Peace Academy Campaign that resulted in the U.S. Institute of Peace, worked to create an interdisciplinary "science of peacemaking" (Fisher, 1997; Sandole, 1991). Although Wedge (1983) perceived the formal international system as resistant to the new field of conflict resolution, he stressed the importance of linking unofficial intervention with official diplomacy (Wedge, 1987).

Wedge's contributions can be included with that of other unofficial diplomats who work to ease tensions and improve relations in situations of international conflict (Berman and Johnson, 1977). These activities typically involve private individuals or NGOs acting as intermediaries, or regular conferences that bring together influential citizens from antagonistic countries to discuss issues. The former type is exemplified by the conciliation efforts of the Quakers, members of the Society of Friends, who attempted to open up communication, clear up misperceptions, and change destructive and violent relationships into constructive and cooperative ones so that negotiations may be more successful (Curle, 1986, 1990; Pettigrew, 1991; Yarrow, 1978). The latter type involves ongoing meetings such as the Dartmouth Conference (Cousins, 1977; Stewart, 1987) and the Pugwash Conference (Kaplan, 1984; Rotblat, 1972), which for decades have brought together influential scientists and professionals to discuss world issues, particularly East-West ones during the period of the Cold War.

The domain of unofficial diplomacy took an important step forward in the early 1980s when Joseph Montville, a former U.S. Foreign Service Officer, coined the term "track-two diplomacy" and described it as unofficial, non-structured interaction between members of adversarial groups or nations directed toward conflict resolution by addressing psychological factors

(Davidson and Montville, 1981-82). Thus, the work of scholar-practitioners in conflict resolution was seen as complementary to official, or track-one, diplomacy. Montville (1987) broadened his definition to include interactions to develop joint strategies (with special attention to the problem-solving workshop), activities to influence public opinion toward reducing victimization and supporting conciliatory moves, and the mobilization of resources through cooperative economic interactions.

Another former member of the U.S. Foreign Service, Ambassador John McDonald, has played a key role in developing unofficial diplomacy and increasing the linkages with official work (e.g., McDonald and Bendahmane, 1987). McDonald (1991, this volume) proposed the concept of "multi-track diplomacy" to reduce confusion around the proliferating meanings of track two, and initially proposed four different unofficial tracks, all involving citizen efforts to help deescalate and resolve international conflict. In a joint study with Louise Diamond, the multi-track system was broadened to include nine tracks, each one dealing with a different sector involved in peacemaking (government, conflict resolution NGOs, business, citizen exchanges, education, activism, religion, media, philanthropic foundations) (Diamond and McDonald, 1991, 1996). Unfortunately, the original study indicated that the nine tracks operate essentially as worlds unto themselves without adequate resources or a systems orientation that would support complementary efforts. Diamond and McDonald followed their own recommendations for building cooperative relationships and legitimizing the field by founding the Institute for Multi-Track Diplomacy in Washington, D.C., in 1992. Their work thus stands at the leading edge of efforts to establish unofficial diplomacy in a comprehensive and systematic manner.

The Psychodynamic Approach

One stream of ICR finds its theoretical base in concepts drawn from psychoanalysis and other areas of psychiatry. This is in contrast to the conclusion eventually drawn by Wedge (1983) that psychiatry actually has little to offer international conflict resolution. Making the contrary assumption, a group of psychiatrists associated with the American Psychiatric Association organized a series of six workshops from 1979 to 1984 that brought together Egyptians, Israelis, and later Palestinians to discuss the psychological aspects of the Middle East conflict (Julius, 1991). Most prominent among this group was Vamik Volkan, an American psychiatrist of Turkish-Cypriot origin who is director of the Center for the Study of the Mind and Human Interaction (CSMHI) at the University of Virginia, established to study psychological factors in intergroup interactions and to undertake practical applications to address intergroup conflict.

The workshops involved various "influentials" (e.g., former politicians, diplomats, academics, psychiatrists) and emphasized the role of psychodynamic factors in processes such as dehumanization, victimization, mourning and forgiveness. Along with Volkan and Julius, Joseph Montville served as a core member of the third-party team that facilitated the sessions. Julius (1991) maintains that the healing approach of psychiatry allowed participants to discuss painful conflicts in a way that worked out problems rather than perpetuating them. A number of tangible outcomes are also attributed to the workshops, including a network of "influentials" across the lines of the conflict, an Israeli academic center in Cairo, and a collaborative project at an Israeli university (Volkan, 1988).

In the late 1980s, conferences on the East-West conflict at CSMHI led to collaboration with Russian institutional partners that laid the basis for a major ICR project focusing on conflicts in the Baltic states of Estonia, Latvia and Lithuania. A series of workshops in the 1990s were organized with influential representatives from the different states and Russia, often looking at the uneasy relationship between the majority ethnic groups and the Russian minority left after the dissolution of the Soviet Union. Volkan and Harris (1992, 1993) present detailed descriptions of the initial workshops as well as the psychoanalytic assumptions and interpretations that guided and informed their work. Later reports from CSMHI (1995a, 1995b) describe continuing workshops and strategies and activities to link the workshop outcomes with the broader processes of democratization and institution building to help promote a civil and peaceful society in the former Soviet republics. The current phase involves three communities in Estonia where mixed groups of Estonians and ethnic Russians first engage in dialogue workshops and then plan and implement joint projects to improve their community and the relations between their groups. In this way, the workshop effects continue to be linked to concrete action outcomes.

A Public Peace Process

Harold Saunders served on the U.S. National Security Council in the White House and in the State Department, and he concluded his diplomatic career as an assistant secretary of state and a member of the Camp David team that brokered the peace agreement between Egypt and Israel in 1979. In the early 1980s, he attended one of the workshops on the Middle East conflict organized by Vamik Volkan, and he has since participated in numerous workshops organized by Volkan and others, including the continuing workshop on the Israeli-Palestinian conflict led by Herbert Kelman and Nadim Rouhana. This combination of official and unofficial experiences led him to advocate new ways of thinking about how nations relate—i.e., as whole societies in continuous interaction—and to develop informal forums for dialogue and analysis that focus on relationship issues (Saunders, 1991a).

Saunders is a longtime member of the Dartmouth Conference, established in 1960 to provide for policy-relevant, citizen-to-citizen dialogue on relations between the United States and the U.S.S.R. (thereafter Russia) (Saunders, 1991b). In 1981, Saunders became cochair of a new task force to analyze regional conflicts and to provide insights to policy makers. Over a ten-year period, the task force also spent considerable time discussing the perceptions and relationship between the superpowers as reflected through their involvements in regional conflicts; this analysis contributed to the "new political thinking" articulated by Mikhail Gorbachev that ultimately led to the demise of the Cold War (Chufrin and Saunders, 1993). Based on this experience, Chufrin and Saunders articulated a "public peace process" (Chufrin and Saunders, 1993) which follows a series of developmental stages.

Saunders is now director of International Affairs at the Kettering Foundation and is working with social psychologist Randa Slim and Russian colleagues from the Dartmouth Conference to carry out a long-term dialogue project on the conflict in the former Soviet republic of Tajikistan (Saunders and Slim, 1994; Slim, 1995, 1998). This dialogue was initiated in 1993 and has held meetings approximately every two months with influential but unofficial representatives of the various factions and regions, roughly split between government and opposition. Following the five-stage model of the public peace process, Saunders and Slim have provided a detailed and integrated picture of this form of ICR. The dialogue has made both intangible and substantive contributions to the prenegotiation stage, to the negotiation process, and to the successful outcome of negotiations. Among other products, the dialogue has contributed a memorandum on national reconciliation in Tajikistan, and it is now developing ways to contribute to the building of a democratic, civil society. The challenges are great, but this systematic, long-term, concerted effort stands as a model to be emulated in the field of ICR. Saunders (1998) has recently provided a comprehensive statement of the methodology of sustained dialogue with applications to both intergroup relations in the United States and to international conflicts.

Conclusion

The history of ICR presents a rich tapestry of approaches and applications, with continuous development over the past thirty-some years. The leading contributors share a common methodology, and yet each has added his or her unique adaptation and interpretation to the approach. In addressing many of the world's most perplexing conflicts, there has been a trend toward replacing one-time interventions with a continuing series of workshops involving the same participants. This not only builds learning among the workshop group but increases the potential for the positive transfer of effects to decision and policy making, both between workshops and in the longer term. There is also increasing attention to project designs that integrate the workshop process into peacebuilding activities in the wider societies. In addition, the method is increasingly seen as complementary to official, traditional third-party interventions, rather than as supplanting or contradicting them (e.g., Fisher and Keashly, 1991). All of this speaks to a growing sophistication about the limitations and yet the realistic contributions that ICR has to make to international conflict resolution writ large.

Elsewhere, I have discussed the critical developmental issues and the primary challenges facing the development of the field (Fisher, 1993, 1997), and I will only summarize some of the main points here. In order to demonstrate its applicability to intense conflict and its effectiveness in contributing to de-escalation and resolution, the field of ICR needs to take more seriously the need for assessment and evaluation. Most work is not well documented, with only anecdotal case-study descriptions, and very few interventions involving more rigorous pre/post assessments or the use of comparison groups. While the research agenda should not interfere with practice and ethical requirements, it is clear that funding bodies will increasingly ask for more systematic evaluations. This challenge can be addressed by mounting more demonstration projects in ICR that have an educational and peacebuilding focus rather than a political or peacemaking one, and by drawing on the methods of participative action research and program evaluation (Rothman and Friedman, this volume).

Another issue to be taken more seriously is the cultural generalizability of the consensus-based, participative problem-solving approach to analyzing and resolving conflict. Some proponents of ICR see a universality in the method that transcends cultural boundaries and requires only cultural sensitivity and adaptation in order to be appropriate and effective. Others question this assumption and call for more work on the cultural assumptions of this primarily Western-based method, and for cultural analysis of the conflicts to which it is applied. If we regard each society as having its culturally appropriate ways of defining and addressing conflict, we must take this challenge seriously (Moore and Woodrow, this volume). Even more, when two cultures collide in conflict, we have an intercultural interface, the understanding and management of which will have significant effects on how well the conflict can be analyzed and resolved with outside assistance from yet another culture. While many third-party teams evince cultural sensitivity and accommodation, few have included anthropologists or others who are able to carry out a sophisticated analysis of the host cultures and their interfaces.

In order to continue to demonstrate its applicability and effectiveness, the field of ICR must address some mundane yet critical questions in the areas of funding, training, institutionalization, and professionalization. ICR practice is an emerging multidisciplinary profession that has no clear foundation and every day is in competition with more established disciplines for the resources required to operate successfully. Obtaining funding for mounting adequate and continuing interventions has been a major problem for ICR scholar-practitioners, who must spend large amounts of time seeking funding from both public and private sources, and must do so in the face of numerous "Catch-22s." For example, ICR work should proceed quietly, yet funders like public acknowledgment; ICR work needs to be highly flexible, yet funders like explicit and detailed work plans; ICR operates in a highly charged political environment, yet funders may want public commitments from leaders up front. Nonetheless,

ICR practitioners appear to have been increasingly successful in gaining support, and a serious dialogue with funding bodies would likely increase the level of mutual understanding and commitment.

Having gained funding, it is not always the case that well-trained practitioners are available to carry out the intervention. While there is no standard for comparison, the number of ICR scholar-practitioners who are seen within the field as competent and experienced is small, and very few educational or professional training programs are producing more in any quantity. Very often, individuals from relevant disciplines or institutions come into this work thinking that they can facilitate dialogue, induce conflict analysis, or bring about reconciliation between adversaries, without realizing the complexity and the difficulty of mounting such interventions successfully. Their failures or null effects then reflect poorly on the field and can reduce access to parties and funding opportunities for other practitioners.

Another difficulty is the small number of institutional bases from which to carry out ICR work. Historically, most interventions were mounted from academia, requiring individual faculty members to enact the challenging and unpredictable ICR role within the constraints of their structured duties and limited resources. Recently, more NGOs are mounting ICR interventions, and they are able to do so with greater flexibility and adaptability, although it is a struggle to maintain the necessary financial resources, and the best human resources are not always available or on secure salaries. The ideal institutional structure appears to be a university-based, semi-autonomous, interdisciplinary center for research and practice, which would have credibility, access to human and financial resources, and continuity over time.

A final challenge facing ICR is that of professionalization—fostering educational, associational and eventually regulatory activities for individuals who are committed to the field and its development. Professional associations have been formed in the United States and elsewhere for practitioners interested in domestic conflict-resolution work, but there is no such forum for scholar-practitioners who address intercommunal or international conflicts. Movement in this direction is necessary to affirm that ICR is an emerging profession, with its own knowledge base, its commitment to human welfare, and its ethical standards of conduct. Continuing consideration of professional issues within a context of secure funding, institutionalization and formal training would enable the field to reach its unique potential in helping to address the destructive aspects of protracted social conflicts.

Note

1. Workshops are indicated by the country or region of focus; publications are indicated by partial titles.

II
Strategies for Conflict Transformation and Peacebuilding

5
Interactive Problem Solving as a Tool for Second Track Diplomacy

Herbert C. Kelman

For some years, my colleagues and I have been actively engaged in the development and application of an approach to the resolution of international conflicts for which we use the term "interactive problem solving."[1] The fullest—indeed, the paradigmatic—application of the approach is represented by problem-solving workshops (Kelman, 1972, 1979, 1992, 1996b; Kelman and Cohen, 1986), although it involves a variety of other activities as well. In fact, I have increasingly come to see interactive problem solving as an approach to the macroprocesses of international conflict resolution, in which problem-solving workshops and similar micro-level activities are integrally related to official diplomacy (Kelman, 1996a).

The approach derives most directly from the work of John Burton (1969, 1979, 1984). While my work follows the general principles laid out by Burton, it has evolved in its own directions, in keeping with my own disciplinary background, my particular style, and the cases on which I have focused my attention. My work has concentrated since 1974 on the Arab-Israeli conflict, particularly on the Israeli-Palestinian component of that conflict. I have also done some work, however, on the Cyprus conflict and have maintained an active interest in several other intense, protracted identity conflicts at the international or intercommunal level, such as the conflicts in Bosnia, Sri Lanka, and Northern Ireland.

During the 1970s, as I became more actively involved in work in and on the Middle East, I collaborated extensively with Ed Azar. He was part of our third-party team (see Kelman, 1978), which organized and facilitated problem-solving workshops and other joint activities with Egyptians, Israelis, and Palestinians, and which also traveled together in the Middle East. In the course of these activities, I benefited enormously from Ed's insights into Arab politics, culture, and society. Ed and I shared the view (to be elaborated later in this chapter) that international conflict is not merely an interstate phenomenon but also an intersocietal phenomenon. This view was reflected in Ed's emphasis on development as an essential context of peace and conflict resolution, a theme that ran through the entire body of his work (see, e.g., Azar, 1979) and that greatly influenced my thinking about protracted conflict. In my work, the view of conflict as an intersocietal phenomenon is reflected in the emphasis on the role of unofficial interactions as an integral component of the larger diplomatic process. Intrigued by this potential of interactive problem solving, Ed joined our third-party team, later collaborated with Stephen Cohen and with John Burton in other third-party efforts (see, e.g., Cohen and Azar, 1981; Azar and Burton, 1986), and developed his own "problem-solving forum" approach to track-two diplomacy (Azar, 1990, this volume).

Interactive Problem Solving

Interactive problem solving—as manifested particularly in problem-solving workshops—is an academically based, unofficial third-party approach, bringing together representatives of parties in conflict for direct communication. The third party typically consists of a panel of social scientists who, between them, possess expertise in group process and international conflict, and at least some familiarity with the conflict region. The role of the third party in our model differs from that of the traditional mediator. Unlike many mediators, we do not propose (and certainly, unlike arbitrators, we do not impose) solutions. Rather, we try to facilitate a process whereby solutions will emerge out of the interaction between the parties themselves. The task of the third party is to provide the setting, create the atmosphere, establish the norms, and offer the occasional interventions that make it possible for such a process to evolve.

Although the distinguishing feature of the approach (in contrast, for example, to traditional mediation) is direct communication between the parties, the objective is not to promote communication or dialogue as an end in itself. Problem-solving workshops are designed to promote a special type of communication—to be described below—with a very specific political purpose. Problem-solving workshops are closely linked to the larger political process. Selection of participants and definition of the agenda, for example, are based on careful analysis of the current political situation within and between the conflicting parties. Moreover, the objective of workshops is to generate inputs into the political process, including the decision-making process itself and the political debate within each of the communities. Most broadly stated, workshops try to contribute to creating a political environment conducive to conflict resolution and to transformation of the relationship between the conflicting parties—both in the short term and in the long term.

Practically speaking, this emphasis usually means that problem-solving workshops are closely linked to negotiation in its various phases, although negotiation does not by any means fully encompass the process of changing international relationships (see Saunders, 1988). In our work on the Israeli-Palestinian conflict in earlier years, problem-solving workshops were designed to contribute to the prenegotiation process: to creating a political atmosphere that would encourage the parties to move to the negotiating table. Thus, in planning and following up on workshops, we focused on the barriers that stood in the way of opening negotiations and on ways of overcoming such barriers—for example, through mutual reassurance. With the beginning of official Israeli-Palestinian negotiations in the fall of 1991, our focus of necessity shifted (Rouhana and Kelman, 1994). During the active negotiation phase, workshops can contribute to overcoming obstacles to staying at the table and negotiating effectively, to exploring options for resolving issues that are not yet on the table, to reframing such issues so as to make them more amenable to negotiation, and to beginning the process of peacebuilding that must accompany and follow the process of peacemaking. Workshops can also be of value in the postnegotiation phase, where they can contribute to implementation of the negotiated agreement and to long-term peacebuilding.

Despite the close link between workshops and negotiations, we have been very clear in emphasizing that workshops are not to be confused with negotiations as such. They are not meant to be negotiations, simulated negotiations, or rehearsals for negotiations, or to serve as substitutes for negotiations. Rather, they are meant to be complementary to negotiations.

Binding agreements can be achieved only through official negotiations. The very binding character of official negotiations, however, makes it very difficult for certain other things to happen in that context—such as the exploration and discovery of the parties' basic concerns, their priorities, their limits. This is where problem-solving workshops—precisely because of their nonbinding character—can make a special contribution to the larger process of negotiation and conflict resolution. This special relationship to the negotiation process underlines one of the central differences between interactive problem solving and traditional mediation: Problem-solving workshops are generally not designed to facilitate or influence the official negotiation process directly, although they do play a significant indirect role. Insofar as we mediate, it is not between the negotiators representing the two parties but between their political communities. What we try to facilitate is not the process of negotiation itself but communication that helps the parties overcome the political, emotional, and at times technical barriers that often prevent them from entering into negotiations, from reaching agreement in the course of negotiations, or from changing their relationship after a political agreement has been negotiated.

Central Features of Problem-Solving Workshops

Until the fall of 1990, the Israeli-Palestinian workshops we organized were all self-contained, one-time events. Some of the participants were involved in more than one workshop, and many were involved in a variety of other efforts at communication across the conflict line. For these and other reasons, there was continuity between these separate events, and they seem to have had a cumulative effect in helping to create a political environment conducive to negotiations. However, because of logistical and financial constraints and a lack of political readiness, we made no attempt before 1990 to reconvene the same group of participants over a series of meetings.

In the fall of 1990, Nadim Rouhana and I convened our first continuing workshop with a group of high-level, politically influential Israelis and Palestinians. The full group met five times between November 1990 and August 1993—a period that included the Persian Gulf crisis and war, the beginning of official negotiations, and the election of a Labor party government in Israel (see Rouhana and Kelman, 1994).[2] After the Oslo agreement (September 1993), Rouhana and I initiated a new project, a Joint Working Group on Israeli-Palestinian Relations (see Kelman, 1996b). This group began meeting in 1994 and held a total of fifteen plenary meetings and a number of sub-committee meetings between the spring of 1994 and the summer of 1999. In contrast to our earlier workshop efforts, the working group was designed to generate and disseminate concrete products in the form of a series of concept papers on final-status issues in the Israeli-Palestinian negotiations and on the long-term relationship between the two societies.[3] The group has published three papers: one on general principles for the final-status negotiations (Joint Working Group, 1999), one on the problem of Palestinian refugees and the right of return (Alpher and Shikaki, et al., 1999), and one on the future Israeli-Palestinian relationship (Joint Working Group, 2000). A fourth paper, on Israeli settlements, is close to completion, but there are no immediate plans to publish it.

To provide a more concrete sense of problem-solving workshops and their underlying logic, I shall describe the format of a typical one-time workshop. It should be stressed, however, that most workshops are in fact "atypical" in one or more respects. Workshops (including continuing workshops) conform to a set of fundamental principles, but they vary in some of their details, depending on the particular occasion, purpose, and set of participants. What I am presenting, then, is a composite picture, which most workshops approximate but do not necessarily correspond to in all details.

Most of our one-time workshops have been held at Harvard University, under the auspices of the Center for International Affairs or in the context of my graduate seminar on international conflict. Workshop sessions usually take place in a seminar room, with participants seated at a round table, although in some cases we have used a living room or a private meeting room at a hotel. The typical workshop is a private, confidential event, without observers. The discussions are not taped, but members of the third party take notes.

Participants in an Israeli-Palestinian workshop usually include three to six members of each party, as well as three to eight third-party members. The numbers have been smaller on some occasions. For example, I have arranged a number of one-on-one meetings, with the participation of one or two third-party members. These meetings have served important purposes and have retained many features of problem-solving workshops, although one major feature—intraparty interaction—is missing. In quite a few of our workshops, the size of the third party has been larger than eight. As an integral feature of my graduate seminar on international conflict, I organized an annual workshop, in which the seminar participants—usually about twenty—served as apprentice members of the third party. Only eight third-party members sat around the table at any one session, however: three "permanent" members (including myself and two colleagues with workshop experience) and five seminar participants, on a rotating basis. When they were not around the table, the seminar participants were able to follow the proceedings (with the full knowledge of the parties, of course) from an adjoining room with a one-way mirror. They were fully integrated into the third party: they took part in all the workshop activities (preworkshop sessions, briefings, breaks, meals, a social gathering) and were always bound by the requirements and discipline of the third-party role. Apart from the large size of the third party, the workshops linked to this graduate seminar were similar to "regular" workshops in their purpose and format, and were widely seen as not just academic exercises but serious political encounters.

The Israeli and Palestinian participants in workshops are all politically active and involved members of the mainstreams of their respective communities. Many, by virtue of their positions or general standing, can be described as politically influential. Depending on the occasion and the political level of the participants, we may discuss our plans for a workshop with relevant elements of the political leadership on both sides, in order to keep them informed, gain their support, and solicit their advice on participants and agenda. For many potential workshop participants, approval and at times encouragement from the political leadership is a necessary condition for their agreement to take part. Recruitment, however, is generally done on an individual basis, and participants are invited to come as individuals rather than as formal representatives. Invitees, of course, may consult with their leaderships or with each other before agreeing to come. Whenever possible, we start the recruitment process with one key person on each side; we then consult with that person and with each successive invitee in selecting the rest of the team. At times, the composition of a team may be negotiated within the particular community (or subcommunity) that we approach, but the final invitation is always issued by the third party to each individual participant.

As an essential part of the recruitment process, we almost always discuss the purposes, procedures, and ground rules of the workshop personally with each participant before obtaining her or his final commitment. Whenever possible, this is done during a face-to-face meeting, although at times it is necessary to do it over the telephone. In addition to the individual briefings, we generally organize two preworkshop sessions, in which the members of each party meet separately with the third party. In these sessions, which generally last four to five hours, we first review the purposes, procedures, and ground rules of the workshop. We then ask the participants to talk about their sides' perspectives on the conflict, the range of views within their community, the current status of the conflict as they see it and the conditions and possibilities for resolving it, and their conceptions of the needs and positions of the other side. We encourage the participants to discuss these issues among themselves. We make it clear that the role of the third party—even in the preworkshop session—is to facilitate the exchange, in part through occasional questions and comments, but not to enter into the substantive discussion or to debate or evaluate what is being said.

The preworkshop sessions fulfill a number of important functions. They provide an opportunity for the participants to become acquainted with the setting, the third party, and members of their own team whom they had not previously met, without having to confront the other party at the same time; to raise questions about the purposes, procedures, and ground rules of the workshop; to begin to practice the type of discourse that the workshop is trying to encourage; to gain a better understanding of the role of the third party; and to "do their duty" by telling the third party their side of the story and enumerating their grievances, thus reducing the pressure to adhere to the conflict norms in the course of the workshop itself. The preworkshop sessions also give the third party an opportunity to observe some of the internal differences within each team and to compare the ways in which the parties treat the issues when they are alone and when they are together.

The workshops themselves generally last two and a half days, often taking place over an extended weekend. The opening session, typically late Friday afternoon, begins with a round of introductions, in which the participants are encouraged to go beyond their professional credentials and say something about their reasons for coming. We then review, once again, the purposes, procedures, and ground rules of the workshop, stressing the principles of privacy and confidentiality, the nature of the discourse that we are trying to encourage, and the role of the third party. This review, in the presence of all of the participants, serves to emphasize the nature of the contract to which all three parties are committing themselves. After dinner, shared by the entire group, we reconvene for the first substantive session. On the second day, we have two sessions (each lasting one and a half hours) in the morning, with a half-hour coffee break in between. The same pattern is repeated after lunch.

That evening, there is a dinner and social gathering for all participants, typically held at the home of the Kelmans. On the third day, there are again two sessions each in the morning and afternoon; the workshop closes late that afternoon. Thus, in addition to ten sessions around the table, workshops provide ample opportunities for informal interaction during meals and breaks. Sometimes participants create additional opportunities for themselves.

In opening the first substantive session, the third party—after describing the political context and the focus of the workshop—proposes a loose agenda. The specific agenda must depend, of course, on the stage of the conflict and the character of the group. The agenda followed in most of our workshops prior to 1992 are appropriate for initial workshops (i.e., workshops whose participants are convening for the first time as a group) in a conflict that is still in a pre-negotiation phase. The main task that we have set for our workshop participants in recent years has been to generate—through their interaction—ideas for bringing the parties to the negotiating table, or for negotiating more productively if they are already at the table. To get the interaction started, we ask the participants to describe their views of the conflict and its current status, to define the spectrum of positions vis-à-vis the conflict in their own societies and to place themselves along that spectrum.

We try to move as rapidly as possible from this more conventional, descriptive discussion into the analytic, problem-solving mode of interaction that is at the heart of the agenda. First, we ask the participants on both sides to talk about their central concerns: the fundamental needs that an agreement would have to satisfy and the fundamental fears that it would have to allay in order to be acceptable to their communities. Only after both sets of concerns are on the table and each side's concerns have been understood by the other are the participants asked to explore the overall shape of a solution that would meet the needs and calm the fears of both sides. Each is expected to think actively about solutions that would be satisfactory to the other, not only to themselves. Next, the participants are asked to discuss the political and psychological constraints that make it difficult to implement such solutions. Finally, the discussion turns to the question of how these constraints can best be overcome and how the two sides can support each other in such an effort. Depending on how much time is left and on the prevailing mood, the participants may try to come up with concrete ideas for unilateral, coordinated, or joint actions—by themselves or their communities—that might help overcome the barriers to negotiating a mutually satisfactory solution.

The agenda described here is not followed rigidly but rather serves as a broad framework for the interaction. The discussions are relatively unstructured and, insofar as possible, are allowed to maintain their natural flow. We are careful not to intervene excessively or prematurely and not to cut off potentially fruitful discussions because they appear to be deviating from the agenda. If the discussion goes too far afield, becomes repetitive, or systematically avoids the issues, the third party—usually with the help of at least some of the participants—will try to bring it back to the broad agenda. In general, the third party is prepared to intervene in order to help keep the discussion moving along productive, constructive channels. At times, particularly at the beginning or at the end of a session, we also make substantive interventions, in order to help interpret, integrate, clarify, or sharpen what is being said or done in the group. On the whole, however, the emphasis in our model is on facilitating the emergence of ideas out of the interaction between the participants themselves. Consistent with that emphasis, we try to stay in the background as much as possible once we have set the stage.

Having drawn a general picture of the format and proceedings of a typical workshop, let me now highlight some of the special features of the approach.

Academic Context

In my colleagues' and my own third-party efforts, our academic base provides the major venue of our activities and source of our authority and credibility. The academic context has several advantages for our enterprise. It allows the parties to interact with each other in a relatively noncommittal way, since the setting is not only unofficial but also known as one in which people engage in free exchange of views, in playful consideration of new ideas, and in "purely academic" discussions. Thus, an academic setting is a good place to set into motion a process of successive approximations, in which parties that do not trust each other begin to communicate in a noncommittal framewor, but gradually move to increasing levels of commitment as their level of working trust increases (Kelman, 1982). Another advantage of the academic context is that it allows us to call upon an alternative set of norms to counteract the norms that typically govern interactions between conflicting parties. Academic norms favor open discussion, attentive listening to opposing views, and an analytical approach, in contrast to the polemical, accusatory, and legalistic approach that conflict norms tend to promote.

Nature of Interaction

The setting, norms, ground rules, agenda, procedures, and third-party interventions in problem-solving workshops are all designed to facilitate a kind of interaction that differs from the way parties in conflict usually interact—if they interact at all. Within the workshop setting, participants are encouraged to talk to each other, rather than to their constituencies or to third parties, and to listen to each other—not in order to discover the weaknesses in the other's argument but in order to penetrate the other's perspective. The principles of privacy and confidentiality—apart from protecting the interests of the participants—are designed to protect this process, by reducing the participants' concern about how each word they say during the workshop will be perceived on the outside. In order to counteract the tendency to speak to the record, we have avoided creating a record, in the form of audio or videotapes or formal minutes. The absence of an audience and the third party's refusal to take sides, evaluate what is said, adjudicate differences, or become involved in the debate of substantive issues further encourage the parties to focus on each other rather than attempt to influence external parties. These features of the workshop are in no way designed to encourage the participants to forget about their constituencies or relevant third parties; ideas generated in workshops must be acceptable to the two communities, as well as to outside actors, if they are to have the desired impact on the political process. Rather, these features are designed to prevent the intrusion of these actors into the workshop interaction itself, thus inhibiting and distorting the generation of new ideas.

A second central element in the nature of the interaction that workshops try to promote is an analytic focus. Workshop discussions are analytical in the sense that participants try to gain a better understanding of the other's—and indeed of their own—concerns, needs, fears, priorities, and constraints, and of the way in which the divergent perspectives of the parties help to feed and escalate their conflict. It is particularly important for each party to gain an understanding of the other's perspective (without accepting that perspective) and of the domestic dynamics that shape the policy debate in each community. To appreciate the constraints under which the other operates is especially difficult in a conflict relationship, since the parties' thinking tends to be dominated by their own respective constraints. But an analytic understanding of the constraints—along with the fundamental concerns—that inform the other's perspective is a sine qua non for inventing solutions that are feasible and satisfactory for both sides.

Analytical discussions proceed on the basis of a "no fault" principle. While there is no presumption that both sides are equally at fault, the discussions are not oriented toward assigning blame but toward exploring the causes of the conflict and the obstacles to its resolution. This analytical approach is designed to lead to a problem-solving mode of interaction, based on the proposition that the conflict represents a joint problem for the two parties that requires joint efforts at solution.

Dual Purpose

Workshops have a dual purpose, which can be described as educational and political. They are designed to produce both *changes* in attitudes, perceptions, and ideas for resolving the conflict among the individual participants in the workshop, and *transfer* of these changes to the political arena—i.e., to the political debate and the decision-making process within each community. The political purpose is an integral part of the workshop approach, whatever the level of the participants involved. Workshops provide opportunities for the parties to interact, to become acquainted with each other, and to humanize their mutual images, not as ends in themselves but as means to producing new learnings that can then be fed into the political process. Some of the specific learnings that participants have acquired in the course of workshops and then communicated to their own political leaderships or publics have included: information about the range of views on the other side, signs of readiness for negotiation, and the availability of potential negotiating partners; insights into the other side's priorities, rock-bottom requirements, and areas of flexibility; and ideas for confidence-building measures, mutually acceptable solutions to issues in conflict, and ways of moving to the negotiating table.

Because of their dual purpose, problem-solving workshops are marked by a dialectical character (Kelman, 1979; Kelman and Cohen, 1986). Some of the conditions favorable to change in the workshop setting may be antagonistic to the transfer of changes to the political arena, and vice versa. There is often a need, therefore, to find the proper balance between contradictory requirements if a workshop is to be effective in fulfilling both its educational and its political purpose. For example, it is important for the participants to develop a considerable degree of working trust in order to engage in joint problem solving, to devise direct or tacit collaborative efforts for overcoming constraints against negotiation, and to become convinced that there are potential negotiating partners on the other side. This trust, however, must not be allowed to turn into excessive camaraderie transcending the conflict, lest the participants lose their credibility and their potential political influence once they return to their home communities. Workshops can be seen as part of a process of building coalitions across the conflict line, but the coalitions must remain uneasy ones that do not threaten members' relationships to their own identity groups (Kelman, 1993).

The selection of participants provides another example of a central workshop feature for which the dialectics of the process have important implications. The closer the participants are to the centers of power in their own communities, the greater the likelihood that what they learn in the course of their workshop experience will be fed directly into the decision-making process. By the same token, however, the closer participants are to the centers of power, the more constrained they are likely to feel, and the greater their difficulty in entering into communication that is open, noncommittal, exploratory, and analytical. Thus, on the whole, as participants move closer to the level of top decision makers, they become less likely to show change as a result of their workshop experience, but whatever changes do occur are more likely to be transferred to the policy process. These contradictory effects have to be taken into account in selecting participants for a given occasion or in defining the goals and agenda for a workshop with a given set of participants. In general, the best way to balance the requirements for change and for transfer is to select participants who are politically influential but not directly involved in the execution of foreign policy. The approach can be adapted for use with decision makers themselves, as long as the facilitators are aware of the advantages and drawbacks of participants at that level.

The workshops and related encounters that we have organized over the years have included participants at three different levels of relationship to the decision-making process: political actors, such as parliamentarians, negotiators, party activists, or advisers to political leaders; political "influentials," such as former officials and diplomats, senior academics (who are leading analysts of the conflict in their own communities and occasional advisers to decision makers), community leaders, writers, or editors; and "pre-influentials", such as younger academics and professionals or advanced graduate students who are slated to move into influential positions in their respective fields. The lines between these three categories are not very precise; moreover, many participants who may have been "pre-influentials" at the time of their workshop have since become influential, and some of our "influentials" have since become political actors. Whatever the level of the participants, a central criterion for selection is that they be politically involved—at least as active participants in the political debate and perhaps in political movements. From our point of view, even this degree of involvement is of direct political relevance, since it contributes to the shaping of the political environment for any peace effort. Another criterion for selection is that participants be part of the mainstreams of their communities and that they enjoy credibility within broad segments of those communities. We look for participants who are as close as possible to the center of the political spectrum, while at the same time interested in negotiations and open to the workshop process. As a result, workshop participants so far have tended to be on the dovish ("moderate" or pro-negotiation) side of the center.

Third-Party Contributions

Although workshops proceed on the principle that useful ideas for conflict resolution must emerge out of the interaction between the parties themselves, the third party plays an essential role (at certain stages of a conflict) in making that interaction possible and fruitful. The third party provides the context in which representatives of parties engaged in an intense conflict are able to come together. It selects, briefs, and convenes the participants. It serves as a repository of trust for both parties, enabling them to proceed with assurance that their confidentiality will be respected and their interests protected, even though—by definition—they cannot trust each other. It establishes and enforces the norms and ground rules that facilitate analytic discussion and a problem-solving orientation. It proposes a broad agenda that encourages the parties to move from exploration of each other's concerns and constraints to the generation of ideas for win/win solutions and for implementing such solutions. It tries to keep the discussion moving in constructive directions. Finally, it makes occasional interventions. These may take the form of content observations, which suggest interpretations and implications of what is being said and point to convergences and divergences between the parties, to blind spots, to possible signals, and to issues for clarification; of process observations at the intergroup level which suggest possible ways in which interactions between the parties "here and now" may reflect the dynamics of the conflict between their communities, and of theoretical inputs, which help participants distance themselves from their own conflict, provide them conceptual tools for analysis of their conflict, and offer them relevant illustrations from previous research.

Process observations are among the unique features of problem-solving workshops. They generally focus on incidents in which one party's words or actions clearly have a strong emotional impact on the other—leading to expressions of anger and dismay, of relief and reassurance, of understanding and acceptance, or of reciprocation. The third party can use such incidents, which are part of the participants' shared immediate experience, as a springboard for exploring some of the issues and concerns that define the conflict between their societies. Through such exploration, each side can gain some insight into the preoccupations of the other and into the way these are affected by its own actions. Process observations must be introduced sparingly, and they make special demands on the third party's skill and sense of timing. It is particularly important that such interventions be pitched at the intergroup rather than the interpersonal level. Analysis of "here and now" interactions is not concerned with the personal characteristics of the participants or with their personal relations to each other but only with what these interactions can tell us about the relationship between their national groups.

Social-Psychological Assumptions

The practice of interactive problem solving is informed by a set of assumptions about the nature of international/intercommunal conflict and conflict resolution. These assumptions are meant to be general in nature, although they refer most directly to conflicts between identity groups and may not be equally applicable in other cases. Thus, the problem-solving approach is likely to be most relevant in conflicts in which identity issues play a central role.

In my particular conception of the problem-solving approach, the guiding assumptions derive from a social-psychological analysis, which provides a bridge between individual behavior and social interaction, on the one hand, and the functioning of social systems (organizations, institutions, societies) and collectivities, on the other (Kelman, 1997b). Social-psychological assumptions enter into the formulation of the structure, the process, and the content of problem-solving workshops.

Workshop Structure

Workshop structure refers primarily to the role of workshops in the larger political context and their place within the social system in which the conflict is carried on. In effect, the focus here is on the relationship between the microprocess of the workshop and the macroprocess of conflict management or resolution. Several assumptions underlie our view of this relationship and hence the way in which workshops are structured.

Conflict as an Intersocietal Process

International conflict is not merely an intergovernmental or interstate phenomenon but also an intersocietal phenomenon. Thus, in addition to the strategic, military, and diplomatic dimensions, it is necessary to give central consideration to the economic, psychological, cultural, and social-structural dimensions in the analysis of the conflict. Interactions along these dimensions, both within and between the conflicting societies, form the essential political environment in which governments function. It is necessary to look at these intrasocietal and intersocietal processes in order to understand the political constraints under which governments operate and the resistance to change that these produce. By the same token, these societal factors, if properly understood and utilized, provide opportunities and levers for change.

This view has a direct implication for the selection of workshop participants. To be politically relevant, workshops do not require the participation of decision makers or their agents. In fact, as proposed in the earlier discussion of the dual purposes and dialectical character of workshops, the ideal participants may be individuals who are politically influential but not directly involved in the foreign-policy decision-making process. The important consideration is that they be active and credible contributors to the political debate within their own communities and thus be able to play a role in changing the political environment.

Another implication of the view of international conflict as an intersocietal phenomenon is that third-party efforts should ideally be directed not merely to a settlement of the conflict, but to its resolution. A political agreement may be adequate for terminating relatively specific, containable interstate disputes, but it is an inadequate response to conflicts that engage the collective identities and existential concerns of the societies involved.

Conflict Resolution as Transformation of the Relationship

Following from the stress on the intersocietal nature of conflict is the assumption that conflict resolution represents an effort to transform the relationship between the conflicting parties. This assumption has direct implications for the type of solutions that third-party intervention tries to generate. First, solutions must emerge out of the interaction between the parties themselves: the process of interactive problem solving itself contributes to transforming the relationship between the parties. Second, solutions must address the needs of both parties, thus providing the foundation of a new relationship between them. Finally, the nature of the solutions and the process by which they were achieved must be such that the parties will be committed to them: only thus can they establish a new relationship on a long-term basis.

Diplomacy as a Mix of Official and Unofficial Processes

Another corollary of the stress on the intersocietal nature of conflict is the view of diplomacy as a broad and complex mix of official and unofficial processes. The peaceful termination or management of conflicts requires binding agreements that can only be achieved at the official level. Unofficial interactions, however, can play a constructive complementary role, particularly by contributing to the development of a political environment conducive to negotiations and other diplomatic initiatives (Saunders, 1988). Problem-solving workshops and other informal efforts, as pointed out at the beginning of the chapter, can make such contributions precisely because of their nonbinding character. In such settings—in contrast to official forums—it is much easier for the parties to engage in noncommittal, exploratory interactions, which allow them to test each other's limits, develop empathy, or engage in creative problem solving. Accordingly, many of the features of problem-solving workshops are specifically geared to maximize the noncommittal nature of the interaction: the academic context; the assurance of privacy and confidentiality; the absence (at least in our earlier work) of expectations of specific products; and the emphasis on interactions characterized by exploration, sharing of perspectives, playing with ideas, brainstorming, and creative problem solving— rather than bargaining.

Impact of Intragroup Conflict on Intergroup Conflict

A further assumption relates to the interplay between intragroup and intergroup conflict. In many international and intercommunal conflicts, internal divisions within each party shape the course of the conflict between the parties. This phenomenon represents a special instance of the general observation of continuities between domestic and international politics. Understanding of the internal divisions within each party is essential to the selection of workshop participants, since the political significance of workshops depends on the potential impact these participants can have on the internal debate. The internal divisions in each society are also a major focus of concern within workshops, particularly when the discussion turns to the political and psychological constraints against compromise solutions and ways of overcoming these constraints.

More generally, I have already alluded to my conceptualization (Kelman, 1993) of workshops and related activities as part of a process of forming a coalition across the conflict line—a coalition between those elements on each side that are interested in a negotiated solution. It is very important to keep in mind, however, that such a coalition must of necessity remain an uneasy coalition. If it became overly cohesive, it would undermine the whole purpose of the enterprise: to have an impact on the political decisions within the two communities. Workshop participants who become closely identified with their counterparts on the other side may become alienated from their own conationals, lose credibility, and hence forfeit their political effectiveness and their ability to promote a new consensus within their own communities. One of the challenges for problem-solving workshops, therefore, is to create an atmosphere in which participants can begin to humanize and trust each other and to develop an effective collaborative relationship without losing sight of their separate group identities and the conflict between their communities.

The World System as a Global Society

At the broadest level, my assumptions about international and inter-communal conflict rest on a view of the world system as a global society—a term used here not only normatively but also descriptively. To be sure, the global society is a weak society, lacking many of the customary features of a society. Still, conceiving of the world as a society corrects for the untenable view of nation-states as sole and unitary actors in the global arena. Clearly, nation-states remain the dominant actors within our current global society. The nation-state benefits from the principle of sovereignty and from its claim to represent its population's national identity—perhaps the most powerful variant of group identity in the modern world. (In intercommunal conflicts within established nation-states, the ethnic community is seen as representing the central element of identity and seeks to restructure, take over, or separate from the existing state in order to give political expression to that identity.) Despite the dominance of the nation-state, the world system has many of the characteristics of a society: it is formed by a multiplicity of actors, including—in addition to nation-states—individuals in their diverse roles, as well as a variety of subnational and supranational groups; it is marked by an ever-increasing degree of interdependence between its component parts; it is divided along many complex lines, with the nation-state representing perhaps the most powerful, but certainly not the only, cutting line; and it contains numerous relationships that cut across nation-state lines, including relations based on ethnicity, religion, ideology, occupation, and economic interests. The embeddedness of the nation-state in a global society, in which ethnic and other bonds cut across nation-state lines, accounts in large part for the continuity between the domestic and foreign policies of the modern state.

The view of the world system as a global society provides several angles for understanding the role of interactive problem solving within a larger context of conflict resolution.

First, the concept of a global society with its emphasis on interdependence suggests the need for alternative conceptions of national and international security, which involve arrangements for common security and mechanisms for the nonviolent conduct, management, and resolution of conflicts. Such arrangements and mechanisms, in turn, call for the development of governmental, intergovernmental, and nongovernmental institutions that embody the emerging new conceptions of security. Interactive problem solving can be seen as the germ of an independent (nongovernmental) institutional mechanism, which can contribute to security through the nonviolent resolution of conflicts.

Second, by focusing on multiple actors and cross-cutting relationships, the concept of a global society encourages us to think of unofficial diplomacy in all of its varieties as an integral part of diplomacy and of a larger process of conflict resolution, and not just as a side-show (as it tends to be viewed in a state-centered model).

Finally, the multiple-actor framework central to the concept of a global society provides a place for the individual as a relevant actor in international relations. Interactive problem solving uses the individual as the unit of analysis in the effort to understand resistance to change in a conflict relationship despite changes in realities and interests, and in the search for solutions that would satisfy the human needs of the parties. Moreover, interactive problem solving is a systematic attempt to promote change at the level of individuals (in the form of new insights and ideas), as a vehicle for change at the system level.

Workshop Process

Several social-psychological assumptions underlie our view of the kind of interaction process that workshops are designed to promote.

Direct Bilateral Interaction

One assumption follows directly from the structural analysis that has just been presented on the role of workshops in the larger political context. Somewhere within the larger framework of conflict resolution, there must be a place for direct, bilateral interaction between the parties centrally involved in a given conflict—such as the Israelis and the Palestinians, or the Greek and the Turkish Cypriots. Such direct, bilateral interactions are not a substitute for the multilateral efforts that are almost invariably required for the resolution of protracted conflicts. Greece and Turkey cannot be excluded from negotiations of the Cyprus conflict, nor can the Arab states and major world powers be bypassed in efforts to resolve the Israeli-Palestinian dispute. Within this larger framework, however, there must be an opportunity for the parties immediately involved—the parties that ultimately have to live with each other—to penetrate each other's perspectives and to engage in joint problem solving designed to produce ideas for a mutually satisfactory agreement between them.

Opportunities for interaction at the micro-level can also contribute some of the needed interactive elements at the macro-level: a binocular orientation, such that each party can view the situation from the other's perspective as well as from its own; a recognition of the need for reciprocity in the process and outcome of negotiations; and a focus on building a new relationship between the parties.

Emergent Character of Interaction

A second assumption underlying the workshop process is that products of social interaction have an emergent character. In the course of direct interaction, the parties are able to observe at first hand their differing reactions to the same events and the different perspectives these reflect; the differences between the way they perceive themselves and the way the other perceives them; and the impact that their statements and actions have on each other. Out of these observations, they can jointly shape new insights and ideas that could not have been predicted from what they brought to the interaction. Certain kinds of solutions to the conflict can emerge only from the confrontation of assumptions, concerns, and identities during face-to-face communication.

The emergence of ideas for solutions to the conflict out of the interaction between the parties (in contrast, for example, to ideas proposed by third parties) has several advantages: such ideas are more likely to be responsive to the fundamental needs and fears of both parties; the parties are more likely to feel committed to the solutions they produce themselves; and the process of producing these ideas in itself contributes to building a new relationship between the parties.

In keeping with our assumption about the emergent character of interaction, we pay attention to the nature of the discourse during workshops (see Pearson, 1990). How does the way parties talk to each other change over the course of the workshop? What are the critical moments in a workshop that have an impact on the continuing interaction? How do new joint ideas come to be formulated in the course of the interaction?

Exploration and Problem Solving

Workshops are designed to promote a special kind of interaction or discourse that can contribute to the desired political outcome. As noted in the earlier discussion of the nature of the interaction, the setting, ground rules, and procedures of problem-solving workshops encourage (and permit) interaction marked by the following elements: an emphasis on addressing each other (rather than one's constituencies, or third parties, or the record) and on listening to each other; analytical discussion; adherence to a "no-fault" principle; and a problem-solving mode of interaction. This kind of interaction allows the parties to explore each other's concerns, penetrate each other's perspectives, and take cognizance of each other's constraints. As a result, they are able to offer each other the needed reassurances to engage in negotiation and to come up with solutions responsive to both sides' needs and fears.

The nature of the interaction fostered in problem-solving workshops has some continuities with a therapeutic model (Kelman, 1991b). The influence of the therapeutic model can be seen particularly in the facilitative role of the third party, the analytical character of the discourse, and the use of "here and now" experiences as a basis for learning about the dynamics of the conflict (as mentioned in the earlier discussion of process observations). It is also important, however, to keep in mind the limited applicability of a therapeutic model to problem-solving workshops. For example, the focus of workshops is not on individuals and their interpersonal relations but on what can be learned from their interaction about the dynamics of the conflict between their communities. Furthermore, there is no assumption that nations can be viewed as equivalent to individuals or that conflict resolution is a form of therapy for national groups.

Establishment of Alternative Norms

The workshop process is predicated on the assumption that the interaction between conflicting parties is governed by a set of "conflict norms" that contribute significantly to escalation and perpetuation of the conflict (Kelman, 1997b). There is a need, therefore, for interactions based on an alternative set of norms conducive to deescalation. Workshops are designed to provide an opportunity for this kind of interaction. As noted earlier, the academic context provides an alternative set of norms on which the interaction between the parties can proceed. The ground rules for interaction within the workshop make it both possible and necessary for participants to abide by these alternative norms. The safe environment of the workshop and the principle of privacy and confidentiality provide the participants with the protection they need to be able to deviate from the conflict norms.

Individual Change as Vehicle for Policy Change

Finally, workshops operationalize a process that is social-psychological par excellence: a process designed to produce change in individuals, interacting in a small-group context, as a vehicle for change in policies and actions of the political system (Kelman, 1997a). Thus, workshops have a dual purpose—educational and political, or change and transfer—as discussed above. This dual purpose at times creates conflicting requirements that have to be balanced in order to fulfill both purposes. I have already illustrated how such conflicts may affect selection of workshop participants and the atmosphere of trust that workshops seek to engender. The relationship between change at the individual level and at the system level—which often lends a dialectical character to problem-solving workshops—is at the heart of the workshop process.

Workshop Content

A set of social-psychological assumptions also informs the substantive emphases of workshop discussions. These emphases include human needs, perceptual and cognitive constraints on information processing, and influence processes, as these enter into conflict relationships.

Parties' Needs and Fears
The satisfaction of the needs of both parties—as articulated through their core identity groups—is the ultimate criterion in the search for a mutually satisfactory resolution of their conflict (Burton, 1990; Kelman, 1990). Unfulfilled needs, especially for identity and security, and existential fears about the denial of such needs typically drive the conflict and create barriers to its resolution. By probing behind the parties' incompatible positions and exploring the identity and security needs that underlie them, it often becomes possible to develop mutually satisfactory solutions, since identity, security, and other psychological needs are not inherently zero sum. Workshop interactions around needs and fears enable the parties to find a language and to identify gestures and actions that are conducive to mutual reassurance. Mutual reassurance is a central element of conflict resolution, particularly in existential conflicts where the parties see their group identity, their people's security, and their very existence as a nation to be at stake.

Escalatory Dynamics of Conflict Interaction
The needs and fears of parties involved in a conflict relationship impose perceptual and cognitive constraints on their processing of new information. One of the major effects of these constraints is that the parties systematically underestimate the occurrence and possibility of change and therefore avoid negotiations, even in the face of changing interests that would make negotiations desirable for both. Images of the enemy are particularly resistant to disconfirming information. The combination of demonic enemy images and virtuous self-images on both sides leads to formation of mirror images, which contribute to the escalatory dynamic of conflict interaction and to resistance to change in a conflict relationship (Bronfenbrenner, 1961; White, 1965).

By focusing on mutual perceptions, mirror images, and systematic differences in perspective, workshop participants can learn to differentiate the enemy image—a necessary condition for movement toward negotiation

(Kelman, 1987). Workshops bring out the symmetries in the parties' images of each other and in their positions and requirements, which arise out of the dynamics of the conflict interaction itself. Such symmetries are often overlooked because of the understandable tendency of protagonists in a conflict relationship to dwell on the asymmetries between them. Without denying these important asymmetries, both empirical and moral, we focus on symmetries, because they tend to be a major source of escalation of conflict (as in the operation of conflict spirals) and a major reason that conflicts become intractable. By the same token, they can serve as a major vehicle for de-escalation by helping the parties penetrate each other's perspective and identify mutually reassuring gestures and actions (Kelman, 1978, 1991a).

Mutual Influence in Conflict Relationships

Finally, the content of workshop discussions reflects an assumption about the nature of influence processes in international relations. Workshops are predicated on the view that the range of influence processes employed in conflict relationships must be broadened. It is necessary to move beyond influence strategies based on threats and even to expand and refine strategies based on promises and positive incentives. By searching for solutions that satisfy the needs of both parties, workshops explore the possibility of mutual influence by way of responsiveness to each other's needs. A key element in this process, emphasized throughout this chapter, is mutual reassurance. In existential conflicts, in particular, parties can encourage each other to move to the negotiating table by reducing both sides' fear—not just, as more traditional strategic analysts maintain, by increasing their pain. At the macro-level, the present approach calls for a shift in emphasis in international influence processes from deterrence and compellence to mutual reassurance. The use of this mode of influence has the added advantage of not only affecting specific behaviors by the other party but contributing to a transformation of the relationship between the parties.

The expanded conception of influence processes that can be brought to bear in a conflict relationship is based on a view of international conflict as a dynamic phenomenon, emphasizing the occurrence and possibility of change. Conflict-resolution efforts are geared, therefore, to discovering possibilities for change, identifying conditions for change, and overcoming resistances to change. Such an approach favors "best-case" analyses and an attitude of "strategic optimism" (Kelman, 1978, 1979), not because of an unrealistic denial of malignant trends but as part of a deliberate strategy to promote change by actively searching for and accentuating whatever realistic possibilities for peaceful resolution of the conflict might be on the horizon. Optimism, in this sense, is part of a strategy designed to create self-fulfilling prophecies of a positive nature, balancing the self-fulfilling prophecies of escalation created by the pessimistic expectations and the worst-case scenarios often favored by more traditional analysts. Problem-solving workshops can be particularly useful in exploring ways in which change can be promoted through the parties' own actions and in discovering ways in which each can exert influence on the other (Kelman, 1991a, 1997b).

Relevance of Interactive Problem Solving

The principles of interactive problem solving have some applicability in a wide range of international conflict situations. Indeed, I would argue that problem-solving workshops and related activities—along with other forms of unofficial diplomacy—should be thought of as integral parts of a larger diplomatic process. This type of intervention can make certain unique contributions to the larger process that are not available through official channels—for example, by providing opportunities for noncommittal exploration of possible ways of getting to the table and of shaping mutually acceptable solutions. Moreover, the assumptions and principles of interactive problem solving can contribute to a reconceptualization of international relationships at the macro-level by encouraging shifts in the nature of the discourse and the means of influence that characterize international relations today (Kelman, 1996a). Nevertheless, it must be said that problem-solving workshops, particularly in the format that has evolved in our style of practice, are more directly relevant in some types of conflict than in others and at certain phases of a given conflict than at others.

Since my primary case has been the Israeli-Palestinian conflict, it is not surprising that my approach is most relevant to situations that share some of the characteristics of that conflict. The approach is most directly relevant to long-standing conflicts in which the interests of the parties have gradually converged and although large segments of each community perceive this to be the case, they seem to be unable or unwilling to enter into negotiations or to bring the negotiations to a satisfactory conclusion. The psychological obstacles to negotiation in these cases are not readily overcome despite the changes in realities and in perceived interests.

Interactive problem solving is not feasible if there is no interest among the parties—or significant elements within each party—in changing the status quo. It is not necessary if there are no profound barriers to negotiations; in that event, other forms of mediation—designed to enhance negotiating skills or to propose reasonable options—may be equally or more useful. However, when the recognition of common interests is insufficient to overcome the psychological barriers, interactive problem solving becomes particularly germane. These conditions are likely to prevail in intense, protracted identity conflicts at the international or intercommunal level, particularly conflicts in which the parties see their national existences to be at stake. The Israeli-Palestinian conflict, the Cyprus conflict, and the conflicts in Northern Ireland

and Sri Lanka clearly share these characteristics. There are many other conflicts, however, that can benefit from a process designed to promote mutual reassurance and to help develop a new relationship between conflicting parties that must find a way of living together.

Since the goal of workshops is to help the parties translate their interest in changing the status quo into an effective negotiating process by overcoming the barriers that stand in the way of such a process, it is necessary to select workshop participants from those segments of the two communities that are indeed interested in a negotiated agreement. They may be skeptical about the possibility of achieving such an agreement and suspicious about the intentions of the other side, but they must have some interest in finding a mutually acceptable way of ending the conflict. In addition, workshop participants must be prepared to meet and talk with members of the other community at a level of equality within the workshop setting, whatever asymmetries in power between the parties may prevail in the relationship between the two communities. Thus, "participants from the stronger party must be *willing* to deal with the other on a basis of equality, which generally means that they have come to accept the illegitimacy of past patterns of discrimination and domination; participants from the weaker must be *able* to deal with the other on a basis of equality, which generally means that they have reached a stage of confrontation in the conflict" (Kelman, 1990: 293-294). In their interactions within the workshop setting, it would be inappropriate for members of the stronger party to take advantage of their superior power, as they might in a negotiating situation. By the same token, it would be inappropriate in this setting for members of the weaker party to take advantage of their superior moral position, as they might in a political rally or an international conference. Workshop interactions are most productive when based on the principle of reciprocity.

As emphasized at the beginning of this chapter, workshops are not intended to substitute for official negotiations, but they may be closely linked to the negotiating process. Thus, our work on the Israeli-Palestinian conflict during the prenegotiation and early negotiation phases helped lay the groundwork for the Oslo agreement by contributing to the development of the cadres, the ideas, and the political atmosphere required for movement to the table and for productive negotiation (Kelman, 1995, 1997c). At a point when active negotiations are in progress, workshops may provide a noncommittal forum to explore options, reframe issues to make them more amenable to negotiation, identify ways of breaking stalemates in the negotiations, and address setbacks in the process. They may also allow the parties to work out solutions to specific technical, political, or emotional issues that require an analytical, problem-solving approach; such solutions can then be fed into the formal negotiating process. In the postnegotiation phase, workshops can help the parties address issues in the implementation of the agreement and explore a new relationship based on patterns of coexistence and cooperation.

The Israeli-Palestinian workshops that we have conducted over the years have suggested some of the ways in which workshops and related activities can contribute to the peace process, helping the parties to overcome the fears and suspicions that keep them from entering into negotiations or from arriving at an agreement. Workshops can help the participants develop more differentiated images of the enemy and discover potential negotiating partners—to learn that there is someone to talk to on the other side and something to talk about. They can contribute to the formation of cadres of individuals who have acquired experience in communicating with the other side and to the conviction that such communication can be fruitful. They enable the parties to penetrate each other's perspectives, gaining insight into the other's concerns, priorities, and constraints. They increase awareness of change and thus contribute to creating and maintaining a sense of possibility—a belief among the relevant parties that a peaceful solution is attainable and that negotiations toward such a solution are feasible.

Workshops also contribute to creating a political environment conducive to fruitful negotiations through the development of a deescalatory language, based on sensitivity to words that frighten and words that reassure the other party. They help in the identification of mutually reassuring actions and symbolic gestures, often in the form of acknowledgments—of the other's humanity, national identity, ties to the land, history of victimization, sense of injustice, genuine fears, and conciliatory moves. They contribute to the development of shared visions of a desirable future, which help reduce the parties' fear of negotiations as a step into an unknown, dangerous realm. They may generate ideas about the shape of a positive-sum solution that meets the basic needs of both parties. They may also generate ideas about how to get from here to there—about a framework and set of principles for moving negotiations forward. Ultimately, problem-solving workshops contribute to a process of transformation of the relationship between enemies.

The continuing workshop that Nadim Rouhana and I convened in 1990-1993 (Rouhana and Kelman, 1994) enhanced the potential relevance of interactive problem solving to the larger political process. A continuing workshop represents a sustained effort to address concrete issues, enabling us to push the process of conflict analysis and interactive problem solving farther and to apply it more systematically than can be done with self-contained, one-time workshops. The longer time period and the continuing nature of the enterprise make it possible to go beyond the sharing of perspectives to the joint production of creative ideas. Moreover, the periodic reconvening of a continuing workshop allows for an iterative and cumulative process, based on feedback and correction. The participants have an opportunity to take the ideas developed in the course of a workshop back to their own communities, gather reactions, and return to the next meeting with proposals for strengthening, expanding, or modifying the original ideas. It is also possible for participants, within or across parties, to meet or otherwise communicate with each other between workshop sessions in order to work out some of the ideas more fully and bring the results of their efforts back to the next session. Finally, a continuing workshop provides better opportunities to address the question of how to disseminate ideas and proposals developed at the workshop most effectively and appropriately.

The Joint Working Group on Israeli-Palestinian Relations that Nadim Rouhana and I initiated in 1994 has addressed the issue of dissemination more directly. This project was initiated with the express purpose of producing and disseminating joint concept papers on the final-status issues in the Israeli-Palestinian negotiations and on the future relationship between the two societies and the two polities that will emerge from the negotiations. The participants are politically influential members of their respective communities, some of whom have held official positions in the past and/or may hold such positions in the future. The working group has followed the general principles and ground rules that have governed our previous problem-solving workshops. The principle of confidentiality and nonattribution has prevailed, as in other workshops, until the group has decided that it was ready to make a particular product public. However, the anticipation that there would ultimately be published papers has focused the discussion more tightly and reduced the noncommittal character of the interaction. It is a price worth paying if it yields products that reflect the joint thinking of influential, mainstream representatives of the two communities and that can be disseminated under their names to decision makers and the wider public on both sides.

The continuing workshop and the joint working group represent important new steps in the development of interactive problem solving. The entire field, for which Ronald Fisher (1993, 1997, this volume) and others use the term "interactive conflict resolution," is still at an early stage of development. A relatively small number of scholar-practitioners around the world are engaged in this kind of work, and the experience they have accumulated is still quite limited. However, the field is maturing. The number of centers devoted to this work is increasing. A new generation is emerging. My students, among others, are actively engaged in research and practice in the field and are taking increasing responsibility for organizing their own projects. By establishing their personal identities as scholar-practitioners in the field, they are giving the field itself an identity of its own. Both the older and the younger generations are establishing networks, whose members engage in collaborative work and are beginning to think systematically about the further development and institutionalization of problem-solving approaches to the resolution of international conflicts (see Fisher, 1993, 1997). Among the issues that need to be addressed and that are, indeed, receiving increasing attention are: the evaluation of this form of practice, the training of new scholar-practitioners, the requirements and pitfalls of professionalization, the formulation of principles and standards of ethical practice, and the development of institutional mechanisms that would strengthen the contribution of interactive problem solving to the resolution of intractable conflicts.

Notes

1. This chapter is adapted from an essay entitled "Interactive Problem Solving: Informal Mediation by the Scholar-Practitioner," schedulded to appear in *Studies in International Mediation: Essays in Honor of Jeffrey Z. Rubin,* edited by Jacob Bercovitch and published by Palgrave Publishers Ltd., New York. It appears here by permission of the editor and publisher.

2. The continuing workshop was supported by grants from the Nathan Cummings Foundation, the John D. and Catherine T. MacArthur Foundation, the U.S. Institute of Peace, and Rockefeller Family and Associates. We are greatly indebted to these organizations for making this work possible and to the Harvard Center for International Affairs for providing the institutional base for it. Nadim Rouhana and I were joined on the panel of third-party facilitators by Harold Saunders of the Kettering Foundation and C. R. Mitchell of George Mason University. We are very grateful to them, as well as to the members of the third-party staff, which included Cynthia Chataway, Rose Kelman, Susan Korper, Kate Rouhana, and William Weisberg.

3. The Joint Working Group is a project of PICAR, the Program on International Conflict Analysis and Resolution (Herbert C. Kelman, director; Donna Hicks, deputy director), which was established at the Harvard Center for International Affairs (now the Weatherhead Center) in 1993, with a grant from the William and Flora Hewlett Foundation. The Hewlett Foundation's support of PICAR's infrastructure is deeply appreciated, as is the support of the working group itself by grants from the Nathan Cummings Foundation, the Carnegie Corporation, the Ford Foundation, the Charles R. Bronfman Foundation, and the U.S. Information Agency, as well as the Hewlett Foundation, the Renner Institut in Vienna, and the Weatherhead Center. The third-party team, chaired by Nadim Rouhana and myself, has included Donna Hicks, Kate Rouhana, Rose Kelman, and (in 1994-1995) Eileen Babbitt. Their dedication and skill have been indispensable to the project.

6
Power, Rights, Interests, and Identity: Conflict Management Strategies for Building a Democratic Peace

John Davies

This chapter explores seven broad strategies, identifiable across cultures, for the management of social conflicts, internal and external. It proposes that each strategy reflects a different perspective or set of normative expectations regarding forms of relationship on both individual and collective levels. Three general approaches to conflict management (power-based, rights-based and interest-based) are seen as complementary to each other if in proper balance. A more detailed analysis breaks them down into seven distinct strategies or perspectives differentiated along two dimensions: forms of relationship (dependence, independence or interdependence) and levels of collective identity (contact groups, cultures/nations, or world/humanity as a whole).

The seven perspectives may also be differentiated according to the complexity of social reasoning implied, consistent with the pioneering cross-cultural research of Kohlberg (1981) and others. These perspectives are often poorly differentiated; most theorists are content to distinguish only two—autocratic versus democratic, or collectivist versus individualist—and then often on the basis of institutions rather than the cultural norms on which the institutions depend. One perspective is generally preferred as more civilized, the other(s) rejected, with no further perspective to bridge them.

Yet while the perspectives may be seen as distinct moral paradigms, they are better viewed not as mutually exclusive but as complementary and balanced by others, each optimal under different circumstances requiring different levels of complexity. Political cultures (or leaders) who incorporate a wider selection of the seven as normative—who are willing to "think out of the box" of currently dominant paradigms—have more options for constructive adaptation to complex and changing environments, as in the present era of rapid globalization and technological change, with less violence, injustice and marginalization. The combination allows an expanded realism or enlightened self-interest that takes cultural norms, identities and aspirations into account in interaction with the dynamics of power. Tensions between proponents of leading-edge versus simpler or more familiar strategies may best be regarded as healthy symptoms of a normal political process, motivating critical social debate on how best to adapt to change, rather than as requiring suppression.

The seven-strategy model is useful in understanding intercommunal as well as international interactions and the dynamics and dangers of democratic, predemocratic or market transitions. Effective conflict transformation, peacebuilding, democratization and development diplomacy require facilitating exploration of both strengths and limitations of currently dominant or conventional strategies, and development of new or improved strategies accessible in the context of the host political culture(s), rather than just promoting or imposing a cloned form of institutional democracy. The proposed framework reconciles several competing models of conflict management behavior, and it extends current theory supporting the efficacy of integrative negotiation in conflict transformation and of democratic norms and institutions in conflict resolution and prevention.

In the following two sections, we review some basic concepts and theoretical assumptions regarding conflict, conflict management, political culture, democratization and development, and consider their inter-relationships. In the third and fourth sections, we examine in more detail the power-rights-interests and the dependence-independence-interdependence frameworks, integrating them in the following section in terms of related dimensions of identity and development (see figure 6.2). We then look at each of the seven strategies or perspectives in more detail, considering the strengths and limitations of each in relation to the development of political culture. Finally, we consider the dynamics of intergroup interactions and misperceptions across these paradigmatic boundaries, and how a better understanding of these may enhance our capacity to build peace and promote sustainable development and democracy.

Conflict Management and Political Culture

All of the more than 30 wars being fought at the turn of the millennium involve nonstate communities whose *identities* (autonomous existence or equal status with neighboring groups) are in some way contested. Even by definition, any protracted *social conflict* may be understood as involving distinct collective identities,[1] plus a perception that their respective aspirations (rooted in needs, interests and values) cannot be simultaneously achieved (see Gurr and Harff, 1994; Rubin, Pruitt, and Kim, 1994).

Most analyses of alternative approaches to managing conflict tend to focus on the second aspect of this definition, concerning competing aspirations, and on how they may be addressed, either by preferring the needs and interests of our own community or those of another (powerful or highly valued) group, or by integrative or balanced consideration of both (see Rubin, Pruitt, and Kim, 1994). While it is often recognized that identity needs can be powerful motivators (see Azar, this volume; Rothman, 1997c), little consideration is given to the first (collective-identity) dimension of social conflict, how it is constituted and how it interacts with these alternative options for prioritizing or reconciling competing interests. Yet, especially since collective identity is never one dimensional, it is essential to ask whose shared aspirations are being prioritized or reconciled with whose in each case. A consideration of these two dimensions in relation to each other points to a broader array of distinct strategies for managing conflict, strategies that may be better attuned to the perspectives of the parties rooted in their various collective identities.

Using the term *conflict management* (rather than conflict termination or resolution) implies an acceptance of conflict as an inevitable part of the dynamics of normal life and as having a potentially positive role in motivating developmental change to accommodate better threatened needs or interests. Conflict management generally does, however, aim to contain or minimize violence (including structural violence or social injustice—Galtung, 1969; Galtung and Jacobsen, 2000), or (if it is assumed that violence is also an inevitable part of the human condition) at least to ensure that it does not work to one's own disadvantage, however broadly or narrowly conceived. The more specific term *conflict transformation* also implies an acceptance of conflict as normal or inevitable, but not of violence: the aim here is to reduce or remove the underlying motivation for either direct or structural violence through addressing needs and interests, and thus to transform conflict systems from destructive violence to constructive, integrative, bottom-up as well as top-down efforts for sustainable development and stable intergroup relations.

Political culture may be defined in terms of the *norms* (shared values, accepted rules, assumptions) that guide our behavior toward each other and our expectations of how we will be treated by others in situations of actual or potential conflict. It is these norms of conflict management, more than the formal laws and institutional structures of society that depend on them, that determine a community's capacity to prevent or contain violence (see Maoz and Russett, 1993; Powelson, 2001). They provide the essential conditions needed to permit growth in *human capital* (knowledge, skills, motivation) and *social capital* (stable, cooperative relations based on trust, both within and across groups) as required for fulfilling aspirations and hence for sustainable economic[2] and political development (Coleman, 1990; Putnam, 1993). *Political development* itself may thus be defined in terms of improvements in a community's capacity for constructive management of conflict and change (i.e., with minimal direct or structural violence), leading to further improvements in human and social capital and enhanced quality of life (as reflected, for example, in the UN Development Program's annual indices).

Democratization and Development

Discussion of political development tends to be dominated by the concept of democratization, or movement from autocratic to democratic forms of governance. Both are typically defined in terms of institutional rather than normative structures; Gurr and Jaggers (1998) for example, define *democracy* in terms of relative openness of political institutions, with executive power being held accountable through institutional constraints, and with transfer of executive power being regulated based on open and competitive elections. *Autocracy* is defined in terms of closed political institutions lacking such accountability and regulated transfer of executive power; other regimes are classified as mixed, transitional, disrupted or collapsed.

Such definitions have proven valuable in facilitating critical debate informed by empirical research. A key research finding has been that democracies do tend to have far fewer violent conflicts than autocracies, especially within and among themselves (see Maoz and Russett, 1993; Esty et al., 1998; Gurr, Marshall and Khosla, 2000). This is consistent with our definition of political development as enhanced capacity for conflict management. But the same research also highlights the finding that transitional or democratizing communities tend to be far more unstable and violence prone than even autocracies, and that new democracies (so defined) thus have a high failure rate (see Gurr and Davies, this volume).

These findings suggest that we need a deeper understanding of what democracy means and how it can be developed. If we assume that a democracy is defined by its institutions rather than its political culture, we may make the mistake of thinking that those institutions can be imposed or imported without regard for the strength or weakness of the internal norms needed to adapt and sustain them or to allow them to function in a genuinely democratic manner. We may also make the mistake of treating conventional (Western) democratic institutions as a universal prescription for all societies, without any basis for evaluating whether it is appropriate to the local cultural context or achievable in the near term. Such prescriptions are likely to be resisted as Western cultural imperialism, and to the extent that democratic institutions are imported rather than appropriately developed or adapted through engaging the internal dynamics and normative dialogue of the indigenous culture (see Harris and Reilly, 1998), this resistance is entirely understandable.

We propose that a more differentiated understanding of democracy and autocracy is needed, one that is rooted in an understanding of the normative perspectives or strategies for conflict management that constitute political cultures. At the same time, this understanding of democracy would have to be applicable across cultures, if it is to be relevant to the aspirations of all communities, providing a normative basis for efforts to promote political development internationally (Powelson, 2001).

As a first step, it may be useful to redefine autocracy and democracy in terms more of the norms that sustain them than of their institutional superstructure. Autocracy depends on the norm or expectation that, in conflict situations, needs and interests are best protected through loyalty or deference to those with power and resources, at least to the extent that one does not have the power to avoid or challenge them. Democracy, on the other hand, requires norms by which needs and interests are generally better protected by upholding rights or principles that have been broadly agreed upon as a just basis for settling conflicts of interest, and hence for constraining and regulating the acquisition and exercise of power (including state executive power). There is a considerable gap between these two political cultures, which may be called *power based* and *rights based*. It will be argued that transition from the first to the second and the long-term stability of the second are only possible through a third normative approach to conflict management, which may be called *interest based*.

Power, Rights, Interests, and Identity

It may be that a shift in *collective identity* is also required for a democratic culture to take root. Individuals may be said to develop multiple *collective identities*, each more or less salient under different circumstances (Tajfel and Turner, 1986). These reflect reference communities including: (a) *contact groups,* such as families, clans, villages, work groups or personal networks; (b) larger *cultures, peoples or nations* sharing common values, assumptions and expectations (but not, for the most part, direct contact), such as professions, trades or castes, provinces or cities, ethnic, cultural or ideological groupings, peoples or nations, religions or civilizations; and (c) the inclusive identity of *humanity as a whole*. While there are many alternative identities that can be structured within each broadly defined level, these three levels appear to correspond with the above three perspectives or categories of political culture.

Power-based political cultures tend to be organized around normative expectations that security and other needs are best served through taking care of personal relationships (local and extended contact groups/networks), particularly those with individuals who wield greater power and resources, since those are the people who are expected to make the decisions required to manage conflicts affecting the larger community. Personal loyalties are important, as are personal status (face) and awareness of one's place in the hierarchical web of relationships. If and when these networks become unclear or disrupted (at least in postsubsistence economies), it may be that order and clarity can only be restored on the basis of competitive assertion of power—power being defined in terms of human, social and economic capital as well as political and military resources, and as including "soft" (persuasive) power as well as hard power exercised through threats and coercion. The potential for protracted violence and recurrent disruption through such reordering processes is great, and awareness of this will tend to reinforce norms of collectivism and conservatism.

Rights-based political cultures, on the other hand, tend to be organized more around normative expectations that our needs (including those for security, effective participation, identity, justice, well-being—see Azar, this volume) are best served by adhering to normative or agreed-upon rules for managing conflicts in ways that protect the rights of others. Whereas in power-based political cultures rules are legitimized because they serve to make predictable the avenues through which power will be exercised and transferred, in rights-based cultures the legitimacy of the rules derives more from their efficacy in equitably protecting the rights of all or most members of the community. To the extent that these rules are linked to shared cultural or ideological values, it is possible for a national collective identity to become prominent (over the clan or contact-group-based identities that are more critical to those in power-based cultures), expanding the possibilities for social capital as needed for modernization.

In more complex rights-based cultures, the rules (laws and norms) are held to be more sacred than the rulers, who can therefore be held to the same standards as others (rule of law). The rules (and institutions through which legislative, executive and judicial power can be exercised to protect rights) provide a context in which competition for power and resources and other forms of conflict can take place with minimal threat of violence and disruption of social order. This encourages the broad economic and political participation, based on principled competition, that is characteristic of stable democratic cultures and open market economies capable of long-term growth. It also tends to foster greater respect for individual enterprise, adaptability to change, and competing ideas than in power-based cultures, and it provides a basis for scientific and technological progress and sustained economic growth.

Each of these political cultures can provide a self-reinforcing normative context or paradigm that reasonably protects the security and basic needs of its members. Each can be applied and sustained for communities of any size: in the case of power-based cultures, through the maintenance of nested hierarchies of contact groups as needed to link together a larger society.

However, as a society chooses to move away from a stable agrarian economy toward industrial- and even information- or service-oriented economies, the consequent need for population mobility, openness to international trade, and constant adaptation to change (all of which disrupt established networks of relationships) clearly favors the rights-based cultures, adding to their affluence, power and quality of life relative to power-based cultures. The subsequent sense of relative deprivation and inequity, brought home with the help of the global revolution in information and communication technology, is profoundly destabilizing, weakening the national identity of the power-based cultures and the relationships of respect that hold them together.

A reasonable strategy for redressing this state of affairs is to promote development of rights-based, democratic political cultures. The problem is the huge gap between power-based and rights-based normative frameworks. Simplistic efforts to introduce democracy by fiat (establishing competitive elections and other democratic institutions modeled on those in the West) are not sufficient to promote a corresponding shift in the underlying norms, particularly when imposed from outside (e.g., as a condition for needed aid). More likely, the institutions will be adapted to serve existing (power-based) norms, providing international legitimacy, for a time, of existing elites' grip on power, while deeper changes are resisted in the name of cultural integrity and resistance to neo-imperialism. Worse, multiparty elections may serve to deepen existing ethnic or tribal divisions, with the winning group taking the prize of state power with little sense of responsibility for other groups (e.g., Moi's Kenya or Mugabe's Zimbabwe).

A better strategy to address this dilemma is to use a third, *interest-based* approach to conflict management distinct from both of those considered so far. This approach is rooted not so much in those levels of identity which correspond to contact groups, or to cultures, but in an understanding and acknowledgement of our shared identity as human beings.

Where the resources and legitimacy of power networks have become uncertain and there has been no development of a normative consensus on rules for managing conflict nonviolently, conflicts cannot be efficiently managed on the basis of determining either who is more powerful, or who is right and who is wrong. However, it is possible to look for an understanding of the motivations driving each party to the conflict—their interests, including basic human needs, as well as values and specific interests derived from their needs in the context of cultural influences and individual experiences. If we assume only that human intelligence implies rationality, exercised in order to promote or satisfy interests, we can still look for areas of convergence (shared or complementary interests, values, needs) which can provide a basis for mutual understanding and respect, and hence willingness to work cooperatively where this may help to address shared problems (expanded social capital). Where interests diverge, a joint effort can be directed toward finding ways of bridging or trading off interests for positive-sum outcomes, or toward agreement on principles that would allow the parties to respect a zero-sum outcome that at least avoids destructive, negative-sum scenarios and maintains stable, long-term relations.

This interest-based approach may be seen as an essential complement for maintaining the health and sustainability of any power- or rights-based system, and, of course, it is at the core of second track diplomacy. Where the exercise of power is guided by agreed rules of the game that protect rights, and where consensus on what those rules and rights should be—and on how they should be upheld and applied institutionally—is achieved and constantly refined and adapted through an interest-based methodology, the stability and adaptability of the political culture is maximized. Where no consensus on authority or rights exists, or when the consensus needs extension, the interest-based approach provides an efficient mechanism for developing it. It does not require common personal loyalties or even shared cultural values, only an understanding of the common humanity or intelligence of the parties. Such awareness of common humanity may not define the boundaries of group or national identity, but it may be a necessary ingredient for any group's long-term stability in a changing world.

The bulk of this book is an exploration of how this interest-based approach can be applied in managing protracted intergroup conflicts. The focus in this chapter is more on understanding its relationship to the more conventional strategies, and how all three strategies occur in different forms. These relationships and differences, which may be critical in assessing what strategies will be effective in implementing adaptive change in different contexts, can best be appreciated with the aid of a cross-cutting framework for understanding strategies for managing conflict.

Dependence, Independence and Interdependence

If we focus on conflict management specifically in terms of how competing interests are reconciled, three primary strategies for managing social conflict (or four, to the extent that avoidance or withdrawal may also be considered as managing) may also be distinguished as occurring across cultures, and as requiring different degrees of complexity of social reasoning (see Pruitt and Carnevale, 1993): yielding, adversarial and integrative. These three strategies correspond to three forms of relationship possible between individuals or identity groups (or four if we add absence of relationship): dependence, independence and interdependence.

Yielding behavior appears to be the simplest strategy, requiring least effort (acceptance of the claim presented to us, perhaps after comparison with a competing interest or perspective of our own). It can be satisfactory (rational) when the other party is trusted, valued or depended upon for resources or at least for restraint of power, to the extent that any competing interests of one's own would appear to be outweighed by respect for the other's greater power or capacity to address shared interests, or by concern for a greater apparent interest or need of the other. This strategy, while not exclusive to any culture, is thus likely to be emphasized more in collectivist cultures (as distinct from individualist cultures—see Triandis and Gelfand, 1998).

Adversarial or contentious behavior requires more effort and complex reasoning, in that an independent position of one's own must be identified and preferred to that presented by the other party (which may, though not necessarily, be ignored or discounted), and the risks of opposition weighed. It can be rational, however, when the other party to the conflict is not trusted, valued or feared, the conflict is seen as zero sum, one's own interest or need is perceived to be more substantial or more worthy than that of the other party, and/or the other party may be induced to yield or withdraw without inflicting damage disproportionate to the value gained (emphasized more in individualist cultures and *realpolitik* perspectives organized around the primacy of one's own or national material interests).

Integrative behavior requires more effort and complex reasoning again, in that it goes beyond the simple dualistic reasoning of identifying which position (and risk structure) is preferred over the other. It considers the positions of both (or several) parties, takes the interests of both (or all) substantially into account, and seeks to identify any positive-sum (win-win) solutions that may be achievable through separate or collaborative action. For example, a fight over rights to a certain tract of land may be resolved (transformed into a mutually respectful or supportive relationship) when it is recognized that the primary interest of one party is simply to have a right of way through (or symbolic sovereignty over) that land, which can be granted without major disruption to the farming and other pragmatic interests and activities of the other party. The interdependence implied here thus includes or upholds the interests and independence of both parties (the "dual concern" model—see figure 6.1), thus transcending polarities between dependence and independence, individualism and collectivism, concern for self and for others, winning and losing.

Figure 6.1 Strategic Choices in Managing Conflict: Dual-Concern Model

High	1. Yielding		2. Integrating
Level of concern for other group's interests		3. Compromising	
Low	4. Avoiding		5. Contending
	Low	*Level of concern for own group's interests*	High

Integrative behavior is rational when the parties are recognized to be, in some sense, interdependent,[3] so that any sacrifice in accepting less than 100 percent of what one aspires to in the immediate conflict situation (e.g., exclusive use of the land) may be more than made up for (at least in the longer term) in two ways. First, the solution agreed to will be more stable, as something for which the parties are jointly responsible and from which they jointly benefit; and second, future relations with the other party are likely to be more productive than if adversarial (win-lose) or yielding (lose-win) behavior had been used to one party's cost. Even if a positive-sum solution is not found to the immediate conflict, the collaborative effort to find a fair solution (a zero-sum compromise or avoidance, based on respect for needs and on mutually recognized standards) can still bring these long-term benefits, and in that sense be a positive-sum outcome. Galtung and Jacobsen (2000) thus point to the value of switching from the conventional (power- or rights-based) axis (options 1, 3 and 5 in figure 6.1) to a perpendicular axis representing a range of possible balanced outcomes (options 2, 3 and 4 in figure 6.1), including creative use of avoidance or compromise when integrative (positive-sum) options appear out of reach.

The emphasis in conflict transformation then, as discussed in this book, is usually to facilitate a shift from adversarial tactics to integrative tactics in circumstances where the needs or substantive interests (and capacities) of both sides are perceived as too great to permit either to yield, rendering continued adversarial tactics less effective than integrative tactics. In some cases, though, it may first be necessary to focus on facilitating a move from yielding or passivity to a culturally appropriate form of advocacy or adversarial tactics, in order that a community can begin effectively to discuss and seek redress for its felt needs or grievances. An ability to express and be firm in standing for one's interests (the role of advocates or activists—see Lederach, 1995) is a prerequisite for effective integrative tactics; in other words, independent thinking is a prerequisite for interdependent thinking by both parties.

A fourth strategy—to ignore, withdraw, or step back from a conflict—may also be a rational one where perceived interests on both sides are too minimal to warrant time or attention, or where there seem to be alternative paths to satisfying interests without engaging the other party (e.g., instead of yielding or arguing over the rights to one piece of land, we look for a better option elsewhere). This may work well where the parties are nondependent on each other—that is, neither dependence nor interdependence is an issue (in contrast to independence, where dependence is actively rejected and thus is an issue). Otherwise, withdrawal may equate with one of the other three modes of conflict management, depending on the specifics of the relationship and the expectations attached to it; if the owners of the land do not feel it is possible to entrust it to anyone else, withdrawal may be seen as adversarial behavior.

In social conflicts that we cannot easily ignore, withdrawal may still have a critical secondary role, in that we can benefit from stepping back from a conflict temporarily (or habitually, in conjunction with another primary coping strategy) better to reflect on or analyze the situation, to evaluate which management strategy to follow, before committing ourselves to it (or before altering course to adopt a new strategy). Such a *reflective* strategy is thus important primarily as a transitional phase in improving the effectiveness of conflict transformation, particularly in facilitating a shift from one preferred strategy to another more complex one (see Rothman, 1997c; Kaufman, this volume).

All these strategies may be found in some form in any society (or even any individual), with each being valued as normal, or morally acceptable, in different specific situations. However, we can distinguish people in terms of which strategies they broadly prefer or regard as normal, and the same may be true of different communities (Chilton, 1988). The broader the range of approaches accessible, and hence the more complex the reasoning in the dominant or normal approaches, the more likely that conflicts can also be managed in ways that sustain the interests, relationships and development of the parties involved, minimizing the likelihood of structural or direct violence.

As with the earlier power/rights/interests framework, it is useful further to differentiate the strategies emphasized within this framework. Either of these two frameworks may be useful for planning a conflict management initiative; however, in the more complex and detailed planning needed for a sustainable peace settlement, they are inadequate. There are critical differences, for example, between yielding to powerful individuals and yielding to commonly held principles; between principled and unprincipled competition; between rights based on national ideology and those based on universal human needs. These differences will become more apparent when we look at how one framework intersects with the other.

Identity and Development

The relationship between these two frameworks or sets of normative strategies can best be understood by considering the relevance of identity. We have suggested that identity is a universal need across cultures and that it is a necessary constituent of any social conflict. The fact that all current wars involve at least one nonstate community (i.e., a group whose independent identity is being asserted but not recognized formally or internationally) also suggests that identity needs are of central importance in conflict dynamics.

The political significance of dependent (yielding), independent (adversarial) and interdependent (integrative) strategies depends on how those employing them see themselves in relation to others. Who, for example, is asserting independence from whom?

Identity is multidimensional. Collective identities may be defined in relation to physical and behavioral similarities (e.g., dress, size, color), similarities of thinking (e.g., family, friends, villages, contact groups), similarities of value systems (e.g., nations, cultures, religions, civilizations), or the globally shared similarity of human nature or intelligence.[4] Each more abstract identity implies that more individuals and groups are like the self, having interests, values and needs that are worthy of respect or accommodation. In other words, they represent increasing degrees of interdependence. Each of the four levels of identity interacts with each of three primary strategies for managing conflicting interests—yielding (dependence), adversarial (independence) and integrative (interdependence). Thus instead of three, we may find it more useful to distinguish twelve strategies for managing conflict, of which nine would be relevant to adult communities (the physical self-concept being primary only in childhood),[5] rooted in different perspectives on the nature of our relationships with others. All these strategies are likely to be available in any community (more or less accessible for different individuals and cultures, and differently expressed by each), though again some will carry greater normative weight as representing conventional wisdom for dealing with specific types of conflict.

While all of these strategies can be found in any community, the differences among them in terms of complexity is reflected in the finding that in the process of individual development of social or moral reasoning, it is apparent that the three basic modes of relationship emerge and predominate sequentially in relation to each more abstract level of identity or self-concept. In relation to each level of identity, interdependence (integrative mode for managing conflicts) is achieved but is followed by a realization that on a deeper level of identity one is still dependent (unable to distance or distinguish oneself in terms of the more abstract modality), thus beginning a new cycle in a continuing spiral of development (see figure 6.2). The emergence of each more complex level of reasoning (and corresponding strategy for managing conflict) does not displace the earlier ones but complements them and adds to the options available for managing conflict and for lowering the risk of violence.

The sequential predominance of these strategies in individual development is evidence of their increasing complexity and also of the distinct rationality of each within its own frame of reference (assumptions about the nature of human relations). In any large society, all strategies may be found at any time, and different strategies are likely to predominate regarding different issues or contexts and to shift over time. Political development is thus better assessed in terms of an increasing range of strategies broadly available (indicating greater conflict-carrying capacity) rather than in terms of a sequential "stage" model analogous to individual development.[6] As this normative range increases or decreases, however, there will typically be a leading-edge strategy relating to key issues, with normal political tensions between its proponents and those of simpler and more familiar strategies, each group being convinced of the moral superiority, or the greater realism, of its preferred paradigm or perspective.

Earlier, we associated the different levels of identity with power-based, rights-based and interest-based approaches to conflict management, respectively. However, figure 6.2 offers a more fine-grained analytical framework. Power-based strategies may be divided into two broad types: the first oriented toward obedience and deference to the powerful (collectivism), the second and more complex version oriented toward independence, instrumental exchange, and unregulated competition to satisfy one's own interests (individualism).

Figure 6.2 Normative Strategies for Managing Conflict: Expanded Model

Levels of Collective Identity: ⬇	Forms of Relationship		
	Dependence (Yielding)	**Independence** (Contending)	**Interdependence** (Integrative)
Contact groups (personal law)	1. Obedience, deference to those in power, collectivist ***Power-based***	2. Instrumental exchange, unregulated competition, individualist, realist ***Power-based***	3. Personal caring, family/network responsibility and commitment ***Interest-based***
Cultures, nations (value systems, national law)	4. Shared values/ principles, national laws, ethnocentric, modern nationalist ***Rights-based***	5. Principled competition, democracy, rule of law, free/fair trade, human rights ***Rights-based***	6. Pluralism, humanitarianism, cultural interdependence ***Interest-based***
World/ humanity (natural law)	7. Globally inclusive, transcending polarities, proactive, visionary, natural law (universally shared dynamics of human intelligence) as reference point: ***Interest-based***		

Rights-based approaches may similarly be divided into two types: the first emphasizing deference to shared moral values and rules for managing conflict and differentiating right from wrong behavior, as needed for building a national or societal consensus; the second emphasizing principled competition among interest groups, ideologies, even cultures, with rule of law more valued than any specific leaders' claims to embody the societal norms. Thus, both yielding and adversarial strategies can be found as subtypes within both power-based and rights-based cultures; in the latter case the emphasis will be in yielding to shared norms or laws rather than to powerful people as such, and adversarial strategies will emphasize lawful or principled competition, as exemplified in adversarial legal processes or scientific debate.

Interest-based strategies are represented in three different forms, the first representing interdependent perspectives capable of bridging the interests of competing parties in a power-based culture, where loyalties to individuals or contact groups are still prior to value systems or shared cultures. We regard this strategy as critical not only for constructively addressing intergroup conflicts in power-based societies but also for promoting successful transition from power- to rights-based political cultures (democratic transitions), providing a mechanism for reaching or consolidating a legitimate national consensus on principles and rights. The second is a more complex strategy required for managing conflicts across cultural divides, where there is internal but not cross-group consensus on shared values, or conflicts where one or more groups are marginalized, lacking the knowledge or other resources to engage effectively in principled competition or to assert rights.

In the third interest-based strategy, common humanity (or "world society"—see Kelman, this volume) is not asserted just as a means for bridging the interests and values of different groups but represents in itself the primary identity or reference point for action. We believe that this highly integrative perspective may be key to providing leadership not only for transforming conflict situations toward sustainable development but more broadly for promoting development and societal coherence in ways that prevent violent conflict from arising at all. This perspective points to possibilities for a more robust democracy accessible for any culture, and for a peaceful world that honors the values of all cultures as the unique and constantly changing expressions of human intelligence or natural law.[7]

Development of Political Culture

We have argued that the prevalence in any society of norms reflecting more of these seven perspectives, or strategies, is an indicator of greater conflict-carrying capacity, and hence capacity for adaptive change, sustainable development (expanding human and social capital) and dynamic peace.

We look at each of these strategies in turn, in the order that they emerge in the context of the development of individual social reasoning. Each more complex perspective or strategy of social reasoning expands on the simpler strategies, rather than replacing them, allowing a broader range of adaptive options for resolving conflict. All strategies are to some extent represented or accessible in all cultures, and by all individuals, although the larger the gap between a currently dominant strategy and a more complex one for the same issue, the less easily the latter will be understood or applied.

No single model of development or of modes of social reasoning will be optimal for all purposes. Even using the concept of development in relation to political cultures can evoke images of cultural imperialism. Nevertheless, we argue that a transcultural, normative model of development is essential if we are to develop a consensus on what forms of social change are worth working for in a dynamically changing, multicultural world.

While the strategies differ in terms of complexity and hence capacity for managing more complex conflict situations, all are rational, and no strategy as such is morally superior to any other. Relevant norms thus deserve equal respect: societies in less complex and more stable contexts may not feel the need to adopt more complex norms, and any attempt to prescribe or impose them from the outside is likely to meet with misunderstanding and resistance. Such attempts imply a too-narrow focus on one (usually rights-based) strategy as being "correct," which limits effectiveness in managing conflict cross-culturally just as surely as does an exclusive focus on simpler *realpolitik* strategies. The addition of new normative strategies to broaden the repertoire of any society in conflict should come as a result of internal debate and should draw on existing cultural norms, with external support for process, not prescriptive pressure.

Strategies 1-2 (Power-Based)

1: Obedience to Authority

The simplest strategy, organized around norms of obedience to leadership by powerful or resourceful individuals, requires only the concrete operational thinking acquired in late childhood.[8] Conscious decision making on conflict issues that require more reflective thinking is likely to be deferred to leader(s), who control resources and may punish the disobedient.

This perspective has advantages in terms of simplicity of organization and decision making, with minimal time or effort lost in argument between competing viewpoints. Stable family, village or business groups founded on the strength, skills, knowledge or resources of an undisputed leader (patriarch, chieftain, sheik, etc.) may do very well based on the simple norms of obedience and deference conceived from this perspective. Larger organizations or communities can become established through simple iteration of this leader-follower relationship into larger pyramidal pecking-order or food-chain networks under the aegis of a paramount ruler (monarch, governor, emperor, dictator, etc.). Even in postagrarian societies, clear chains of command can be an advantage especially in threatening situations requiring swift decision and response, such as in simple military or paramilitary organizations.

However, emphasis on the virtues of deference and conformity may radically reduce opportunities for initiative and creative contributions from the mass of the community and even among the elite. In the absence of competent leadership, group inertia means that change and adaptation will be slow and uncertain. When the community is too large and complex for effective personal rule, or too much in flux for stable networks to be maintained, or when leaders seek to exploit their positions at the expense of group members or otherwise seek to exercise power and authority beyond their ability to do it well, this perspective is unlikely to support the group's needs and interests for long. Nor, when it is unclear who has legitimacy to lead and make decisions, can there be efficient resolution of disputes concerning leadership and responsibility.

Worse, because might and right are not easily separable here (the mystique of personal power), dominance may rightly be protected from challenge through punishment, physical coercion, threats and extortion (Kohlberg's,

1981, "punishment and obedience" stage of moral reasoning). Massive waste of human and social capital can become institutionalized in the form of genocide, enslavement, imprisonment or the creation of underclasses through a combination of direct and structural violence. Hitler, Stalin, Pol Pot, Idi Amin, or any of a host of dictators have exemplified the downside of this strategy— though these were in many ways canny leaders who knew how to appeal to some of the more complex norms as well. As long as their victims count themselves as powerless, morally or practically unable to change or challenge the status quo, such predatory regimes can persist, but they are vulnerable to challenges premised on more complex norms.

As the simplest strategy, it also becomes the most likely default (along with passive avoidance) for those who have been traumatized or feel depressed or overwhelmed by fear or losses from war or other forms of disaster or abuse. Those who feel victimized thus tend not to see possibilities for promoting constructive change, which leads to inertia and makes recovery, development and peacebuilding extremely difficult following protracted war. Recovery efforts thus need to emphasize helping people to move beyond victimhood toward reconciliation (see Borris, this volume).

2: Instrumental Exchange and Competition

From this perspective, accessible from adolescence,[9] adversarial modes of managing conflict appear more rational, as awareness of our own interests and needs become sharper than awareness of those that others present to us. We may often find it reasonable to resist, question or actively avoid (in such ways as may be allowed by the cultural context) the claims of others, which appear to lack merit or conflict with our own. Rather than automatic obedience, right behavior now means acting or competing to meet our needs and interests, and expecting that others will do the same. *Realism,* rather than loyalty or deference, becomes the primary virtue. Conflicts can thus be managed or resolved through instrumental exchange, whether of goods or threats ("bads"— including normative threats of punishment for noncompliance). Any tactics designed to satisfy one's own desires at the expense of others, whether through argument, bribery, hiding or falsifying relevant information, blaming or demonizing the other, blocking access to others' sources of support, etc. fit within this broad strategic perspective (see Rubin, Pruitt, and Kim, 1994). If applied subject to principles of nonviolence or respect for law or human rights these tactics would fall within Strategy 5, though the difference may be lost on those habituated to power-based systems.

This perspective provides the basis for societal norms upholding free trade and barter. Political and social conflicts can now be resolved through competition. Compliance (votes or other forms of cooperation) can be bought through use of bribes, patronage, aid, economic or political favors, or through threats, either on an issue-by-issue basis or as a stable, longer-term arrangement. If power is imposed or goods taken without exchange, just retribution or revenge may be sought ("an eye for an eye" reflects the logic of this perspective). Again, through simple iteration of such instrumental exchange relationships, a relatively stable lattice of relationships can be built up, organized around those with greatest capacity for patronage or threats, thus creating a status system which limits and controls the aspirations of the disadvantaged communities, tribes, classes, castes or gender groups.

On the international level, in a system that is anarchic to the extent that it lacks more complex norms for managing conflicts, this has led to *realpolitik* reliance on military and economic power, to arms races, and to client states dependent on the protection or support of regional or superpowers (e.g., Zaire under Mobutu, or satellite states during the Cold War). Where there is no agreement on guiding principles, bribery (e.g., the United States with North Korea, or with Israel and Egypt) and/or the threat or application of economic sanctions or military force (e.g., with Saddam's Iraq and Milošević's Yugoslavia) may be invoked as a normal ("realist") aspect of diplomacy.

Settlements and political structures based on such instrumentalist thinking, particularly when threats are relied on more than bribes (see Freedman, 1981), are brittle. In a changing world, where power relations are ambiguous and shifting, they are subject to recurrent power struggles, terrorism and vicious cycles of revenge, and they are at risk of deteriorating into protracted violence (e.g., between warlords or competing tribes or communities, as now in Sudan, Somalia, Angola, Burundi, Congo, Israel/Palestine, Sri Lanka, Burma, Chechnya, Colombia—see Azar, this volume). Leaders may play on and exacerbate the fears of their communities, buying popularity or militant mobilization at the cost of further destabilizing and polarizing relations with other groups, blaming or scapegoating others to direct frustration away from themselves. Normative instrumentalist strategies also tend to deplete the environment and marginalize or leave at risk those individuals or groups without sufficient resources to exchange in order to meet their needs (or without sufficient human and social capital to generate those resources). As exploitative political and economic structures inevitably break down, we are left with a level of political underdevelopment reviled by Thomas Hobbes as "the war of each against all."

Strategy 3 (Interest-Based): Caring and Personal Responsibility

The ability to put oneself in another's shoes, to understand and respect the conflicting interests of others, to protect and care personally for those who are unable to compete, fend for themselves or offer concrete exchange for needed help is the defining trait of this mode of social reasoning[10]—the "golden rule" norm that is found at the core of all the major cultures and traditions. It is important to recognize the rational nature of this behavior and associated norms of responsibility and commitment. The norm is to treat familiar others on a par with ourselves (in contrast both to yielding, where the other is put first, and to adversarial behavior, where one's own interests are put first); although strict expectations of instrumental exchange (immediate self-interest) are no longer insisted on, there is still the probability of benefit from the long-term relationship building and mutual protection that occurs with this strategy. We can expect also to be helped when in need, and this enlightened self-interest leads to increased social capital and a simple form of civil society. The expected benefit may not be just from the person being cared for but from anyone in the community, especially those aware of our own adherence to community norms. Nonadherence can be effectively regulated in political cultures organized around this perspective through shaming, or even banishment—an extreme sanction from this perspective, where personal relationships are primary to identity.

However, while these norms may be present to some degree within one or both communities in conflict with each other, the existence of violent conflict is clear evidence that they are not operating effectively at least across group lines. This strategy is thus the usual or primary focus of second track diplomacy, using Strategy-3 appropriate or "alternative" dispute-resolution mechanisms (i.e., alternative to submissive or adversarial options, whether power- or rights-based). Integrative problem-solving techniques, as discussed elsewhere in this volume, are used to facilitate a strategic shift by the parties, with the aim of developing sufficient understanding, respect, sense of responsibility and trust (social capital) to allow the parties to become aware of, and to work together to find ways of satisfying, the needs and primary interests of both sides. This may be accomplished with or without the support of third-party neutrals, and may involve a cooperative search for additional resources ("expanding the pie"); ways of compensating for or cutting the costs of concessions; trading off different interests, allowing each party to achieve its higher priorities while conceding on lower priorities ("logrolling"—see Brams and Taylor, 1996); or ways of dovetailing or "bridging" the parties' underlying interests so that both may be substantially if not fully satisfied.

For example, the United States-brokered Camp David accords between Israel and Egypt in the 1970s were able to resolve the dispute over the Israeli-occupied Sinai territory by finding a formula that addressed the primary Egyptian concern for sovereignty as well as the primary Israeli need for security, by returning the land to Egypt under conditions that prevented future surprise attacks or Egyptian military presence. The respect and trust generated by the normative application of integrative negotiation processes, as well as the discovery of specific positive-sum outcomes through such processes, together provide a basis for sustainable development and a more durable peace than is achievable with the strategies discussed earlier.

While findings vary according to specific context, research indicates that in general people both prefer conflicts to be settled through an integrative process respecting the concerns of both parties, and that such a process leads to higher joint outcomes than do adversarial processes, with yielding strategies producing lower joint benefit than either of the other two (see Pruitt and Carnevale, 1993).

It is possible through iteration of personal connections of mutual trust and commitment to build a lattice of social relations that can undergird sustainable development and peace even in large societies. A political culture based on Strategy 3 may thus work well either in small, stable communities interacting with outsiders only at the fringe, or where there are stable links among local communities via trust relationships among leaders or elites. However, it will not work so well with large communities in flux, as in the postagrarian world, where most people live in cities, where they are strangers to most of those around them. Trusting and supporting only those we know may not get us far, especially in the press of the anonymous megacities to which displaced villagers and former farm-workers gravitate in search of new jobs.

The problem is that interactions with those outside one's clan, contact group or network, with whom such personal trust has not been established, may by default still be conducted on the basis of instrumental exchange, subject to the same vicious cycles of threat and revenge discussed above. Communities of trust based on extended families, clans or shared interests (e.g., those of local landowners, nomadic tribes, guilds) will still be prone to zero-sum conflict with rival groups that may lead to protracted violence or structural injustices through domination by the more powerful groups. Examples abound, in predatory or exploitative elites recently in power in countries such as Guatemala, Pakistan, Burundi, the Philippines or Indonesia. Power and ultimate responsibility for managing conflict are left to individuals, and maintained on the basis of personal loyalties (cronyism and nepotism), not subject to any overarching respect for law or broadly shared values.

If integrative problem-solving techniques are to be effective in resolving violent conflicts between large and complex communities, particularly those with contrasting cultures, it is necessary to look beyond the effort to establish understanding, commitment and trust only on the level of personal relations and to focus also on the value systems that define and divide the larger communities in conflict. Newly won personal understanding and trust can too easily evaporate in the face of negative stereotypes and mutual distrust more deeply woven into the value system of the larger societies in conflict, if the dynamics of these larger systems are not understood and addressed.

Strategies 4-5 (Rights-Based)

4: Deference to a Common System of Rules or Values

Kohlberg's (1981) research indicates that in most people across a wide range of different cultures, there is a cognitive developmental shift in adulthood where the primary reference point moves from the operational thinking process to the evolving system of principles, rules, assumptions or values which he/she has gradually taken on, constructed or come to understand (consciously or otherwise) as guiding that thinking process.[11] While in large part shaped by our cultural context and experiences, our value system comes to be experienced primarily as an internal point of reference. Principled or moral conduct favoring the social good is effectively self-monitored at this level as a matter of duty or conscience, with relatively little need for threats and bribes (Perspective 2) or shaming and personal loyalty (Perspective 3).

When integrative conflict managers fail to find a win-win solution to their conflicts, it is useful to identify commonly held principles or values that can provide the basis for a solution that, while maybe zero sum, can be respected by both parties as fair and thus preserve or strengthen the relationship. For example, if there is only a finite amount of land to be divided between two communities and no acceptable trade-offs for the land can be found, the dividing line will be respected more if it is agreed on the basis of principles respected by both sides rather than imposed based on the greater strength or determination of one side. It may still be necessary for one or both parties to yield some land, but the outcome will be more stable if the yielding is not to the greater power or will of the other side (Strategies 1 or 2) but rather to a mutually respected law, principle or value seen as promoting the common good. Examples of such principles might be equality, first occupancy, proportionality to resources invested, or the need to protect the basic needs and long-term economic viability of both parties.

More efficient for many purposes than a strategy which requires integrative, issue-by-issue negotiation among interdependent thinkers, and/or the establishment of trust-based relationships directly or indirectly with all members of a large community is the strategy of constructing or adapting, reaffirming or refining an agreed set of rules, principles or values which all parties agree to refer to as the basis for managing their conflicts.

This strategy allows another big expansion in social capital, because trust can be based primarily on adherence to *(dependence on)* value systems that can be developed, shared and stabilized through very large, diverse and mobile communities or nations (common *cultures*) whose members are for the most part unacquainted with each other. The value system may evolve as a set of traditional, cultural norms honored or revered by community members, or it may be promoted more quickly by a forward-thinking elite and formalized in part into a set of written rules (community or national laws) that members are willing largely to accept as legitimate and worthy of respect.

There is no loss of interdependence—rather, dependence on a shared value system or political culture allows expansion of the range of interdependent relationships to much larger, more fluid and anonymous communities. It thus becomes possible and advantageous to build nations based on shared national values and interests that, because of the expansion in social capital, have greater potential for sustainable development and satisfaction of members' needs and interests (Hobbes's *Leviathan*). Given this expansion of social capital, an employer, for example, can now hire the person from the larger community who is most qualified for a job rather than choose only from an extended family, clan or other contact community that he/she personally trusts. A government can establish regulations or laws that are in harmony with the shared value system and (in contrast with regimes organized around normative Strategy 3) can reasonably trust its public servants to apply them dutifully for the common good of a large community, without taking advantage of their positions to enrich themselves and their families and personal friends (Max Weber's bureaucratic ideal), allowing substantial control over the corruption and bribery that may flow unchecked in the absence of strategy norms.

In the wake of transition from an agrarian to a modern industrial or postindustrial society, where large population transfers become routine, and cities and broad, impersonal communication networks predominate over traditional village communities, such a shift in political culture becomes essential for long-term stability. Application of shared norms will reduce the likelihood of violent conflict, and where conflict does break out, it may be dealt with institutionally, according to law or custom. An important part of conflict management, particularly where secession has become an issue, may be to identify applicable laws or standards, and/or to agree on what adjustments to these rules may be needed for both parties to reaffirm their identities as part of the larger nation (e.g., Montenegro in Yugoslavia, or Aceh in Indonesia).

Leadership at this level is legitimized less on the basis of personal loyalties than on that of the ability to model, apply and conform to the sociomoral order, and uphold and apply the law or doctrine in order to satisfy needs effectively and manage conflict. However, leadership will still typically be vested in and by members of an elite or higher caste, who may be regarded as uniquely qualified to understand and apply the moral order as a principled autocracy (e.g., religious hierarchies, hereditary nobility or ruling classes, traditional chiefs or sheiks, communist *nomenklatura*). Leaders who fail to come up to standard can be held somewhat accountable to the community and/or remaining elite, and even be replaced, as having lost, in the Chinese idiom, the "mandate of heaven."

The large, bureaucratic institutions that become possible at this level tend to be highly centralized, top-down affairs (e.g., communist command economies, inquisitorial courts, theocracies), that may become isolated from new or unconventional ideas from either inside or outside the broader community. The expectation is that newcomers will be assimilated or will adapt or melt into the larger social order rather than maintain distinct (sub-) cultures. Nevertheless, this strategy of national consensus on values and rules of behavior (such as the "Asian values" promoted by Singapore's Lee Kuan Yew) represents a significant advance beyond the limitations of personal rule, essential to the establishment of a modern state, which is often not appreciated by Westerners focused exclusively on rapid democratic reform. Because it is still in a sense autocratic, this form of governance is too often confused with power-based personal rule; rather, it should be valued as a necessary prerequisite for, or element of, smooth and sustainable democratic and market transitions. Preliminary analysis of democratic transitions conducted at CIDCM suggests that countries with these predemocratic, Strategy-4 norms of governance already in place tend to be those able to introduce Strategy-5 democratic institutions without substantial violence or reversals (e.g., South Korea, Taiwan, Poland; see also Dalpino, 2000).

A major limitation of this fourth strategy is that those who do not adhere to the shared value system or laws may be mistrusted and marginalized as deviants, madmen, criminals, apostates, primitives or enemies of the state, who may be denied access, respect, or the opportunity to satisfy their needs or exercise their basic human rights. Because those subscribing primarily to Strategy 4 are closely identified with (dependent on) the value system, it is not easy for them to step back and compare it to alternative cultural worldviews which may appear to conflict with it, or to uphold the value of both their own and alternative systems. The point of law and normative behavior is to protect the moral order. Value systems can thus become rigid ideologies or dogmas, resistant to new ideas that may facilitate adaptive change and development, and they may be used to justify violence (war, colonization) directed at less virtuous outsiders. Outsiders should be assimilated into the culture or excluded from it—there is little patience for cultural, political or economic pluralism. International affairs still tend to be conducted according to the Strategy-2 *realpolitik* principles, relying on the judicious exercise of power to protect and advance national interests and values.

Leaders in Strategy-4 cultures no longer rule arbitrarily on the basis of personal power and networks of patronage or personal loyalty, but they still in a sense protect and embody the law rather than being fully subject to it, and hence still tend to be replaced only on their death (e.g., postrevolutionary presidents in Iran), and then only by other members of the elite. It is more difficult to achieve a consensus that a living leader has lost his legitimacy, and effecting his replacement can create dangerous instability. In other words, to some extent, the mystique of power characteristic of Strategy 1 can still operate in favor of those who present themselves as the guardians of national values.

However, the more basic problem with national ideologies is that any individual, particularly in mobile, urban, information-age communities, will tend to have several identity groups, with distinct shared values. We may see ourselves as part of an ethnic or linguistic minority group, a religion, a gender group, a profession, etc., as well as a nation, with one or more of these identities becoming salient according to context or need. Particularly when the integrity of a nation, or even the well-being of some of its people, is threatened, affected citizens may well look for reaffirmation of shared values by scapegoating members of such secondary identity groups or subcultures as being alien, outside the common culture, even when there has been no breach of national laws (e.g., Baha'i's in Iran). Where a nation has become polarized and the boundaries among subnational groups have become rigid, it may become very difficult to reestablish trust and common ground within the confines of this strategy.

5: Principled Competition, Rule of Law, Democracy

The ability to step back from the value system that has been adopted as one's own, to recognize that, while it has validity at least for one's own community, it is only one of many possible systems worthy of respect, is characteristic of postformal systems thinking or dialectical operations. The dialectic, in this case, is among differing worldviews, cultural perspectives, value systems or ideological systems. While no longer identified with any single value system (independent from it), this perspective still upholds the values and laws of the home community as having validity, based on the recognition that they represent a *duty or social contract with utilitarian value* for the members—a rational and principled (if not necessarily conscious) calculation or intuition, based on the greatest good for the greatest number.

Laws, norms and values are now seen as relative to culture and social context. They are therefore not adequate as a basis for relations between distinct cultures or value systems, or for a cross-cultural consensus on what types of social change should be preferred. In order to go beyond the postmodernist trap of nihilistic relativism, the logic of Perspective 5 (and of postmodernism) leads us to look for a principled basis for such relations. From this has developed the concept of universal human rights (principles to guide human interaction which elicit respect across cultures) and other rules or laws consistent with these universal rights for which cross-cultural consensus has or can be achieved. On the basis of such mutual respect among those representing different value systems, ideologies, nations or cultures, a dialectic, debate or principled interaction among groups with competing perspectives becomes possible, without violence or threat to the core identity, security or developmental needs of any party.

This ongoing dialectic of principled interaction provides a dynamic through which competing perspectives can be evaluated and adapted by the parties—similar to Popper's view of the function of scientific debate—allowing more dynamic evolution of norms, laws and institutions within the context of each culture or community, as well as in the larger international community.

In the political sphere, this perspective or strategy constitutes the core of the liberal democratic process, a civic culture (Almond and Verba, 1963; Apter, 1987) allowing broad-based participation in governance and open debate among competing viewpoints, protected by laws or norms of freedom of speech and belief. It requires accountability according to law of rulers to the general population affected by their decisions (rule of law), and an orderly, open and broadly inclusive process of choosing successive leaders and decision makers, thereby ensuring continuing legitimacy of government. The strategy is a rational one, likely to be adopted as elites come to realize over time that the cost of suppressing political opponents with competing viewpoints exceeds the cost of tolerating and engaging them in principled or regulated competition (Lijphart, 1977; Diamond, 1994; Powelson, 2001).

The core of a democracy is the open, principled and nonviolent processes through which leaders are elected, rights and laws for managing conflict openly discussed and agreed, and appropriate institutions developed to administer them—not the specific institutions themselves. The laws will require constant interpretation, revision and adaptation as new situations develop, and so it is the process through which this is accomplished, more than the specific (and never final) laws that may come out of that process, that sustain the democratic consensus. Institutions play a critical role insofar as they embody or express the norms upholding the democratic process.

There is a wide range of institutions that may qualify as democratic, but their effectiveness depends on their appropriateness in the context of the host culture and social conditions, and the legitimacy of the process through which they were established. A strong president elected through multiparty, winner-take-all elections may work well enough for France, for example, but may spell disaster for divided societies such as Angola, where more inclusive, power-sharing institutions are needed before warring factions will be willing to buy in. Nor do "elections" have the same meaning in traditional societies with low literacy levels and no expectation of policy debates or accountability. Harris and Reilly (1998) not only review several options for postconflict democratic institutions that might be adopted, but also emphasize that a pre-requisite for any of these to succeed is that it be agreed on as a national consensus through an inclusive, culturally appropriate, interest-based process—which requires both Strategies 3 and 4.

The same strategy, in the sphere of economics, may be seen as Adam Smith's "invisible hand," whereby broad access to principled, competitive participation in a free market economy ensures fuller mobilization of available human and social capital, and more efficient utilization of diverse comparative advantages, to sustain economic growth in a way that is beyond the grasp of a centralized command economy lacking rule of law. Rule of law also differentiates this type of free and fair market from the bandit capitalism of Strategy 2, or the crony capitalism of Strategy 3. Too often the concept of a free market does not distinguish among these different forms, leaving us puzzled by the fragility of free market economics in places like Russia and Indonesia, where Strategy-4 or -5 norms and institutions are still weak.

Rule of law means that contracts or agreements are no longer dependent on the goodwill of those in authority (revocable any time at their discretion) but, if made according to law, can be relied on and, in case of dispute, interpreted and enforced through appeal to impartial arbitrators or courts respecting the rights of the parties. A continuing process of developing and adapting the body of agreed rules or laws to address new issues in ways consistent with general norms is also a necessary element for the long-term success of this strategy.

Because the same general logic or strategy of principled competition, supported by rule of law, underlies both democratic politics and principled free market economics, it is not surprising that the existence of a democratic culture is highly correlated with sustained economic development and growth (Lipset, 1981; Inglehart, 1990). Success with a new strategy in one area—say, principled free trade—is likely to inspire application elsewhere, such as democratic reform, as many proponents of China's entry into the World Trade Organization argue.

Conflicts between different peoples or identity groups are less likely if members are able to recognize their common membership in a larger or cross-cutting group, representing values that can be appealed to by both parties as a basis for resolving disputes (e.g., Ireland and Britain are part of a larger European or Western identity; Israelis and Palestinians part of a larger Abrahamic tradition; Abkhaz and Georgians part of the Caucasian peoples). Thus even within this broad value-system level of identity, shifts to include larger or overlapping reference groups or identities may enhance the capacity for constructive conflict management. The capacity for such shifts is much greater within the dynamics of this fifth perspective, and management of intergroup conflicts within Perspective-4 cultures will be most effective if it explores and models an appropriate Strategy-5 process, locating principles for dispute resolution that transcend differences in culture and that can be equally respected by both parties.

Principles that transcend cultural contrasts, such as nonviolence and respect for human rights, provide a basis for strategic nonviolent action, typically (and most effectively) aimed at political elites in Strategy-4-dominated cultures. Activists are more likely to be successful when they can attract broad public support based on contrasting their own principled activity with power-based suppression of cultures or interest groups that are perceived by authorities as illegitimate because they do not assimilate to the Perspective-4 values consensus. Such support is more likely in a society which already embraces rights-based norms and may help expand these to Perspective-5 norms. Hence the struggle for Tibetan autonomy in China has so far not had the impact of the campaigns to oust Milosevic in Yugoslavia or Pinochet in Chile, or Gandhi's struggle for an India independent of Britain (see Gurr and Davies, this volume).

The great achievement of this perspective (liberal democratic culture) is that for the first time, the needs and rights of all people can be respected independently of their personal and cultural loyalties. The law is less concerned with moral or victimless crimes; even those accused of acting violently against others' needs or rights can debate the charges and evidence, and expect fair treatment through legal institutions or processes aiming to balance the needs, rights and interests of all involved. The potential for violence erupting from conflicts within or among communities at this level is thus enormously reduced. Indeed, nonviolent conflict management is sometimes taken to be the defining characteristic of a democratic culture (see Maoz and Russett, 1993), reflecting the finding that democracies tend to fight fewer wars both within and among themselves, and to settle more wars through negotiated accommodation (see Gurr and Davies, this volume)—the concept of democratic peace. On this basis it is possible to contemplate the possibility of moving beyond the *realpolitik* assumption of international anarchy and of disrupting historical cycles of international and intercommunal wars based on an evolving international consensus organized around democratic and free market norms and institutions (see Fukuyama, 1992; Gurr and Davies, this volume).

Nevertheless, there are critical limitations to this strategy for conflict management. First, it is not likely to be successful in areas where the parties have had little or no prior experience with the application of at least Strategy 4, in relation to similar issues. To a society based primarily on Strategy 3 norms of personal responsibility, the competitive norms of Strategy 5 can be too easily confused with the unprincipled, instrumental competition of Strategy 2. Working in such societies, we receive several offers to help resolve the apparently out-of-control conflicts raging in Washington, D.C., or in courts all over the United States and other democratic countries—and many expressions of puzzlement or distaste. Strategy 4 (developing a national consensus on the rules of the game), on the other hand, is much more accessible in such communities and will usually provide a more productive focus for conflict management efforts than any exclusive preoccupation with Strategy 5. We will return to this point later, in considering the general issues surrounding shifts between normative strategies.

A second limitation is that, just as those without the resources to compete under norms based on instrumental exchange became victimized or oppressed, so also, even with norms of principled competition, individuals and communities without the resources (relevant education, language skills, wealth, technology, etc.) to compete or participate effectively are greatly at risk of becoming further marginalized and dependent on others. The Marxist critique of capitalist-dominated societies, elaborated in dependency theories and, to a lesser extent, in world-system theories, may still have validity in this sense— although not, of course, the attempt to avoid the evils of such free market capitalism through breaking down institutions upholding principled competition in favor of the coercive and regressive imposition of Perspective-4 command economies and ideologically driven authoritarian states. It is possible with Strategy 5 to develop consensus on norms and laws that moderate the competitive disadvantages of the poor and constrain the narrowly self-serving exercise of economic and political power to avoid the emergence of monopolies and narrow concentrations of power in elites. However, there will always be pressures to return to an elitism more common with Strategy 4, and these may not be fully contained without the emergence of Strategy-6 or Strategy-7-based counterpressures.

Third, even rule-of-law-based economic competition, particularly in the industrial sphere, can still have a devastating impact on the environment and ecology (the tragedy of the local or global commons), in some cases posing as severe a threat as that of Strategy-2 bandit capitalism. While the rights and needs of all may be recognized in principle, and competitive actions are thus constrained within the norms of civic culture, there may be insufficient understanding to motivate active concern and responsibility for common pooled resources and for often anonymous individuals or communities who, while not being directly victimized, are nevertheless negatively impacted or pushed aside in the competitive process (Gilligan, 1982; Chilton, 1988: 54).

Strategies 6 and 7 (Interest-Based)

6: Pluralism, Humanitarianism, Cultural Interdependence
Just as from Perspective 3, it becomes possible to understand or empathize with another's thinking or put oneself in his/her shoes while simultaneously honoring one's own competing viewpoint, so from Perspective 6 the same thing is possible in terms of competing value-systems, worldviews, cultures or communities of interest.[12] Rather than integratively coordinating just two dimensions of interest at a time (mine and yours: Perspective 3), now the coordination of multiple dimensions of interest, within and across cultures, is seen as achievable and for the common good. Interdependence is recognized as ultimately universal, so that mutual care and responsibility for all others' needs is assumed, in balance with one's own—a higher order application of the golden rule (Kohlberg, 1981: 203-204).

The trend away from top-down imposition of rules by overarching authorities toward more broadly participatory and distributive decision making with each more complex strategy can be continued further with Strategy 6. Strategy-6 cultures and institutions are likely to develop through local or highly issue-specific initiatives as part of the maturing of democratic cultures. While habitual Perspective-6 thinkers may be a small minority in any culture, they may have an influence disproportionate to their numbers by taking on leadership and responsibility for the tough issues and problems that others have avoided as intractable, finding ways to mobilize support among the much larger constituency who can recognize and apply Strategy 6 when occasion demands.

To make the claim (as Chilton, 1988, does), that no states have as yet developed political cultures based primarily on norms from this perspective, is missing the point. Forms of democracy that emphasize inclusive participation by minorities rather than simple majority rule (e.g., through consociation as in Switzerland, regional autonomy as in South Africa, or more modestly through preferential voting as in Estonia, proportional representation of ethnic groups as in Mauritius, or language pluralism as in Lithuania), are drawing on Strategy-6 norms of pluralism and mutual accommodation and are likely to allow smoother democratic transitions for ethnically or culturally diverse societies (see Harris and Reilly, 1998). Dominance of Strategy 6 is not the point but rather the utilization of Strategy 6 where it is needed in conjunction with Strategy 5, etc., to better manage the concerns and disputes of minorities in diverse societies, protecting the effectiveness of their political and economic participation and guarding against the risk of an exploitative majority.

The critical influence of pluralist or internationalist perspectives is apparent in debates, policy shifts and initiatives over a variety of complex national and global issues, ranging from recognition of the collective rights of marginalized or victimized cultural minorities to restorative justice for those displaced or otherwise impacted by war, to protection of the global environment, to initiatives providing empowerment and support for culturally appropriate economic development, to enhancing the capacity for the poor to compete more effectively and meet their aspirations. The thousands of private volunteer organizations (PVOs) and other NGOs and government or IGO agencies providing relief services for war victims, refugees, homeless or displaced communities that local governments and businesses have not managed to care for are a sign of strengthening Strategy-6 norms that are not fundamentally constrained by state or cultural boundaries.

Such organizations have been able to provide mediation services across cultural divides (see Moore and Woodrow, this volume), access to information and media, human rights monitoring, and preventive or unofficial multi-track diplomacy to intervene in intrastate ethnic conflicts where states and intergovernmental organizations are able to do little (see Lund, 1996; McDonald, this volume). Gurr and Davies (this volume) point to the impact of emerging global norms on protecting minorities and of the engagement of NGOs and international agencies in sharply reducing the number of ethnic wars now being fought. These organizations also contribute to an increasing extent in recovery and peacebuilding initiatives, providing models for communities struggling to establish norms and institutions that will sustain development and peace in the longer term.

A basic application of Strategy-6 norms is in developing intergroup and cross-cultural dialogue that allows strengthening of more inclusive identities at the national and regional levels to complement those that have been primary in past conflicts. This is essential for strengthening national identity particularly in multicommunal states, and also for strengthening international relations at the regional and global levels, not only among states but also among nonstate communities and organizations. As states recognize their interdependence and realize the opportunities for mutual gain through more collaborative policies, such rights-based institutions as the World Trade Organization, International Atomic Energy Agency, European Union or Organization for African Unity (now African Union) can help to assure minority communities of their place in a diverse society and improve chances for mutual accommodation at the intercommunal level. Thus, for example, Ireland's and Britain's membership in the European Union has reduced the distance between the parties to the conflict in Northern Ireland, through reducing the gap in economic opportunities, granting freedom of movement and migration between states, and providing clearer formulation, protection of individual and minority group rights, etc. In contrast, as the Soviet and Yugoslav states broke up, minorities within newly independent states felt more threatened and inclined, in the absence of serious Strategy-6 dialogue, to fight for their autonomy.

Commercial organizations also may take the initiative in dealing with community divisions and social problems in their areas of operation—for example, through hiring and investment practices that benefit local communities rather than only centralized, often corrupt state administrations. They may empower local entrepreneurs through microlending programs, build schools or infrastructure, or clean up the environment, providing models for efficient, integrative and just administration for public as well as private sectors. Too often, however, multinational corporations deal only or primarily with largely autocratic state authorities, strengthening existing power-based norms rather than contributing to the evolution of more inclusive political and economic cultures.

Similarly, the investment and lending programs of major international institutions, particularly of the IMF, are frequently accompanied with detailed policy prescriptions derived with too little consultation with, or involvement by, the target communities (even local elites, let alone the nonelite communities most impacted). This implies Perspective-4, top-down strategies rather than the more inclusive, distributed decision-making characteristic of level-six perspectives—with all the risks and limitations inherent in that fourth perspective. While conditionality in lending will usually be necessary to ensure constructive use of funds, appropriate conditions can be identified only by or in close collaboration with those who deeply understand the often unique needs, risks and norms of affected communities.

Again (as with Strategy 3), the rationality of this strategy should be emphasized: it is not a matter of idealism but of enlightened self-interest to understand the ways in which the quality of life in each community or culture deeply impacts that in others, particularly in an era of global trade and economics, communication and media, and travel. The despoiling of Ogoni and Ijaw homelands in the oil fields of Nigeria, for example, undercut the economic and political viability not only of local communities but also of the larger Nigerian and African region, as well as the longer-term investments of the international oil companies themselves.

The emergence of internationalist perspectives and multilateralism in political and economic theory and practice is evidence of the growing influence of Perspective 6 (see Klare and Chandrani, 1998). There is still some distance to go, however, in developing an international system characterized more by integrative consultation, respect for group rights and mutual support among localized centers of decision making than by the systemic dominance of great powers and multinational corporations.

A limitation of this perspective is that the focus tends to be on dealing reactively with the problems of the victimized, marginalized or oppressed, or with ongoing or potential violent conflicts among distinct social groups. Too exclusive a preoccupation with such problems and with the reactive provision of humanitarian assistance may distract our attention and energy from the many possibilities for more proactively developing human and social capital and quality of life, thus preventing, or reducing the likelihood of, violence, injustice, economic collapse or environmental degradation even before it occurs. Preventive strategies are more cost effective, yielding much greater return than do the tens of billions of dollars per year now being spent in humanitarian relief and military peacekeeping operations (Lund, 1996).

7: Natural Law Orientation, Inclusiveness

A yet more fundamental level of individual identity than value systems is awareness itself, variously described as consciousness, being, life or spirit, as distinct from the thoughts, feelings or value systems which are the content of awareness and generated from it (Alexander, Davies et al., 1990). When awareness is experienced as distinct from any content ("postconceptual" experience), rather than differentiating oneself from anyone else, it connects one intimately with all human beings, since they share the same reality as the core of their humanity. From this perspective, we are no longer defined merely in exclusive, localized or conceptual ("us/them") terms or bound by limited self-interpretation. This universal perspective is not only reflected in, but also widely regarded as central to, all the great cultural and spiritual traditions (in the Western tradition, the writings of Plato, Descartes, Plotinus, Kant, Hegel, Jung, A. Maslow and K. Wilber are influential examples).[13]

Just as value systems provide a structured context supporting and guiding our operational thought processes (which in turn provide a context guiding our behavior), so awareness itself may be understood as providing a structured context for the evolution and adaptation of our value systems or worldviews. Although awareness, as distinct from its content, may not be experienced as a structure, yet its structure is implicit, just as abstract quantum fields, which are said to underlie all matter and energy in the universe, are held (even in their unexpressed ground state) to have structure which can be identified indirectly through the regularity and predictability of their expressions in the phenomenal world. These regularities are the natural laws, which we seek to identify in every field of science (including social and cognitive sciences) as well as through art or religion, and which constitute the primary context of our lives. The same relationship appears to hold true between awareness and the regularities identifiable in the dynamics of human motivation, cognition and experience, as studied in the psychological sciences.

From Perspective 7, which complements and recontextualizes the other six perspectives, rather than replacing them, the emphasis is more on appreciating or understanding what is, less on evaluating as authoritative or weak, friend or enemy, good or bad, right or wrong. Because we do not see ourselves as fundamentally separate from anyone else, such comparisons are no more helpful than labeling parts of our own body as good or bad, etc. From this inclusive point of view, there are no major external threats to human needs for security, identity, effective participation, etc. and there is no longer an option for avoiding responsibility for what we do not like or understand in ourselves by projecting it on to others (as bad, wrong, enemy, etc.).

Rather than seeing ourselves as the product of circumstances in large part beyond our control, we take full responsibility for where we find ourselves, including both strengths and weaknesses, since from this perspective we are continually generating ourselves and our relationship with others, individually and collectively. In this we are dependent only on the natural laws from which life is structured (or from a religious viewpoint, the divine laws that express the will of God), and which give us ample capacity to manage and develop resources to meet needs and aspirations. The same perspectives of dependence, independence and interdependence appear to be repeated in relation to development of identity at this level as awareness or being,[14] but differentiating among these three perspectives in terms of normative political culture will add little to our discussion at this point.

Dependence here on natural law may be contrasted with obedience to specific *conceptions* of natural (or divine) law formulated or expressed by others—inevitably flavored by language and cultural context—which would constitute the more doctrinally oriented dependence of Perspective 4.

Dependence only on natural law, as that structure which dynamically connects us with all of life, reflects a higher degree of both independence and interdependence than Perspective 6 (where identity is still structured primarily in terms of culturally-based value systems), allowing a still more broadly participatory process in political and social life within and between cultures, and a more stable and dynamic peace.

As we have seen with the earlier strategies, the risk of violence is primarily with those outside our identity group: we are not prone to harm ourselves or (other things being equal) those we currently accept as like ourselves, if we can help it. To the extent that our primary identity is inclusive of all human life (or "world society"—Kelman, this volume), there is no person or community left outside our identity group, so the risk of violence, injustice or blocked development is even less than with Strategy 6. All cultures and value systems are respected as derived from natural law, through the lens of personal and collective experience in diverse historical and environmental contexts, and therefore, at root, not in conflict with us or each other. Each community and all individuals are seen as responsible for creating their own lives and deserving of our support if we can give it. Violence and injustice come not from human nature as such, or from any supposed shortage of resources, but from lack of knowledge of how to satisfy needs, how to make best use of material, human and social resources, and thus how to manage conflicts in more efficient ways that are not ultimately self-defeating. Ultimately, there are no basic conflicts of interest, because all are natural expressions of ourselves, of the desire to satisfy universally shared human needs. This implies that social capital is no longer limited to those who share the same culture or perspective—all are potential partners based on shared needs and shared dynamics of human intelligence.

In comparison to the earlier perspectives, attitudes and behaviors are guided not so much by history and polarities of strong/weak, good/bad, mine/yours; rather, we are free to consider what is, and what is possible and desirable. The focus is proactive in envisioning and generating new possibilities that satisfy and harmonize with all that we are. This strategy frees us both from the inertia of fear and powerlessness (feeling shaped by history and circumstances), and from the consuming effort of resisting, changing or denying whatever we think is bad or wrong (usually projected as outside ourselves), to invest our energy in discovering opportunities for generating what we do want—individual and collective interests. This will have the tendency to prevent or minimize risk of violence without focusing on problems or violence as such, because no one's interests are excluded or seen as fundamentally competing with our own. In this sense we agree with Cahill's (1996) characterization of a preventive approach to conflict management as one of the supreme creations of the human spirit, a far more effective guarantor of the quality of human life than even the humanitarianism of Strategy 6.

This perspective, while not sustainable for most people most of the time, provides an essential part of our strategic repertoire for management of complex conflicts. In the transitional *reflective phase* of conflict transformation and integrative problem-solving processes (see Kaufman, this volume), for example, a primary function is to hear the concerns motivating each of the parties without judging them, to aid in identifying the needs, fears and values driving the communities in the conflict, and to help the parties recognize that they are not just victims or enemies but free to accept responsibility for where they are and to use their time and resources for creating a more desirable and sustainable future. Recognition that, at root, the human needs that motivate the parties are universally shared highlights the common humanity of the parties and provides the ground for genuine reconciliation.

Another technique for discovering common ground is to engage representatives from each of the parties in envisioning a desired possible future for the region in conflict, again while suspending critical evaluation, in order to identify shared goals for which they could work together (see Kaufman, this volume). While these techniques are available for responding to conflicts from earlier interest-based perspectives, Strategy 7 supports them by providing a common identity or reference point even across wide cultural divides, facilitating a stepping back from, or transcendence of, differences. It also implies the ongoing and proactive application of such techniques as a normal part of life, preventing the emergence of future violence.

Much of the recent work of John Marks and Search for Common Ground (SFCG) exemplifies this perspective. Emphasis is placed on bringing groups in conflict together by creating music, radio and television shows, classrooms, after-school centers, sports events, newspapers, magazines etc., created by popular and skilled professionals from the different groups working in partnership. People of all ages are attracted by the quality of the work which expresses the human spirit and transcends cultural differences, while incidentally being exposed to models of integrative behavior, learning to appreciate the contribution of the other groups and unique cultures to the common good (even, in some cases, learning their language), and absorbing the message that everyone gains through such cooperation and mutual respect. As a result, for example, twice as many people as before express willingness to invite members of other groups into their homes (SFCG, personal communication).

Natural law also provides a basis for developing, reforming and adapting national and international laws in the face of new challenges. *Natural justice* has become an essential, if sometimes abused, reference point in many legal systems for interpreting laws, or filling in the gaps between statutory laws, in ways that promote the common good. It also provides a supportive framework for efforts to define and achieve consensus on broadly or universally applicable human rights, more recently including group rights. Once formulated, application of such explicit laws or rights is a Strategy 4, 5, or 6 process. With

Strategy 6, justice takes the form of *restorative justice:* the point is not (as with earlier strategies) punishment or retribution, deterrence or protection of people, the moral order or human rights but restoring or enhancing the capacity of victims to lead productive and responsible lives. In Strategy 7, restorative justice expands to include not only victims but everyone else, including perpetrators—whose violence may be seen as driven by lack of understanding of better options for satisfying interests.

The influence of actions from this inclusive perspective will generally be to strengthen coherent and interdependent relations in any community. Strategy 7 is thus an important asset for leadership. Many of the most courageous and insightful breakthroughs for a just and dynamic peace have been by leaders (such as Gandhi, King, Sadat, Mandela) who have acknowledged being inspired to act from experiences of this transcendental perspective (sometimes emerging during long prison terms), allowing them to forgive and engage constructively with former enemies. They, in turn, inspire others at every level of society. However, Perspective 7 does not imply any particular desire for acquiring the positions of power that we usually associate with leadership: from this perspective, leadership may equally be expressed in a grassroots or egalitarian process.

For example, there is strong empirical evidence that as the proportion in any community regularly accessing this perspective through meditation increases beyond a critical threshold, political and criminal violence consistently decrease and other quality-of-life indices improve (see Orme-Johnson et al., 1988; Alexander et al., 1990; Hagelin et al., 1999). Such nonintrusive but powerful contributions to the collective good represent an expansion in social capital and a level of decentralization of power and capacity for sustainable peace beyond even that achievable with Strategy 6. Such meditative practices have their place in all the major cultural and spiritual traditions, and these findings are a reminder of their potentially critical role in peacebuilding both within and across cultures.

These practices can also help those involved in peacemaking or peacebuilding, often working with people under stress and caught in cycles of fear, blame and resistance, to regain and maintain their own balance, their capacity for empathy, understanding, and awareness of integrative possibilities in any situation. It is difficult to be effective in promoting integration and peace if we are not experiencing it within ourselves, or if we have not released any blaming or polarizing stances in our own conflicts.[15]

The proactive generativity and inclusiveness of Strategy 7 represents an opposite pole from the powerlessness and victimhood to which we are vulnerable if relying too much on Strategy 1, and from the alienation and disintegration that may follow overuse of Strategy 2. It frees us from moral arrogance, projection and divisiveness which may follow from focusing just on rights-based approaches, and even from the often burdensome responsibilities of

Strategies 3 and 6. Strategy 7 flows naturally from the experience of the self as all-inclusive, unbounded, one with the world or universe.

Any effort to impose it exclusive of other strategies would imply either misplaced idealism (as with some forms of libertarianism or nonviolent anarchism) or a power- or rights-based strategy in the guise of Strategy 7 (e.g., the divine right of kings; scripture as national law backed by state sanctions). Nevertheless, it gives us a larger perspective, from which it is possible to envision a better world and to promote progress toward a broader, more robust democracy and economy at home and internationally. It enables us to live more in a way that promotes a just and sustainable society excluding no one, preventing or minimizing violence and environmental degradation without being consumed by the scale and complexity of the problems and associated tensions, promoting an integrative balance complementing and reframing rather than resisting the other normative frameworks.

Dynamics of Development and Peacebuilding

In individuals, the dominant or preferred strategy tends to shift over time and with broadening experience in the direction of greater complexity of social reasoning, with simpler strategies retained as alternatives. Chilton (1988) argues that something analogous happens also in political cultures, with norms of social reasoning or conflict management tending to shift in the same way, providing the basis for political development.

Even on the individual level, however, a more complex perspective will not become dominant in application to all areas of social behavior at once. It will take time for insights achieved in one area of social activity to be applied to others—a phenomenon referred to as horizontal *décalage*. Thus, a preference for rule of law and fair competition in free market economics (Strategy 5), for example, may not immediately correspond to a similar preference in the political sphere. Social norms for groups will be even less sharply focused at any one perspective, with a much broader horizontal *décalage* across issues and areas of activity, as consensus shifts slowly and unevenly through public debate or discussion (Chilton, 1988 explores these dynamics in some detail).

Applying such a model of individual development of social reasoning directly to the development of political culture is problematic. Too easily it can lead to characterizations of cultures as monolithic, with some societies held as inferior, more primitive, or less worthy of respect than other more developed cultures, which may, in turn, assume a right to prescribe or impose their own norms on societies seen as less capable of governing themselves.

The reality is more complex: any large culture will have individuals functioning at all levels of development, with some normative support for application of each of the seven strategies of conflict management in different social contexts. Consensus is always far from complete. It not only happens that those preferring a simpler strategy have difficulty understanding and respecting the reasoning of those favoring more complex strategies, but the same can happen in reverse. Just as a society emphasizing norms of personal caring and responsibility (Strategy 3) over the unbridled competition of Strategy 2 may have difficulty appreciating the value of the often fiercely competitive norms of more individualistic democratic cultures (Strategy 5), so liberal democratic cultures may overlook the value of political systems built around personal loyalty and responsibility, and overestimate the potential for rapid democratic reform. In either case there is a failure of understanding and a loss of adaptability and capacity for conflict management.

A better standard for measuring development than identifying the dominant strategy for dealing with conflict might be the breadth of the repertoire of normative strategies available in public discourse, from which it is possible to identify that strategy most suited to a given context. Simpler is often better; any one of the seven primary strategies may be the best strategy under certain conditions, alone or in combination, and so their combined availability, rather than the dominance of any one, should be the better guide to political health.

Pressure for normative developmental change regarding any social issue comes when a conflict over that issue does not appear tractable in terms of current norms; new options are needed. Resistance to such change typically comes from those who are advantaged by currently conventional norms, who may attack and stigmatize more complex reformist ideas as representing an alien culture, to be rejected by all. Also, more complex forms of reasoning than one's own will generally not be recognized as such—particularly reasoning more than one step of complexity beyond the currently dominant perspective (Kohlberg, 1981). Rather, they are likely to be understood reductively in terms of the current perspective, or interpreted as lower-level or faulty reasoning. Thus, while it may be advantageous for those wishing to influence a community to be operating from a more complex perspective than the dominant norm for the group, it will be necessary for them to also be able to communicate with the group in terms at or close to the dominant norm.

The analytical framework illustrated in figure 6.2 helps to clarify the ways in which each normative strategy may be most easily misconstrued—usually the more complex being misperceived as the less complex, but sometimes the reverse (e.g., when power-based processes for affirming leadership are passed off as rights based through rigged elections to satisfy donors). Adjacent cells (whether vertically or horizontally) are more likely to be confused than diagonals or separated cells. Thus, power-based, rights-based or interest-based strategies may often be confused within each of these three broader categories (e.g., promotion of Strategy 5 democratic norms may be seen as Strategy 4 Western imperialism). Deference to shared principles (Strategy 4) may be confused with deference to people (Strategy 1); principled competition (five) with unprincipled (two); or deference to natural law (seven) with deference to written laws or to religious or cultural ideology (four). Being alert to the need to clarify these distinctions and to communicate them in terms accessible from currently dominant perspectives can avert much frustration for those seeking to support culturally appropriate efforts for reform and development.

Conflicts between cultures are more difficult to manage than those between groups within the same culture, in that there will be cultural differences in the ways that the same perspectives or strategies for conflict management are realized or normatively expressed in the two cultures. The tendency to interpret reductively ambiguous actions or too-complex communications by others in terms lower than (or at least not higher than) one's own normative level ensures plenty of room for misunderstandings to occur as a result of cultural differences, even where levels of complexity are equivalent. Another group's actions are thus easily perceived and demonized as irrational, or more primitive (and hence more dangerous) than one's own.

Those interested in providing support for conflict transformation, development or peacebuilding are likely to be wasting their time if they are espousing norms or institutions that do not make sense in terms of the current norms of the culture. A necessary first step in such cases will be to elicit from the target communities a detailed expression of their current perspectives, capacities and needs, and then to support them in identifying culturally and developmentally accessible options for resolving their own current conflicts or issues (Lederach, 1995). Imposing from outside, as a condition of desperately needed aid, Western-style institutions, such as multiparty elections, on a society without attention to the more immediate issue of shifting from predatory or exploitative to responsible personal leadership (from Strategies 1 or 2 to 3), or from personal leadership to more inclusive rule based on values or laws shared across clans, castes, tribes or subcultures (from 3 to 4), risks undermining the legitimacy and coherence of existing forces for reform and at best wastes resources that otherwise might promote genuine, endogenously driven development—as recently in Angola, Burundi and Cambodia.

It is much better in these cases to think of democracy in broader terms, rooted in participatory, interest-based processes and endogenous adaptation of cultural norms, rather than just Strategy-5 institutions. Imposition of democratic institutions is likely to be self-defeating if accomplished primarily through nondemocratic exercise of power, since it provides a model to reinforce autocratic, nonparticipatory norms. Appropriate and sustainable democratic institutions are more likely to emerge as an outcome of inclusive, interest-based processes, which also seek to define shared national values (Strategies 3 and 4 included as the basis for 5) and to include and empower marginalized groups, affirming their common humanity (Strategies 6 and 7).

The relative success of the transition from a white-dominated apartheid regime to a potentially sustainable (if still imperfect) democracy in South

Africa, for example, may be attributed to such a broad-based peacebuilding process that gave the needed legitimacy to the institutional outcomes. The absence of equivalent processes in Bosnia, Kosovo and Cambodia, for example, has led to weak institutions not yet capable of upholding democratic norms.

Conflict transformation work normally takes place where each party perceives the other as using at least some Perspective-2 adversarial tactics, obliging it to respond in kind rather than in terms of more civilized norms valued for relations within itself or with other valued groups. The primary focus of most conflict transformation efforts is thus to identify and facilitate the application of integrative or problem-solving strategies (Perspective 3). However, other options should be considered, preferably in combination with Strategy 3. If the political culture of an oppressed community is focused on Strategy-1 norms of obedience, it may be necessary first to identify and make explicit what forms of advocacy or argument exist within the culture and how they might be used as a basis for training in improved advocacy skills (e.g., persuasive argument, projecting firmness, dealing with threats, drawing local and international support) and for exploring how such limitations might be remedied to ensure against a tendency to yield to unsustainable demands.

Conflict analysis may also point to the need or potential for conflict transformation to facilitate a shift of emphasis not just from the second to third strategies but also to strategies which go beyond individual cooperation to promote (or even institutionalize) more broadly interdependent relations between their communities. Too often individuals return home from workshops in which integrative collaboration was achieved on the personal level only to find themselves unable to translate that in terms of the higher-order relations needed for sustainable peace between cultures (Strategies 5, 6 and 7), and to find their new Perspective-3 insights giving way in the face of pressure to conform with existing community attitudes (e.g., at Perspective 4).

Conversely, if facilitators emphasizing Strategy 6 are not careful to differentiate it from Strategy 3 and to avoid relying on strategies more complex than required, workshop participants from communities more used to Strategies 1 or 2 may have difficulty on reentry in explaining their new insights on interest-based conflict management. Or if the complementarity of the different strategies is not made clear, it may be difficult for participants to promote interest-based insights or initiatives while at the same time respecting existing power-based or rights-based norms. Without the continued support of workshop partners, new insights and commitments may soon fade if seen as contradicting longer-established norms.

If representatives from both communities can be helped to recognize the presence of more complex norms internal to each other's societies, a more complete and balanced approach to conflict transformation and peacebuilding becomes possible. This may involve, for example, promoting a Strategy-4 emphasis on identifying shared goals, values, principles or laws (reflecting a deeper cultural identity common to the parties); Strategy-5 formulation of laws and institutions promoting principled competition and respect for human rights; Strategy-6 policies to ensure that these institutions address security and access needs in poor or marginalized communities, and identity needs in distinct cultural communities; and/or Strategy-7 constructive projects toward common or superordinate goals perhaps unrelated to present disputes.

These latter strategies (4 through 7) take our attention from short-term conflict transformation efforts to longer-term peacebuilding, or promotion of sustainable development, in the absence of which frustration and violence will recur, even in "developed" (Perspective 5) countries. They are more likely to be beneficial when used in complementary ways and sequentially in a longer-term democracy-building strategy. This emphasis on complementarity also ensures that normative strategies currently in use are respected as part of the larger picture, and it keeps us in touch with the realities of power-based norms; all seven should be recognized as essential elements in a realistic, comprehensive, and internally driven approach to achieving a stable peace.

Concluding Remarks

We have argued that sensitivity to the political cultures of communities in conflict, as reflected in their normative perspectives on conflict management, can significantly enhance facilitation of conflict transformation processes, peacebuilding and development diplomacy. Efforts are likely to be more effective if they focus on promoting not only a shift in predominant norms from dependency or contention to include more integrative strategies of conflict management but also a shift toward increasing the salience of shared values and broader social identities. Broad-based peacebuilding processes which provide a model through a balanced inclusion of elements of all seven conflict management strategies are more likely to engage and earn the respect of all the relevant interest and identity groups. They are also more likely to generate sustainable outcomes, with culturally and situationally appropriate democratic institutions supported by shared national norms as well as norms of mutual respect and accommodation among groups, both internally and internationally.

We have proposed that political development or democratization may be understood in terms of movement toward a broader and more balanced array of norms for managing conflicts, such that violence and injustices can be progressively minimized, human and social capital enhanced, confidence in the future and opportunities for effective participation broadened, and quality of life improved. The conceptual framework offered includes and expands the narrow realism of more power-oriented theories and the constructivism of culturally oriented theories, while avoiding the traps of idealism out of touch with the dynamics of power and self-interest. It points to more appropriate methodologies for providing effective leadership and for aiding and stabilizing democratic transitions, avoiding the traps of imposing democratic institutions (such as majority voting and majority rule) without first strengthening norms of interest-based accommodation and a national consensus on shared values as needed for a rights-based political culture and identity to emerge. Further, it emphasizes the need for democracies not only to rely on principled competition but also to strengthen multi-track, interest-based processes that bring interest groups and cultures into integrative partnerships which can ensure those principles are constantly reevaluated, adapted to changing conditions and strengthened. Finally, it points to the richly diverse community that can emerge rooted in an inclusive human identity, free from the polarities and "us/them" projections that otherwise shut us off from most of the enormous human and social resources in the rest of the world, as well as within our own community.

The framework outlined here requires more systematic testing and refinement. Our preliminary research at CIDCM confirms our expectation that the presence of broader and more complex norms for conflict management are reliably associated with lower susceptibility to war and other forms of political violence (an expansion and refinement of the democratic peace hypothesis). More rigorous testing might be accomplished through systematic analysis of the policies and statements of leaders, journalists or other reflectors of community norms in periods of conflict or transition, to assess the correlation of different normative patterns with levels of violence and with the effectiveness of different types of intervention in each context.

Notes

1. Separate identities are most often established on the basis of distinct ethnic, linguistic, religious or other ascribed cultural differentials, mobilized in response to perceived comparative disadvantage, threat or distrust.

2. Even in predicting growth in a country's gross domestic product, economists no longer apply the classical formula by which growth was seen as a function only of physical capital and labor. These factors cannot account for the sustained growth occurring in advanced economies, and they account for less than half the variance observed in economic growth generally. The remaining variance (and sustainable growth in advanced economies) may be understood as a function of human and social capital (e.g., Romer, 1986).

3. Interdependence may also be contrasted with codependence; in the latter case, the parties have not effectively asserted their independence and thus tend to yield to each other without being firm in defending their own needs.

4. The simpler identities will be accessible and preferred at younger ages but remain along with more complex or abstract identities. Thus in childhood (to about age five or six), identity tends to be experienced in terms of physical appearance, action and speech (Piaget, 1971). In adolescence (about ages six to twenty-four years in the United States), identity is typically experienced more in terms of operational thinking and in terms of relations with others with whom thoughts can be shared (ibid.; Kohlberg, 1981). In adulthood, identity tends to be experienced more in terms of value systems,

which then may become accessible for comparison through habits of higher-order intellectual or feeling-intuitive functioning, called systems thinking, postformal operations or dialectical operations (e.g., Alexander, Druker and Langer, 1990; Commons et al., 1984; Kegan, 1982; Kohlberg, 1981). Those sharing similar value systems will be more likely included within one's social identity. A further shift in adulthood occurs (though not with much stability for most of us) to a point where identity is experienced primarily in terms of being, a globally inclusive reference point (see Alexander, Davies et al., 1990).

5. A developmental sequence of dependent, independent and interdependent perspectives in relation to physical-behavioral identity is observable across cultures during the first six years or so of life, from preverbal babies to the independence of the two-year-old able to express desires and walk around at will, to the cooperative play of the five-year-old.

6. In contrast, Chilton (1988) argues for a simpler, normative stage model of political development, closer to the sequence of stages of social reasoning found in individual development.

7. These seven perspectives correspond closely with Kohlberg's (1981) stages of moral reasoning—the seventh is introduced by Kohlberg and Ryncarz (1990). The first six of these are also the basis for Chilton's (1988) normative stage theory of political development. This paper draws support from their work and from the extensive cross-cultural research which Kohlberg's work has generated (see Rest, 1986), though preferring the language of distinct perspectives or strategies linked to levels of identity, rather than importing the language of stages into the realm of collective development. While it is possible to draw more specific distinctions between natural law-dependent, independent and interdependent subperspectives within the seventh perspective, for present purposes it is enough to distinguish this from the other six strategies.

8. The concrete operator finds it difficult to step back and mentally compare one set of thoughts or concepts with another. He/she learns new concepts best by imitation, repetition, conforming to the ideas received from others perceived as competent, powerful or attractive, without yet having the option of systematic questioning or evaluation, and in this sense necessarily depends on their wisdom and good will.

9. As adolescents, we typically develop a stronger capacity and preference for thinking reflectively *about* thoughts and concepts in their own right, separate from their concrete referents, thus moving from concrete to formal operational thought. We can begin to compare critically and to assess ideas, interests, values and principles independently, distinguishing those which are acceptable as our own from those which are not. Personal identity is now based on what we think and value, more than on the ideas or approval of others. This new independence of thought allows for reasoned defense against ideas and expectations in conflict with our own but does not yet allow much room for simultaneous empathy with such conflicting points of view.

10. The stage of social reasoning typically becoming primary in early adulthood and forming the basis for minimal norms or conventions of adult social responsibility is marked by a tendency to empathize with the thoughts, interests and needs of other valued individuals, while still honoring our own, even when the two are in apparent conflict. This allows, for the first time, the option for sustained, integrative coping strategies that meet or respect the interests of both parties in conflict. It provides the minimum requirement for responsible parenting and mentoring, or for care of elderly, sick, disabled or disadvantaged individuals within the family or contact community.

Rather than ignoring, exploiting or blaming the vulnerable, helping or empowering them within the contact group becomes a core value.

11. This represents the beginning of a new cycle of dependence-independence-interdependence in the spiral of development of social reasoning (see figure 6.2), as we come to recognize that while our thinking may be independent or interdependent, on a deeper level it is still dependent on the underlying value system. Such systems thinking is thought to involve massively parallel, nonlinear pathways, engaging primarily the prefrontal lobes of the cortex and the limbic system.

12. A later stage of dialectical or systems thinking is referred to by Fowler (1981) as "synthetic operations," or by Cook-Greuter (1990) as "unitary operations," reflecting the shift to an integrative (synthesizing) or interdependent orientation.

13. Kohlberg and Ryncarz (1990) describe a seventh, highest stage of development of moral reasoning based on transcendental experience of the self as more than thoughts and values, beyond the six Kohlberg had identified earlier. To the extent that it was not recognized as a sustainable perspective but rather glimpsed as a temporary experience only, they labeled it as a "soft" rather than "hard" stage, fully distinct from Kohlberg's Stage 6. In light of more recent evidence for the stabilization of this perspective (see Alexander, Davies et al., 1990; Mason et al., 1997), we would argue that Stage 7 be treated as a distinct hard stage—though some reconceptualizing is needed.

14. Dependence in Perspective 7 is in relation only to natural law (or from a religious perspective, divine law). In postconventional individual development, if we distinguish separate stages, independence in Perspective 8 reflects a dynamic tension between the self as awareness or being, and experience of universal being or intelligence as distinct from the self. Interdependence (Perspective 9) is achieved in the balanced integration of these two aspects of being (see Alexander, Davies et al., 1990, for a more detailed analysis of these perspectives in relation to individual development).

15. A simple centering exercise, for example, is to sit comfortably, eyes closed, and sweep one's attention slowly from the top of the head to the center of the chest, then in turn from the hands, from the feet, from the base of the spine and from the surrounding space again to the center of the chest, as if gathering one's energy there in a silent, boundless ocean of awareness or light, away from the usual chatter of the mind. Any tension or holding in the head or body is consciously released, including from the eyes, jaw, tongue, shoulders, fingers, toes, anus, back and diaphragm. Each thought or distraction or renewed tension that comes, when noticed, is allowed to fall away again into silence, subsiding effortlessly back into the ocean, neither encouraged nor resisted, without judgment or effort. Even ten minutes or so of this process can leave one feeling relaxed, alert and refreshed. Other metaphors may be preferred to aid in letting go of tensions and thoughts, and similar exercises can be found in any cultural tradition, though each with its own unique flavor and impact: I have had good results using the Transcendental Meditation, or TM, technique, whose efficacy has been extensively researched and validated (see, e.g., Alexander, Rainforth and Gelderloos, 1994).

7

Mapping Cultures: Strategies for Effective Intercultural Conflict Resolution

Christopher Moore and Peter Woodrow

"We are hopelessly lost!" exclaims the weary traveler. "I don't recognize any landmarks, and without a map we'll never find our route, or a place to stay for the night!" Lacking familiar landmarks, a map, or a friendly person to help them locate themselves and identify possible routes to their destination, travelers often feel lost and overwhelmed in unknown territory.[1]

Similarly, people interacting with people from other cultures often feel lost. Lacking familiar attitudes, beliefs, behaviors, procedures or structures that shape day-to-day interactions, people in cross-cultural situations often get disoriented, make mistakes and spend time and energy merely surviving rather than understanding and appreciating the differences they encounter. They also often fail to resolve serious conflicts due to cultural misunderstandings.

Intercultural negotiators and conflict resolution professionals need general principles to guide their negotiation or mediation strategies and a cultural map that helps them to:

- Identify the general "topography" of cultures: the beliefs, attitudes, behaviors, procedures and social structures that shape human interactions;
- Identify potential hazards, obstacles and pleasant surprises that intercultural travelers might miss if they did not have a trusty guide;
- Select responses that will promote successful interactions and outcomes.

Unfortunately, few analytical frameworks identify, interpret and respond to cultural differences. Few maps describe how different cultures solve problems, negotiate agreements or resolve disputes. This chapter will help address this gap.

Defining Culture

> Culture is the cumulative result of experience, values, religion, beliefs, attitudes, meanings, knowledge, social organizations, procedures, timing, roles, spatial relations, concepts of the universe and material objects acquired or created by groups of people, in the course of generations, through individual and group effort and interactions. Culture manifests itself in patterns of language, behavior and activities and provides models and norms for acceptable day-to-day interactions and styles of communication. Culture enables people to live together in a society within a given geographic environment, at a given state of technical development and at a particular moment in time (adapted from Samovar and Porter, 1972).

When we think of culture, we often think of the national cultures reported in the international media. However, culture is much broader and encompasses the beliefs, attitudes and behaviors of diverse ethnic groups, clans, tribes, regional subcultures or even neighborhoods. Culture differentiates people by religious or ideological persuasions, professions and educational backgrounds. Families also have cultures, as do the two largest cultural groups in the world, men and women. Companies, organizations and educational institutions also demonstrate unique cultures. With all of these cultural variables and significant variations within cultures, how can we develop any common understanding, general hypotheses or conclusions about how a particular person or group from any one culture might behave in conflicts or negotiations?

Specific cultures do contain clusters of people with fairly common attitudinal and behavioral patterns. As indicated in figure 7.1 below, these clusters occupy the middle portion of a bell-shaped curve (Trompenaars, 1994).

Figure 7.1 Distribution of Cultural Patterns in a Specific Group

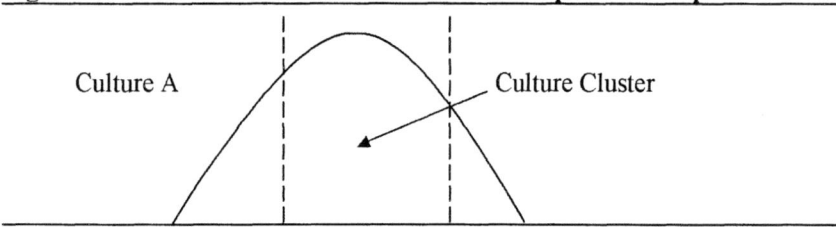

However, every culture includes outliers, people who vary significantly from the norm. While still contained within the range for their culture, their views and behaviors differ significantly from those of their peers and may even look similar to those of other cultures. For instance, a businessman or engineer from a developing country who was educated in England may have more in common with his or her peers in Europe than with his countrymen (see figure 7.2).

Figure 7.2 Similarities and Differences among Members of Cultures

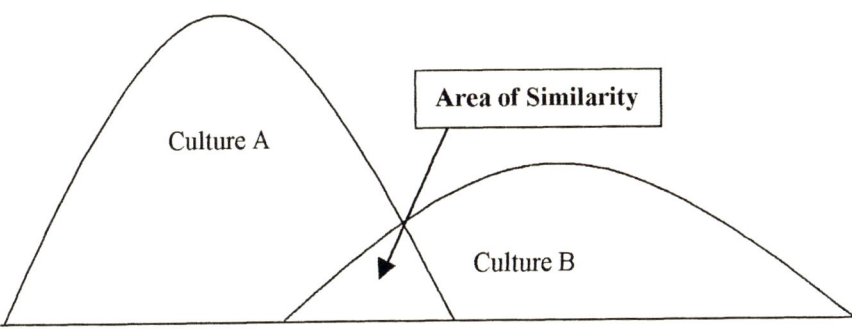

For this reason, we must be wary of generalizations about how people from a specific culture may think or act. Rigid notions about a group's cultural patterns can result in inaccurate stereotypes, gross injustices to the group and possibly disastrous assumptions or actions. Common cultural patterns found in a group's central cultural cluster should be looked upon as clues to the ways a cultural group may think or respond. But the hypothesis should always be tested and modified after direct interaction with the group. We may well encounter an outlier who seems more similar to us than we ever expected.

With these cautions in mind, we consider two intercultural situations and present guidelines for developing effective intercultural strategies.

The journal entry and e-mail message in boxes 7.1 and 7.2 illustrate some of the difficulties of cross-cultural work. The journal writer encounters a group that expends considerable effort in getting to know its potential business partner, devoting time to meals, tours and informal opportunities to talk. He worries that concrete negotiations may never get started. The writer of the e-mail message has a similar dilemma, but in his case, formal ceremonial events, a confusing decision-making process and unclear power dynamics have him stymied. We will address these issues further below.

Box 7.1 A Traveler's Journal

April 27, 1999

I finally have a few minutes to catch my breath and jot down some events of the last week. These days have been hectic, starting with two days of trying to get everything done before leaving, a very long plane ride and jet lag. We had no sooner arrived than we were whisked off to a big party arranged by our counterparts. I've never been so tired in my life!

The next day we started what I thought were to be negotiations, but it was only the first of a number of welcoming meetings attended by anywhere from ten to twenty people. I didn't know so many people were interested in this deal, although I am not at all sure how everyone fits in. We finally had a meeting where we each made an opening statement. Theirs was quite long and with lots of flowery words about creating a special friendship that would help overcome the past decades of

Box 7.1—Continued

tension between our two countries. I tried to move the conversation toward business at hand and made a statement that was short and to the point.

It felt like we were just getting started when they told us that they had arranged a tour of the city and the facility. After the tour, we had a late ceremonial lunch and lots of informal talks, only some of which related indirectly to the deal. After a break in the afternoon for us to go back to the hotel to refresh ourselves, we held another brief meeting that gradually moved toward the substance of our negotiations but stayed very general. Then another large meal! I was beginning to wonder if/when negotiations were ever going to start.

The next three days were crazy. They asked us for a proposal, which we readily presented, and then began both to take it apart and to ask myriad questions. They didn't reject our ideas, only asked questions and remained stoically distant. It was not clear to me what they were up to.

Well, it is 11:30 P.M., and I'm off to bed. Hope to get more sleep than in the last few nights. I am finally adjusting to the time zone and tomorrow is the weekend. Maybe I'll get some time to myself and not have to be the good guest all the time!

Box 7.2 An E-mail Home

To: gangatoffice@develop.org
Subject: Progress on Water Development Talks

This is an update on how the talks are proceeding. In my last message I told you we had to meet the local leader to proceed. Well, that meeting happened, and it was quite an event! We were met by a whole group of notables and what must have been his bodyguards all decked out in uniforms. We proceeded to a small but sumptuous audience hall and were served refreshments and carried on small talk. One of our colleagues raised the issue of the project, but the leader said that we should discuss it later with some of his colleagues. We took the hint and returned to small talk.

Upon adjourning we were shown into another large room and seated at a table at the front. About 25 men and three women filed in behind us and took their seats in a fairly large circle. A number of subordinates also stood around the outside of the circle, constantly coming in and out delivering messages to their bosses. Occasionally, a cell phone would ring, and the recipient of the call would rush to the back of the room. We were asked to make our presentation, while everyone listened politely. Then they began a long and elaborate discussion that didn't seem to have much focus on either us or on the project proposal.

For long periods they seemed to be arguing among themselves. They occasionally asked us questions, but the discussion focused on several men who made fairly long vociferous speeches.

They seemed to circle the question without ever explicitly supporting or rejecting it. I guess they got all the views out and assessed the lay of the land without committing themselves. When it seemed appropriate, we added our comments and tried to answer the questions. Finally, one of the older men said he liked our ideas, made a general counter-proposal and suggested that talks continue next week. I guess this will take longer than I figured! Please change my return air reservations to late next week. That's all for now.

Preparing for Intercultural Conflict Resolution

The next section will be divided into what can be done to prepare before dialogue or negotiation begins, and strategies that can be used during actual problem-solving activities to accommodate different cultural patterns.

Understand How Culture Can Make a Difference, and Pay Attention to It

People just starting to work across cultures, and even some with extensive experience, often make one of two significant mistakes. First, they assume that all of us are basically the same, that underneath our multipigmented skin, exotic clothing and diverse languages and practices, we all have identical wants and desires and similar approaches to negotiations and conflict resolution. Those who assert the basic similarity of cultures assume that "if we can just communicate," all problems will evaporate.

While this view is less common than it used to be, it is still frequently found in people with little experience working in diverse cultures. It is also prevalent among those who, when abroad, spend most of their time in international enclaves or tourist havens, and among members of dominant cultures who have never had to accommodate or adapt to the cultures of other groups.

The second common mistake, currently in vogue, is to romanticize culture and diversity and to treat other cultures as exotic, sacred and deserving of protection from "cultural imperialism." Followers of this approach often overemphasize differences between cultures, try to "go native," make extreme efforts to be "culturally correct" and try hard to avoid unpardonable errors.

Both views of culture hold some truth; there are many similarities between cultures, and cultures are unique and precious. However, each view represents an unhelpful extreme; the truth probably lies somewhere in between. Cultural differences are important factors in the success or failure of intercultural interactions, yet there are also many similarities among human beings. We must accept that culture plays an important part in interactions between groups, learn how to identify cultural similarities, build upon them and develop strategies that will help to bridge the important differences.

Develop an Awareness of How Cultural Differences Influence Problem Solving and Conflict Resolution

A framework for analyzing the impact of cultural differences on negotiation and problem-solving dialogue can be useful for understanding both our own and other cultures. The Wheel of Culture map (figure 7.3) identifies cultural factors that shape the ways members of societies bargain for their interests and respond to disputes:

Figure 7.3 The Wheel of Culture Map

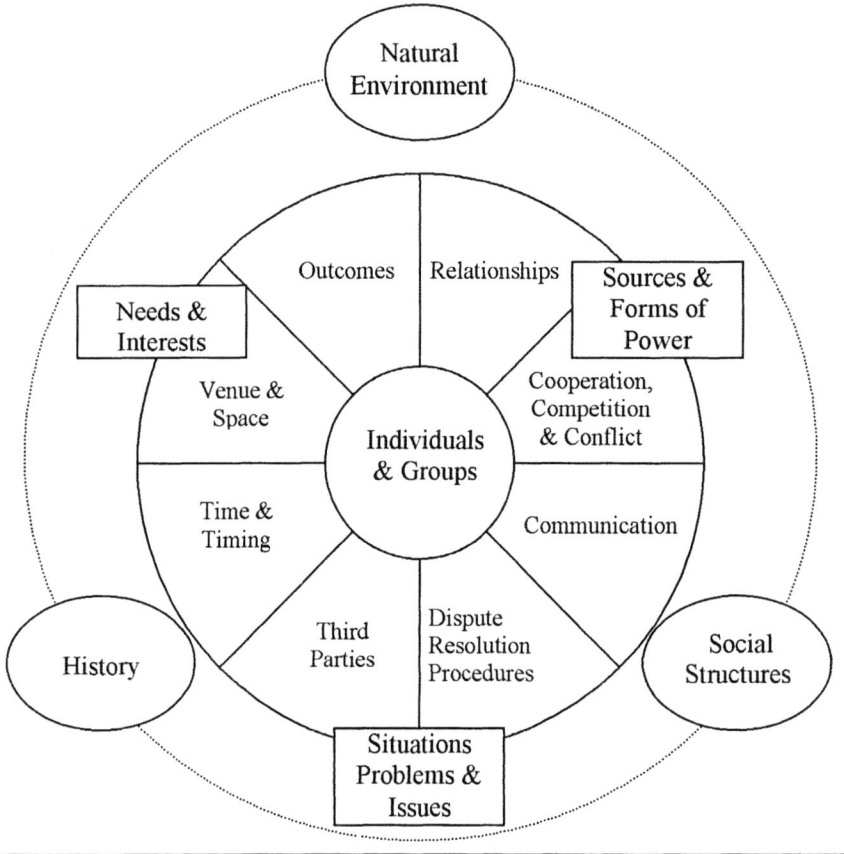

The Hub: Individuals and Groups

At the center of the wheel are individuals and groups who interact when problems are to be solved, negotiations conducted or disputes resolved. In general, cultures can be defined by how much emphasis their members put on the individual versus the group or collectivity (Hofstede, 1980) with cultures falling along an individualism/collectivism continuum of orientations.

Cultures oriented toward individuals generally value individual autonomy, initiative, creativity and authority in decision making. Those oriented toward collectivism generally value group cohesion, harmony and decision making that involves either consultation with group members before deciding, or consideration of the well-being of the group over that of the individual. Before entering a dialogue or negotiation it is helpful to know whether a culture is oriented toward individualism or collectivism, in comparison to your personal or organizational culture.

The Outer Rim

This section of the wheel identifies the broad external factors that influence the development of a specific group's cultural approach to negotiations and conflict resolution. These elements include:

- The natural environment;
- History, events, trends and adaptations that have occurred over time;
- Social structures, both intellectual and physical, that people create to adapt to or survive in their environment.

These three factors continuously interact and influence one another and the members of any given culture. In order to understand why people think and act the way they do, it is helpful to understand how the natural environment and history have shaped their values, views, behaviors and social structures.

The Inner Rim

The individuals or groups engaged in conflict resolution each demonstrate:

- Situations, issues or problems that must be addressed;
- Needs or interests they wish to have met;
- Sources of power and influence.

A culture significantly affects how its members define the social situations they face, the problems they encounter and the issues or topics that are or are not discussed. The situations that members of any given culture have to handle are often quite similar: raising or buying food; securing shelter; obtaining work to support oneself or a family; contracting marriages; purchasing other needed goods; and interacting with peers, subordinates and superiors. However, the meanings and importance which members of a culture place on these situations varies greatly. This causes problems when people from diverse cultures attach different meanings or importance to similar situations. An important element of preparation for any dialogue or negotiation is to develop a clear understanding of how the other party defines the situation and the issues to be discussed.

Needs and interests describe what individuals and groups require, expect or desire. They range from those critical for human survival, such as food, shelter, health and physical security, to identity needs such as meaning, community, intimacy and autonomy (Mayer, 2000). In the negotiating process, parties naturally advocate for their interests and needs. At times, the extent and manner of meeting relevant interests may be quite negotiable and flexible. At other times, when an individual or group feels that basic survival or fundamental identity is at risk, it may make rigid demands or intimidating statements.

While all cultures have similar minimum biological needs for survival, they differ significantly as to what they consider to be adequate satisfaction of these needs. All individuals have generally similar identity needs, but they differ significantly regarding how these can be addressed. Therefore, another critical element of preparation is to develop a tentative understanding or preliminary theory about the needs and interests of the parties (or the other party), and to become clear about your own.

Power and influence have been defined as "the ability to act, to influence an outcome, to get something to happen (or not happen), or to overcome resistance" (Mayer, 2000). Culture influences the preferred forms and sources of power and influence, and how and when they are to be used. It often determines the options available when a party has more or less power than another. A slight to someone's spouse by an unknown person in some cultures may result in giving the commenter the "cold shoulder" or a quick verbal retort. Others may consider it an attack on the spouse's honor that can be righted only by a physical fight or, in extreme cases, the death of the offender. A follower of Gandhi who believes that his or her rights have been violated may respond with *satyagraha*, or nonviolent resistance, a far different reaction than that of Tamil Tiger guerilla fighters in Sri Lanka. Good cultural analysis seeks to identify what forms of power and influence are likely to be used by whom and in which situations.

The Spokes

The spokes of the wheel represent specific culturally based patterns of belief and behavior that influence the interactions between individuals and groups. These factors are strongly influenced by the natural environment, social structures and the history of a cultural group, as well as by the specific situations or problems to be addressed. The spokes include cultural beliefs, attitudes and behaviors concerning:

- *Establishing, building and maintaining relationships:* How are relationships established, with whom, and involving what activities? What factors help build or change relationships?
- *Orientation toward cooperation, competition and conflict:* What are the common patterns of conflict behavior? Is overt conflict acceptable?
- *Appropriate and effective communications:* Should communication be direct or indirect; explicit or implicit; expressed emotionally or nonemotionally; and should it involve only one-at-a-time talk or overlapping talk? What reliance is placed on nonverbal communication?
- *Problem-solving or negotiation processes:* What are the roles of relationships and trust? Is positional bargaining or an interest-based negotiating style assumed? How are the stages of problem solving or negotiation handled?
- *Preferred outcomes to problems or conflicts:* What is the orientation toward "winning" or success? What preferences are there concerning the substantive, procedural or psychological components of outcomes? What other culturally acceptable or sanctioned norms exist about outcomes?
- *Roles and functions of third parties (go-between, facilitator, mediator):* What relationship to the parties is preferred, and what procedures are

normally used? Should the third party be partial or impartial; involved in the substance or just process?

- *Management of time and timing:* What are the expectations concerning duration, timing of activities, and timing allowed for agreements?
- *Use and setup of venue and space:* Should it be a public or private space; indoors or outdoors; formal or informal? How should the space be set up?

The Wheel of Culture is an analytical tool that can be used as a guide. It enables the effective negotiator or mediator to analyze cultural responses that are considered appropriate in his or her own culture in each of the above areas and to begin to identify cultural norms held by the parties or by the counterpart (potential partner, buyer/seller, authority, opponent or ally).

Educate Yourself about the New Culture

Once you have a general understanding of potential cultural similarities or differences in the context of dialogue or negotiations, it is often helpful to do more detailed research and exploration regarding the other culture. Some things that can be done to prepare for direct interactions include:

- Read a variety of books, magazines, news articles or Internet sources about the culture you plan to engage. Read authors from both the other culture and your own. Compare and contrast the views of different authors. If possible, include novels, which often reveal the most about cultural differences.
- See movies or rent videos about and from the other culture. Visual media can help you anticipate and prepare to operate in diverse settings and situations, acclimate you to hearing another language and present issues, themes and common cultural responses. However, "Hollywood" treatments do not necessarily present real life; documentaries and movies made in other cultures may come closer.
- Find and talk with members of the other culture. One of the best preparations for working with members of another culture is to meet someone from their context prior to conducting negotiations or initiating conflict-resolution efforts. Foreign students or faculty at universities are often very willing to talk, and they often welcome the opportunity to converse with others from another culture. They can be invaluable sources of information and orientation, since they have usually encountered both your culture and their own. Also, look for local cultural events sponsored or attended by the cultural group of interest. Go, observe, meet people and get to know some of their cultural behaviors in social settings.
- Talk with members of your own culture who have lived or worked in the other culture. Focus especially on people who have had experiences with the other culture that are similar to those you expect in the future.

Develop a Conflict-Resolution Plan Appropriate to the Situation

Based on what you have learned in the earlier steps, develop a preliminary plan concerning how you might initiate dialogue or negotiations, and then respond as the situation evolves. Consider how to:

- Establish contacts and build relationships that will be compatible with the other culture and your own;
- Develop appropriate forums and formats for interactions;
- Comply with their negotiation or dispute-resolution protocols in a way that is comfortable for all parties;
- Start discussions or negotiations on substantive issues;
- Conduct information exchanges and mutual education;
- Decide how you might respond to their more positional approaches or demands;
- Develop strategies for encouraging more interest-based approaches;
- Manage timing for the dialogue or negotiations as a whole, including relationship building, substantive discussions and timing of offers;
- Consider the Wheel of Culture spokes related to problems you might encounter and develop possible strategies for addressing them.

Flexible Responses

Following the above steps of preparation, you will need a flexible approach to your interactions with the other party in the midst of negotiations or conflict-resolution efforts:

Recognize When Something Different Appears to Be Happening

Once dialogue or negotiations have begun, participants need to "put up their antennae" to observe possible cultural differences that may emerge. The categories of the Wheel of Culture map should make it easier to identify such differences. Some questions to ask yourself include:

- What is similar or different about the setting of the meetings or negotiations than would be found in your culture?
- How are the situation, problems or issues that are being addressed similar to or different from those that might be common in your own culture?
- What behavioral similarities or differences do you see?
- Based upon what they say, do you have any clues about what their beliefs, attitudes or expectations are about the relationship or process being used?
- Are you interacting with an individual or a group? If the latter, is their behavior concerning who talks, what they talk about, how they express

themselves or how they interact with one another different than what might be expected in your culture?

Analyze and Interpret What is Happening and Develop an Appropriate Response

Once you perceive that cultural differences are influencing the course of dialogue or negotiations, figure out why the interlocutors might be thinking or acting in a particular manner. Apply insights gained from pre-entry study, research and interactions, and:

- Clarify what is happening;
- Develop a hypothesis about why it is happening and what the beliefs, attitudes and behaviors being expressed may mean to those exhibiting them;
- Decide how to respond and develop two or more strategies to try.

We have identified five basic strategies for conducting cross-cultural negotiations or problem-solving dialogues. The five strategies are based on the variables regarding the first party's willingness or ability to adapt to its counterpart's culture and the counterpart's willingness or ability to do the same. The resulting choices are: *adhering; avoiding-contending; adapting; adopting; and advancing.* We will discuss each of these in more detail.

Figure 7.4 illustrates how these choices arise out of interactions between the two parties' approaches. If the first party has a low willingness or ability to adapt to its counterpart's culture, two possibilities result. If the other party is more flexible, the first party can stick to its own way of doing things, the *adhering* strategy. If, on the other hand, the other party is also unable or reluctant to change its approach and the first party wants to persist in its cultural approach, the two parties will engage in an *avoiding-contending* mode. This pattern of interaction is marked either by competition regarding whose way of doing things will prevail (contending), or by the parties' avoiding interaction, with the potential for miscues and misinterpretations.

Figure 7.4 Strategic Choices in Cross-Cultural Interactions

High	Adhering		Advancing
Other Party's Ability/Willingness to Adapt to First Party's Culture		Adapting	
Low	Avoiding-Contending		Adopting
	Low	First Party's Ability/ Willingness to Adapt to Other Party's Culture	High

In a situation where both parties are somewhat knowledgeable about each other's cultures and are fairly compliant toward each other, they may arrive at a strategy of *adapting*. Each compromises a bit, probably adhering in some areas and adopting the counterpart's ways in other matters, resulting in a mixed set of procedures.

If the first party is willing to adapt to the other culture and knows something about it, a different set of choices presents itself. If the other party demonstrates unwillingness or inability to move toward the first party's way of doing things, while the first party is more flexible, the first party will end up *adopting* the cultural norms of the other. This is the *adhering* strategy with the roles reversed.

An intriguing fifth option is also available. If both parties know each other's cultural norms pretty well and both exhibit real willingness to adapt to another way of doing things, they can move into the *advancing* mode. In this mode the parties invent a third way that is based wholly neither in one culture nor the other. This shares some attributes with the *adapting* model but goes beyond a series of compromises to advance shared norms for interaction that are completely comfortable for both parties.

Select and Implement a Strategy

Once you have decided on a strategy, try it out. Observe the responses of the other party. See if your strategy is effective. If not, try another strategy or go back to your analysis and see if another interpretation of the situation or difficulty might be more accurate. If so, develop new strategies and try them. Remember to:

- Use a trial-and-error process to develop strategies or responses that help achieve your desired ends;
- Be flexible and consider using multiple possible responses;
- Remain open to doing it their way if it will achieve the results you want and it does not go beyond your comfort level.

Working across cultures can be frustrating and fascinating. We hope the thoughts presented here regarding preparation and flexible response prove helpful and that the road map offered may guide your way to successful cross-cultural interactions.

Note

1.   This chapter is adapted from a paper by the authors in the South African journal *Track Two* 8, no. 1 (July 1999), a publication of the Centre for Conflict Resolution.

In a situation where both parties are somewhat knowledgeable about each other's cultures and are fairly compliant toward each other, they may arrive at a strategy of *adapting*. Each compromises a bit, probably adhering in some areas and adopting the counterpart's ways in other matters, resulting in a mixed set of procedures.

If the first party is willing to adapt to the other culture and knows something about it, a different set of choices presents itself. If the other party demonstrates unwillingness or inability to move toward the first party's way of doing things, while the first party is more flexible, the first party will end up *adopting* the cultural norms of the other. This is the *adhering* strategy with the roles reversed.

An intriguing fifth option is also available. If both parties know each other's cultural norms pretty well and both exhibit real willingness to adapt to another way of doing things, they can move into the *advancing* mode. In this mode the parties invent a third way that is based wholly neither in one culture nor the other. This shares some attributes with the *adapting* model but goes beyond a series of compromises to advance shared norms for interaction that are completely comfortable for both parties.

Select and Implement a Strategy

Once you have decided on a strategy, try it out. Observe the responses of the other party. See if your strategy is effective. If not, try another strategy or go back to your analysis and see if another interpretation of the situation or difficulty might be more accurate. If so, develop new strategies and try them. Remember to:

- Use a trial-and-error process to develop strategies or responses that help achieve your desired ends;
- Be flexible and consider using multiple possible responses;
- Remain open to doing it their way if it will achieve the results you want and it does not go beyond your comfort level.

Working across cultures can be frustrating and fascinating. We hope the thoughts presented here regarding preparation and flexible response prove helpful and that the road map offered may guide your way to successful cross-cultural interactions.

Note

1. This chapter is adapted from a paper by the authors in the South African journal *Track Two* 8, no. 1 (July 1999), a publication of the Centre for Conflict Resolution.

TRC participants themselves are reviewed, and conclusions are drawn on the effectiveness of the reconciliation process in South Africa.

What Is Reconciliation?

Reconciliation is a complex, multifaceted and multilevel process, and different conceptual frameworks have been used to define it. Generally speaking, reconciliation is a collective turning from a conflictive past toward a commitment to build a positive future. The reconciliation process engages all parties involved in the conflict to work toward decreasing the level of conflict behavior and improving attitudes toward the "other." Relationships are central to reconciliation: they provide the basis of conflict and are at the heart of its long-term solution. The fundamental challenge is that of building new, constructive relationships, representing a profound healing process.

In order to provide an opportunity to redress past trauma and dehumanization, history needs to be clearly exposed, and a future must be envisioned. Given collective memories of animosity and suffering, it is difficult for people to transcend the past, even if they have forgiven their enemies for old transgressions. Reconciliation requires that people listen to one another and give each other the opportunity to express the trauma, grief and anger that accompany the painful memories of former injustices. Acknowledgment through listening to one another's stories validates experiences and feelings, and represents the first step toward restoration of the person and the relationship (Lederach, 1997).

Reconciliation allows for a new complex of positive feelings and perceptions to develop toward the "other." In that perception, possibilities for forgiveness grow as former antagonists learn that they can live together. Reconciliation happens over time and requires a level of maturity where parties accept their shortcomings, take responsibility for their behavior and follow through with positive actions for the rebuilding of relationships.

Ultimately, reconciliation implies a change in a group's fundamental values and a transformation of its identity. A radical approach to reconciliation does not simply change the attitudes among conflicting groups but also changes the boundaries of what it means to be part of those groups. Recognizing that deep-rooted conflict dynamics are centrally dependent on group identity formation, this reconciliation paradigm identifies group identity as a target for intervention (Van der Merwe, 1999).

Van der Merwe (1999) focuses on aspects of relationships that need to be addressed in the reconciliation process, including identity, patterns of interaction and related values and attitudes. At the heart of reconciliation is the recognition that we all have a right to exist, so issues of identity and recognition become paramount. How a group defines itself is often deeply connected with how it defines the "enemy." If an antagonistic relationship has existed over centuries, the sense of who one is may be directly related to how one's group has interacted with the "other." Expanding the boundaries of group identity thus implies a change in the way a group defines itself and the "enemy." Such a loosening of identity boundaries can allow a shift in values to those supporting a new moral order based on consensus and cooperation. These values determine what are acceptable forms of behavior and appropriate ways of dealing with conflict and disagreement. As behaviors change, attitudes change, impacting patterns of interaction. When there is positive reciprocal behavior, it feeds into a progressive trust-building process.

Substantive components to the reconciliation process include the parties' needs for security, justice, truth, and healing. Van der Merwe (1999) suggests adding truth and justice (from Lederach, 1995, 1997; Shriver, 1995) to security and healing (from victim-offender mediation), as the key components to be addressed through interaction and exchange. Lederach (1995) focuses on reconciliation as the place where the paradoxical concepts of truth and forgiveness, justice and mercy intersect. The integration of these elements is reconciliation, and the manner in which they are addressed is fundamental in determining how much change will happen. If communities are to have hope for the future, the truth must be revealed and mutual security assured. People need to experience a sense of justice and know that injustice is being addressed. They also need to sense that healing is taking place through acknowledgment of victimization, the restoration of dignity and the management of trauma.

Finally, underlying much of the conflict over different justice and reconciliation approaches is a tension between looking at the issue either from an individual (bottom-up) or national (top-down) perspective. Individual approaches focus primarily on those victims who are set apart from their groups by the extreme forms of victimization that they have experienced. They find themselves not only alienated from the enemy but often from their own groups. Reconciliation between communities has features similar to reconciliation between persons but contains an additional element: a whole people may be held collectively responsible for the miseries of another people suffering collective injustices.

Hence, national reconciliation is seen in terms of relationships among different identity groups or across ideological divisions. It requires changing the ways that political leaders relate to each other, how they mobilize support, and how sectors of society identify themselves in relation to these categories. The approach involves promoting constructive interparty interaction aimed at improving attitudes among party leadership and between ethnic groups, and generating a sense of a unified national identity. From this top-down perspective, the strategy lies in maximizing impact at the national level, whether the focus is on behavior control or on social values. Individual cases are addressed in order to create national awareness of the consequences for perpetrators and to build national consensus around values.

The bottom-up approach addresses the needs of each individual or each community as a unique concern. It is the individual victim and offender involved whose circumstances and needs have to be addressed. A lack of change in the their behavior, attitudes, values and identity would render the intervention meaningless. Each community is seen as a unique concern: the local dynamics cannot be seen as the outflow of national group division. Each community is infused with specific local events, personalities involved in the conflict, and unique individual victims. The choice of reconciliation approach affects which components (justice, truth, security, healing, etc.) should be treated as essential and at what social level they should be pursued.

The South African Truth and Reconciliation Commission

When the African National Congress came to power in 1994, many of its leaders believed that reconciliation was the best way to begin a new democracy. Immediate concern focused on the future of apartheid functionaries, from death-squad members and spies to simple office workers. Should there be Nuremberg-style trials, or some other legal remedy for atrocities carried out under apartheid? Apartheid leaders were calling for amnesty. They wanted assurance that the new government would not prosecute them for the thousands of assassinations they had committed to keep power. Nelson Mandela did not want to tear the country apart and risk the destruction of the transition by whites, who still ran the police and military. From the beginning, Mandela placed reconciliation and forgiveness as his top priorities, even above justice. Amnesty was agreed to, subject to certain conditions.

In this, the South Africans drew from the experience of a few other countries recently in transition to democracy, taking their greatest lead from Chile. There, a truth commission made up of respected citizens from across the political spectrum had interviewed thousands of relatives and victims of the dictatorship, written their collective story, and also made recommendations for reparations and for the prevention of future abuses. While many felt that amnesty would rob society of justice, at least the truth commission would make public the dictatorship's crimes. Victims would have the satisfaction of seeing a state that had always denied involvement in any flagrant human rights violations acknowledge responsibility for torture and murder.[1]

The Promotion of National Unity and Reconciliation Act of 1995, in establishing the Truth and Reconciliation Commission (TRC), states: "Amnesty shall be granted in respect of acts, omissions and offenses associated with political objectives and committed in the course of the conflicts of the past" between March 1, 1960, and December 5, 1993, and which have been disclosed by the perpetrators. The act effectively gave the president discretion to grant amnesty to individuals who had acted with political intent and whose release might promote peaceful solutions, simply by publishing the name, the act and the date of release. Since its inception, the TRC has aimed to give voice to the experiences of victims, witnesses and perpetrators of apartheid-era violence so as to understand, as far as possible, the causes, nature and extent of past abuses.

The three main short-term objectives of the TRC were: (1) to restore the human and civil dignity of the victims by giving them an opportunity to relate their own accounts of the violations; (2) to grant amnesty to those giving full disclosure of politically motivated crimes; and (3) to make recommendations to Parliament on reparation and rehabilitation measures, including measures to prevent the future commission of human rights violations. The long-term goals of the TRC were: (1) to help heal the victims of political violence in the apartheid years; and (2) to help heal society and create a new culture of respect for human rights, where such things could never happen again.

What differentiates South Africa from other countries is that the idea of trials was combined with that of a truth commission. Amnesty would only be granted to individuals who earned it by telling the truth. Anyone who had committed a politically motivated crime could tell his story to the Truth Commission, including all details and the names of other perpetrators. If that happened, the person could be granted amnesty: otherwise, they, along with those who did not apply for amnesty by May 10, 1997, could be prosecuted.

In evaluating the success of the South African TRC, we consider its effectiveness in relation to each of four critical components of reconciliation discussed above: justice, truth, mercy and healing.

The South African TRC and Justice

Social psychologists have long argued that people have a need to believe that they live in a just world (Lerner, 1980). People experience justice as a basic human need, without which healing and reconciliation are impossible. How justice is perceived and restored is critical: how it is defined by the parties and how a common understanding of appropriate forms of justice is developed goes to the core of the reconciliation process (Van der Merwe, 1999).

Most commonly, especially in protracted conflicts, the term "justice" is used in a narrow, retributive sense, without reference to its broader restorative function. Not only is restorative justice supportive of reconciliation and forgiveness, but the longer-term development of social justice depends on it.[2]

There has been a great deal of criticism concerning an assumed low salience of the issue of justice for the South African TRC. This criticism reflects a preoccupation with justice in the narrow sense of prosecution and punishment of individual perpetrators through the formal justice system. The options for this were limited, in part because the transition from apartheid to democratic rule was a negotiated one. The National Party refused to relinquish power without some form of guarantee that its members and those who had defended the government would not be prosecuted (Simpson and Van Zyl, 1995). On the other hand, the ANC and other parties would not agree to grant a general amnesty: a compromise was needed in order to move forward.[3] These preconditions led to the framing of the TRC and the related constitutional agreement to grant conditional amnesty.

Criticisms of the TRC concerning justice also reflected a conflict between the interest in individual justice and the general interest in social justice. "Justice" typically functions not only to protect against wrongdoing and promote rectification at the individual level but also more broadly to protect individual rights generally against state actions (Lotter, 1993, 6-7). Amnesty often feels very unfair to the victims: why should people who have committed such horrific acts only need to acknowledge their guilt and then be allowed to walk free? Many victims feel revictimized when perpetrators are not only set free but are allowed to have positions of power while many of the victims still live in poverty. But the essential point is that the TRC was created to assist in the political transition from autocratic to democratic rule. Granting amnesty is the price South Africa had to pay for the common good, for the negotiated settlement. As the minister of justice, Dullah Omar, stated,

> We have a nation of victims, and if we are unable to provide complete justice on an individual basis—and we need to try and achieve maximum justice within the framework of reconciliation—it is possible for us to ensure that there is historical and collective justice for the people of our country. If we achieve that, if we achieve social justice and move in that direction, then those who today feel aggrieved that individual justice has not been done will at least be able to say that our society has achieved what the victims fought for during their lifetimes. And that therefore at that level, one will be able to say that justice has been done.
>
> Reconciliation does not replace or exclude justice. However, it is also unacceptable to make it totally subject to satisfying justice's legal requirements. Reconciliation builds the foundation of commonality that makes it possible for justice to be done in the spirit of openness and acceptance of the other in the interest of our common future. Reconciliation replaces the culture of revenge, not the culture of justice. In this view justice is not punishment but restoration, not necessarily to bring things back to the way they were, but to the way they should be. It is about restoring people's lives, restoring peace and harmony (Omar, in Rwelamira and Werle, 1996: xii.).

Even though the South African TRC did not give a blanket amnesty and in certain situations did give the right to redress for qualified cases, the likelihood of people not being punished for their crimes could create an explosive environment. The current high crime rate is arguably linked to victims' unresolved feelings of anger, hurt and grief. When criminals are exempt from punishment it may set off within others a "need for retribution[:]. . . a profound sense of moral equilibrium impelling us to demand that people pay for the harm they have done to others" (Jacoby, 1985). This sets up a tension between retribution and reconciliation.

At the heart of the issue is a moral conflict between justice, as embodied in the criminal justice system, and values such as truth, reconciliation, peace and the common good, underlying this kind of commission. The critical point is that criminal justice is not the only social goal, nor always the ultimate value. In the context of a fragile transition to a stable democracy, political compromises like conditional amnesty might be justified for the sake of the common good.[4] If retributive justice were maintained, not only peace would have been threatened, but also truth. Very few people would have come forward willingly to tell their stories if they had feared retribution. Wilhelm Verwoerd (1997) comments that

> The argument that retributive justice would be imprudent at this transitional stage of South African history is not to be "soft" on perpetrators of indefensible crimes. It is not to throw justice out of the window for the sake of peace. It is to argue, instead, that (further) sacrifices by the few are (unfortunately) necessary for the sake of the many. Amnesty is, primarily, a means to prevent further and highly probable future injustices—i.e., the gross violations of human rights resulting from (continued or renewed) civil war.

Another important consideration is that the criminal justice system is set up to prosecute individuals or small groups of conspirators where there is a clear causality between the crime and the intent of a given individual. In cases of political crimes where large numbers of people are involved, determining legal responsibility becomes increasingly difficult, as illustrated by the Nuremberg trials. During the Nuremberg (and Tokyo) tribunals, even with very strong evidence, few Nazis were found guilty. These trials illustrated the difficulty in finding out what happened in large numbers of gross human rights violations and the difficulty in producing sufficient evidence to convict specific individuals for such crimes. Recognizing these obstacles to prosecution and punishment, conditional amnesty may be seen in a different light as the only means left to satisfy society's—and especially the victims'—need for finding out the truth.

Political crimes present problems not only in terms of prosecution and punishment but also in the rehabilitation process, because political motivation leading to crimes cannot be rehabilitated through jail terms and special treatment.[5] The challenge of rehabilitation goes beyond dealing with individual perpetrators. As we saw during the Nuremberg and Tokyo war tribunals, concentrating on a few prominent human rights violators addresses only the tip of the iceberg. It became clear that entire institutions, such as the security organizations that were responsible for many of the gross human rights violations, had to be transformed. This shift in focus from individual to social and institutional transformation was central to the TRC's contribution toward greater social justice in South Africa.

The South African TRC and Truth

Revealing the truth is crucial to the healing function of reconciliation: it allows victims to be acknowledged, to be brought out of shame and isolation and to have their humanity and civil dignity restored. It allows the emergence of a common memory to replace the relative truths promoted by former enemies, and a larger moral climate that encourages forgiveness and reconciliation. Becker (1990) writes:

To advance the process of social reparation, it will be necessary to publicly establish the truth of the victims' experiences. Truth, in this case, means the end of denial and silence. It means facing pain, loss, and conflict that have been intentionally avoided in the belief that if things are not mentioned they cease to exist and that wounds not reopened will allow social peace. Establishing the truth is necessarily linked to demands for justice, but the process cannot and must not end there. Clarifying responsibilities for what has happened is a necessary but not a sufficient condition for obtaining truth. At both the individual and collective levels, the capacity for being moved ethically and emotionally must be recovered.

When one walks into the room where the public hearings of the Truth and Reconciliation Commission were held, one cannot escape seeing a banner which reads, "Truth: the Road to Reconciliation." This banner expresses the purpose of facilitating a truth-recovery process, the telling of stories that have long been kept silent. The truth is often relative, especially for enemies with different political or ideological dispositions. But the intent of the TRC was to give voice to the experiences of the victims, witnesses and perpetrators, to uncover as complete a picture as possible of the causes, nature and extent of past abuses. Until people know where responsibility lies for atrocities committed and are given information such as the location of missing loved ones, obstacles to reconciliation will remain.

A vivid illustration is provided by the Rev. Frank Chikane, general secretary of the South African Council of Churches, who related a story in which he narrowly escaped death in 1989. He had been poisoned several times in the space of a few weeks, with a common insecticide that has an effect similar to that of nerve gas. The episodes all took place when he was travelling extensively, the poison being placed on his luggage. Reverend Chikane likened the role of the TRC to that of the confessional, and as such, he cautions,

> There can be no absolution without confession. My plea to those who were involved in my poisoning is that they disclose this information not only for their own peace of mind, but to relieve me as well from the pain of wanting to forgive but not knowing who to forgive (Miller, unpublished paper).

While amnesty greatly reduces the risk that a peace process may be derailed by those willing to revert to violence rather than be punished, even being confronted with the truth of one's own acts can be threatening. The South African TRC has thus been criticized as a witch-hunt, for tracking down people to find out what really happened. Yet to know truth is to counter the deceit which characterized so much of South Africa's history. Finding out the truth is about remembering. A reconciled society and common identity implies a joint memory of the past and joint recognition that the losses of both sides are the losses of society as a whole. Developing a collective memory is an essential step in affirming a common identity.[6]

Without acknowledgment, wounds cannot be healed. The philosopher George Santayana once commented that those who forget the past are doomed to repeat it. If wounds are not healed we will pay for the failure in the future with the continuance of vengeance. To accept national amnesia would also leave its scars, in effect victimizing the victims a second time by denying something that contributes to their identity, their sense of who they are.[7]

Truth is about revealing that which is hidden. Through recounting the horrific events of the past, the human and civil dignity of victims is restored. South Africans have the opportunity to tell and hear horrifying stories so that they can share in a new common humanity born of pain and suffering. In sharing their stories, victims overcome feelings of isolation, ultimately forgiving and shedding the burden of shame. Those witnessing the storytelling gain an authentic depth of understanding that breaks down barriers in ways which would be almost impossible by any other means.

Truth indicates honesty and revelation, the longing for acknowledgment of wrong and the validation of painful losses and experiences. Without truth, conflicts cannot be resolved. Although speaking the truth may leave the protagonist feeling vulnerable and unworthy, this vulnerability opens up the possibility of healing. It provides a picture of the psychological landscape. Victims can be acknowledged and empowered, giving groups and states the option to forgive. The search for truth can thus create the moral climate in which reconciliation and peace will flourish.

The South African TRC and Mercy (Forgiveness)

Why did the Truth and Reconciliation Commission deal with the question of impunity in the way it did? Why were so many people willing to choose forgiveness rather than demand retribution? This had a lot to do with the concept of *Ubuntu*, which is part of the fabric of the South African culture. It is a concept difficult to define in Western terms. Basically, it conveys the view that "My humanity is caught up, is inextricably bound up, in yours. A person is a person through other persons" (Tutu, 1999). We belong to a greater whole, and when others are dehumanized or diminished, we are all dehumanized or diminished. To forgive becomes practical, as the best form of self-interest (see also Davies, this volume).

Mercy, as a concept related to *Ubuntu*, is an important component of the reconciliation process, especially in relation to amnesty, which, at least within the South African context, had to be embraced on practical grounds. There is a condition to the grant of amnesty in which mercy plays a pivotal role. Amnesty has to be seen as more than a formal judicial decision, and certainly not as the victory of the perpetrator, but rather as a gracious gift of the victims. Amnesty then becomes an act of mercy, a gift toward our common humanity. Herein lies the empowerment of the victim. The victim alone can give or withhold mercy; the perpetrator is a moral supplicant.

Mercy, or forgiveness, is a particularly difficult aspect of the reconciliation process, since it is impossible to achieve if little or no healing has yet taken place. Telling one's story, expressing one's feelings, and having a sense of being heard are necessary steps in the forgiveness process. The circumstances and the individuals involved (especially their spiritual inclinations) will influence their readiness for expressing forgiveness. Another determining factor is whether remorse is expressed from the other side. Not all people have a predisposition to forgiveness, and not all people can easily accept responsibility for their actions. However, the degree to which these steps can be taken will determine the depth of healing and ultimately the depth of reconciliation that can occur.

The South African TRC and Healing

Healing requires not just readiness to forgive, but acknowledgment by perpetrators of the pain they have caused and expression of true remorse.[8] One of many examples of such healing through the history of the TRC involved Eugene de Koch, former head of Vlakplass. This feared man stood before a crowd in Port Elizabeth and spoke of his crimes, leading to a powerful moment when he showed sympathy toward the widows of his victims and asked for forgiveness. The crowd responded with applause. Extending forgiveness in this way produced a catharsis for everyone involved, forging a new relationship between survivors and perpetrator.

Another example of healing took place when the daughters of those slain in the St. James Church massacre chose to meet with the perpetrators (APLA cadres). By the end of the meeting not only did the daughters offer forgiveness, but they expressed understanding for the killers. The daughters were able to suspend their preconceptions, gain insight into their traumatic event, and, in discovering the humanity of the other side, release long-held pain and anger. Forgiveness is key to such shifts in perception and to the release of pain, fear and anger that otherwise keep people trapped in cycles of resistance and revenge.

Unfortunately, not everyone in South Africa has been provided with the psychological and social support required to embrace reconciliation. Factors such as satisfaction of needs for justice and security, and whether remorse and forgiveness have been expressed, determine if and how long it may take for reconciliation and healing to occur.

One factor that has hampered healing and reconciliation for some is the "reconciliatory compromise" (Winslow, 1997) reached in the negotiation process, which, for many, has preserved the status quo in the new dispensation. Many victims and survivors are retraumatized by sunset clauses that protect the jobs of police and military who may have been involved in human rights violations, reinforcing a continued sense of powerlessness, anger and fear.[9]

An unexpected turn of events not anticipated by the TRC, however, was that survivors recognized their need to become more actively involved in the amnesty hearings for their own healing. Where they once felt powerless, now they were assuming the role of interrogators, with the former torturers now at their mercy.[10] In this regard the amnesty process became the chief vehicle for reconciliation (Winslow, 1997). It allowed the victims and survivors to get answers about the past directly from the perpetrators, especially concerning gross human rights violations. That, in turn, not only helped in healing but exposed the horrific forms of torture that had taken place, helping to prevent them from happening again. It broke the "culture of silence" and shattered old myths and beliefs so there could be no turning back. A national healing process, though uneven, had begun.

Both victims and victimizers have expressed extreme feelings of anger over the hidden past revealed by the TRC. There has been denial and avoidance from all sectors of the population, remorsefulness from some of those complicit in violations, indifference from others, and enormous feelings of guilt, pain, and sadness for many. For those who testified, psychological difficulties and symptoms of posttraumatic stress disorder (PTSD) are common, ranging from crippling self-blame, enormous anger (sometimes exacerbated by the granting of amnesty), and unresolved grief, to a host of social and interpersonal problems. These consequences have not always received adequate attention by the TRC.

One weakness of the TRC comes from inadequate preparation for the long-term processes of healing. People who have testified and opened up their personal Pandora's boxes have not always been provided with services or referrals following the hearings. Situations of this nature may lead to momentary relief but can leave people feeling retraumatized months later.

There have been similar problems faced by perpetrators, amnesty applicants and their families, who have received very little therapeutic support. There is a tendency not to include perpetrators in the same healing circle as the victims. If we do not include the perpetrators, healing will be incomplete at best. The issue of treating perpetrators is morally complex in a country that has so recently emerged from violent conflict, and many providers and institutions may also feel limited by their inexperience with such work. Because of the horrific acts committed under apartheid, the plight of the victims was given first priority, which has made access for perpetrators and their families difficult.

Making the situation even more complex, there are those who can be seen as both victims and perpetrators. This group has been given even less psychological support. The youths that were involved in intracommunity conflict in the early 1990s, for example, had limited interactions with the TRC, often due to an assumption implicit in the TRC process that one is either a victim or perpetrator. Only over time, as more information became available to the TRC, did a more complex set of relationships and roles surface.

It is perhaps ironic that although reconciliation was a macro-theme of the TRC's work, there was no apparatus in its structure to achieve it (Winslow, 1997). For example, there was a committee to uncover the truth, a committee to explore methods of redress for survivors of human rights violations, and a committee to consider amnesty for perpetrators. There was no provision made for a committee on reconciliation, let alone healing. So how could the TRC be expected to heal or to reconcile? The logic becomes one of process. The TRC uncovers the truth about gross human rights violations. This acknowledgment of the past serves as a catalyst for a host of reactions along "the road to reconciliation," as proclaimed in the commission's banners, bringing catharsis to those who have suffered, and justification for offering reparations to victims as a form of restorative justice.

Clearly, healing has taken place, and beneficial changes are apparent in the national psyche. The country is facing the ugliness of the past thirty years, and the old norms, myths and beliefs no longer hold true for many South Africans. A new nation is being born with new norms and realities to shape its history and motivations, allowing it to move on and build a new future and new moral order. The TRC has contributed to this healing in several ways.

First, the TRC has normalized the symptoms of trauma and exposure to gross violence. The TRC has made it socially acceptable to talk about pain in public, to mourn the loss of loved ones with emotion, and to seek counseling to overcome past traumas. By building up public awareness of the consequences of trauma and suffering, the TRC has assisted survivors in grappling with their pain and possibly removed some of the stigma of mental health issues.

Second, the TRC has created platforms for survivors to experience the humanity of their perpetrators through amnesty hearings. Regardless of the outcome of the hearings, survivors had the chance to see their tormentors in an entirely new relationship of power, where the balance is tipped in favor of victims. At amnesty hearings, survivors finally saw their former prison guards and torturers not as powerful security-force members with the power of life and death in their hands but as ordinary human beings, no longer the objects of fear and now subject to the rule of law. This equalization of power in a changed, reconciled environment carried the potential for healing.

Third, the TRC has promoted healing through its emphasis on prevention of future human rights violations.

Fourth, the TRC has had the potential to remove some of the most powerful cues and reminders of past human rights violations, which otherwise would have contributed to sustaining survivors' trauma. The TRC could insist that police generals implicated in human rights violations not be in control of the police. The TRC could recommend changing the names of notorious police stations, prisons, and torture facilities. And the TRC could propose the creation of parks, monuments, and other symbols of reconciliation. By dismantling or rendering impotent the symbols of past repression and constructing new reference points with new meaning, the TRC could help facilitate the nation's healing.

It should be remembered that healing may take place before reconciliation, rather than as a result of it. Survivors may need to reconcile their experience within themselves before feeling ready to tackle reconciliation with another person, let alone a perpetrator. Trudy de Ridder, a clinical psychologist at the Trauma Center, which works with survivors from the TRC, explains it this way:

> As long as survivors of human rights violations entertain secret emotions of revenge, the perpetrators will maintain their control and power over their lives. Survivors need to let go of the perpetrator inside themselves by releasing their anger. If they don't then the perpetrator still controls them, still haunts their memories, and still controls their destiny. They are still victims—powerless to effect change in their lives. Our job as therapists is to channel that anger in a healthy and balanced way in order to bring about healing and inner reconciliation (Winslow, 1997).

Lessons Learned from South Africa

There is no question that the TRC had a profound psychological impact on South Africans. Yet different experiences have meant different reactions toward the TRC, depending on whether one was a perpetrator, a victim, or just complicit with the apartheid system. Evaluating the impact of the TRC is a complex challenge.

Hamber (1998) and the Center for the Study of Violence and Reconciliation (CSVR) conducted eleven reconciliation and rehabilitation workshops between August 1997 and February 1998 to elicit the views of the victims/survivors regarding reparations and rehabilitation and to broaden the discussion about the TRC reparation policy in order to make proposals for further intervention on a local level.[11] The workshops revealed many different perspectives on the impact of the TRC with respect to local reconciliation initiatives before, during and after the TRC hearings, and several additional issues that the survivors in the workshops felt still needed to be addressed.

Perspectives

The term "reconciliation" meant different things to different people across different provinces. Four major viewpoints emerged. The first dealt with truth as a precondition to reconciliation. Many victims felt that they needed to know the truth in order for reconciliation to take place, and that they could not forgive people who did not come forward. This group also felt that the process of truth telling and breaking the culture of silence was the beginning of a more complex reconciliation process.

The second viewpoint dealt with reconciliation as justice. The participants in this group felt that perpetrators should contribute materially and financially toward the reparation and rehabilitation of victims. Justice and punishment were favored over amnesty.

Third, some felt that reconciliation is a deeply personal process and that each case had to be dealt with individually. Perpetrators had therefore to be held accountable individually and be accessible to the victims.

The fourth viewpoint coupled reconciliation with specific reparation. It was stated by most survivors that reconciliation and reparation were integrally linked, which was apparent in the slogan "No Reconciliation without Reparation" echoed throughout the workshops.

Issues

There were many problems expressed in the workshops concerning the actual process of reconciliation. Most participants felt that the TRC process had not overcome the divisions created by the conflict, especially at the community level. They felt that the commission had not sufficiently permeated local communities and that the TRC had not always dealt with inter- and intracommunity conflict. Race was seen as an issue perpetuating division and was thought not to have been completely addressed through the TRC. There seemed to be an absence of white people at TRC meetings, giving the perception that blacks and whites were still living in separate worlds.

Another factor seen as hampering reconciliation was that survivors felt that the TRC was very lenient toward the perpetrators, who were benefiting from the system because of amnesty while the victims were still suffering from the effects of apartheid. There was a perception that despite survivors' having named perpetrators in their statements, the commission had done little to follow up the accusations, leaving some who committed the atrocities against them still in positions of power in the government and police services.

Some of the survivors wanted to meet with their perpetrators. They felt that the commission had done little in this regard, since there was no comprehensive victim-offender mediation program in place. Survivors also wanted to be more active in the amnesty process. Some raised the criticism that they had been informed through the media about an amnesty application that was relevant to them before the TRC made contact with them.

There was the perception that ordinary victims were discriminated against in favor of high-profile victims. Many communities felt that they were left out and that other communities were favored over them. Many survivors said, "Our area was the only one ignored." Also of concern was the lack of processes set up to provide support to help survivors deal with the past as revealed by the TRC.

The greatest overall concern was the need for transformation within specific institutions, particularly the police force. Survivors felt that a number of issues not adequately addressed by the TRC were critical to a healing and reconciliation process. The first dealt with police officials' not making any meaningful contribution to transforming their role from that of sustaining apartheid to protecting individuals' rights. The participants felt that those in the police force who did appear before the TRC had not fully acknowledged or accepted responsibility for committing gross violations of human rights. They felt that the police who did come forward shifted the responsibility to those higher up in the hierarchy and ignored their own roles.

Second, survivors expressed the need to establish a police service that is human-rights-oriented in its actions and not one that uses old strategies against the so called "new enemy," i.e., criminals. Third, many believed that there were perpetrators of abuses named by victims still present in the ranks of the police and magistrates.

Fourth, concerning symbolic reparation, many spoke out strongly for the need to transform offensive symbols of the past in their communities. These dealt with local and national symbols, public holidays and the history of the country. Participants felt that the newly elected democratic government did not succeed in changing the image of the institutions they inherited. For example, various local institutions, schools, towns, and official buildings still retained the names of notorious apartheid leaders. National symbols still carried a pervasive cultural heritage of "white supremacy." It was felt that the monuments representing this legacy should be destroyed or kept in museums. There was the perception that several public holidays still carried connotations of the past, commemorating events that symbolized the history of narrow sectoral interests.

Finally, the history of South Africa as written for the public and found in school textbooks was seen as biased, impugning the dignity of victims of the previous government. It was felt these textbooks should be rewritten to correct the distortions and give a more accurate and balanced view of the country's past.

Recommendations

Participants listed a number of recommendations to be presented to the TRC. The first recommendation was that the TRC honor criticisms expressed as part of its mandate to receive and suggest ways to rectify reconciliation issues. It was felt that the TRC needed to acknowledge that, although some processes had begun, reconciliation had not been achieved, and in some cases existing conflicts had been exacerbated. The victims/survivors suggested that a card be issued granting freely accessible psychological and medical services.

Many survivors felt that the issue of perpetrators needed to be dealt with more fully. Many still felt unsafe and feared repercussions from perpetrators. It was recommended that the security concerns of the victims be addressed through the establishment of a special police task group under the auspices of the body that is to implement police reparations. This body could be mandated to investigate allegations and concerns where survivors feel their security is at risk and ensure that people receive appropriate protection. They also expressed the need for civilian oversight and for victim/offender mediation programs maintained by credible institutions to help deal with the legacy of the past.

Survivors were adamant about removing perpetrators of past abuses from public office, to give space for newly trained personnel. They felt that police officers should be retrained in the protection of human rights and that the TRC should include in its report a detailed chapter on the role of the police in apartheid atrocities. This chapter should form part of the basic police training.

Many survivors recommended that no people granted amnesty for gross violations of human rights should be employed within the police or in the government at all.

Another theme was that continuing inter- and intracommunity racial divisions created through apartheid need to be addressed. For this, perpetrators and beneficiaries of crimes need to show remorse. It was suggested that this could be done by giving money to a reparations fund, by doing community service, or by being actively involved in the ongoing process of national and community reconciliation. Meetings, workshops and public forums between previously segregated groups and conflicting communities should be facilitated, and the TRC should develop mechanisms for this work after the disestablishment of the TRC.

The survivors felt that there needed to be acknowledgment that the TRC was a generous process for perpetrators who committed abuses that were condemned all over the world. There is still the feeling that justice has not been done and that this lack needs to be rectified before a new society can be created. There is a strong voice recommending that criminal prosecutions be pursued against all perpetrators who carry responsibility for past human rights abuses, especially those who did not take the opportunity to apply for amnesty. It was further recommended that a mechanism be put in place to assist victims to pursue civil claims against perpetrators who did not apply for amnesty.

Questions were raised about ongoing investigations in which survivors were unclear about the status of their case or in which the TRC had not reported back to the survivors. Others felt that not all of the truth had come out, despite the efforts of the TRC. They recommended that the TRC report in detail to all individuals and communities on the status of their cases and that mechanisms and resources be put in place so that survivors can continue investigations if they wish.

The participants of these workshops who belong to the Khulumani Support Groups/CSVR acknowledged that their relationships with the TRC had been strained. This is the consequence of the legitimate demands the victim support groups placed on the TRC to deliver reparations and services more effectively to survivors. It is important that the TRC recognize that such criticism is beneficial and part of the TRC process. The survivors therefore recommended that survivor support groups be set up or maintained to address ongoing problems resulting from the TRC and the conflicts of the past. Groups will serve as a living memory of the TRC while mobilizing more resources for the empowerment of victims. The TRC should give its full support to such groups, acknowledge their role and contribution to the TRC and the reconciliation process, and find constructive ways both to maintain present groups and develop new ones.

Human rights education is essential in the rebuilding of South Africa. The impact of apartheid, the violence that destroyed so many communities and lives, cannot be ignored. The survivors recommended that the history of South Africa be presented in school textbooks in such a manner that the suffering of victims across the political spectrum is recognized. The TRC should write recommendations that fit with current restructuring of the Education Department and ideas for a new curriculum. It was also recommended that programs that provide intensive human rights education to the general public be encouraged and institutionalized within schools and universities. Human rights education should be started at the earliest age possible.

Finally, symbolic ways of representing the past and future were considered critical for most survivors. There was a discussion that new national symbols should not be built around representations of heroism and the courage of a few individuals. Rather, these should be oriented toward recognizing the dignity and strength of the many who have suffered and sacrificed for the realization of a free society. Local institutions should be renamed not after "new heroes" but in a manner that restores dignity to victims and the community as a whole.

Some Closing Thoughts

Truth requires a breaking of the code of silence so that painful experiences can be expressed, a shared understanding of what took place can be achieved, and responsibility can be accepted for the suffering that has been caused. Restorative justice requires an agreement between survivors and perpetrators on some form of restitution. Such acknowledgment and empowerment make forgiveness possible, which, in turn, allows healing and reconciliation.

When we finally embrace reconciliation, it is because we realize that our pain comes from a limited understanding of reality, from not appreciating the psychological forces which have led to hatred and violence. We have not been able to rise above the battlefield to understand the fear that has motivated our own and others' behavior, the wounds that have fueled the violence. By choosing to view ourselves as victims, we have created more pain. People at peace within themselves do not seek to hurt, victimize or murder; only those who carry the burden of unhealed wounds, who feel impoverished, victimized and vulnerable within themselves are likely to perpetrate more violence. Acts of violence are the projections of fear and guilt which we attempt to suppress or deny lest we feel more pain. We find a target to dump it on, and this target becomes our enemy and the repository for all that we cannot accept about ourselves. Then our enemy is likely to return the favor by projecting their fears and attacking back. This is why violence begets violence; instead of taking responsibility for our past and looking at our part in the perpetuation of violence, we direct our hatred toward the other.

The evil face of the enemy is an externalization of the viciousness of the enmity that rages inside us. In order to reduce our conflicts in the outside world, we have to confront successfully the internal conflict that unleashes our own destructive energy. In order to move toward transcendence of those boundaries that fragment humankind, we must "bridge the gulf that cleaves the human psyche" (Schmookler, 1988: 250).

This is where forgiveness plays a critical role. As long as we maintain that all our problems are out there in the world, we remain on the course of destruction. Only when we can acknowledge that the roots of anger, hatred and violence lie within us can we pave the road toward peace. Yes, there are real threats and danger in the world, but just as violence can be cycled into a system at any time, so can peace. Just as trauma can create wounds that lead to vicious cycles of revenge, so too can a sincere movement for healing and reconciliation lead to cultures of peace. What is required of us as peacemakers is a coming to terms with our own human imperfections.

Reconciling with our inner demons through facing our guilt and shame shifts our relationship to the world in a more productive direction. When we deeply understand that all of us are capable of committing terrible crimes, that no one is immune to acting violently, we can deal with the actions of others in a more humane way. Peace will come only from those who accept our human condition with humility. This is the spiritual task that lies before us and that provides the opportunity to build a more durable peace.

Then what is reconciliation? It is not only about building a bridge toward others with whom we have been in conflict. It is about building a bridge within our own psyche and healing the wounds within us. It is embracing our wholeness by integrating all the different aspects of our hearts and minds. Only to the extent that we can achieve this within ourselves can we bring about reconciliation and a harmonious integration of our larger society.

The basic lesson is that the larger the gap there is within us, the shakier the foundation on which to build relationships with others. Without knowing the truth of our experience and what we feel, we cannot feel compassion toward others. If we cannot embrace our own true emotions, we will not be capable of opening our hearts to others. In not feeling, we deny knowing the truth about ourselves. We cannot trust ourselves if we do not know the truth about ourselves, and without trust in ourselves we cannot trust others. Knowing the truth and building trust is at the core of developing human bonds. Without that we cannot build the bridge of reconciliation. Without understanding why our differences bring out so much intolerance and destructiveness, we will be unlikely to know how to reconcile. If we look at the problem as being only between us and not within us, we will never come to a lasting solution of our difficulties.

When we reconcile, we transcend our boundaries to create a larger whole, reaching toward unity with others. Only when we come from a place of humility can we prepare ourselves to connect with something larger than ourselves. For many, there is a sense that it is not "I" who is doing this but a greater, more powerful reality that brings along with it a vast sense of peacefulness. This "something greater than ourselves" is what the spirit of forgiveness is about, and forgiveness is a prerequisite for reconciliation. Only when we can forgive ourselves for being what we are and embrace all of who we are will we be able to forgive one another and be open to constructive transformation. The greatest tragedy of humanity may be that the wounds that history has inflicted on us make us all vulnerable to inflicting the same violence and pain on others. When we worship strength for such destruction, we have lost touch with what can bring us true or sustainable security. Stopping these self-perpetuating patterns requires ongoing psychological or spiritual transformation in our global society.

Reconciliation may serve as a collective form of forgiveness. It requires that we let go of the past to build a future, to put aside our anger and hatred and to practice mercy for the greater good. In order to make the leap over the fence of hatred to a new place of abiding hope, a community must come to recognize that there is a better way than violence. How much pain and suffering we must go through before this is recognized, we do not know. One thing is sure: reconciliation through truth, restorative justice, forgiveness and healing is not just an option in the twenty-first century. It is necessary for our survival.

Notes

1. Dullah Omar, the minister of justice, spoke of the formation of the Truth and Reconciliation Commission as "A pathway, a stepping stone toward the historic bridge . . . whereby our society can leave behind the past of a deeply divided society characterized by strife, conflict, untold suffering and injustice, and commence the journey toward a future founded on the recognition of human rights, democracy, peaceful co-existence, and development opportunities for all South Africans irrespective of color, race, class, belief or sex" (Hansard, 1995: 1339-40).

2. Pope John Paul II emphasized this: "The command to forgive does not precede the objective demands of justice, but justice in the correct sense of the word is actually the ultimate aim of forgiveness" (Encyclical XIV, quoted in Bronkhorst, 1995: 41).

3. As ANC MP Willie Hoffmeyr explained, "We had to accept very early on that we would not get complete justice. In the negotiation process, several compromises had to be made, and I would defend them very strongly in the interests of peace in this country. We could have chosen the revolution and overthrow route, but we chose the negotiation route, and that means having to live and work with and rebuild the country together with people who have treated us very badly in the past and against whom we have very strong feelings" (Graybill, 1996: 258).

4. Kadar Asmal, a key architect of the TRC stated, "We must deliberately sacrifice the formal trappings of justice, the courts and the trials, for an even higher good: truth. We sacrifice justice, because the pains of justice might traumatize our country or affect the transition. We sacrifice justice for truth so as to consolidate democracy, to close the chapter of the past and to avoid confrontation" (Hansard, 1995).

5. Jorge Correa (1992), who served as executive secretary of the Chilean TRC, comments that sending human rights violators to jail is not a very effective device because political motivation cannot be rehabilitated through special treatments. He believes that most of these people, once they have recovered political power, are likely to violate human rights again.

6. The philosopher Niebuhr (1941) has eloquently described this: "Where common memory is lacking, where men do not share in the same past there can be no real community, and where community is to be formed common memory must be created. . . . The measure of our distance from each other in our nations and our groups can be taken

by noting the divergence, the separateness and lack of sympathy in our social memories. Conversely the measure of our unity is the extent of our common memory."

7. Ariel Dorfman's Chilean play, *Death and the Maiden*, tells of a woman whose husband has been appointed to his country's Truth Commission. While she is busy in the kitchen someone who has been helped by her husband enters the house. She does not see him but recognizes his voice as that of the man who tortured and raped her when she was in detention. She holds a gun to him and is ready to kill him because he denies strenuously that he could have done this. His denial hit at the core of her being, at her integrity, her identity. Eventually he admits that he was the culprit, and, strangely, she lets him go (Tutu, 1999).

8. "To truly heal we must say our truth, not only our regret and pain but also what harm was caused, what anger, what disgust, and also what desire for self-punishment or vengeance was evoked in us" (Estes, 1995).

9. Winslow (1997) reports one Worcester youth capturing this sentiment succinctly when he compared his status with a former torturer who still retains his job and rank as a policeman: "Today he has stars on his shoulders, and I am nothing."

10. One of the most poignant examples was at the amnesty hearing of Jeff Benzein, where the notorious wet-bag method of suffocation was demonstrated. Benzein was challenged by many of his victims to admit to the cruelty he inflicted on so many people and to name others who took part in executing this torture.

11. There were 560 participants from the Khulumani Victim Support Group, including mainly survivors, family members and some representatives of community organizations. The ratio of men to women was approximately one to five, from black residential areas in four provinces, balanced between rural and urban, where high levels of conflict had occurred. The report does not claim to represent the views of all victims. Most of the participants involved have had interaction with the TRC; therefore, the views expressed represent those of relatively more informed and politicized survivors. If they express confusion about the TRC process, most likely this confusion is more heightened in other provinces.

III
The Innovative Problem-Solving
Workshop

9
Sharing the Experience of Citizens' Diplomacy with Partners in Conflict

Edy Kaufman

The two following chapters present a practical application of well-researched collaborative problem-solving methods to deal with the world's conflicts, including political, ethnic, religious or local. In the literature on these sometimes intractable issues, words such as "resolution," "reduction," "management," "regulation," "transformation," "dissolution," "settlement," and "containment" are all used to illustrate different preferred outcomes of problem-solving exercises. The methods of dealing with conflict consist of mainly two types:[1] resolution or transformation, and settlement or containment. This book is concerned with the former, stressing cooperation through information sharing, relationship building, and joint analysis to address the root causes of conflict. We are of the school that seeks resolution, because if underlying causes are not dealt with in a settlement, another conflict can spring up where the first one left off.

Track-two diplomacy has been developed mainly in the United States for this purpose. I have found that the term "track two" often has a different connotation in the South, however, referring to unofficial negotiations by a small political elite. "Citizens' diplomacy," as used in the title of this chapter, is the term preferred particularly by my Latin American colleagues,[2] prominent civil society activists who use these techniques to empower them both in generating advice for the elite and for engaging in grassroots-level dispute resolution.

The practices outlined in this section for conducting innovative problem solving workshops (IPSWs)[3] are offered as one model for working with unofficial citizen representatives of the parties as "Partners in Conflict." They are designed to facilitate resolution of a conflict based on transformation of the parties' perceptions and attitudes, and on addressing not only potential elements for settlement of the present dispute but also its underlying causes through a reconstruction of the relationship between the parties (Bloomfield, 1995). Complementary to classical diplomacy, second track or citizens' diplomacy is considered an effective means especially for dealing with protracted communal conflicts—prolonged identity-driven disputes accompanied by fluctuating and sometimes high levels of violence. It is difficult to convey in writing the richness and validity of this type of program, and we are aware of no other attempt to present it in such detail.[4]

What brings us to share some of our learning experiences is a sense of urgency in the desire of those who have participated in the workshops to have written materials to build on in furthering the process of conflict resolution in their communities. Workshops have been held by and with Partners in Conflict from Middle Eastern civil society as well as from Central Asia, the Caucasus, Southeast Asia, Africa and Latin America.

I have been eager to disseminate our IPSW model also for personal reasons. My experiences working in the 1980s with fellow Israelis and Palestinians at the Truman Institute for the Advancement of Peace in the Hebrew University of Jerusalem made it clear how vital this information could have been for maximizing the effectiveness of our work. During this time, and throughout the first *Intifada* (Palestinian uprising), we managed to maintain a sustained dialogue between the two parties, without any professional tools save our sensitivity, sense of equality and respect, and political judgment. I believe that in returning to Jerusalem now after developing facilitation skills in track-two diplomacy as developed in the United States, I am better able to help those who are committed to renewing or moving forward a difficult peace process. This chapter thus represents a lateral transfer of expertise from my work as a scholar-practitioner in the Israeli-Palestinian conflict (South-South transfer of experiences), which has been enriched by my work elsewhere while based at the University of Maryland's Center for International Development and Conflict Management.

The term "Partners in Conflict" is intended to underline a common identity among participants in our workshops, such as a shared occupation or profession (e.g., academics, journalists), attributes (e.g., gender, religion), mutual concerns (e.g., environment, development), or common region (e.g., Caucasus, Middle East, Andean countries). This common identity must be based on dimensions different from those that are used to characterize the conflict (such as ethnicity, religion, language, and territory). When a peace accord has been reached and the participants are brought together to assist in its implementation and sustainability, we have referred to them as "Partners in Peace" (e.g., Israelis and Palestinians in the late 90's; Northern Ireland Catholics and Protestants).

The program of exercises for Partners in Conflict[5] (hereafter called "Partners") is for the purpose of building bridges across sometimes wide divides, by stressing commonalties. It is also meant to develop an "epistemic community"—a group of individuals who share collective understanding relating to their own issues and problems. Emphasizing commonalities and a shared identity while acknowledging basic differences encourages the establishment of a solid link between the two groups. An interesting example is bringing together people who live on each side of a border between countries in conflict. These individuals, in spite of their differences, share a certain frontier identity. Often ignored in the peace process, which is negotiated by diplomats and politicians in the capitals, these citizens can play a major role in the consolidation of a lasting peace.[6]

Such "team building" requires not only technical input. It goes much deeper, exploring ways for Partners to transform their relationships with one another by awakening empathy and learning to move from adversarial to collaborative attitudes. It is not our purpose to erase the border between groups in conflict, as this would only make conflict resolution more difficult to achieve. As Rouhana (1995) argues, "The strength in the new relationship between the two teams is based on each team's unshakable group identity and commitments" (see also Kelman, 1993).

In the following pages we highlight a sample day-to-day curriculum that has been developed over a decade of experimentation. For each topic we explain the rationale and practical application of the IPSW approach. Often there is a degree of skepticism in trying alternative dispute-resolution methods, either from pragmatists who come from a *realpolitik* school of thought (e.g., Bercovitch, 1984; Zartman and Touval, 1985) or from those suspicious that it may be a "group therapy" approach, not seen as having much value outside North American culture). To overcome this skepticism, we suggest sharing the program's rationale to provide transparency and encourage full participation.

In broad terms, the program moves from the establishment of a working relationship among the Partners to the establishment of a cooperative problem solving attitude, through building skills for a creative thinking process and then applying them to the concrete issues at stake (Deutsch, 1998). Transitions from one stage to another cannot be rigidly structured, because the rate of participants' progress determines the rhythm of the workshop. Further, this ambitious menu could be devoured in an intensive two weeks; however, in the face of financial and temporal constraints, selection is usually required. We simply provide an optimal IPSW, leaving to the creativity of the organizers the task of adapting it according to their needs and experience. Those readers who are anxious to begin experimenting with the workshop without familiarizing themselves with the *know-how* of workshop planning, may go straight to the *show-how*, beginning with the section entitled Day 1.

Preparations

The planning of a project in citizens' diplomacy starts with a needs assessment defining the issues at stake and the dynamics of the conflict to be addressed (see Gurr and Davies, this volume). Normally, this requires working with local Partners (co-organizers or cofacilitators) and a visit to the area to engage in dialogue with stakeholders and potential participants. The facilitators may explain the IPSW and its value as part of a longer-term process, and even provide a short demonstration.

Location

The meeting place for IPSW should have, if possible, an established tradition of peacemaking, lending an atmosphere that calls on the Partners to make meaningful contributions to the workshop. This is preferable to a modern hotel, which often masks rather than reflects the country one is in. Success in the workshop is directly related to the participants' state of mind, and having the proper surrounding conditions is not a trivial matter.

Near Jerusalem, for example, the Tantur Ecumenical Institute has become a symbol of dialogue and tolerance. It is located next to a check post, one gate facing Jerusalem and the other looking to Bethlehem in the West Bank. It is enough to see the landscape from the roof of the building to obtain a sense of the urgency in seeking solutions to a sad surrounding picture. In Italy, Santa Anna di Stazzema, the site of the assassination of more that 500 women and children by retreating Nazi troops, has been transformed into a welcoming National Peace Park.

A live-in setting too can often provide an intensive workshop environment that a nonresidential setting cannot (Cohen et al., 1977). Joint accommodations for Partners can be a source of trust building, but they must be planned carefully. Explicit criteria other than the conflict itself should be advanced for selecting who will share accommodations with whom, such as by gender, profession, or even lottery. I am reminded of a summer camp in Italy for Israeli and Palestinian teenagers, and the excitement of a fourteen-year-old boy from Tel Aviv about the fact that upon arrival he had been put in the same room as a Palestinian child. "I am sure Shamir [at that time prime minister of Israel] never slept with a Palestinian in same room," he told us.

The main meeting space should normally be arranged in a circle of chairs, with easy access and moveability as required. A circle is nearly universally appreciated as nondivisive, and it can expand to include all or shrink to keep people together when others may be absent. The facilitators should be seated in the circle with everyone else. A flipchart should be available.

Meals and parties are also important times for trust building, as they provide a friendly and unstructured setting for discussion; they may also be designated for small-group meetings or planning sessions. The Partners should also have common areas where they can spend nonorganized free time together.

A commitment should be made to absolute confidentiality, and the workshop location should enable this to be honored. Conducting the workshop in the city of residence of the participants is a source of disruption, even if it is safe. A resort or distant university campus generates a positive predisposition for experimenting and learning. Being away from the conflict and the Partners' usual places of living and working is strongly recommended, at least for the initial stage.

Level of Conflict

There has been much debate in the field about the best time to intervene in a conflict, and to what extent the conflict needs to have "matured" in order for these types of workshops to be effective. Does it need to be a manifest, rather than latent, conflict? Can the workshop be conducted before widespread violence erupts, or is it necessary to wait until hostilities become stalemated? This latter stage is the point at which parties to the conflict are likely to be most receptive, but preventive action is always the better option. Protracted communal conflicts, like those in Northern Ireland, Sri Lanka, or Israel/Palestine, are particularly suitable to this approach to conflict resolution. Our experience has been that IPSW can be used at different stages, with the objectives and techniques used adapted to the relevant conflict level. In more than one case unforeseen tragic events have occurred during the workshop, and it is better to plan in advance, based on a good needs assessment, how to respond to such crises.

While emphasis has been put on track-two diplomacy preceding official negotiations, it is also important to support track-one peacemaking with the more flexible collaborative problem-solving process. The Oslo accords between Israelis and Palestinians demonstrated the potential of such back-channel communication for stalemated official discussions (Kriesberg, 1996). The informal negotiations that preceded this agreement were eventually endorsed and worked out in detail through traditional diplomacy. At that time, peacebuilding efforts among members of the broader civil society were assumed to be no longer needed but were recognized as a priority once more after Yitzhak Rabin's assassination and threats to the lives of Hosni Mubarak and Yasser Arafat from extremists in their own societies (Kriesberg, 1996).

We have also experimented successfully with IPSW in border disputes that have been latent, as with our Ecuadorian/Peruvian Partners at the prenegotiation stage following their 1995 war, during track-one negotiation and postpeace accord. Even when violence is sporadic and of low intensity, it can help the cause of peace if the weaker side or "underdog" (very few conflicts are among contenders of equal weight) is at least recognized as a proper partner for informal dialogue and has an opportunity to respond to pressures from the other side.

The IPSW workshop can also be applied to "ethnic tensions" at a level below what is recognized as ethnic conflict. However, the Los Angeles riots and more frequent incidents of violence in Jerusalem are not separate issues so much as points on a spectrum. The methods described here are pertinent to both.

The degree of maturity of the conflict determines, in part, the selection of exercises. If no face-to-face contacts have occurred, for example, more work needs to be invested in ice-breaking and trust-building aspects in the initial stages. In the words of Patrick Regan (1996), "although characteristics of the conflict affect the probability of success, policy makers seeking to maximize this probability would do better to focus on how to intervene rather than when."

Types of Participants

The IPSW training lends itself best to candidates from similar sectors of the competing groups. Their status may range from influential formal or informal policy advisers and public figures to professional groups (journalists, educators, young diplomats) and grassroots activists (representatives of human rights organizations, trade unions, students). An ideal participant for second track diplomacy would be someone who is close enough to the center of power to have some sort of influence over decision makers, political elite, and/or public opinion, without suffering the downside of being constrained by an official position in the governing structure (Rouhana and Kelman, 1994).

Collaborative problem solving is not as strong an option for official diplomacy, because policy makers are generally too aware of their constituencies to risk going through an open-ended process of change, or to role-play or otherwise engage closely with adversaries. Exceptional cases do occur, but in general, the approach does not appeal to officials.[7] However, in the post-Cold War era, military and diplomatic forces in peacekeeping operations or in border areas with guerrillas or paramilitary forces need to utilize dispute-resolution techniques to placate the tensions endemic to such regions. Within this scope, collaborative problem solving is indispensable as a supplement to governmental mediation efforts.

The program is applicable to Partners in domestic as well as international or ethnopolitical disputes. Examples from our experience include convening the proponents and opponents of separating schools for speakers of the Kazakh and Russian languages; the World Bank's and Inter-American Development Bank's ambitious plan of education reform in Bolivia, opposed by the strong teachers' unions; the militant taxi drivers' and indigenous groups' strike in Ecuador against government gasoline price increases; and the debate between the government and the church in Peru on the use of contraceptives. Other interstate issues suitable for second track workshops include control over common-pool resources such as rivers, aquifers and international waterways, and other ecological disputes.[8]

It is also possible to use these techniques for pedagogic purposes, attracting university students or other interest groups to normal classes or mock workshops. This is an excellent approach for broad-based skill building. Simulations require knowledge of the history of both societies and their conflict in order to generate serious and realistic solutions (Rouhana and Kelman, 1994). It may require more preparation to engage efficiently the participants in some aspects of role-playing, but this can be achieved within the structure of a regular class.[9]

The inclusion of a few "real" Partners in such simulations can add value for both sets of participants, with many points for cross-fertilization. At the University of Maryland, we have had exciting experiences involving our students in projects with their peers from Israel and Palestine, at College Park and in Jerusalem. In pluralistic societies one often finds local constituencies (in this case American Jews and Arabs) who identify with the actors of the distant conflict. This not only brings the dispute closer to home but also presents to the facilitator/teacher the challenge of developing empathy toward the perspectives of the other side as needed to bridge the gap between the Partners.[10]

Selection of Participants

To make sure that the best candidates are chosen from a large pool, it is important to rely on objective criteria and to avoid personal preferences. Before the selection process, consider what would be the optimum group composition, including "mirror" types from the two sides and the best balance of age, experience, gender, etc. of potential participants. Care is needed with ethnopolitical conflicts where there may be different cultural norms regarding roles of gender, age or occupation groups. Ensuring equal status and the ability of participants to meet over extended periods and under difficult circumstances are vitally important.

Particularly in cases where Partners are brought from areas of conflict to workshops held in affluent societies, additional motives for their traveling—such as sightseeing, shopping, and saving per diem stipends for families in precarious circumstances—cannot be ignored. To a large extent, these are legitimate secondary motives, and organizers may need to allow some free time for sightseeing, etc., before or after the workshop. At the same time, the facilitators must be sure that participants understand and are committed to the real purpose behind the workshop. They are not expected to attend a regular conference with papers and discussions, but they are expected to be open to new ideas, personal growth, and possible changes in their points of view. When selecting participants, it is difficult to evaluate attitudes and personalities via correspondence or telephone interviews. One "wrong" person can spoil an entire group. The best way to reduce this risk is through a personal, in-depth interview on location after a spoken and/or written presentation. Another advantage of face-to-face communication is that it is easier to obtain binding commitments from participants and to achieve personal relationships with them that will enhance facilitators' credibility (Cohen et al., 1977). If relevant organizations see third-party involvement in choosing participants as infringing their autonomy and insist on nominating the candidates, there should be careful discussion of criteria.

Rouhana and Kelman suggest several additional criteria for the choice of participants. First, those being selected should enjoy credibility in their own society or group. This allows them to pass on what they have learned to the communities they represent, thus giving the workshop legitimacy and impact. If Partners are to achieve such trustworthiness, they must share mainstream political views with their groups or societies. Within this range, it is advantageous to have a broad spectrum of outlooks, to enhance the realism of the workshop, while avoiding candidates who hold strong political or personal antagonisms toward each other. The organizers should strive to also secure participants whose knowledge, experience, and personal integrity will help them respect the other side (Rouhana and Kelman, 1994; Kelman, this volume; Cohen et al., 1977). While we find it more important to help rebuild the "negotiating middle," workshops including more enlightened representatives of two more polarized parties may work within these criteria.

We have stressed the need to select candidates who are in a sense already Partners in spite of the divide between them, in that they share one attribute already. We have also been successful bringing together matched sets of Partners from different professions or vocations. For example, a group of ten Ecuadorians and ten Peruvians we convened to deal with their border dispute included two environmentalists, two human rights activists, two heads of business organizations, two journalists, and two leading members of universities. Fairly early in the workshop they started to work across their divide in "affinity groups," which were later very valuable in the brainstorming and reentry stages of the project. The potential contribution of the Partners was recognized by both governments when five out of the twenty members of "Group Maryland" were "co-opted" into the official negotiations. Once the peace accords were concluded, some returned to our track-two efforts to build sustained support for the implementation of the agreements.

Number of Participants

The ideal number depends on many factors. In general, a small group of between ten and twenty members works best, including equal numbers from each side - if numbers are unequal then it is best to have the "underdog" over-represented. If there are three or more parties, some other criteria for balance may be important. For instance, in an international waterway dispute over the Nile River basin, with ten riparian states, it may be better to have a higher number of participants representing the key players, with percentages allocated based on the importance of the resource to each country. The total number of participants should not be lower than eight or greater than thirty. If the participants are together for an optimal period (fifteen days to a month or more) the facilitators can work more intensively with a core group and enlarge the number of Partners for special activities.

Despite any differences in the number of representatives, the consensus-building nature of the process ensures that all parties carry equal weight. No solutions are to be imposed on the weaker parties. At the same time, when brainstorming for policy-relevant solutions, participants are encouraged to take into account power politics and the real asymmetry of forces outside the workshop which are normal in conflict situations.

Organizers/Facilitators

The first generation of facilitators was raised in the United States and other Western countries. We are now increasingly finding facilitators from areas of conflict who are more familiar with the limits and possibilities in each case and with the specific regional cultures.

Criteria for facilitators include first, relevant personal expertise derived from practical experience. Second, they must be regarded as trustworthy ("honest brokers") by both sides to the conflict (Rouhana and Kelman, 1994). Third, facilitators' personal traits need to be considered, including need for control, need for structure, capacity for empathy, etc., since they will influence the management style of the workshop (Boardman and Horowitz, 1994).

Normally, facilitators, one or more as needed to ensure an adequate mix of relevant knowledge and experience, come from a third party. When anyone from a party to the conflict is included, the honest-broker criterion requires facilitators from both sides. They can often work better with each of the participating groups, as well as serving in specialized roles within the workshop, providing feedback and support to other facilitators, or serving as recorders. Facilitators may adopt a "process-content role division," where one focuses on the content of the discussion and another pays more attention to the interactions of the group and its dynamics.

They may adopt an active-passive approach, whereby one acts in a traditional role and others in a more passive role, mainly identifying with the Partners and thus providing necessary feedback (Auvine et al., 1978; Polzer, 1996). A staged approach to IPSW may start with organizers/facilitators assigning responsibilities to cofacilitators, chosen as the most suitable and interested among the participants.

At minimum, local advisers from the area of conflict should be involved in preparing the program. I have seen facilitators ask participants to hold hands, or take deep breaths and stretch. This may be useful, but unless it fits the context of culturally relevant experience, it may be rejected outright as superficial and thus reflect negatively on the entire project.

On the other hand, each culture will have its own customs that are worth using; for instance, working with Partners from the Caucasus made us familiar with the institution of a *tamada*. This involves having a "toastmaster" walk around the room at a meal or celebration, speaking to a number of good causes and honoring different people. Such traditions can be valuable in providing messages of unity in diversity and for reducing tensions among participants.

It is preferable that facilitators be chosen who have lived in foreign countries for a time, preferably in the region of the participants, and that they speak a foreign language, even if the exercises are conducted in English. A facilitator who has not only been exposed to but interacted with other cultures tends to have a less limited perspective of the conflict at hand and to be perceived by participants as open-minded.

Even with support from cofacilitators, facilitators should keep their own diaries as they work, so that they can add their real-time thoughts to the ongoing process of evaluation. They should also be aware of participants' interactions, not only during the formal sessions but throughout other socializing opportunities. This is not a nine-to-five job. We have found that appointing one of our team members (preferably with similar ethnic background to the Partners) to be in charge of personal and social issues that come up during the workshop helps to improve relations among the Partners.

Duration

This model IPSW fifteen-day workshop is offered as optimal but will need to be adapted to cultural contexts and real-life demands. We have been able to host Partners anywhere from two days to several months. Hence the model is offered as a manual, or cookbook, from which facilitators should prepare their own menu, selecting recipes according to their needs assessment, type of participants, level and stage of conflict, etc. A systematic review of all aspects can determine the time to spend on each phase: trust building, skill building, consensus building, and reentry. Usually, it is advisable to plan for two or three consecutive workshops in the period of a year or so—possibly one in a third party's country, followed by one in each of the Partners' states, or in a border area, with equal time between sides. Such cases allow us to use the first workshop to socialize the participants into the general ideas behind the IPSW and to prepare a specific agenda for dealing with the specific conflict in subsequent workshops. To continue the first activity with subsequent face-to-face gathering is crucial for sustained commitment.

In this manual the days are not divided into sessions, since the timing must be decided according to the circumstances and types of participants, and must be sensitive to the progress being made. It may be necessary to improvise and slow down the process. The sequence of stages, such as moving from training steps to immersion in the participants' own conflict, is what counts.

Frequently a tendency exists among participants to pressure the facilitators to "come to the point" and deal with the specific conflictive issues that brought them together. While sympathizing with this sense of urgency, facilitators do need to secure feedback that indeed most are ready to use their acquired skills to deal effectively with their own disputes. In general, the period of training should cover about a third of the initial workshop. Ample time must be allocated for the Partners to absorb the material and social experiences, and to feel comfortable. Coffee and smoking breaks should be allowed every one and a half hours or so, since if participants have to break ranks and leave the room individually, this could disrupt their rapport and the intensity of their work.

Preparation of the Participants and Facilitators

The participants should have a fairly good picture of what is expected of them when they arrive, and if more than one are from the same place, they should meet prior to the workshop, with the facilitators if possible. When such a visit has not been possible, we have at times been able to communicate with the help of video-conferencing equipment, arranged through the U.S. Information Service. On such occasions, we were able to speak *separately to each team* about technical details (location, weather, and degree of informality) and the role that the Partners would be expected to play, and to secure agreement on the ground rules. After having shared a draft program, we asked for suggestions and/or clarifications. It is important that if a visit is paid to meet with some of the Partners, the facilitators make every effort to meet with the other Partners as well (Rouhana and Kelman, 1994).

In cases of asymmetries between Partners' levels of international experience, negotiation skills, or language fluency (the workshop may be held in a common foreign language, such as English, Russian or French), the organizers should empower the weaker side with some previous training,. Separate intraparty meetings may be required in situations of extreme hostility and violence, to build trust before the intergroup work.

We have frequently been asked if it is appropriate for the participants to meet government representatives (such as foreign ministry officers) for a preliminary briefing. We have tended to discourage this, unless we know it is an option available to both sides and that the officials will share information about related track-one negotiations without requiring the Partners to restrict themselves to the official positions. Nonetheless, often the authorities not only need to know about the workshop but also may deter their own nationals from participating without prior authorization.

The organizing team and facilitators must prepare a well-thought-out program with an explicit agenda to share with the potential candidates. Any relevant feedback should be incorporated before the workshop begins. As Auvine instructed, "Know exactly what you want to accomplish and make sure everything on your agenda relates to that goal" (Auvine et al., 1978). He also offers a checklist of seven ground rules for the construction of an agenda. *First*, select content that is relevant for the group; *second*, present material in a logical order; *third*, plan the time and know what exercises to drop if the time runs short, or to include if there is time left over; *fourth*, plan the workshop's agenda so that there is a variety in pace; *fifth*, use different types of exercises involving all the senses; *sixth*, have a clearly defined beginning and end for the workshop as a whole and for every session; and *seventh*, do not forget to give the middle a meaning (Auvine et al., 1978).

Cofacilitators from parties involved in the dispute should be included in the planning of workshop activities earlier than other participants, since their feedback is usually crucial in setting up the program in a way that meets the needs and expectations of the participants.

Planning the Evaluation Process

Among the important issues to consider in project design are the standards by which a project is evaluated, who does the evaluation, and the extent to which it is a central part of implementation. The ARIA group (Rothman and Friedman, this volume) has developed interactive software that can help organizers check the internal consistency of goals between the facilitators, organizers, participants and funders.[11] In a nutshell, action evaluation is meant to provide real-time, ongoing evaluation during the project, following criteria developed jointly by the participants and facilitators, helping Partners take ownership of the process.

Unless an alternative has been decided on, there should be fifteen to twenty minutes at the end of each day for a short evaluation and debriefing. Responses to an instrument such as the "One-Minute Evaluation" (box 9.1) should be analyzed every night by the organizers and the most interesting comments reviewed the next morning.

Box 9.1 One-Minute Evaluation

1. What is the most useful/meaningful thing learned during this session?

2. What questions remain uppermost in your mind as we end this session?

Workshop Day 1: Getting to Know the Place and Each Other

This first day is about orientation. The Partners should be made familiar and comfortable with their surroundings and the procedures of the workshop. Participants should be shown about the premises and given some basic information. Visits as a whole group can be made to interesting nearby sites, or there can be a reception for the group at other institutions.

Being introduced as a group to others can generate interesting team-building dynamics among Partners. At this point, participants are perceived by others as a unified foreign team, whatever the cleavages among them. They are often identified by locals through a common attribute (e.g., the Middle Easterners, the Caucasians). The president of the University of Maryland, planning to give a short speech to Israeli and Palestinian students, told me that he could not find a clear physical distinction among them and asked if it was proper to mention this. Clearly, it was positive for the Partners to be recognized by their commonalities. In another workshop where Arab, Jewish, and African Americans worked together to encourage dialogue between their Israeli and Palestinian peers, they became the delegation from the University of Maryland, welcomed in Jerusalem as "the Americans," something they stressed afterward.

This may also be a time for uninational meetings, particularly if the participants from one or the other party did not have the opportunity to meet as a group previously. There may be strong grievances and deep mistrust toward the other side, and it may be important for the facilitators to hold a session with each side separately in order to give an opportunity to communicate such concerns and learn how best to address them during the workshop.

In addition to an inspirational introduction to the site, practical information should be provided about house rules, routines, facilities, etc., so that in the following days the participants can concentrate on the substance of the program.

The remainder of the first day should be open to allow for adaptation to the new environment. This generates opportunities for groups of different origins to come together informally, sharing meals, overcoming jet lag, reading material provided to them, talking with the organizers about the program, etc. This is important because once the workshop is fully under way, the atmosphere may become more intense as details about resolving the conflict are thrashed out, and lighter moments may not be so frequent.

Day 2: Getting to Know Each Other and the Program

Objective and Rationale of Trust Building

The introductory segment needs to be used by participants to familiarize themselves with each other's names, to discover similarities across the divide, and to set a participatory tone by encourage all participants to interact. Building trust is essential for a constructive workshop environment. This requires a breakdown of negative images, so that participants can enter into a critical dialogue.

There are many techniques available for the introduction of participants. Some traditional methods, such as simply stating names and affiliations, seem to be rituals to which people are not inclined to listen closely. Small nametags are not visible enough and may be perceived cross-culturally as a commercial gimmick. Instead of nametags, displaying a person's name on a large sign attached to a table tends to attract more attention. Even with some creativity, there is a limit to what formal introductions can do. The exercises below are designed to break the ice more effectively and to allow the Partners to begin to see some commonalities between them. Depending on the amount of time available, what is culturally appropriate, and the dynamics of the group, several of these ice-breakers should be used.[12] Some exercises are more appropriate for informal settings such as a relaxed dinner; others can be conducted within the classroom. Rather than telling the participants that they are about to conduct an "ice-breaker," since the word itself is a reminder of frozen or cold relationships, it is best to introduce it as "Getting to Know Each Other."

Regardless of the combination of exercises chosen, it is important to establish early the role of the facilitators as a tool for the Partners to ease any communication difficulties between them.[13] It should be made clear that the facilitators are not there to run the show but that the Partners themselves are responsible for doing the work and achieving results. The facilitators' own presentations in front of the group are critical for a healthy workshop environment. The facilitators should introduce themselves not only as "experts," with relevant experience that may validate their roles, but also as "people," in order to lay the foundations for an egalitarian atmosphere in the workshop (Auvine et al., 1978). One creative way to arrange the seating not according to the sides of the conflict, a natural tendency in the initial stages, is to suggest to the participants to find their place in the circle according to their birthday (ask who has been born during the current month, help order them according to the date and then ask the rest to find out by themselves where to sit, by talking to the others).

Getting to Know Each Other (Ice-breaker Exercises)

Interviews
We can start the day by asking each individual to interview another participant whom he did not previously know and then have each pair present each other to the group. (This suggestion presents less abrupt means of creating familiarity among the participants than asking individuals to introduce a member of the other team.) For the interview it has been suggested to ask: Who is he or she? Where does he or she work? What is one thing that it is not apparent about him or her? and What skill or ability does he or she bring to the workshop?

Introducing Your Neighbor (A Variation on the Theme)
The participants should be paired by number and asked to introduce themselves to their neighbors for a few minutes and prepare introductions of them for the group. Facilitators can provide some guidelines for the introductions, including characteristics relevant to the workshop. For example: What is it in his or her life

story that brought him or her to take an interest in conflict resolution? What position has he or she held in a governmental or nongovernmental organization? What are some pertinent activities in his/her home country?

Name Histories (A Personal Favorite)

This is best conducted over a meal or in another informal setting. We ask the Partners in turn to tell us all they know about the origins of their first and family names, and nicknames as well, if they so desire.[14] The best manner of applying this methodology is to ask if first names relate to a historic or religious figure, or an important relative, if the Partner was given a nickname and if he/she enjoys being called by it. The family name may have an interesting background, often related to a trade, place, or perhaps another fascinating story. Usually, even when some of the participants did know each other previously, in a superficial manner, they never had the chance to explore this part of their identities. A facilitator should take notes and provide some comments, stressing linkages and common trends between the names' backgrounds. More than once, one finds that the participants do indeed have shared names, based on common linguistic origins, as is prevalent in Semitic languages. Once the facilitators have completed the tour around the room, including the hosts, the Partners themselves should be encouraged to ask each other questions and contribute to an analysis of the revealed patterns.

This activity can bring out some interesting commonalities. In a gathering of Middle Easterners, we found out that the names of all nineteen participants, whether they were in Farsi, Turkish, Arabic, or Hebrew, had a historical or literal meaning behind them, often describing virtues that the holders of the name were proud to emulate in their own lives (the Just, the Compassionate, the Generous, the Happy, the Grateful, the Blessed).

Ups and Downs (Another Personal Favorite)

This activity requires that participants who share an announced attribute (e.g., women) stand up, while the rest of the group remains seated and applauds. Then the inverse occurs. We usually spend fifteen to twenty minutes finding out many unknown shared qualities or characteristics, such as first-generation university graduates, places of birth, religions, numbers of siblings (up to twelve or fourteen sometimes), marital status, number of children, languages, travels abroad, etc. Those who are left standing together with an impressive accomplishment (such as speaking eight languages) should get a round of applause. Facilitators can opt for stressing a certain order that will give more salience to the "underdog." This can be done by praising those with the higher numbers of siblings (calling for those who are the only child to stand up; one brother/sister, two, three, up to five, up to ten) or newcomers (asking for those who are three or more generations in the country to stand up, two, first generation; or third or more university graduates, two or first generation to rise). In the end, we ask the participants if there are any questions they would like to pose to the group. Sometimes they are interested to learn who is a vegetarian, or left-handed, but in other cases the search for common denominators includes painful experiences such as a relative lost in the war/confrontation, or having been a prisoner. In each instance, the facilitators need to think how to ask sensitive questions while at the same time maximizing the power of this exercise.

On one occasion, after going through some initial ups and downs, we asked Partners from Palestinian and Israeli universities to stand up if they had been born in a village or agricultural settlement. Then we asked those born in a city to rise, and then an additional question for those born in Jerusalem. We found ourselves clapping for a small group of young Israelis and Palestinians who felt united in their recognition by the others. To what extent this little moment helped for the later brainstorming session on the future of Jerusalem is hard to say, but it definitely created a productive atmosphere for subsequent discussions on the subject.

After completing this exercise, some time should be spent speaking about the importance of recognizing overlapping identities, and how in a situation of violence people tend to be defined only by one attribute that separates them (almost always nationality or ethnicity). When the Partners start to communicate with each other in the workshop, they soon find that they share much more than they had assumed, so that it becomes difficult always to pigeonhole each other into a dichotomy of one collective against another. In most nonviolent environments, we are inclined to recognize several important dimensions of our identities. To illustrate the variety of overlapping loyalties that people tend to develop in pluralistic societies, a definition of diversity such as that used by our diversity program at the University of Maryland might be circulated and discussed:

> Diversity is "otherness," or those human qualities that are different from our own and outside the groups to which we belong, yet are present in other individuals and groups. It is important to distinguish between the primary and secondary dimensions of diversity. Primary dimensions are the following: age, ethnicity, gender, physical abilities/qualities, race, and sexual orientation. The secondary dimensions of diversity are those that can be changed and include but are not limited to: educational background, geographic locations, income marital status, military experience, parental status, religious beliefs, and work experience.

While this definition calls for respect of differences, facilitators should stress the unifying elements and the value of attaching importance to more than one of these identities, such as gender, across the ethnic divide. For the participants it is perfectly all right to express a strong unifying identity (normally national or ethnic); at the same time it is also all right to explore other shared identities with the Partners that cross the divide. In principle, questions for "ups and downs" can include any of the parameters in the definition, but facilitators must remain sensitive to the Partners' cultures. For example, asking heterosexuals or homosexuals to stand up is not appropriate in most contexts. Discussion of explicit criteria behind the exercise is recommended to explain why certain qualities are not used, at least for the present (Auvine et al., 1978).

First Jobs

Another simple but user-friendly ice-breaker is to ask participants to share what were their first jobs. Offering one of the facilitators' experiences first and going round the room generates a warm climate and often stresses a commonality of humble origins or creative occupations.

Cultural Treasure Hunting

This icebreaker allows fifteen to twenty minutes for each person to wander around the room, talking to the others, and drawing out commonalities (hobbies, musical preferences or playing abilities, month of birthday). A gratifying outcome of the use of this exercise occurred when a Palestinian participant discovered he shared the same birthday as an Israeli woman. The resulting bond became very special, with the woman later offering the man home hospitality over a couple of days when he had to postpone his flight back home because of sudden heart problems. A second illustration of the success of this technique came out of a workshop near Quito, wherein two leaders of indigenous groups on both sides of the Peruvian/Ecuadorian disputed area met for the first time. When the two presented their seventh shared commonalty, they said, "We both feel that if, instead of the central governments, we were to have been asked to resolve the conflict, we would have done it long ago and at a much lesser price."

Name and Hobby

Fun for young people: we stand in a circle, and the first person gives his/her first name and illustrates with a movement his/her hobby (basketball, piano, reading, etc.). The second repeats the name and hobby of the first and adds his/her name and hobby, the third includes the previous two and adds his/her own. The more we move on, the more difficult it is to remember; the other participants help the introducing person to remind him/her with their signs and body language. It is a nice, unplanned team effort.

Jokes

In some extroverted cultures it may be worth suggesting an evening sharing jokes, humor being potentially a powerful means to overcome inhibitions and deal with stereotypes. In the Latin American context, I was amazed to see the degree of openness and self-exposure involved in the national, ethnic and gender jokes shared.

Presentation of the Program

Objective and Rationale

The introduction to the program should be detailed and include discussion, making sure the ground rules are fully comprehended and accepted. Sharing the rationale behind the agenda is crucial for setting the right mood behind each activity, and it should be repeated as often as necessary. The need to be engaged in a learning mode prior to beginning the actual problem solving must be stressed. The approach to introducing the subject ought to promote a predisposition in the participants to open up to new ideas in the field, as well as to personal growth. At this stage, a few minutes should be put aside to acquaint the Partners with the basics of collaborative problem solving, the rules for consensus, and the adaptation of dissenters (all are explained below).

Why Do It?

The Partners may be wondering what they will gain from this workshop. We suggest listing the following five expected short-term outcomes. Firstly, they will be learning new skills which can be advantageous in private and/or public life. Secondly, links will be strengthened with others across conflict lines. Thirdly, the experimentation with problem solving will lead to the search for solutions, which ideally can be conveyed to policy makers and/or to the public at large. Fourthly, at a more intimate level, this may lead to personal transformation and new perceptions or attitudes toward the present adversary and toward conflict in general. Fifthly, the follow-up after reentry allows options for new activities that may open up new possibilities in professional lives and voluntary activities.

In general, a useful way to present the material is to request cooperation from the Partners for learning beneficial life skills and in giving the facilitators feedback on whether this process could be made to work in their own societies and environments, and on whether they want to, or may be able to, use this in their own right as educators or facilitators. For purposes of evaluating the achievements of the workshop at the concluding stage (day fifteen) we can also encourage the Partners to write for themselves their revised expectations from the workshop, now that the "deal" is clearer in their mind. An even better way to get the participants involved in the process is through the use of "action evaluation," a method conceived by Ross and Rothman (1999; Rothman and Friedman, this volume), where the goals are interactively determined and articulated together with the participants, as they evolve during the workshop and longer-term follow-up activities.

This may also be a time to say a few inspirational words, making all aware of the uniqueness of the opportunity as well as its timeliness. Though culturally bounded, and perhaps superfluous in some low-context societies, it is always good to find some metaphors or expressions in the local language or traditions that can help the facilitators to reach out from the beginning.

A Note on Facilitation

One should not explain all the logic of the exercises before they are done, so as to prevent the participants being influenced by expectations and to allow them to discover how they act on their own. A post-facto examination is necessary, since we are working with people who are potential multipliers of these techniques. The premium time for this is briefly at the end of each day. In terms of personal transformation, introspection and self-assessment is left to individuals, although they may be encouraged to reflect out loud at a summing-up and evaluation session at the end of the entire program.

Often, participants will ask when discussion of their own conflict will begin. Only once the whole group is impatient is it time to move to the next phase. We avoid focusing prematurely on the Partners' conflict, by making the transition gradual. Facilitators can give examples from their experiences in other workshops.

If it is not yet time to start the search for consensus on innovative solutions, one way of bringing the discussion home is by asking participants to give examples from their own conflict while still in the trust-building or skills-building stages of the IPSW. The idea here is to avoid premature closure, or exposing Partners to more challenging situations without first obtaining deeper knowledge of the principles and techniques of conflict resolution. The move from conceptual understanding of the field to working together toward solutions can begin as soon as the facilitators sense it is appropriate.

When the threat of violence at home is high, it is essential to tackle the issue a priori, so that an unforeseen act (terrorist bombing, massive killings by soldiers) will not wreck the entire exercise. Not long ago, we had a workshop with Egyptians, Israelis, Jordanians, and Palestinians in the Sinai the same day that Israeli bulldozers began to turn the earth to build at Har Homa on the Palestinians' Jebel Abu Ghnaiem land. We were all concerned about an outbreak of violence, particularly a Palestinian professor from Bir Zeit University. We discussed how we would react were anything to happen, and this professor monitored the news during every break. Nothing dramatic occurred, and the workshop continued. A few weeks later I witnessed, as a participant in a Middle East second track meeting in Helsinki, just the opposite take place. A few hours after beginning we heard the news about a bombing in a Tel Aviv cafe. We Israelis took in the news from all possible sources, including calling our families. Some participants wanted the meeting to continue, business as usual; others suggested that an Egyptian former diplomat and myself prepare a text expressing concern and based on commonly agreed principles. However, the atmosphere was too confrontational, and it was enough that one participant opposed such moves to prevent us going ahead. The lesson learned is that when the likelihood of disrupting acts is high, it makes sense to prepare the Partners up front for such an eventuality, rather than be shocked and disheartened by it and have the entire exercise made unproductive. The need to learn how to share the grief of the other when violence and terror occur in real-time situations needs to be incorporated into the IPSW (as discussed more fully below under the section on "acknowledgment and healing").

Finally, the facilitators should also consider the possibility of granting a certificate or diploma of participation or successful conclusion of the IPSW to the participants, if this works as an incentive and is appropriate to the nature of the workshop. Such an action brings a sense of cooperative pride, can help in fostering a sense of achievement that can be shared by all the participants, and breeds a feeling of togetherness.

Introducing Facilitation

Depersonalizing the facilitators' own roles in the workshop can be helped by introductory remarks on the role of facilitation, stressing widely recognized standards for such functions. It is worth explaining the different levels of third-party intervention, which range from early neutral evaluation to conciliation, facilitation, mediation, nonbinding arbitration, and, for official processes only, to power mediation, settlement conferences, and binding arbitration. It should be explained that facilitators are expected to play a much more proactive role than the traditional function of chairperson or moderator. I sometimes recycle a story learned from Bill Ury in the context of creative thinking but adapted to the role of the facilitator.

An old Bedouin at the verge of departing from this world calls his three sons and tells them of his will to leave to the older half of his camels, one-third to the middle and one-ninth to the youngest among them. They promise to respect his wish, but when he dies the counting of the camels totals seventeen, and they get into a futile argument and fail to divide the possessions as promised. At this time, a wise camel driver comes along and inquires as to the nature of the dispute. He then tells the sons: "Take my camel." First, the sons feel embarrassed about dispossessing the poor camel driver of his camel, but he insists, and then something unexpected takes place. The older takes his half (nine), the second his third (six) and the younger his ninth (two)—totaling seventeen. The experienced old "facilitator" takes off with his camel and tells the sons: "Perhaps you can now solve problems by yourself."

Partners should be encouraged to pay close attention to the methods of facilitation. When the Partners are back in their own countries, if they want to organize similar IPSWs, using the arts of facilitation will be necessary, and it is best that they try them as fully and early as possible. This includes motivating participation, eliciting alternatives, welcoming different points of view, setting an example of sensitive listening, maintaining an equal-time principle for the participants who wish to speak, summarizing ideas while stressing common ground, initiating and ending meetings on a positive note, etc. It is useful to have a handout on facilitation ready, since many participants consider themselves as potentially filling such a role. Occasionally, if there is good progress during the workshop, we have encouraged Partners to take over a session and cofacilitate with others. This experiment provides a team-building effort and consolidates the skills learned.

Facilitation may be very proactive, and perhaps it is best to be up front about it. Facilitators coming from other areas of conflict where negotiations have been successful (such as in South Africa and, for a while at least, the Israeli/Palestinian conflict) may bring added legitimacy and may use it to take more active leadership in moving Partners ahead more quickly. I sometimes apologize in advance for what may amount, at times, to hyperactive behavior on my part. If we build trust, such well-intentioned excesses can be understood by the participants and forgiven.

Humor and entertainment may be used by facilitators and are often beneficial in several ways, such as tension release, face saving, and as a means to reduce threat levels. However, the facilitators must be careful with the use of humor. Timing, ethical considerations, and power balance, as well as one's own limitations need to be considered (Wimmer, 1994).

Debriefing is a unique opportunity for the facilitator to make transparent to the Partners the meaning of each exercise performed. Given the experiential nature of the workshop and the tendency to avoid lengthy introductory lectures, the purpose here is to get the help of the participants in making explicit the implicit learning that may or may not have fully clicked in everybody's minds. We want them to take ownership of the process both in terms of being able to replicate the activity back home as well as in becoming convinced that we are using adequate vehicles to build trust, skills and eventually consensus.

Last but not least, facilitators should help simplify the process by which Partners bring insights and skills developed over the course of the workshop back to their communities. Toward this end, facilitators should make explanations easily understood, so that Partners will have the ability to conduct their own workshops.

This is best done when two cofacilitators, one from each party, can do the job. Such cofacilitation is a phenomenon that has taken off with some Israeli Jewish and Arab facilitators who have decided to use their experience together. The legitimacy they have in pressing for tangible results for the workshop is much higher, though it may take a while to establish their record as honest brokers.

A valuable way to end the day is for participants to fill out a One-Minute Evaluation form (box 9.1) and to be asked for any last thoughts or questions. This form may be presented at the start or end of each following day, providing a constant participatory evaluation process that is of utmost importance to the success of the workshop. While the friendships, attitude changes, and insights that the Partners may gain from this experiment are important both for themselves and for the promotion of a conflict resolution perspective, the evaluation forms contribute to the practical success of the workshop itself. They do so by giving the facilitators information on what was effective and what was not during the day's exercises, and on what should be added, changed or cut altogether. Although this evaluation and adaptation step is not listed again at the end of each day's activities, it should nonetheless be remembered as an integral daily part of any successful workshop.

A reentry workshop, when the Partners meet for a second time or more, still requires some Day 2 ice-breakers, and allowance for airing the many grievances that may have accumulated in the interim. We can have a session in which people can speak their minds, most likely in an adversarial manner. It might be programmed as "Status of the Peace Process" or, as was done in a reentry workshop after the outbreak of the Al Aqsa *Intifada* in 2001, as "What Went Wrong" (WWW).

Day 3: Conflict Resolution in Theory and Practice

Once the Partners are fully immersed in the spirit of the location, have warmed up to one another, and understand the rules of the IPSW, the facilitators can proceed to a systematic presentation of the methods to be used and map it within the general area of alternative or appropriate dispute resolution (ADR). Exceptionally, given the experiential nature of our work, at this time, as we move toward skills building, we need to make a persuasive presentation of our underlying philosophy as well as the concrete product toward which the workshop is directed.

Introductory Lecture

Rationale and Methodology

This presentation should be structured according to the facilitators' own approach. As a rule of thumb, more time should be spent on prognosis (possibilities for resolution) than on diagnosis (historical roots of the conflict). Playing back the video of the long history of fighting is not going to change the script, and while it is important at times to let participants express their adversarial feelings, the process that we are about to experiment with is essentially forward looking. The lecture need not be brief, and Partners should be encouraged to raise questions or comments. One can elicit interaction by making reference to common preconceptions or controversial statements they may have heard.

Outline of a Sample Lecture

Information on the dynamics of complex conflicts, and the history, process and applications of collaborative problem solving can be drawn from several of the chapters in this volume. Some points that I feel are important to include are:

1. Conflict can be seen as a constructive or destructive driving force, mostly depending on how it is managed. The term "transformation" should be distinguished from resolution, management, reduction, and termination (though in the workshop we may use them as synonyms). "Transformation" is most suitable for our IPSW method, since the expectation is to influence an attitudinal change and provide tools to help both sides cope with the tensions and problems arising along the road to reconciliation..

2. To help Partners understand how conflict can be viewed constructively, when culturally suitable, I have used sex as an analogy to conflict. Exceptionally, some individuals can sublimate or refrain from sex, but both sex and conflict are natural phenomena. Rather than repress them, the aspiration should be to make best use of them. A nonviolent outcome is preferable and is best when one channels it in an effort to obtain maximal progress toward satisfaction for both parties.

3. Asymmetry in power relations is a factor that needs to be recognized, and in conflict the temptation to act unilaterally is powerful. Such independent, one-sided behavior, however, may end in unstable outcomes: the stronger party may win a war but have difficulty in gaining peace. A lion cannot easily kill a fly; the weak have their own weapons and can make life for an oppressor untenable by means of terror, uprisings, and obstructionism. The fragile nature of coalitions among states and nations induces changes in configurations over time, and a single powerful country can eventually be forced to confront a group of individually weaker, but collectively stronger, actors. Hence, impartial reasoning requires that we put ourselves in the shoes of the "other." Bill Ury has often quoted Gandhi as stating that practicing "an eye for an eye . . . we all go blind."

4. Facilitators should present their own normative approach to conflict resolution. While advocating nonviolence as a priority goal, I would admit

that war may sometimes be legitimate, such as in the case of self-defense or rebellion against tyranny, but it should be used only as a last resort, when all attempts to negotiate or apply nonviolent strategies have failed. And what about litigation, bringing the other side to a court of justice? Even if we respect the outcome to be fair—and this is not always the case—the nature of the system is that we either win or lose. We call it adjudication, and it may tell us "You are right," but it also means, for the other, "You are wrong" and that your minimal expectations cannot be met. So it is better to try alternatives to both power politics and litigation (Davies, this volume). This appeal is surely justified when we try to reduce levels of conflict in our workplace, neighborhood and family. If we are bound to live together, we know that inflicting pain through one-sided impositions is not a good recipe for a durable friendship. My own conviction is that appropriate dispute resolution is not a panacea but is worth trying first, and for the long term, as it may often take time to bear fruit.

5. Do we need a third party to intervene? Agreed, the preference is that both parties in conflict should find ways of overcoming the conflict on their own by educating themselves on methods such as "principled negotiation."[15] However, it is not easy for parties that are in the escalation phase of a dispute, and often before or after a fight, to cool down by themselves. In many cases, a third party is needed to help them move to a resolution. Depending on the authority and resources of this third party, he/she can decide for the parties (arbitration), assist the parties to reach a compromise (mediation), or provide the two sides with the tools and skills that will enable them to invent jointly new options to deal with the immediate dispute and others as they appear in the future (facilitation). The first two may be more appropriate when dealing with single-issue, interest-based disputes; the third is recommended for dealing with identity-driven, complex conflicts. Often tangible and nontangible traits are part and parcel of the conflict, and a formalistic solution may not touch upon the more in-depth needs or help to improve the larger relationship.

6. Facilitators may conceive of their roles differently. Some emphasize the enormity of the problem, suggesting ways to learn how "to live with the conflict." Others confine themselves to generating "dialogue groups" to continue over time, with the objective of reducing misperceptions and building personal trust. Our approach is more ambitious, since it moves on from this into consensus building toward action. The expected relative advantages provided by this interactive problem-solving approach, can be summarized as follows:

a. Many problems are not necessarily zero sum but can be developed into win-win solutions.

b. Often we do not recognize the real needs hidden behind publicly stated positions.

c. Good will, sensitivity, and learned intuition are all necessary ingredients for finding common ground. But professionalization and a good knowledge of available techniques can make a real difference.

d. More formal ways of negotiating do not allow for full expression of creativity, exploring new ideas and putting ourselves in the shoes of the other.

7. As a corollary of this last point, mention should be made of the growing importance of track-two diplomacy with the end of the Cold War and the persistence of ethnopolitical conflicts that have deep roots and require the addressing of needs for recognition, security, perceived survival, dignity, or well-being (Gurr and Davies, this volume). These identity-driven hostilities are often exacerbated by irresponsible leadership, seeking legitimacy or power through playing on the fears of their own people, creating extremists even among intellectuals, academics, and professionals. Often, the bloody acts of fanatics and fundamentalists paralyze the diplomatic process; deep-rooted animosities call both for peacemaking among leaders and for broader joint reconciliation efforts.[16]

Track-two diplomacy has also increased as a result of the process of globalization, which has expanded cross-border and international interaction, while also making involvement in international affairs more accessible to individual citizens and more relevant to their daily lives. There is an intrinsic difference between track-two and "back channel" negotiations, often run in parallel or in preparation for official negotiations. The latter is mostly conducted by emissaries of the governments, often security/intelligence agents or messengers with no authority to discuss issues. Track two, on the other hand, is conducted by nonofficial individuals, with the objective of generating new options, putting themselves in the shoes of the other, testing the limits of the possible. They may report back to officials in their respective governments, bring the new shared ideas to their peers within civil society, or try to affect public opinion through the media and other informal channels.

The Image of the Other

Objectives and Rationale
How one party to a conflict views the other side is a critical factor, affecting the way they deal with each other on all levels. Too often, different cultures or ways of life are seen as mutually exclusive, defined by contact with each other, and this polarity tends to reduce a conflict to "us" versus "them" terms. Ethnic prejudice and other forms of discrimination, based on gender, religion, social class, age, sexual orientation, language, and so on, have the same root. Polarization is more extreme when the image of the "other" is tainted by the use of violence, confirming the presumption that "they" are unreasonable and incapable of change (Cohen, 1994). This session should focus on showing how possible solutions are missed or undermined due to prejudice, fear or even hatred of the "other." Focusing on the universality of this problem helps Partners to understand that their conflicts are not

unique and are thus more likely to be solved as others have been. In most cases, there will be a resolution. The main issue here is using history to learn from previous conflicts and cases: not "if" but "when," how and at what price. Our goal is to find ways of bringing the resolution closer, and thus reducing the cost in human suffering. The mechanisms of demonization of the enemy lead to "a scapegoating of him, the creating of a stereotypic picture. It tends to be one-dimensional, certainly not three-dimensional or fully based on reality" (Moses, 1996).

Exercise: "The Faces of the Enemy"

Sam Keen's *The Faces of the Enemy* video, book, and guidelines for discussions[17], made during the last years of the Cold War, is a remarkable tool for creating awareness of the image of the adversary.[18] It can be used as a starting point for a discussion of propaganda and demonization.

The *Faces of the Enemy* lays out many tools for structured discussions on the image of the other. Facilitators can choose from a menu of points and questions. If pressed for time, I would suggest a discussion based on two of his questions: "Do we need enemies? If we didn't have them would we have to invent them to have somebody to blame for our problems?" and: "Why do we automatically suspect people who are different from us? Is the unknown always evil, dangerous, fearful?"

Exercise: Creating Your Own Exercise on Demonization

If one is not able to obtain *The Faces of the Enemy*, one can construct one's own activity by finding demonizing cartoons or film clips in libraries, newspapers or, most easily, on the Internet. The cartoons do not need to be relevant to the particular conflict (it may actually be beneficial if they are not related, so that the Partners can look at them more clinically), but they should clearly illustrate how one side demonizes the other. The Partners can break up into groups to analyze the material and present the stereotypes found. The facilitator should elicit some observations, showing, for instance that each side more often then not demonizes the same things in the other

Deescalating Exercise

This is an important skill to develop. We can start with the Partners' sharing their past or present experience of a conflict situation that got out of hand (e.g., *Intifada Al Aqsa*), when misperception of the other's intentions and domestic politics resulted in tragic unintended consequences. Often there is not much time to look for optimal solutions, and one way to start down the ladder is by small gestures, often initiated unilaterally by the stronger side. The other could respond with another symbolic measure, and eventually these one-time gestures could become permanent rituals. But, as Kenneth Boulding used to say, "It is easier to do harm than to do good," and Partners are reminded with dismay of their own sad experiences. In the discussion, provide illustrations of spiraling up ("You force me to do it," "I am only defending myself") and deescalation ("We are both engaged in a self-destructive cycle," "What can I do to decrease the level of fear that would not be perceived as a sign of weakness?").

A proven method of deescalating the disconsolation inherent in such a discussion, while at the same time keeping to the topic, is provided by a beautifully illustrated book by Dr. Seuss called *The Butter Battle Book*. This children's story is of two friendly neighboring nations, whose disagreement over which side of the bread should be buttered escalates to a potentially nuclear confrontation. It is a parody that affords neither a happy nor an unhappy ending. The Partners themselves can go around the circle reading each a page of the story; then give ten minutes for putting on paper what they can imagine for one last extra page to the book, providing deescalation scenarios. We end the session by again going around and each reading his/her suggestion for a "happy end."[19] We find out that preventing a situation from becoming extremely violent requires, among other things: investigating incidents to clarify what actually happened; forming a group of people from across the divide, a group that could be representative of people of good will from all parties involved; religious figures calling for dialogue under their auspices; controlling rumors to correct misunderstandings; third-party shuttling between opposing sides; asking sides to make pledges that such incidents will not recur; asking sides to offer reparation, restitution or compensation; and setting up agreed mechanisms to pre-empt a new crisis (Fisher et al., 2000).

It may have been a heavy morning and afternoon, and the participants should spend a little extra time digesting the information. If they require some fresh air for a late afternoon or early evening outing, this is a good time to call it a day.

Day 4: Dealing with Our Own Conflicts

When we start training ourselves in conflict resolution skills, it is important to underline that we do not want to change the ideologies, identities or basic values of the Partners. Our work is at two levels: firstly, to find a more balanced way to view the image of the "other," renewing our attitudinal prism by taking into account how, in the process of socialization, we have been strongly influenced by common stereotypes and prejudices. Secondly, we aim for an improvement in the channels of communication. Bad news travels fast, and with a loudspeaker; good news needs to be retransmitted time and time again. In order to reduce misperceptions, we need to educate ourselves how best to articulate the message, how not to be distracted by the surroundings and how to listen effectively and elicit a sincere and clear response. Before going into the relevant exercises, some attention on setting a relaxed and confident tone is appropriate.

Confidence-Building Measures

Objectives and Rationale

While the atmosphere is normally calm and polite when dealing with conflicts at large, the closer the Partners come to their own issues the more tension enters the room and begins to affect the stakeholders. Anxiety should be met creatively.

Before moving into these more sour moments, the facilitators can suggest to the participants that they adopt some relaxation or confidence-building measures based on acknowledged positive gestures toward each other. We can discuss examples, such as President Sadat's decision to come to Jerusalem as a statement to the Israeli public about his peaceful intentions. This and other stories are skillfully analyzed by Mitchell (2000).

Possible Exercise

A recommendation culled from the field of marital counseling is that each team may be offered a bouquet of flowers of a different color. For every "good deed" enacted by one side throughout the workshop, the other party should offer a flower. This way, it may be that after a week one group may have obtained a large number of flowers of the color of the other group, or vice versa. This is perhaps too romantic for some cultures, but the principle of providing confidence-building measures during the workshop may help the participants to generate more effective reciprocal empathy toward each other when engaging in reflective analysis or brainstorming at a later stage. In a deeper sense, signaling conciliatory intentions increases flexibility in the process, and it can be done through acknowledging specific interests of the other party, willingness to change, showing the flag of the other, using a vocabulary that includes politically correct language of the other party, volunteering to conduct an activity, etc.[20]

Focusing on Our Own Conflict

Objectives and Rationale

The Partners must now start to come to terms with their own conflict. This is a difficult session, as the Partners will be extremely sensitive to perceived biases in the presentation. Nevertheless, this is the time to start airing these conflicting points of view. I have often drawn a cone shape to illustrate how misperception of the real problems behind conflicts arises from an attitudinal prism structured from the belief system (values, ideology, religion), social constructs (prejudice, stereotypes, images), and (mis)communication. We do not directly work with the belief system but on building skills to overcome obstructions from distorted social constructs and miscommunication. The focus is now on dealing with the image of the "other" that we perceive as enemy, creating awareness for prejudice and stereotype reduction, and sensitivity toward the personal suffering that the conflict generates among participants themselves.

Exercise

To start the discussion, a documentary or interesting speaker on the conflict should be presented.[21] Most protracted conflicts have generated films and documentaries, and the Partners can be encouraged to bring videos produced by their own governments or groups. Biases can be balanced by showing videos from both sides. One can also ask Partners on both sides to present their communities' views of the conflict. We must be clear in asking the speakers to introduce only official or generalized positions, rather than their own personal views. This avoids putting them on record, possibly in a confrontational mode, and perhaps hindering their ability to change their opinions or attitudes at a later time.

An unstructured discussion should follow, in which the mood, fatigue, and general predispositions of the participants will determine when they may begin confronting each other over their shared problems. Within the limits of previously agreed ground rules appropriate to the culture, the discussion should be allowed to flow and run freely. It may often lead to escalation and confrontational interchanges, unless these have been proscribed. If it does, our hope is that the participants will begin to notice and realize how futile this type of exchange can be. If there are participants who show a predisposition to act as peacemakers, they may be encouraged to take an active role in reaching out to other, more adamant and difficult Partners.

Dealing with Our Stereotypes

Objective and Rationale
Stereotyping is a common phenomenon. We all have a tendency to generate prejudicial perceptions of the groups that we consider threats, particularly to our security needs. These deep-rooted images are part of the nontangible dimensions of the conflict, and without raising awareness they are difficult to change. As we develop a new image of the other party as similar or equal to us in important ways, we should also expect to find that they have had a low opinion of us. The following exercise can be used to generate an awareness of the Partners' own limitations in judging the intentions, ulterior motives and designs of the other party. As a whole, the atmosphere produced from this session is usually tense but somewhat comical, with laughter often erupting as each side hears the perceptions held by the other.

Exercise: Mirror, Mirror on the Wall—Our Own Stereotypes
The group is divided into teams. Each party divides into an A team and a B team. The facilitators ask team A in both parties to provide a list of negative stereotypes of the other party. Rather than think about their own images, they are asked to look for the lowest denominator of prejudice and even bigotry in their own societies, to identify prevailing attitudes (focusing, at this stage, on negative aspects and terms).[22] B teams are asked to conjecture what perceptions of their own people might be listed by the other party's team A. After ten to fifteen minutes, the information can be shared. The A teams count the number of stereotypes and analyze the similarities and differences. Many interesting findings are likely to be revealed, including some shared images of the other. The same is done for B teams with a discussion on the high or low correlation between As and Bs.

The teams then return to their smaller groups but this time focus on positive stereotypes. This usually entails a discussion on whether it is possible to describe positive stereotypes, or if the term is used only for negative aspects. The same analysis should be done, but this time a comparison of good and bad stereotypes should be included. Often in a conflict situation the negative images accumulate far more than the positive. Does a shorter list of the latter in one group imply an asymmetry in the conflict? Does the weaker party tend to have more negative images attributed to it than the dominant party? Do we tend to project more negative images of ourselves as reflected in the eyes of the other (B teams) than the list provided by the other (A teams) would indicate?

A note to facilitators: In some cases, particularly in high-context cultures where strong wording about the other can result in long-standing uneasiness during the workshop and beyond, an alternative format can be explored, in which the sides are asked to imagine the traits of an "ideal" neighbor, implying that the imagined qualities do not reflect the current situation.

Exercise: Images of the Other

An alternate exercise (Blake, Shepard and Mouton, 1964) has the two groups write a brief description of themselves and their relationships with the other group. They are also asked to jot down how they perceive the other and its behavior. Each can be summed up in five or ten points. Usually the participants find it easier to develop the image of the other rather than that of themselves and are made aware that they are not so sure about their own conduct. In the next phase, the groups' self-images as well as their observations about the other are made public. This allows for a comparison, which many times will show astonishing differences. The Partners may ask questions of the other group to ensure they understand correctly, and then discuss the different images. Sharp accusations may be voiced at this stage, and should be kept within agreed ground rules.

A self-diagnosis phase follows, with each group asking itself why its opponents perceive them as they do. Once a thorough discussion is conducted within each group, all meet again to share their diagnoses. It is hoped that this will lead to a more open and insightful debate, followed by a change in each group's perceptions of themselves and the other party. Even if all the issues raised are not resolved, the participants are still given a more critical view of their perceptions. This may be summed up with a presentation on the problems arising from perceptions and how they can be worked through to lessen or change their negative impacts.

At this stage, there may be a strong residue of hostility if only, or mainly, negative representations were drawn out. Focusing on a discussion of mirror images or similarities can minimize this. There is no need to pretend that this stage must have a happy ending, particularly in light of the phase that follows. These mirror images show the enemy as the coward and us as the brave. Often, the side that perceives itself as the weaker and as seeking to redress the status quo has sharper and more negative images of the other. For example, while Ecuadorians historically have more grievances about Peruvians, the latter have more critical attitudes toward Chileans, whom Peruvians generally consider to be aggressors. Nations can select their main "enemy" and minimize the importance of others.

A note to facilitators: Debriefing can maximize the effectiveness of this exercise. First, it allows participants to internalize the main lessons of the exercise, making some of the implicit findings more explicit to all. Second, it provides participants with a clear-cut bottom line. An exercise in Ecuador on "feminist" and "macho" Latinos showed not only the prevailing stereotypes but also the feelings that were partially shared by participants themselves.

Discrimination and Prejudice—A Personal View

Objective and Rationale
Partners are asked to personalize their view of the conflict. Fear for personal safety and security can be a much more powerful driving force than nationwide goals. Fears are easily projected onto groups seen as competing for scarce resources, especially those with less familiar cultures, leading to dehumanizing of the other side and polarized "us versus them" thinking, with each group defining itself by affirming attributes not shared by the problematic other. Personalizing the conflict helps the Partners to more clearly see the human beings on the other side.

Exercise
The Partners are encouraged to share personal experiences, or those of friends or family, in which an element of discrimination, racism, bigotry, prejudice or negative stereotyping occurred. This is a time for sad news, perhaps mild cases of racial or national discrimination, or in protracted communal conflict, oftentimes cases of atrocities, prison experiences, torture, and death. When there is an asymmetry in the power relations between the disputants, that will usually be reflected in asymmetry of suffering.

If both sides have stories to share a more evenhanded evening will follow, but balance cannot be created artificially. In a workshop on "Coping with Terror and Violence: Learning to Share the Grief of the Other" that took place in Bethlehem, we heard numerous personal and family stories from our Arab participants and specially invited guest relatives of the "martyrs." "Fortunately" (and I use this word with some irony), we did have a couple of cases on the Jewish side. For example, one involved a former airplane hostage from Entebbe, Uganda, whose hospitalized mother had been murdered by Idi Amin when he (Amin) was told of the successful rescue operation performed by the Israelis.

In addition to describing the incidents, the participants should be asked to recall if there was any attempt to deal with the events after the fact. More often than not, people let it pass, unattended, leaving bitter feelings to smolder. These wounds are cumulative and usually kept raw by aggravating remarks about the victim's people. In some cases we have had "better" stories of acts of violence that led to offers, by some among the victimizers, of help and partial redress for the injustice committed. In case participants are slow to open up, the facilitators or local organizers can be prepared to share some of their own stories. For example, I have a short CNN news tape of my family involved in supporting the Palestinian family of a former domestic helper, father of four, who was killed by Israeli Border Police while working a small plot of land in his village.

This exercise can be used to generate discussion about human suffering and to analyze its effects on ethnopolitical conflicts; the cycle of violence generates feelings that can easily become stronger than those engendered by the original causes of the conflict. At this stage there may also be an opportunity to deal with issues of accepting responsibility for the actions of one's own community, rather than continuing to deny and to attribute only negatives to the other party.

A note to facilitators: Facilitators should assess if it might be premature to evoke such strong reflections of the Partners' own conflict and consider bringing them up at a later stage, during the exercises on "healing." On the other hand, when teaching students from a country without a significant level of conflict, if the class is diverse enough, we often find ethnic tensions reflected in stories of discrimination or prejudice. Rather than simulate a case study, it is best for them to talk about their own life experience.

Intercultural Communications

Objective and Rationale

Partners should understand and develop skills to address the difficulties raised by intercultural communication, even when the Partners in many ways share the same cultural milieus.

Introductory Remarks

In addressing the barriers generated by distinct languages and cultural traditions, we should place them in the wider context of the way we talk and listen. How to improve the way we express ourselves is addressed below; the receptivity issue is integrated both in the "active listening" exercises suggested for the reflexive stage and in a section on understanding body language during the adversarial stage (see chapter 10).

As a short demonstration of intercultural barriers to communication, ask each group to prepare in a few minutes five hand, head or body gestures and see how many of them are recognized by the other side. This can also alert Partners to avoid the mistake of downplaying the significance of cultural differences in their case.

The demonstration can serve as a bridge to a brief exploration of two contrasting paradigms of communication: one is common in individualistic societies (such as the United States, Israel), associated with predominantly verbal and explicit, or low-context communication styles; the second is predominant in more collectivist, interdependent societies, characterized by a nonverbal and implicit, or high-context style (Cohen, 1997b). Based on a thorough analysis of these cultural differences, Cohen provides ten recommendations for international negotiators, which are also instructive for citizen diplomats—box 9.2 (see also Moore and Woodrow, this volume, for more detailed guidance in cross-cultural work).

Even where cultural differences are of minimal concern, it is important to educate ourselves to develop the elements of an optimal communication process: effective expression by the speaker, accurate reception by the listener, and the feedback required in a group setting to ensure a high quality of dialogue.

Box 9.2 Ten Principles

1. Prepare for a negotiation by studying your opponents' culture and history and not just the issue at hand. Best of all, learn the language. Immerse yourself in the historical relationship between your nations. It may explain more than you expect.

2. Try to establish a warm, personal relationship with your interlocutors. If possible, get to know them even before negotiations get under way. Cultivating contacts and acquaintances is time well spent.

3. Do not assume that what you mean by a message—verbal or nonverbal—is what representatives of the other side will understand by it. They will interpret it in the light of their cultural and linguistic background, not yours. By the same token, they may be unaware that things look different from your perspective.

4. Be alert to indirect formulations and nonverbal gestures. High-context societies put a lot of weight on them. You may have to read between the lines to understand what your Partners are hinting at. Assume they will not come right out with it. Be careful in your own words and body language. Your Partners may read more into them than you intend. Do not express criticism in public. Do not lose your temper. Anything that leads to loss of face is likely to be counterproductive.

5. Do not overestimate the power of advocacy. Your interlocutors are unlikely to shift their positions simply in response to good arguments. Pressure may bring short-term results but risks damaging the relationship. Facts and circumstances speak louder than words and are easier to comply with.

6. Adapt your strategy to your opponent's cultural needs. On matters of inviolable principle, attempt to accommodate their instinct for prior agreement with your preference for progress on practical matters. Where haggling is called for, leave yourself plenty of leeway. Start high, bargain doggedly and hold back a trump card for the final round.

7. Flexibility is not a virtue against intransigent opponents. If they are concerned to discover your real bottom line, repeated concessions will confuse rather than clarify the issue. Nor is there merit in innovation for its own sake. Avoid the temptation to compromise with yourself.

8. Be patient. Haste will almost certainly mean unnecessary concessions. Resist the temptation to labor under artificial time constraints; they will work to your disadvantage. Allow your opponents to decide in their own good time. Their bureaucratic requirements cannot be short-circuited.

9. Be aware of the emphasis placed by your opponents on matters of status and face. Outward forms and appearances may be as important as substance. For face-conscious negotiators, an agreement must be presentable as an honorable outcome. On the other hand, symbolic gains may compensate them for substantive losses.

10. Do not be surprised if negotiation continues beyond the apparent conclusion of an agreement. Implementation is unlikely to be automatic and often requires continuing discussion. To assist compliance, it may help to build a system of graduated, performance-based incentives into the original contract.

Exercise 1

The facilitators can ask participants to represent their own cultures or to play another, having first identified its key values and cultural norms for behavior. A skilled assistant, prepared to role-play a fictional culture with highly contrasting but still positive values and behavioral norms, can dramatize the miscommunication and confusion that arises from lack of awareness of the nonuniversality of our cultural assumptions. Sensitivity is required in order to avoid offending anyone through exaggeration or ridicule.

Exercise 2

An alternative is to use a film developed by Edward Stewart, a pioneer in this area, showing an American businessman arriving in a South or Central Asian country, committing gaffes in his impatient dealings and relationship with a local partner. Identifying their misunderstandings can be fun, and it is useful to track the departures from the recommendations in box 9.2.

This may be followed by a "Cultures in Conflict" game of role-playing two or more different types of culture, based on a set of prepared "culture cards." These cards specify contrasting behavioral traits relating to personality, privacy, conversation topics, approaches to the opposite sex, behavior at home and outside, body language, etc., so cards can be assigned to small groups in any combination to define contrasting cultures. Participants are unaware of the nature of the traits of the other group(s) with whom they have to communicate, and they will quickly appreciate the profound misunderstandings that can arise.

The "values continuum" (box 9.3) can be used to analyze the cultural learning that took place in this exercise, or it can be used to compare the Partners' cultures, by placing each culture along a continuum between each set of contrasting values.[23]

Box 9.3 Values Continuum

Control	Adaptation
Confrontation	Harmony
Individualism	Interdependence
Conscience as guide	Norms as guide
Resources expanding	Resources limited
Explicitness	Subtlety, respect
Change, progress	Continuity
Action, doing	Experience, being
Future oriented	Past oriented
Youth valued	Age valued
Problem solving	Relationship building
Competition	Consensus
Equality	Hierarchy
Linear limited time	Circular open time
Mechanical world	Spiritual/organic
Analysis, reason	Synthesis, wisdom
Truth is relative	Truth is absolute
Informality	Formality
Trust institutions	Trust relationships
Constrained contact	Intense contact
Constrained expression	Expansive expression

The Way We Express Ourselves

Nonviolent Communication—Objective and Rationale

Marshal Rosenberg (1983) has developed an interactive model for learning to express and listen effectively, with an emphasis on "empowering evaluations."[24] The accent here is on providing a more objective, empathic, compassionate way for the parties to understand each other. His exercises encourage us to focus on four sets of issues, which are useful to adapt and role-play:

1. *What we observe:* Change expressions that confuse observation and evaluation (e.g., "You are too generous") to examples separating observation and evaluation (e.g., "When you give all your lunch money to others, I think you are too generous"). Also, change failure by generalization (e.g., "Blacks don't cut their grass or repair their houses") to more specific instances about person and place (e.g., "I have not seen the black family at 1679 Ross Street cut their lawn or fix the shingles of their roof"). Another example: replace "White people can't dance" with "Remember the white couple in the club last night? Both were poor dancers." Rather than stating, "All men are pigs," say "The man who lives next door cheats on his wife."

2. *What we feel:* Rather than criticizing others or their behavior ("You are wrong"), use the words "I feel" to focus on and share your own experiences ("I feel that I am right"). Rather than expressing only feelings ("I feel uncared for"), add words that tell more about why you think they occur ("When you don't call for a week I feel hurt, because I interpret it as you not caring for me"). Express how you experience the behavior of others impacting you rather than criticize the behavior itself.

3. *What we value:* Our feelings result not only from what we observe, but also from how we react to what is important to our cultural and personal values. Different people (and cultures) attach different values to the same acts or expressions. One method of clarifying our values is by adding to an observation a "because I" statement. This method transforms the sentence from "You always yell at me when we disagree" to "It's hard for me to discuss things when you yell, because I think youre angry at me and don't want to hear what I have to say." To "This country is so disorganized," we should add, "I have a hard time figuring out how things work here because I come from a place where structure and punctuality are important."

4. *What we are requesting:* This fourth piece of information elucidates what we are requesting as a positive action. Expressions such as "I want you to respect my right" or "I want some understanding" work better than negatives ("I want you to stop attacking me") but still are not sufficient. It is more effective to give voice to what you *do* want if you are specific. It is a good idea to express feelings ("I would like you to be honest with me") if they are accompanied by an appeal ("I would like you to tell me what I've been doing that you don't like").

Nonviolent Communication Exercise

Participants are divided into four groups, and for twenty minutes each group should prepare four or more wrong and right statements about the conflict from their personal experiences. Each group can take one of the categories or compete for the best examples for all four. We then read the statements, sharing them with the other groups, who are asked to pick statements that best highlight the different categories. This gives them tools to talk about the conflict without exacerbating relations through misunderstandings.

Hot Buttons Exercise

Susan Potziba has suggested that some phrases or slogans that we inadvertently use have a very negative connotation to the other (e.g., comparing Israeli behavior to "Nazi" behavior; using the term "terrorists" when referring to Palestinians; using "Orientals" for people from East Asia). Usage of such terms immediately blocks the comprehension of the rest of the sentence or discourse, and people are best advised to refrain from using them. The exercise requires the individuals (or team) to write down over ten minutes a list of such explosive expressions when used by the adversary, and perhaps also expressions that are embarrassing when used by their own peers against the other party. The negative catchwords should then be shared in the group, usually discovering some that were not originally considered as such. The Partners should then be invited to make a commitment to avoid hurting each other by pressing such "hot buttons."

At the end of the day, reflect for a few minutes on the events that have occurred, taking care to defuse whatever tensions remain, to avoid carrying over any hostile attitudes to the following day.

Day 5: Experimenting with Conflict Resolution

An option at this stage is to consider alternative approaches to collaborative problem solving within the broader field of ADR.

Mediation

Objective and Rationale

Mediation training may be introduced, briefly in theory and then in practice through simulations, as a way of demonstrating how integrative problem-solving methods can also be used to help decision makers come to a mutually acceptable agreement. It is best to focus on a scenario that is realistic for the participants, such as one relating to perceived discrimination in the workplace. If possible a mediation practitioner should be brought in to run this session. Sometimes we ask participants to bring examples from their own personal lives, or a couple of participants may be asked to role-play a prepared scenario, giving them ample room for improvisation.

Simple (nonpower) mediation is widely used for resolving single-issue disputes with two or few parties involved. In the context of complex, protracted conflicts or distributional disputes involving larger numbers of groups or stakeholders, or stakeholders without experience in methods of face-to-face negotiations or in working with each other, it will usually be better to use second track collaborative problem-solving methods such as IPSW first, or in parallel with official mediation. Protracted conflicts tend to multiply the issues under dispute, involve disjoined conglomerates on both sides and asymmetries in power relations, with violence resulting in widely shared feelings of victimization on both sides, and failed initiatives. These issues must be addressed before official mediation can be effective.

Exercise

A good scenario for demonstrating mediation concerns a policeman who has been decorated for a recent act of bravery but is going to court to sue a journalist who covered the story. In the process of gathering information, the journalist had learned that the policeman is a homosexual, and this added news value got the story to the front page. The journalist's defense was that the information was accurate and that his purpose had been noble, namely, to show the entire city that the gay community includes dedicated and heroic policemen, and by so doing to help destroy negative stereotypes. Yet, the life of this particular plaintiff was ruined: his peers no longer liked to work with him; they mocked him, and eventually he had to take a leave of absence and may possibly be obliged to resign. As the mediator goes through the different stages of resolving the conflict[25], she/he may organize a "fishbowl" with the rest of the participants, encouraging them to provide questions to the parties or suggestions to the mediator.

Other Exercises

The facilitators might also, if time permits, familiarize the participants with other methods used, from elite interaction through first track diplomacy, down to peer mediation with children. For instance, they might discuss the nature of mediation efforts with Croatian, Bosnian and Serb leaders in Dayton, Ohio (what is the impact of deadlines, or pressure from a power-mediator, on the parties?); or Jimmy Carter's experience with Egyptian and Israeli representatives at Camp David; or "notebook diplomacy" as used recently in Haiti (carrying a text via laptop from one side to the other for refinement can be an efficient way of reaching an accord).[26] Other ongoing issues of diplomacy in crisis situations may be discussed.

Introducing the concept of peer mediation with children in schools, with locally trained children as presenters, if available, may have an extraordinary inspirational power. If they can do it, why can't adults? A good discussion can bring up the notion of adapting this tool to the professional circles of the Partners.

Alternatively, highlighting an elicitive approach, the participants can also search within their own cultures for traditional mechanisms of mediation and problem solving. How have Japanese, Arab or other traditional societies, been effective in regulating levels of conflict using time-honored customs involving the family, the workplace, or elders?

Our Shared Vision: An Exercise in Foreseeing the Future

Objective and Rationale

This exercise is designed to create a positive foundation from which Partners can work toward a desired future, at the same time clarifying the dangers of allowing events to continue as they have in the past. The goal is to generate a creative tension by highlighting a plausible positive scenario for the future and then a plausible negative scenario, as a motivating force toward resolution of immediate disputes.

Exercise

Collective vision building involves asking the Partners to look ahead twenty to thirty years (older Partners prefer to go for a longer period ahead) and to share with the group the best realistic scenarios for their regions or the communities in conflict. Some time should be spent encouraging the participants to be forthcoming and creative, going around the room and eliciting responses from everybody. The atmosphere tends to be rather pastoral and constructive. Clearly, it is easier to find common denominators two decades ahead.[27] Younger participants tend to place themselves and their career objectives within the wider picture, while older groups normally envisage the future that they wish for their children. Realistic optimism is encouraged here, taking into account both constraints and possible future opportunities for peacebuilding, sustained structural reform, social change and economic growth. Facilitators may also have to provide a reality check when participants stray too far into fantasy, as when a woman from one of the poorest countries in the world visualized each of the Partners' families as having a Mercedes-Benz. As a whole, this exercise tends to generate harmonious and inspired discussion, and the elements of a shared vision (perhaps more than one) should be registered on a flip chart and summarized in a handout for the Partners.

Next comes an anticlimactic moment, as the facilitators ask the participants to switch gears and now think of the worst plausible scenarios of twenty years hence. There is normally a reluctance to do so.[28] Some assert that things cannot be worse than they are, but others disagree. The atmosphere grows heavier as the Partners are reminded where they are coming from. They speak about higher levels of conflict, economic stagnation, increasing dependence on humanitarian aid, guerrilla warfare, terror, massive loss of life, hunger and mass starvation, chaos, the emergence of new latent ethnic conflict, and other such disheartening scenes.[29] These should also be written on the flip chart and summarized in a handout.

The aim of the exercise is to see if it is possible to integrate or agree on alternate plausible positive scenarios in one "vision statement" reflecting a coherent collective wisdom of the group. We should encourage a working group or individual Partners to take on this challenge as other agenda items allow. This represents a shared aspiration of the group, and care should be taken to capture a statement that resonates as describing something both achievable and worth investing substantial time and energy to realize.

It is easier to agree on more remote common aims projected twenty years ahead than on ideas to be implemented now. For this tougher task we can use the technique of "backcasting," or backtracking. This brings the thinking about preferred scenarios down to ten years ahead, then five, and serves then as a basis to prepare the agenda for discussions in subsequent days. It is important that the participants themselves table the priority issues to be addressed in the workshop and set a joint agenda.

A common observation has been that Partners come to understand that while "keeping cards close to the chest" may make sense in a zero-sum competition, it may be that both can use the same card to complete their "hands." In a long-term shared vision we are talking about a team who would like jointly to maximize their future gains (good-news vision) playing together against adverse circumstances (bad-news vision). In the Israeli/Palestinian case, for example, if a cooperative two-state solution is the shared vision, it does make more sense to signal it now, allowing the Palestinian side to perceive the light at the end of the tunnel. At the same time, the demilitarized and peaceful nature envisaged for the state, the legitimization and acceptance of Israel as a partner, allows the two parties to feel more relaxed when discussing the tougher and more intricate steps to be taken toward the common goal.

We have now concluded the "prenegotiation" phase of the IPSW and look forward to the main integrative problem-solving exercise, where the Partners attempt to address creatively the issues in dispute and identify potential solutions. The next section of the workshop reviews alternative methods for reaching consensus, then provides a detailed account of our preferred methodology. Spending adequate time building skills pays off as we get into the workshop's "real" purpose.

Notes

1. They are seen by some as mutually exclusive (Bloomfield, 1995: 154), but there have been attempts to construct an integrative model (e.g., Fisher and Keashly, 1991).

2. The negative reaction to track two was exacerbated when this term was used in U.S. anti-Cuban legislation and for covert operations in Chile aimed at undermining Salvador Allende's regime.

3. Shorter versions of the IPSW are available in Spanish and Russian (see Kaufman, 1998).

4. Chris Mitchell and Michael Banks' (1996) "Handbook on the Analytical Problem Solving Approach" is useful more as a conceptual and educational tool, focusing less on concrete and experiential aspects. Ambassador John McDonald has also introduced the general approach in several publications, including his "Guidelines for Newcomers to Track Two Diplomacy."

5. The term is borrowed from the work of my friend Abbe Loewenthal on U.S.-Latin American relations.

6. For instance, the Association of Universities of the South of Ecuador and North of Peru (AUSENP) has been involved in a program on citizen's diplomacy for local conflict resolution, the awarding of a binational peace prize, joint research projects, etc.

7. After learning from Larry Susskind about his work with government and unofficial representatives in an environmental dispute in Ecuador and "parallel informal negotiations" in climate change negotiations I am becoming convinced that you can have a "track 1½," mixing participants from both. In our third workshop of Ecuadorian/Peruvian civil society leaders, one participant from each foreign office was invited in a "personal capacity," and the other participants felt sufficiently comfortable with their presence.

8. We are currently working with upstream and downstream states on the Salween River, with Chinese, Burmese and Thai participants. For a full research strategy on transboundary water disputes, see Kaufman, Oppenheimer, Wolf, and Dinar, 1997: 38-48.

9. Over the last few years I have had the pleasure of team-teaching a course on "Conflict Resolution: The Israeli/Palestinian Experiment" with Professor Manual Hassassian, of the University of Bethlehem. This course has become a powerful testing ground both for exploring the issues and motivating students to move away from adversarial attitudes and search for common ground.

10. For an analysis of such an interactive process with Partners and students, see Leslie Gottert, "An Evaluation of the Israeli-Palestinian Building Bridges: A Christian, Jewish and Moslem Trialogue" (CIDCM, University of Maryland, 1995).

11. The Action Evaluation Research Institute has developed a software program (www.aepro.org) that allows organizers of conflict resolution activities to connect interactively with the ARIA group for guidance on the evaluation process. The first analysis is free, then the ARIA group can become involved at different levels of consultancy throughout the project.

12. As Fisher notes, it is important during the introduction section for the participants "to articulate their value base, since cultural differences in assumptions, expectations, and preferences abound in the practice domain of conflict resolution" (Fisher 1994b).

13. Dialogue of itself promotes mutual confirmation of the parties, serving their basic human need to be recognized as individuals with values and and valued identities (see Azar, this volume). However, trust cannot be assumed: it must be built. Joe Montville defines trust in terms of willingness to risk increasing vulnerability to another whose behavior is beyond one's control, based on confidence that the other will not exploit that vulnerability.

14. A Filipino peace activist who had just tested its transcultural applicability in Sri Lanka gave me this idea. I replicated it immediately with a group in the Peruvian military.

15. "Principled negotiation" as a method for parties in conflict has been developed by Roger Fisher and Bill Ury (1991); it provides the parties with ideas how to move from rigid positions into the exploration of underlying interests, looking for integrative options which give better outcomes than unilateral actions or positional bargaining.

16. During World War I the number of civilian casualties was only 5 percent; it went up to 50 percent in World War II and reached 90 percent in the 1990s.

17. The study guide may be used in connection with Sam Keen's (1986) PBS documentary film *Faces of the Enemy,* available from Catticus Corporation, 2600 Tenth Street, Berkeley, CA 94710, tel. 415-548-0854.

18. On the image of the enemy, see Jervis, 1976; Volkan, 1988; and Moses, 1996.

19. A specially designed class on Dr. Seuss's *Butter Battle Book* has been designed by Carrie Shaw for the "Partners in Conflict in the Transcaucasus" program and is available upon request from this author at CIDCM.

20. Lewicki, 1994: 194 provides a list of conciliatory signs.

21. For the Israeli/Palestinian conflict we have used the PBS documentary *Arab and Jew,* narrated by David Shipler, author of the book of the same name.

22. Well educated Partners, or Partners from high-context cultures, may often not feel comfortable expressing negative stereotypes of the other. We can ask them to recollect the abuses used by the lowest strata in their own society.

23. This set of contrasting values was provided to me by John Davies.

24. For a full description of these techniques, see Rosenberg (1983).

25. Simple mediation requires first building trust among the parties; setting the agenda; asking in-depth questions; reframing the issues; meeting with the parties separately to explore options in confidence; bringing them together to discuss options that may satisfy the concerns of both parties; confirming agreement in principle; and finally drafting an agreement.

26. A variation on the "single-text procedure" (Susskind and Cruikshank, 1987: 124).

27. "By thinking of the longer term, it is possible to exchange a small loss now for a large gain in the future" (Susskind and Cruikshank, 1987: 88).

28. The option of reversing the order and starting with the "bad news" scenario has the advantage of ending the session with a positive note. But participants may be reluctant to begin by contemplating a future situation worse than the already depressing present.

29. This was the worst scenario of participants from the Caucasus.

10
Toward Innovative Solutions

Edy Kaufman

Searching for Common Ground

In chapter 9, the focus was on preparing the Partners for applying principles and methods of collaborative problem solving. Only in the last two days did the Partners begin to address their own conflicts. Building on the trust and insights gained in the previous days, the Partners should now be ready to look for common ground and innovative solutions. We shall illustrate several consensus exercises on Day 6 and then focus in more depth on our preferred methodology, developed from Rothman's (1997c) "ARIA" approach.

The final phase of the workshop is concerned with preparations for the Partners' reentry into their own communities; it covers some of the first post-workshop steps that are best done while participants are still together. By this time, they will have accumulated enough experience and skills to conduct an IPSW on their own and to involve themselves in conflict resolution in general.

Day 6: Consensus Exercises

Collaborative problem solving is based on the search for consensus as an alternative to enforced solutions or poor compromises. Consensus implies decision making that is based not on majority rule but rather on ensuring that everyone's concerns are heard and dealt with before decisions are made. This means that all participants' opinions must be given equal weight and consideration. Below are several types of consensus-seeking exercises that can be used to illustrate the approach.

Some Illustrations

Exercise 1: TOWS/FODA

   TOWS/FODA (external Threats and Opportunities, internal Weaknesses and Strengths) is an instrument adapted at the University of Costa Rica for corporate training (FODA is the Spanish acronym). Participants are asked to brainstorm on a particular theme of shared concern (e.g., occupational career prospects for Costa Rican businesswomen), each person coming up with a list of difficulties and opportunities. They are then asked to prioritize the listed items according to their importance either as maximizing positive factors (opportunities and strengths) or as minimizing negative factors (threats and weaknesses). Each person turns to the participant on his/her right, takes his or her list and eliminates all but the top three choices. The same is done for those on the left. These choices are compiled, and the resulting shared list is the group's consensus.

Exercise 2: Bridging the Gap

   A current controversial issue that divides the group fairly evenly but not by community membership (such as capital punishment) is identified.[1] Partners are asked to wear a tag corresponding to their beliefs (blue for yes, yellow for no) and to stand in two separate groups. The individuals from each group should then spend ten minutes in close proximity, trying to persuade those on the other side to change their views. At the end of the session, people who have changed their minds are asked to change their tags accordingly. Usually in this first phase none will.[2]

   Then the Partners are asked to find possible points of agreement and move toward a "lesser evil" alternative. A third division should be added for those who agree on a new alternative (such as "no capital punishment but mandatory life imprisonment without parole for more egregious offenders"). Participants finding themselves in this group then trade their yellow or blue tags for a green tag and place themselves in the middle of the two polarized groups. Others can remain where they originally were. The "greens" (mixture of blue and yellow) should now try for ten minutes to persuade others to join them by bringing up more new proposals (such as "voluntary preference for capital punishment or life imprisonment accepted," or "assassination of prison mate by former assassin punishable by death").

   The point is that when people are brought to a confrontation between two opposing positions, they tend to become more polarized than when asked to come up with alternative shared solutions.

   A note to facilitators: In case the result is not as expected, one can discuss with the group whether they have used the negotiation skills that they have just learned. This game can be fascinating and take up much time, so facilitators should be careful to budget plenty of time for addressing the Partners' own conflict. Shorter "competition versus cooperation" exercises include: placing people in a circle (or two) and asking them all to touch a ball as quickly as possible, the best strategy being not passing it around but for all to place a hand or even a finger on it at the same time; or, providing all with numbers and asking them to order themselves accordingly without talking, coordination once more being the way to succeed.

Exercise 3: Finding Minimal Common Denominators

In this exercise the two parties are asked to role-play themselves in their own conflict. They are given a well-known specific issue of divergence within their larger conflict (e.g., the Arab refugee problem for Israelis and Palestinians). Each team (1 and 2) should focus in a separate room for twenty minutes on finding at least five major concessions that they could live with, followed by a list of five (or more) bottom-line minimal demands to be expected from the other side, and write them on a flip chart.

The two sides are brought back together and asked to post their respective positions. If there is goodwill between the parties, it is to be expected that some points may overlap, but more often this is not the case. The Partners then split into two mixed teams (3 and 4), take the options offered by teams 1 and 2, and attempt to work out an accommodation over the next twenty minutes (again in separate rooms). The dynamics in teams 3 and 4 in their desire to achieve results may provide a greater chance of success, and either one of these teams, or both, may come back with a shared resolution.

If the members of these teams still do not agree, we can introduce a process to promote more principled negotiation, guiding the Partners through consideration of situations elsewhere which are analogous to their own conflict. This technique has been used for work at CIDCM on three conflicts in the Transcaucasus involving separatist regions (Abkhazia, South Ossetia and Nagorno Karabakh) calling for at least a large degree of autonomy, if not full independence. Lateral thinking led us to research the characteristics of existing independent microstates and to offer the Partners a summary of their attributes[3] to stimulate new ideas for their own conflicts.

Later, in preparation for a workshop on the Transcaucasus that we conducted in Aland, Finland—one of the oldest and best examples of autonomy—our Partners researched similar cases elsewhere and identified a list of mutually agreed-on successful options, using Lapidoth's (1997) systematic framework of autonomies. In a paper, "Diffusion of Power: Options for Societies in Transition," we described the cases of three successful regions with substantial autonomy: the Aland Islands in Finland, the Generalitat of Cataluña in Spain, and the Commonwealth of Puerto Rico in the United States. We disaggregated the relevant agreements according to different functions: cultural, political (executive, legislative, judiciary), economic, religious, language, infrastructure, etc. We then asked the Partners as individuals to draw out the five preferred and five "lesser evil" attributes of possible solutions, reminding them again that they should take into account as much as possible the preferences of the other party to their conflict.

The expectation here is that the groups will produce a statement that will include attributes mentioned in the agreements that could represent principles shared by all the Caucasian Partners. This is easier to achieve than bilateral statements from the Partners to each of the three conflicts. More agreement was reached than anticipated, although the larger units (the states of Azerbaijan and Georgia) gave more concessions than the smaller units (Abkhazia, South Ossetia, and Nagorno-Karabakh). The Partners agreed on what became the First Regional Proclamation of Principles for Conflict Resolution in the Transcaucasus (now translated by them to all regional languages). Evaluation of this experiment is currently in progress.

Exercise 4: Unilateral Best Offers

In cases where one of the parties is domestically deeply divided and thus prevented from developing middle-ground propositions, the other side may design a best offer that "can't be refused." Given the confidential nature of our exercise and the nonbinding characteristics of our deliberations, there is nothing to lose if a tempting and generous proposition is made as a "trial balloon." The Partners from the other party should be allowed time to consider it and eventually to join discussions on this basis, or based on a counteroffer triggered by the unilateral best offer. A problem-solving dialogue process similar to "laptop diplomacy" can now begin, with facilitators shuttling from team to team.

Preparations for ARIA

Rationale and Motivation

The approach we use most frequently to facilitate a transition by the parties from an adversarial stance in the conflict to an integrative one is the ARIA technique (Adversarial, Reflexive, Integrative, Action), developed by Jay Rothman (1997c). In this session, the Partners should be introduced to the concepts behind the approach and engaged in an exercise that illustrates how different approaches to conflict can result in different outcomes.

An Overview of ARIA

The first (adversarial or advocacy) phase focuses on the parties' positions on the major issues in the conflict, bringing out *what* points each Partner would like to make on behalf of his/her nation or group. The second (reflexive) stage is meant to bring to the fore the underlying needs and interests of each party, and to answer the questions of *why* they hold the positions they do and why they stress these points over others in adversarial arguments. The needs that motivate such stances are thus identified. Once the motivations behind the formal positions of each party are understood, points of convergence become apparent (shared needs and compatible interests), providing a basis for the third (integrative) stage. At this time, both parties brainstorm together and look for consensual ideas. They elaborate jointly answers to the question of *how* to resolve the conflict or selected conflict issues and consider action steps for how these or other integrative ideas may be promoted.[4]

In introducing ARIA to a group (mostly hydrologists) from riparian states with conflicting upstream/downstream interests, I used the following example. An egg has rolled down a hill to a neighboring farm, getting stuck in the dividing fence. At the adversarial level, the neighboring family declared that for years, any eggs that had rolled down the hill to its property were its own, and it had documents to prove it. The other family argued that the reason it had put up the fence in the first place was because its sloping land prevented it from keeping the eggs laid by the free-ranging hens. They argued that the neighbors had never taken possession of any egg, even if such right was granted in principle and embodied in a new constitution. The arguments led nowhere, and their pulling and pushing at the fence ended with fragile eggs being smashed. If the families had progressed from adversarial discourse to reflect why each needed the eggs, it might have become clear, for example, that one family was planning to use the yolk for mayonnaise, while the other was interested in the white for meringue. That would allow an integrative discussion on how to accomplish the separation of the elements, perhaps leading to new options for mutual benefit (e.g., the unused shells could be processed by both families to provide nutritive material for feed, which could then be marketed together). This represents an even better solution than a zero-sum compromise based on equally splitting the number of eggs.

Bill Ury uses a similar story about a fight over an orange, where the *why* exploration allowed the discovery that one side wanted its pulp for juice, the other its peel for jam. And if both parties wanted the juice, knowing why may help discovering that one is thirsty—hence best to give him cold water—and the other wanted vitamin C, which may be cheaper to buy in larger quantities while selling the juice. Most problems are more complex than this, but the lesson is a valid one. For example, in an integrative stage the two sides might go farther to address the longer-term needs of the parties. They might both decide to take the seeds that none need at the moment, plant them, and thus each acquire a steady supply of oranges in the future. A more complex scenario can be used to bring it closer to that faced by the Partners.

Day 7: ARIA—The Adversarial Stage

Motivation and Rationale

The adversarial phase should begin with a more detailed explanation of its specific dynamics (see Rothman, 1997c). In this phase, each party should aim to be persuasive, with lines of argument prepared and ready to be articulated firmly and clearly. This phase serves several functions: it makes clear what issues are in dispute and establishes the credibility of the participants as knowledgeable and effective spokespersons for their communities, who might also be effective in persuading their communities to consider new perspectives for resolving the conflict. It also makes clear that neither party can be talked into conceding on key issues, showing where they will stand firm, and making clear that Partners will need to move beyond adversarial habits to get results.

A note to facilitators: There is rarely any need to spend much time training the participants, since oppositional discourse has been the norm in most societies, particularly those with protracted conflicts. However, these norms are not universal. Some Japanese, Burmese and Thai participants we have worked with found it very difficult to articulate arguments in an adversarial manner. In such cases, some training in culturally appropriate advocacy skills may be beneficial. In all cases, organizers should consider the relevant norms for such discourse when planning a workshop and make sure there is a consensus among participants on culturally appropriate ground rules (e.g., no personal attacks or insults, no interruptions) that can be used in structuring this phase of the process.

The Adversarial Exercise

The facilitators should ensure that there is agreement among the Partners by this stage on the topic for discussion. It can be a specific issue dividing the parties within their larger conflict and of particular concern for the Partners (e.g., the status of refugees) or a simulated situation (e.g., a UN Security Council debate on contending complaints) relevant to their concerns. In any case the area of discussion should be clearly defined and agreed.

Facilitators should make clear that any premature shift to problem solving or proposing solutions at this stage will be inappropriate. Until there has been a clear definition of the problem and the points of firm disagreement between the parties, any discussion of solutions is likely to be unproductive. Agreement in second track diplomacy has little value in itself; if it does not fully address the real concerns of the communities, it is unlikely to elicit much interest at home.

Once the principles and ground rules are well understood and questions are answered by the facilitators, each side can be given twenty minutes to prepare its arguments and perhaps an order of presenters, including at least a "pilot" and "copilot" who will start up the discussion and take the lead as speakers until other members of the team feel comfortable participating.

We generally have the contending parties face each other for this exercise; if there are more than five or six representing each party, two chairs for each side are placed closer than the rest of the groups. The dialogue begins with the anchors' opening statements one after the other, beginning with the party challenging the status quo, each talking for just a few minutes. After this there is open discussion, with the copilots joining in, and at any time the other partners may be asked to share in the debate. With larger groups, whenever a Partner wishes to say something, he/she should approach either of the two speaking members of their own team and tap his/her shoulder. That person should then yield the seat to the new speaker and join the rest of the group, returning as desired to speak again.

This lively process generally proceeds for at least thirty minutes, depending on the number of participants (all should be encouraged to take part) as well as the intensity and complexity of the discussion, with facilitators ensuring compliance with ground rules. There is no need to cut this part short, unless either the positions and points of difference are clear or (in the absence of contrary ground rules) it devolves into a shouting match, with both sides pointing fingers, using incriminatory "you" language, interrupting, or making critical remarks about the other. If the debate escalates in this manner, the facilitators may tell everyone to "freeze," often at the point where fingers are being raised, and ask the Partners to evaluate the exercise.

In any case, at the end of the discussion a first assessment is made of what was learned from the process, focusing on the quality and content of the arguments presented. In preparation for a second round, with role reversal, the teams are asked to tell one another any significant points that were left out. There may also be a brief consideration of whether any adjustment of ground rules is desirable at this stage, remembering that what feels like welcome catharsis for some may preclude a good future working relationship for others. Any extended discussion of the value of this phase, however, should be left till after the second round.

Many useful insights can come out of this discussion, in addition to clarifying the positions, grievances and demands of the parties. Disputes over key historical points can be clarified (e.g., who occupied land in dispute when, who started the violence cycle, number of casualties, types of atrocities, or sequences of cause and effect). Issues of rights, law and morality can also be clarified, keeping in mind that the aim of this analysis is clarifying positions, not determining who is right or wrong.

At this point a second round should be organized in the same manner as the first, but with each side arguing the opposite party's position. Often, there is resistance to representing the views of the other party, but since the rules of the game have been agreed in advance, the Partners should be able to overcome this natural aversion and proceed to defend their opponents' arguments energetically. Several interesting developments should be readily apparent to the Partners. More often than not, they submit the most extreme positions of the other, either because they are less able to perceive more moderate arguments or because politically it is more expedient to portray the rival as extremist and resistant to compromise. The presenters tend to be more effective, or at least more uninhibited, pointed or critical of each other. This session can be tense, but it occasionally provokes laughter or a smile at the ability of one side to represent so accurately the excessive views of the other. The facilitators should maintain the seriousness of the simulation, however, intervening if necessary to ask for appropriate behavior within the agreed rules.

The debriefing and evaluation that follows the role reversal should include an analysis of the scope and limitations of the adversarial stage. It may also be instructive to discuss the verbal styles and body language used (facial expressions that convey anger, boredom or suspicion; tone and patterns of voice with high pitch, shouting; and posture and gestures, such as arms folded, eye contact). Similarly metaphors (quoting from holy texts or famous phrases), slogans ("blood on their hands"), and personal criticisms used in the heat of debate ("You don't understand," "You don't know what you're talking about," "That's not right") should be noted. The use of phrases that imply total certainty ("of course," "no doubt") might be noted, and also the tendency to become repetitive (as with propaganda, or when Partners had run out of arguments but could not remain silent). Tendencies to interrupt might be noted, and instances when people disconnected, stopped listening and started preparing a response in the middle of another person's turn. Assumptions may be defined as truth, and the other's position dismissed a priori, showing a determination to be right at all costs. Advocacy of a position can lead one to restrict the argument to strong points or perhaps to resort to half-truths, unchecked figures, dates and "facts," leaving the other side unable to respond with effective evidence to the contrary. Use of the term "you" categorizes the other camp as monolithic.

On the one hand, as evidenced by behaviors such as these, this phase often becomes a dialogue of the deaf and, as such, may only excite each side against the other, affirming preconceived points of view and closed-minded attitudes. On the other hand, this phase fulfills important functions, such as clarifying points of dispute, affirming Partners as committed and effective spokespersons for their communities, and demonstrating ways in which information and insights regarding the perspective of the other party may have been systematically shut out. There is often also a catharsis that occurs, allowing Partners to get out of their systems feelings of grief, frustration or anger that otherwise may hinder the Partners' subsequent work together. It is often easier fully to hear and understand our adversaries once we have been able to verbalize our own convictions in front of them.

Above all, this initial encounter makes a statement and tables the long list of charges from which the Partners can now move in search for a better understanding of the conflict and for possible solutions. The participants can now actively attempt to explain their feelings and assess their attitudes toward the intrinsic value of this stage. Clearly, a common understanding is being sought, and although it may not provide any settlement, this stage is a necessary condition for moving into other stages that will bring the participants closer together. This debriefing should aim to verify that the Partners are not leaving the room alienated from each other. The hope is that having played each other's roles, the Partners feel closer by verbalizing the subjective truths of the other. It may be that they will be ready to forgo the argument on who has more rights and accept that both simply have rights, as reflected in the emotions played out in this exercise and the conflict itself, revealing the parties' determination and dedication to their causes.

Before ending the day, it is a good idea to find a way to explain the nature of the reflexive stage, since it may be difficult for some Partners to get a good grasp of it and participate without prior practice or awareness of its power. Often, conflict situations arise or are made worse by lack of communication and sharing of knowledge. The next day requires an extra effort to reflect on one's motivations, values or needs, to express feelings, and to listen with attention to the other side. To a certain extent, the reversed role-playing has paved the way for putting ourselves in the place of the other, which is a key part of the exercise to follow.

Day 8: ARIA—The Reflexive Stage

Motivation and Rationale

The reflexive stage is necessary because it reframes the conflict not just in terms of the Partners' opposing positions but now at a deeper level of understanding the needs and motivations of each party. It also continues the deescalation of the antagonism that was allowed to surface the previous day.

A note to facilitators: There are a variety of ways to help enhance participants' talking and listening, and their ability to engage in the reflexive stage, since it is the most personal phase and therefore the most threatening for many people. It is particularly difficult in some non-Western cultures. In America, self-examination in public is part of the popular culture, and quite a large number of people feel free to discuss psychological or marital problems no matter who is listening. When dealing with Partners on a worldwide scale, more often than not it is necessary to spend a good deal of time in preparation to adapt the process so that the participants are comfortable with this session. For example, it may be advisable to work in small groups and only at a second stage to share experiences and insights with the entire group. The mood during the reflexive stage is quite different from that of the adversarial stage. Participants are encouraged to use "I" statements, rather than the incriminating "you" from the previous phase, to talk to themselves aloud and to be honest about their feelings. It is important to remind participants that they should provide only as much information as they feel comfortable sharing, while at the same time stressing that opening up is not a sign of weakness. The transition from the adversarial to the reflexive stage implies shifting to a deeper level of empathy for both sides.

Discussion: Conflict Behavior

The day should begin with a presentation on why this stage is included in the workshop. The facilitators should generate an intellectual comprehension of the concept of "needs" through serious discussion. When one contemplates what drives people and nations to the extreme of sacrificing their own lives and well-being for a cause, one can understand that human beings are driven by strong inner forces. Human needs such as physical security, freedom from oppression and discrimination, economic well-being, group identity (recognition, dignity and respect), and access to the social institutions of allocation and exchange are most commonly expressed and appear to be universal (Azar, this volume). Continual frustration in the attempt to improve satisfaction of one's human needs can motivate violence when no better options appear to be available.

The "dual concern" model helps to further clarify the motivational dynamics of conflict (see Davies, this volume, figure 6.1). The model defines conflict behavior as varying according to two dimensions of concern in each situation. One represents degree of concern for self, or salience of one's own needs and interests, ranging from low (leading to a preference for yielding or avoidance strategies) to high (leading to a preference for contending or integrative strategies). The second represents the range of concern for others, from low (leading to contending or avoidance) to high (leading to yielding or integrative strategies). By recognizing that there are two distinct dimensions of concern, for self and for other, that are not contradictory, one can shift from a one-dimensional model focusing only on self versus other (leading to yielding, contending or compromise) to notice a new continuum representing balanced concern for both parties, ranging from low concern for both (leading to avoidance or inaction) through moderate concern (allowing compromise) to high concern for both, which motivates collaborative effort to find a win-win (integrative) outcome. On conflicts over issues (needs) of high concern to both parties, full collaboration creates a stable solution; the other options leave one or both parties partially or completely unsatisfied and thus represent unstable settlements containing the seeds of future conflict cycles.

Exercise: Moving around the Room

A useful exercise for illustrating the theory is to place placards expressing different points of the continuum in corners of the room. Participants then move around the room depending on their personal reactions to a series of issues raised by the facilitators, or their classification of a list of personality attributes. Such methods of learning about conflict behavior help people whose style of learning is more concrete than abstract grasp the importance of this reflexive phase in facilitating a transition from "us versus them" to balanced or integrative perspectives. This progression is essential for joint problem solving to be successful. Experiential learning also has the advantage of promoting interaction among learners, which can help people overcome a number of prejudices. It enables participants to view members of the other party as they do themselves and to realize that their fears, hopes and needs are not all that different from anyone else's.

A Personal Observation

Before we move to exercises designed to reveal the motivations of peoples in conflict, I would like to share a cautionary experience. When prominent members of Ecuadorian and Peruvian civil society once met at College Park, it became apparent in the workshop's initial stages that attitudes toward their border disputes became increasingly more antagonistic when moving from civil society attitudes to governmental stands to military positions. In these cases, the Partners were unsure which level of needs to present in the reflexive stage, and we finally agreed to use active listening techniques to represent each of the three parts of their societies. Interesting contrasts emerged here; in addition to sharing with each other the mostly symbolic expectation of the people (recognition, dignity, respect for those killed in action, and economic well-being), the government had other, more immediate interests (usually political motivations such as elections, prestige), and the military was more concerned with the need to legitimate its function in the post-Cold War era and justify the purchase of new weapons, among other things. Such diversity of motivation across sectors within each party to a conflict is especially common when the level of violence is low; however, in all cases we should be cautious not to overgeneralize what we learn of Partners' motivations to entire peoples.

Active Listening

Motivation and Rationale

Selective hearing through disconnection, lack of knowledge, or highly charged emotions have been highlighted in previous days as barriers to effective communication. Listening skills can be developed in a number of ways. The purpose is to promote more honest and effective communication among the participants, based on respect for the speaker and a willingness to hear and understand the full message being transmitted. The facilitators' responsibility is to help all involved feel that they are being heard, through keeping the group focused, encouraging parties to speak out, clarifying key concepts, asking questions and summarizing main points periodically. They should also validate the willingness of participants to share concerns, fears, needs, values or experiences that may have gone unstated prior to this stage. These concerns are often deep and personal. Therefore, a sympathetic and sensitive atmosphere should be constructed.

Exercise: Robbery Report

Before discussing the active listening techniques, it is useful to demonstrate how the converse works: when one does *not* actively listen, the results can be quite detrimental. In this exercise, three volunteers are chosen and asked to wait outside. After they have left, everyone in the room is given copies of a robbery report. A volunteer is asked to enter and listen as someone reads the report in a voice that conveys urgency, but so that the volunteer can clearly understand what is said. The next volunteer is then asked in, and the report is repeated to him by the first one; the same follows for the last participant, as he/she repeats it to a "policeman" investigating the crime. The Partners should all be taking notes to see how communication can be mixed up and even wrong, if one does not pay close attention to what is being said (UNICEF, 1997). It should be stressed, however, that the volunteers should not be made to feel as though they are terrible communicators but rather that they have now aided in deciphering the factors that make effective listening a difficult act for anyone.

Discussion: Principles of Active Listening

Active listening involves paying attention, eliciting additional information and reflecting back the messages received (UNICEF, 1997). Factors such as atmosphere, body language and patience are also crucial (see box 10.1.).

Box 10.1 Techniques of Active Listening

Paying Attention
1. Face the person who is talking.
2. Notice the speaker's body language; does it match what he/she is saying?
3. Listen in a place that is free of distractions, so that you can give undivided attention.
4. Don't do anything else while you are listening.

Eliciting
1. Make use of "encouragers" such as "Can you say more about that?" or "Really?"
2. Use a tone of voice that conveys interest.
3. Ask open questions to elicit more information.
4. Avoid overwhelming the speaker with too many questions.
5. Give the speaker a chance to say what needs to be said.
6. Avoid giving advice, or describing when something similar happened to you.

Reflecting
1. Occasionally paraphrase the speaker's main ideas, if appropriate.
2. Occasionally reflect the speaker's feelings, if appropriate.
3. Check to make sure your understanding is accurate by saying "It sounds like what you mean is . . . Is that so?" or "Are you saying that you're feeling. . . ."

In order to practice active listening, three approaches may be considered. The Partners can be consulted about which of the following exercises they would prefer. If there is not sufficient time to practice and illustrate the three approaches in consecutive rounds, the Partners may break into pairs or groups of three and explore the different types of active listening simultaneously and then share the experience with the others. The exercises on "nonviolent communication" may also be practiced or at least reviewed at this stage.

Exercise 1: The group is divided into groups of three, and people are asked to speak in rotation. As the first participant speaks, the second listens and then repeats back what was heard to the speaker, avoiding criticisms or passing judgment through changing the use of certain terms. The third member of the triad acts as a coach, paying close attention to both verbal and nonverbal cues, and in this manner helps both the speaker and the listener listen actively. Repeating the exercise three times allows each person to play each role and to feel the benefits that active listening can offer. All the participants then sit in a circle, and one member of each group is asked to report its main findings.

Exercise 2: The teams sit close together, each forming a matching half-circle. Partners on one team listen to what those on the other have to say concerning their experiences and motivations in the conflict, then summarize the needs that were expressed, using fewer words than the original speakers. The roles are then reversed. Paraphrasing can in fact assist in organizing the thoughts of the original presenter and clarify some poorly expressed concepts. During this phase, the Partners' voices tend to be lower, as they fall into a more introspective mood. Since participants are inclined to speak softly of their concerns, the circle should be close. Each talk should last only about five minutes. Suggested topics for discussion might include a problem at work that was resolved successfully or unsuccessfully, past personal experiences in the current conflict, or an example of when the speaker mediated a conflict between others (UNICEF, 1997).

Exercise 3: The goal here is for team members to use counseling skills and reflective phrases to increase understanding. The Partner is encouraged to express feelings that she/he might hesitate to say out loud. Participants from one team speak of their experience and motivations in the current conflict while the other group encourages them, using phrases such as "Tell me more," "I understand but what do you mean when you say humiliation?" or "We all have fears, but what characterizes yours?" Such listening may be therapeutic for the speaker, but it has also been rewarding to see how much more information and insights Partners are able to gain when asking questions in a concerned, helpful manner.

Applying Reflexive Listening

Once the rules of the reflexive phase are clear and the principles explored and understood, they can be applied to the conflict as a whole using at least one of these active-listening approaches. Allow at least one hour for the small group role-rotation, with an additional hour or more for the debriefing in plenary. The rotating coaches in each group have been taking notes during the exercise recording the underlying needs. Presenting their observations to the larger group is an important step toward understanding the group's concerns. The more recurrent needs are clearly priorities that need to be addressed in the next integrative stage

Evaluating What Has Been Learned

This day is extremely important, because it provides a basis for a more thorough understanding of potential areas of common ground, and it should be evaluated at this point. The Partners may be asked whether, if they were to go through this stage another time, they would act differently. Their perception of the relevance and validity of the specific exercises can be assessed, along with their evaluation of the extent to which knowing the "why" behind the Partners' positions may help in moving the problem-solving dialogue process along. Discovering the unexpressed reasons motivating the participants will be valuable for all involved.

It should now be clearer how much misperceptions have distorted the messages of both sides and have inclined each party to expect the worst behaviors and conspiracies of the other. The Partners are now more aware that different individuals and nations tend to express their needs only indirectly, that they have universally recognizable human needs, and that different needs will be more salient to different groups. For example, Israelis are overwhelmingly concerned with security, at the national level as well as at the personal level of daily existence; at the same time, Palestinians most strongly feel the need to master their own destinies and not be controlled by others. Perhaps both needs can be met, since they are searching for different yet potentially complementary outcomes. It is such common ground, based on the evolving understanding of shared or complementary needs, which allows both parties to deal with group problem solving rather than personal issues during the next day.

Introduction and Agenda Setting for the Integrative Phase

Motivation and Rationale

In this section the integrative phase should be discussed so participants will be prepared for the next day. This phase is about maximizing mutual gains, inventing new options while not necessarily committing a priori to their acceptance, and then finding the common denominators. The introduction should also set the agenda for their discussions. Different exercises can illustrate the importance of win-win strategies and seeing things from the other's perceptive.

An important note to facilitators: During this session and in following sessions, the participants should already be sitting together in one semicircle as a group rather than in distinct groups as for the previous two stages.

Exercise: Illustrating Zero-Sum and Win-Win Thinking

To illustrate the difference between zero-sum thinking and a win-win strategy, a number of Partners can be selected for the following game, the more the better. The Partners are paired for a session of arm wrestling, with two small monetary awards for those with the most wins in one minute. While many of the participants struggle to put down their adversary's hand no more than a few times, a team embracing the win-win strategy can come to an agreement to split the two awards in equal shares and then let each one put the other's hand down as many times as possible. While others struggle, they can rack up victories. If no one in the room comes up with this strategy, the facilitators can demonstrate this alternative to adversarial thinking. The idea is to push the Partners into a cooperative mood and open them up to experimentation.

Exercise: Perspectives

A simple way illustrating the importance of perspective is to ask the Partners to focus on a particular part of the room that contains different objects, or a view through a window. When participants describe what they perceive from their viewpoints, it is easy to make the case that multiple points of view provide a much richer picture. Whatever exercise is used, the point is to demonstrate the value of being open to a new way of perceiving the same situation. It is always interesting to the Partners to realize how many different understandings of the same thing there are in a group. These exercises exemplify the value of being open and creative in problem solving.

A Discussion of Brainstorming

"Brainstorming" may be defined as a procedure for idea generation that involves the suspension of judgment and the deferral of evaluation. A brief comment on its origin as currently practiced may also be of interest. Brainstorming was an integral part of Osborne's creative problem-solving process in the 1930's, one stage in a cycle that includes fact finding, problem finding, idea finding, solution finding and acceptance finding. Brainstorming attempts to get the brain's more linear-thinking left hemisphere to work with the more holistic right hemisphere. This requires using techniques that are logical and sequential but also some that are random and freewheeling.

Some methods that have worked well in promoting creativity in my joint projects with Barri Sanders are lateral thinking, backcasting, writing in different colors, circular listening, mind mapping and list exchanges. The number of creativity generators is as extensive as the facilitators' capability for inventing them. Facilitators may discuss some of these ways for developing new ideas and talk about thinking as a self-organized informational system. *Lateral thinking*, for example, may be contrasted with hierarchical or linear (logical) thinking, which may lead to "tunnel vision" perspectives restricted by unexamined preconceptions of what is possible or relevant. Lateral thinking allows us to search horizontally for analogies between situations that seem very different but share characteristics with the conflict being discussed in the workshop. Earlier we discussed an example of lateral thinking in looking for models in existing microstates and autonomous regions, models that might open up the thinking of those dealing with the breakaway regions of Azerbaijan and Georgia.

Another option touched on earlier is *backcasting,* in which participants build back from the earlier "shared vision" exercise, revising the expected positive and negative outcomes of the problem from twenty years down to ten, five and then to the present. Other suggestions include *"expanding the cake"* before cutting it, meaning adding incentives for agreements by injecting assets other than those already under dispute. An example of this principle arises where territorial conflicts can be dealt with through gerrymandering. In the case of Jerusalem, one could define a much wider municipal area covering a hundred square kilometers (the area of the disputed Old City is only one square kilometer), covering what was under the Ottoman Empire the *sanjak,* or district, of Jerusalem, and then divide that into more ample Palestinian and Israeli capitals. Other tools for refocusing on problematic transactions and generating alternative options include: *nonspecific compensation* (one party concedes on the issue in return for some benefit received in an unrelated area), *"logrolling"* (each party concedes on issues that are of low priority to itself but of high priority to the other party), *"cost cutting"* (one party gets what it wants but the other's costs are reduced or eliminated) and *"bridging"* (neither party achieves its initial demands, but a new option is devised that satisfies the most important interests underlying those demands) (Rubin, Pruitt and Kim, 1994). Splitting the overall issue of water rights to a river, for example, not simply according to a percentage entitlements for each state but through identifying more specific values the river affords (irrigation, navigation, fishery, tourism, environment, domestic water consumption, power generation, cooling for industrial use, etc.) and asking stakeholders to assign numeric preferences to each allows these relative values to guide the division of access rights so that each state receives a higher percentage of its desired values than it would have received under a simple percentage split—a positive-sum outcome.

Agenda Setting

The agenda for the next day's brainstorming session can be set in several ways. Ask the participants to identify the most viable and important agenda items they think should be addressed:

1. By getting feedback from the official first-track negotiations and finding either the impasses that have emerged or the points of discord that have been avoided but require addressing before the final agreement;
2. By looking back to the best possible and worst possible scenarios of the shared-vision exercise and backcasting from the future down to the immediate issues that need to be discussed; or
3. By splitting into small groups and reporting their collective preferences back to the plenary.

It is important that Partners build consensus about the topic to be addressed. This is best done through appointing a small preparatory committee early in the workshop to take on that responsibility, since the Partners will already have been identifying potential agenda items through earlier discussions and exercises. Criteria for selection can include: salience, gravity (levels of related violence, arrests, suffering), participants' shared knowledge and expertise, simplicity, relevance for a majority of both communities, and the potential for generating early warning reports with appropriate recommendations.

The committee should meet with the facilitators a day or two prior to the brainstorming session to discuss the likely points. The recommended subject for the integrative phase should be presented to all the Partners during this session so they have time to reach consensus, think about the issue, and sleep on it before the integrative phase starts.

A note to facilitators: It is often obvious in international problem solving that those charged with finding solutions are too rooted in past history and current events to be forward thinking. The workshop has provided a different context, with extrapolation toward the future and reflexive exercises generating a recognition of joint perspectives, and with experimentation in techniques for freeing the imagination to think ahead creatively.

Day 9: ARIA—The Integrative Stage

Phase 1: Brainstorming

Setup

The day can begin with the participants once again seated not facing each other but in a curve facing the problem, which is mapped out on the flip chart or blackboard. Before beginning the creative process, we can help the Partners get into a "brainstorming mood" through brief tales[5] and exercises.

Exercise in Creative Thinking: Thinking outside the Box

This is an effective tool for demonstrating that creative thinking can solve problems that people see as insoluble.

Figure 10.1 Thinking outside the Box

The instructions for the exercise are:

1. Connect all nine dots using no more than four straight lines.
2. The dots cannot be repositioned.
3. The connecting line must be drawn in one continuous stroke: leave the pencil on the paper until all lines have been drawn.

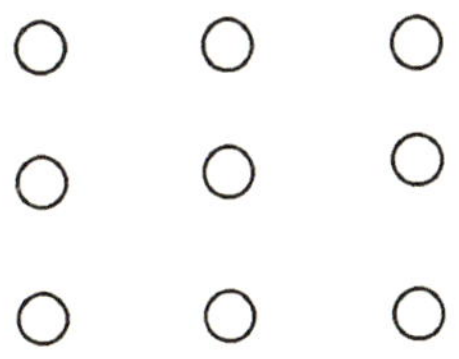

The concept behind the solution is not to allow our thinking to be contained and limited by imaginary boundaries. Thinking outside of boundaries and limitations is what creative thinking is about.

A note to facilitators: The title clearly reads "thinking outside the box," and yet, overwhelmingly, people disregard it and try to draw the four lines *inside* the box.[6]

Once the tone is set (if needed, remind them of the value of unconventional ideas for generating win-win outcomes, perhaps with a story[7]) the attributes of the brainstorming technique should be briefly reviewed and a list of rules for the exercise displayed: (1) all ideas are encouraged; (2) record them for display; (3) no criticisms, justifications or discussion of the merits; (4) avoid passing judgment either orally or through body language; (5) keep adding more ideas, including changing course to new lines of ideas; (6) do not focus on substantive differences; (7) all is confidential; (8) adding a footnote (or "hitchhike") idea is acceptable; (9) combine related propositions or expand propositions with improvements; (10) depersonalize the ideas by not registering the name of the proponent; (11) encourage daring and freewheeling ideas ("the sky's the limit," "think big," "no budgetary constraints") and (12) keep the flow going for as long as possible.

A note to facilitators: It is difficult for many participants to refrain from offering comments or body language about others' ideas. It is critical that the facilitators have the skills to keep this activity on track: reassure them that there will be an opportunity for evaluating the ideas later.

The Brainstorming Exercise

A brainstorming usually lasts from thirty to sixty minutes, depending on the number of Partners and levels of previous knowledge of the issues. Ideas should be stated briefly, since no justification is called for; this keeps the flow going and facilitates recording for later analysis. Two participants or facilitators should write down the ideas, checking to ensure accuracy, with proponents calling on the recorders alternately, so that the writing will not slow the flow of ideas.[8]

If the group seems to be running out of ideas, and the facilitators would like to encourage more, they may announce how many minutes remain in the session, so that an extra effort can be made to generate more. Quantity is no guarantee of quality, but a larger harvest may include more powerful and creative suggestions.

Once this exercise is completed and before the break, all participants should be asked to mark on the charts those ideas they consider useful (for example, ++ for a very good idea, + for a good idea). This will serve to indicate to the small groups what the priorities of the larger group are and which ideas to focus on more. A long break between this phase and the next allows participants to recover from an intensive effort and switch to a different set of thinking skills.

Phase 2: Classification and Evaluation

Motivation and Rationale

In this section the Partners are asked to organize the ideas into thematic areas (such as economic, social, cultural, political, security and humanitarian) and then redraft them to make the language more accessible to people outside the workshop, and to avoid rough or potentially offending "hot button" wording (see exercise from Day 4). Once the solutions are divided into several baskets, preexisting zero-sum assumptions shift. Participants will attach different values to potential gains (and losses) in each of the baskets. Even if there is one basket that seems to have the most important issues at stake, the introduction of several alerts both sides to the potential for trade-offs, which they can get only if they are willing to be flexible on the more difficult and important issues. For example, it may be reasonable to leave for the end the most difficult problems (e.g., among Israelis and Palestinians, the issue of Jerusalem) to be tackled by a special group. Once there has been an accumulation of creative and attractive solutions to the smaller issues, the motivation to deal effectively with the core problems increases.

Classification and Evaluation Exercise

During the break, the facilitators and several Partners should separate the suggestions by thematic categories, according either to major issue areas within the conflict, the professional skills of the participants, or other explicit criteria. After the break the Partners should divide into small mixed groups, each with Partners from both sides. Partners may also be asked to join the group to which they can best contribute based on their professional interests or their personal cognitive strengths (avoiding, competing, compromising, accommodating or collaborating styles).[9] The sense that they are acting in a capacity based not only on their own ethnic, national, or group identity may help open their minds toward dealing with the conflict based on complementarity with opposing Partners. No harm is done if an attractive idea or two is sent to more than one group; each Partner may choose to explore his/her own special area of interest.

Any outside observers who may be attending the workshop may be keen to participate and contribute with their own ideas. Normally, if security and confidentiality are not issues, Partners will welcome the opportunity to invite local observers. This should be encouraged, since a few people with different perspectives can help in defusing any continuing polarization and further expedite the search for common ground.

Group members are asked now to discuss the ideas assigned to them, clarifying them as needed and, taking into account the marks (++ and +) that were placed on the charts next to the ideas, rating them, say, on a five-point scale (five for the best, one for the poorest). Ideas and values assigned to them by the small groups are put on flip charts for the entire workshop. Within one or two hours, with a rapporteur recording the results, the rephrased ideas (usually about ten to fifteen for each group) are listed in order of assigned value, and the preferred notions are brought back to the entire group. Looking again into the fine drafting of the ideas is important, to make sure that they will be understood "out of the room" in the respective societies and to ensure that they are couched in appropriate language.

Phase 3: The Search for Common Ground

Motivation and Rationale

Partners should understand that consensus is not achieved through majority vote or avoidance of objections. Everyone should have his or her concerns brought before the entire group, and only when that participant is comfortable with relinquishing an idea should the group let it drop. In true consensus finding, people actively listen to each other and find ways to satisfy the important concerns of everyone. This takes longer than majority rule, but the resulting buy-in is critical to keep someone from sabotaging the project later. If participants feel unduly pressured, they will have a hard time implementing any ideas they are not happy with.

The Consensus Exercise

The small teams return to the main group, fixing their own chart pages on the walls. The facilitators should present some dos and don'ts of consensus.

Box 10.2 The Levels of Consensus

This ladder illustrates what different degrees of consensus may sound like. It moves from the clearest level of consensus to that showing most concern about the process.
1. "I agree wholeheartedly with the decision. I am satisfied that this decision was accepted by the group."
2. "I find the decision to be acceptable."
3. "I can live with the decision."
4. "I do not totally agree, but I will not block the decision, I will support it."
5. "I do not agree with the decision and would like to block the decision being accepted."
6. "I believe there is no unity in this group. We have not reached consensus."

After the presentation by each small group, the Partners should be asked if there is consensus (it is not a good idea to ask if there are opponents). Where there are major reservations, the person holding them can be given additional clarification by the rapporteur, other members of his/her team and the group at large. There is always room for accommodation by adding, subtracting, or changing the original wording of an idea. Dissenters will feel pressure from their peers to approve the idea even if they do not fully agree; they may yield and let it pass. Although people should not be forced to go along with the majority, and consensus rule gives each Partner a veto, it is not necessarily unhealthy for a participant to drop his/her objection to what other members of the group consider feasible. In some cases, a participant who agrees to let go his/her objections becomes a king/queen for the day; he/she may come to feel good about accommodating instead of being intransigent. On the other hand, if anyone persists in his/her objection and no accommodation can be found, the idea should be dropped and the process moved along, without making anyone feel ostracized or excluded.[10]

Once an approved list is completed, it can be typed up and distributed among the Partners and, if they agree, as a joint statement for other interested parties. The exercise may then be concluded with a short evaluation of the integrative stage and of the ARIA process so far. These three days will have been intense and productive.

Feedback is important, so that the facilitators and organizers can learn what worked and what did not, and see the value of their collective and individual efforts.

A note to facilitators: I have had cases in which consensus has been reached, only to be approached a few days later on behalf of one of the Partners who is unwilling to go along with his/her previously agreed position. One can opt either to talk to the particular individual and explore refinements that the group may accept, or simply redraft the preamble to the joint statement to read "All participants from group A and an overwhelming majority of participants from group B".

Day 10: Practicing Conflict Transformation in the Real World

Adapting the Workshop into the Partners' Own Cultures

Motivation and Rationale

About two-thirds of the workshop has now been completed, and the feeling may be that the most difficult part is over. Thoughts may be shifting to the return home, and there may be some sadness and/or expectations about a new priority or, in some cases, a new career in the field of conflict resolution. The facilitators can now present the results of the previous day much more systematically for comments and discussion on how to follow up the main ideas. Concrete recommendations for policy makers may be discussed at this point, as well as how to formulate these ideas to elicit interest among colleagues and how to translate them into activities aimed at changing public opinion and initiating grassroots action. If the Partners are to promote a culture of conflict resolution in their own societies and train as facilitators to work with colleagues and others in their own environments, there is a need to adapt activities and concepts in order for them to gain value and acceptance.[11] When we speak about adaptation to different cultures, we mean not only at the level of adequate language but also in terms of traditional forms and exercises that need to be identified and integrated with the newly developed techniques.

Discussion of Culture and Conflict Transformation

Moving to a more elicitive approach, the workshop may now also focus on revisiting the strengths and weakness of collaborative problem solving in light of the traditions and existing conflict resolution mechanisms and practices found in the Partners' own cultures. The facilitators should lead a discussion on how the lessons learned can be best applied given the cultures of the Partners. This objective should be pursued in a systematic manner, beginning with basic concepts such as peace, conflict, management and reconciliation. As an example, in a workshop I was involved in, I used the Spanish phrase *tormenta de ideas* as a translation for "brainstorming." A participant from Bolivia informed me that the preferred term was *lluvia de ideas,* or a "rain of ideas," because it sounds less frightening than "storming." It is worthwhile to listen and comment, and try to elicit ideas for adapting the model to help participants develop an integrative approach that will be effective in their communities.[12] In developing their own plans for conducting conflict-resolution training, participants will need to adapt it to the mentality and culture of their own nations, incorporating autonomous elements from local traditions both in the naming and substance of the exercises. Respect for the role of elders in peacemaking may need to be factored in; seniority should not be unnecessarily challenged. Tight social networks make it difficult "to separate the people from the problem," and alternative ways are required.

One of the perceived difficulties is the role-playing in the adversarial stage of ARIA. In some Confucian cultures in particular, the idea of being outspoken and aggressive is contrary to tradition, and often the participants are not able or willing to act along the prescribed lines. In experimenting on adaptation we were able to ascertain that Japanese high school students dealing with the conflicts with the Buraku and Korean-Japanese did not feel comfortable speaking aloud but were willing to write down how they felt. Another adaptation included not sharing personal statements but asking one of each group of Partners to act as a rapporteur or "leader" and bring to the fore the comments expressed by individual members of the inner group who would prefer to remain anonymous.[13] Ground rules such as these can be worked out according to the needs of each culture.

Introducing Information Technology (IT)

Motivation and Rationale

Rapid developments in computer technology and electronic media also require that the IPSW be constantly adjusted, though only within limits set by technical and budgetary constraints in the Partners' countries. In planning how to maintain postworkshop communication and dialogue among Partners, we have found that, paradoxically, in many developing countries our Partners have access to electronic communicative technology via the Internet, while older means of communication (phones, mail, fax) may not yet be available, at least not between the communities in conflict. We have been able to set up an embryonic "virtual community" of Partners that will endeavor to use all Internet channels available (e-mail, home pages, chat groups, video-conferencing).

A Discussion of Tools of Communication

Workshop organizers may arrange a session to present such IT tools and help in efforts to facilitate the Partners' access to them. The advantage of using such non-face-to-face of communication cannot be neglected: when direct meetings are not available in the home region, given the level of conflict between the parties, ongoing discussion of the issues and action steps through the Internet is a valid alternative.

Once, for example, in a workshop at College Park, we were able to familiarize participants with the International Communications and Negotiation Simulations (ICONS) Project, a worldwide, multi-institutional, computer-assisted simulation program used to address issues of concern at the international, regional or dyadic levels. Partners expressed their enthusiasm for experimenting with ICONS as an additional tool to their face-to-face contacts, especially because operations as expensive as workshops can only occur sporadically. The Partners conducted simulations on topical issues at College Park in mixed teams, representing both themselves and the other party, as well as foreign actors (mostly the regional powers). If the workshop participants are academics, they may wish to use the ICONS network in training their students. In any case, if they will be keeping in touch via the Internet in the follow-up stages, they can also be trained in the use of such on-line negotiation simulations and use them as a vehicle for discussion among themselves and others. Adapting ICONS to particular issues of concern to the Partners may be worthwhile, if funding is available. Video-conferencing may also be an option for the follow-up phase, if equipment is available in the region and budget constraints permit.

Most of Day 10 may be spent in informal groups developing ideas for implementation. The facilitators should provide supporting information, such as opportunities and procedures for applying for funding. Representatives of relevant foundations might be invited to come speak, and good impressions of the group's potentials may lay the ground for future funding (see Day 14).

Day 11: Acknowledgment and Healing

Rationale and Motivation

Given the human suffering that accompanies protracted communal conflicts, the Partners will need to develop their skills in dealing with traumatic situations, past wounds, present threats and possible future acts of violence that may derail a prolonged official peace process. Volkan, Julius and Montville (1991: 538) brings up the question of how a person can overcome the sense of past injustice and victimhood, and become compassionate toward the other side. They state that "for the mourning process to occur, [it] requires that the victimizers accept responsibility for their acts or those of their predecessor government and people, recognize the injustice, and in some way ask forgiveness of the victims. In many cases, the contrition has to be mutual" (see also Volkan, 1985).[14]

Social responsibility, contrition and forgiveness are powerful and even necessary elements in dealing with intense conflicts. They may not carry any direct tangible costs, but they can still be extremely difficult to express (Cohen, 1997a). Research and practical exploration on how best to facilitate these processes in real time are still in the early stages. A key issue is how to recognize in suffering an opportunity for reconciliation, rather than leaving it as a festering wound and source of further hatred and animosity. Such actions, often perpetrated by a small extremist minority, have a paralyzing effect, even among Partners who feel great goodwill toward each other under other circumstances.

We have found that due to sensitivity and lack of profound knowledge of the other party's traditions of grief, benevolently inclined people have been unable or unwilling to share their feelings of sorrow and compassion with their "enemies." Acts such as attending a funeral of a victim killed by one's own people not only requires human courage but may in some situations be counterproductive or dangerous. Hence, there is a need to understand the traditions and expectations of the communities involved, and for careful preparation (jointly, where possible) before undertaking such acts.

The problem of healing is relevant not only for dealing with the past but also for the conduct of the workshop. There have been instances when acts of terror or massacres have occurred in the Partners' communities during our workshops. As discussed earlier, explicit ways of coping with the trauma are required, and a discussion on healing should be undertaken immediately. During an Israeli/Palestinian workshop a short time after a Jew (Baruch Goldstein) massacred a large number of Muslims at prayer in Hebron, it was reported on the morning news that many Jews had just been killed in a bomb explosion at a bus station in Jerusalem. In cases such as these, when not everyone may have heard the news already, the facts should be brought in, with sensitivity, and the Partners can be asked what they think needs to be said to each other. They may also discuss the possibility of another such episode occurring, and what should be done about that. A group of Palestinian and Israeli women students once discussed the possibility of sending letters, with a small present or book, to children in the other community wounded in such violence. This, it was hoped, would open a channel of communication so that eventually Arab and Jewish students could together visit the victims of both sides in the hospital. The healing power of such humanitarian acts can also be multiplied if announced in the media.

Even when the majorities of two nations in conflict would like to move on and pragmatically reach a compromise agreement, the extremes of both sides, generating violent acts, can stop the peace process. A handful of fanatics can be a formidable barrier, unless more enlightened sectors of the silent majorities realize that they also need to play a moderating role, particularly, but not only, at the most difficult moments. Partners can brainstorm specific ideas or doable projects that can be included as personal commitments at the reentry stage.

Acknowledgment, forgiveness and healing is essential to short-term, and particularly long-term, reconciliation. In protracted and violent communal conflicts this makes the difference between a cold, fragile peace based on formal cease-fire agreements and the development of a sustainable "people-to-people" relationship. There are no shortcuts on this route. Eventually, the painful experiences of the past must be dealt with. Many such processes of "truth and reconciliation" have been undertaken as a governmental initiative (Chile, South Africa—see Borris, this volume) or at the NGO level (the *"Nunca Mas"*—never again—church-sponsored reports in Uruguay and Brazil). The Partners can discuss planning or cooperating together with such processes, particularly if the workshop is taking place at the postnegotiation stage, after a peace agreement has been signed.

Introducing personal stories can help. The facilitators and participants can ask each other if they have ever felt discriminated against, oppressed or have mourned the loss of friends and relatives as a result of the conflict. If an actual episode of this nature has occurred during or just prior to the workshop, it should be dealt with. If there have been no such cases involving the participants, role-playing can also be a useful alternative.

It has been suggested that acknowledgment of responsibility and actively seeking justice for the other party will produce lasting beneficial effects, though such an undertaking is less likely to happen immediately after a crisis. The potential for this can be discussed at the workshop, though I would not pressure the Partners for such recognition of responsibility in public, nor would I recommend that it occur immediately after an act of violence. This workshop should allow participants to show empathy not only for the humanity of their respective peoples as a whole, but also toward each other as individuals. Receiving faxes or telephone calls from Palestinian Partners and friends has helped in dealing with my own grief. Originating such communications to them has given me a sense of doing the right thing and allowed me, in expressing my concern, to express my gratitude for the concern expressed by them. In an ideal world the training process should empower Partners to make this area an integral part of their lives as peace builders.

Although such spontaneous gestures can be invaluable, protracted conflicts require a network of Partners to address in a systematic and sustained way the challenge of expressing humanity toward each other. From our own experiences we have come to realize how difficult is to agree to share victimhood. Past and present suffering are hard to compare, and so are the isolated but brutal acts of terror inflicted by one side and the sustained and widespread hardship caused by the policies of the other side (structural violence). The fact that this is a difficult mission does not imply that it is impossible. Beyond sensitivity training, organizations on each side can facilitate such expressions by bringing the participants into contact with the victims' families, with the media, and even with the perpetrators of violence or their relatives. To illustrate, in 1997 a group of Israelis and Palestinians set up a HEAL (Healing Early Action Link) network to address on a reciprocal and joint basis the acts of violence committed by official and nonofficial perpetrators of both sides.[15] The activities conducted by this group include visiting victims of political violence, writing letters to victims and relatives, conducting training courses, preparing a manual for wide circulation and joint media appearances. Early action can also include joint writing of press articles. Calls for establishing joint memorials can help achieve healing through association with the past suffering of both communities.[16]

This session may also be useful to introduce the expectations of "justice" by both sides, particularly relevant for those that perceive themselves as the oppressed in an asymmetric dyadic relationship. Human rights principles can provide international standards that are shared by most nations and their governments.[17]

I have seen even young students very moved by the sessions of this day, particularly if an incident has occurred real-time, generating an urgent need to work out a healing process together. Partners' ability to commit to be active in this field upon reentry is crucial in cases of sporadic or continuous violence.

Day 12: Joint Activities before Departure and Reentry

Training for Reentry

Motivation and Rationale

The IPSW should not be an isolated event—that could leave the Partners feeling isolated and lost after reentry. The reentry process has been described as a culture shock attributable both to separation from those who have undergone a similar experience and to exposure to a sort of inquisition from others in a still-hostile environment. Participants who wish to share new and moderate ideas from the brainstorming session may be regarded by some as fools, naive or (even worse), as traitors and victims of brainwashing. Within a Partner's family, tensions can be quite high when discussing how helpful the workshop was and how it has influenced their thinking. To avoid perceptions of proselytizing or preaching, the Partners should offer detailed pictures of lessons learned and actively seek feedback on these new perspectives.

Investment in personal transformation alone, when dealing with Partners in ongoing conflicts, is not justified. The internalization of experiential learning without the added phase of empowerment through follow-up action can result in frustration and inconclusiveness rather than fulfillment and growth. Hence, it is for the benefit of the individual as well that effective means for contributing to community transformation should also be planned. It is relatively simple to conceive of follow-up activities, if participants collaborate and time is allocated. "When reentry is well planned, the lessons learned and the skills developed can be applied back home in beneficial ways, over an appropriate time frame and within a trusting environment" (Eshelman and Standish, 1996).

Box 10.3 Guidelines for Going Home

1. The more intense the experience has been, the greater the chance for distress or dissatisfaction with any questioning about the "new you" when you return. You may need additional time to re-acclimate yourself back home. Adjustment may be aided or hampered by close relationships, personality issues and work stress. Allow more time than you think will be necessary before judging success or failure.

2. Because of the closeness established with other participants in a relatively short period of time, there may be an additional sense of loss when you return home, as well as a sense of jealousy from those close to you upon your return. Be gentle with

Box 10.3—Continued

yourself as well as with people at home. Also keep contact if possible with someone from your new network. They will probably be experiencing some of the same things.

3. Although you have had time to process what you've learned, those at home have not. Remember how skeptical you were initially. Allow the same period of skepticism for colleagues and friends at home. It's a classical case of lag time between learning something in a cognitive way and experiencing it as reality.

4. As you describe what you've learned, be aware of oversimplifying or under-simplifying. Descriptions of past happenings bring visions to you that are inaccessible for those who were not there. Set a scene and then fill in the activity only to the level that you think is of interest. Monitor how others receive your information and modify your descriptions accordingly. If you want to incorporate what you've learned successfully, do not bore people or set unrealistic expectations with any proposed changes.

5. The things that you are bringing back home will be questioned. Avoid defending them or the whole experience as the "right way of life." It may help if you share some negative aspects of your experience as well as the positive ones. It keeps your eye on reality and puts the whole experience in a more acceptable light.

6. Feedback is valuable. People will be more comfortable with you if they can tell you how your stories about your experience sound to them. It also provides an excellent way to modify any ideas that are not accurately reflected.

7. Learning continues long after presentation of material. It is not at all unusual to have "aha" experiences after returning home. This kind of realization is particularly likely after laboratory or experiential learning. It is refreshing to know that learning of this kind is continuous and may be triggered at any time.

8. Seek colleagues and friends who share your concerns and values. It is with these people that you will find the support necessary to implement change. Using allies to best advantage will spread excitement for your ideas farther than you can.

9. The culture of experiential learning is not accepted or understood globally. Be prepared to explain things in a very concrete sense. Avoid buzzwords or phrases and remember that some of the more insignificant aspects of the experience for you might be quite powerful for others. Respect others' learning process as the leaders of your group respected yours.

10. There is never enough time to practice things that you've learned. If you can share, try learning by teaching others. Expect some mistakes, realizing that practice makes perfect.

11. Learning in a classroom or laboratory is temporary and needs to be both nurtured and reinforced before it becomes permanent or institutionalized.

These eleven guidelines are but a few of the areas that need to be reviewed periodically. Be sensitive with yourself and others, and you will find that reentry brings opportunities of which you never even dreamed.

Activities for Reentry

Generally, we suggest starting the reentry stage in the immediate aftermath of the workshop. If in the capital of a third country (such as Washington, D.C.) the Partners can submit documentation of their points of agreement and program of action in a joint delegation to their respective ambassadors. This was done, for instance, by the Peruvian and Ecuadorian participants, who were ceremoniously received in the two embassies. In the case of the Partners from the Transcaucasus, we set up joint lectures at different institutions and universities in the area, generating the opportunity to show to a wider audience their commitment to searching for common ground and avoiding adversarial discourse.

In addition to developing specific small projects, the Partners should consider expected problems upon reentry and how to confront them effectively. A two-hour discussion and advising session is recommended as a debriefing in their habitat or work place upon return. More enthusiastic participants should not be in a rush to share the outcomes and agreements from the workshop but should first give detailed accounts of the intricacies of the IPSW process. If they can remember how skeptical they were on the first day, perhaps they will better understand the need for this delay.

Keeping in touch with other participants inside and outside their own country or community is also extremely useful, so that no one feels alone in the process of keeping alive the commitments undertaken to themselves and each other. Use of IT technology (e-mail, a shared Web site, chat groups, video-conferencing, etc.) needs to be discussed, making sure Partners have access, often by the organizers' making sure that budgetary provisions have been made in the original proposal.

In preparing for reentry, it may be worthwhile to role-play among the Partners an interaction with a friend or colleague from a home community who is skeptical of the IPSW process. A Partner tells the story as the local "friend" increases his/her critical response. Other participants can evaluate the performance and suggest improvements in strategy. Another suggested exercise is to ask the participants to take a few minutes and write themselves a letter, to be mailed by the organizers about two weeks after their return. In the letters, the participants should express their current feeling and willingness to undertake some specific joint actions and projects in the near future. A more collective equivalent is to ask the Partners to write a message for themselves and put all of them in a bottle, to be copied and shared after departure with everybody.

Additionally, it may be worthwhile for participants to organize an informal discussion session at a university, NGO, a friend's house or in a Partner's own home. The emphasis should be on process and content, avoiding buzzwords or phrases that were part of the internal language of the workshop. The experience should be shared with peers, even if it is not as well received as originally hoped. The stimulus for creative efforts to resolve the conflict will be transmitted to the larger community more by deeds than by words.

Team-Building Exercises

In order to stimulate team building, it is suggested that the participants prepare themselves for joint presentations in front of a local or even mixed audience, to write an op-ed together, or to use some other form for joint expression. At College Park we have often arranged for Partners in small groups jointly to visit schools where peer mediation takes place and have them talk to the students about their conflicts and current experiences in addressing ways to resolve them. If they are academics, the Partners can be asked to share the podium at a university or elsewhere (perhaps for a modest honorarium, which can be a helpful stimulus). Being an experienced team-teacher with an exceptional Palestinian Partner, I can confirm that team-teaching in classrooms provides us with adrenaline and empowers us to continue with other concrete activities in putting the collaborative experience into action.

When jointly speaking in public the Partners must take care to minimize the potential for ending the performance in an adversarial manner. One way of doing so is to suggest at least two rounds of presentations. In the first round the Partners speak introspectively and objectively about their own side of the conflict, looking at the performance of their own governments and societies. In the second part, they can comment on the performance of the other side to the conflict and, if necessary, correct any possible biases in the presentation of the other person. This two-staged approach alleviates the uncertainty of going first and attacking immediately, as a pre-emptive measure.

Day 13: Unstructured Social Activities

No matter how well the workshop has progressed, there is normally a need for some private space, away from the sustained intensity of workshop activities. The day may include individual or group activities resulting from participants' special requests, such as visits to museums, shopping expeditions, or just quiet relaxation and reflection. Shared outdoor activities or excursions that require some investment of energy and human resources can also promote team building. The time may also be used for more detailed discussion about the Partners' future cooperation. An optional evening outing to a cultural event or dinner may also be offered.

Basically, this day is a time for collecting thoughts and easing tensions that may have arisen in the workshop, particularly the more intensive stages of ARIA, so that everyone will be refreshed in the last days for discussions on joint projects and the sometimes difficult step of saying good-bye.

Day 14: Finalizing Drafts of Action Plans

The Partners come together again to design and develop action plans and joint projects, with timelines for their future activities and programs. This is a good time to familiarize participants with potential sources of funding, fund-raising issues and the possible involvement of the hosting institution in future plans. The current funders for the project may also be invited for a conversation with the Partners, along with other project development specialists.

The types of projects that can be developed are nearly limitless, but plans must take into account budgetary constraints. It is useful to begin developing a shared mechanism or institution for some of these projects. Loyalty can develop to a transnational joint enterprise or epistemic community that may transcend the original loyalty to the group. Such institutions may take on a life of their own and promote problem solving through the generation of shared values. My own team-teaching with a Palestinian colleague has for several years not only afforded me a good understanding of his arguments but made our views closer and more integrative. It is the recurrent practice of pedagogic activities which unites us, especially when we face hostile environments in our own societies.

There are many training resources for action planning, each often copywriting their own products. We have used different organizing frameworks, mostly based on systematic common sense, dealing with short-term objectives and long-term goals (what?), motivation (why?), division of labor (who?), timeline (when?), activities (how?), and budget (how much?).

When it is possible to involve representatives of foundations in dialogue with the Partners, the latter, in anticipation of possible funding, tend to work harder on their action plans, normally including a summary evaluation of the workshop as well of their prospects for related applied work. This in itself is an accelerator for future cooperation. Some minimal funding is critical for maintaining the Partners' relationships in the future, given the dedication required to work effectively in the often shattered or impoverished societies from which they come.

Day 15: The Last Day

Motivation and Rationale

The completion of the workshop is likely to be an emotional event, as bonds and relationships between participants often grow strong during the project. Its importance can hardly be stressed enough, because the values, experiences and commitments that are developed during these final stages will strongly influence the attitudes of the participants toward future joint activities (Keyton, 1993).

How members terminate the workshop activities affects how they will approach similar situations. Being encouraged to say good-bye allows an opportunity apart from the task to talk about the interaction process and the relational components of that task group. It provides a time to diffuse and assess the emotional impact of the task. It is time to reflect on what has happened and how, a time to take the positive forward, and a time to learn from the negative (Keyton, 1993).

Evaluation

This session should not become an early farewell ceremony, which has a legitimate place at the very end of the workshop. Particularly, in cases were the general feeling is positive, we can easily find ourselves moving from facilitation to felicitation. We need to minimize ritual expressions of gratitude, saying that there will be another opportunity. Ideally, we should have used already the "action-evaluation" technique (Rothman and Friedman, this volume), and therefore the last day should only add incrementally to the revision of the goals and objectives set at the beginning of the workshop. If not, an overall evaluation of the workshop should be conducted in addition to the "one-minute evaluation" forms that have provided immediate inputs on the daily program and the assessment of the ARIA role-playing. Feedback, collected through personal and group interviews, should be gathered on the extent to which the workshop has fulfilled the goals and expectations of the participants. Personal interviews minimize group pressure. At the same time, a critical evaluation of the workshop's effectiveness in furthering group goals requires that feedback also be given in a group setting, since group pressures are part of the reality defining how participants deal with the conflict.

The criteria for evaluation are determined beforehand, so that the workshop is assessed in terms of previously defined intermediate or long-term goals, as well as immediate returns as judged from concrete outcomes and activities (such as declarations, joint lectures in the community, expressions of trust and confidence-building measures offered during the workshop).

Kelman (1997a) provides a long list of intermediate goals, including developing cadres with experience in and commitment to direct communication with the other side; viewing communication and negotiation as feasible; striving for mutually satisfactory agreements for the end of conflict; differentiating the enemy image from reality; identification of Partners from the other side; raising awareness of others' perspectives; developing a deescalatory language; identifying usually reassuring actions and symbolic gestures; generating shared visions of a desirable future; and getting the Partners to the table and overcoming obstacles in the dialogue process.

These individual and group evaluations can be supported by a prepared set of questions, particularly if we would have liked to measure before-and-after attitudinal changes. A complex questionnaire is not recommended. More importantly, the participants should be encouraged to speak aloud about their learning experiences and have them recorded (if they agree), to provide an outlet to express emotions and commitment to the continuing project and to each other. When there is no volunteer to start the oral evaluation, we can ask a couple of the participants to read their answers from the written form, trading places in the center of the room. Often, it may sound self-congratulatory as well as a repeat of expressions of thanks to the organizers, but it is a good idea to let a first round of statements go in this direction and allow for the Partners to express their often genuine sense of gratitude. However, the facilitators should encourage a second round if necessary, for which the participants are reminded how important it is to note what went wrong, how things could be improved, etc.

A note to facilitators: The facilitator needs to take into account that in some cultures (e.g., parts of East and South East Asia) there is a reluctance to express criticism in public, as well as to share feelings. Aware of this, the facilitator may either risk having requests for oral evaluation met largely by silence or request that individual participants talk to him or to a member of the delegation, who will be in charge of providing a list of suggestions without attribution.

Final Team-Building and Saying Good-bye

Some outdoor team-building activities can be included here, according to the age group and culture, from high-ropes to sharing a unique landscape. The physical sense of being one group is an added and lasting dimension. On the departing day of a workshop in Sinai, most Egyptian, Jordanian, Palestinian and Israeli Partners took part in a canyon expedition. One of the Palestinian participants was blind and insisted on walking with everybody else, asking only to be told what the landscape was like. Although at the outset we were concerned about whether he would be able to complete the journey, we soon discovered that his willpower overcame all difficulties. When there was a narrow passage or high slope where he needed active assistance, the main volunteer was a strong Israeli settler, whom the Palestinian sought out when back in the jeep. A Jordanian participant indicated she had vertigo and refused to climb down to the canyon. She was encouraged not to remain behind, and eventually she did join the rest of us, being periodically calmed and supported by the other participants.

Saying a few parting words can be done in different ways, from holding hands in a circle, to just reading from a prepared text. *Abrazos* (hugs), shaking hands, kissing both or only one sex, showing emotions or not—all of these expressions need to be respectful of the participants' cultures and value systems. Holding hands in a circle with a moment of silence to collect thoughts seems to work across many cultures, but it is difficult to generalize on this point. Perhaps it is best to ask the participants themselves to organize the good-bye ceremony, and the facilitators and staff to be invited guests. In the Caucasian tradition, toasting is a nearly endless process, and the vodka glasses tend to be accompanied by ever-deeper expressions of respect, friendship and love. The process of departure sometimes may include private moments, or a moving ceremony with the host community and friends of the participants present as well. Part of the activity could be ceremonial and used to grant diplomas or certificates, which help bind the group together with one more shared identity, as "graduates."

The workshop is now complete, and all that remains is for the Partners to return to their homes and lives. It is hoped that the lessons learned and friendships gained from the workshop will remain with all Partners, fostering a greater understanding of the nature of their conflict and, thus, of potential solutions which may put an end to the human suffering it has created.

Concluding Remarks

It can be argued, quite correctly, that the preceding ideas are based mostly on common sense and experience. Our experience is that their amalgamation creates a powerful process larger than its individual components. The activities described in this and the preceding chapter can potentially enable participants to feel their way through an intense experience of opening up to each other and to a personal transformation which allows them to commit themselves powerfully to working on the resolution of their communities' conflicts. Now it is up to them to experiment and adapt the workshop to the conditions of their own situations. Clearly, it is more a gestalt than a universal recipe, requiring adaptation to the particulars of different cultures and constantly changing circumstances. Although some exercises may appear childish or naive, adults have found humanity in doing them. Most workshops are shorter than the suggested fifteen days, and facilitators will have to make hard choices selecting initial activities of higher relevance to their Partners and completing the cycle in other encounters.

Looking back with the eyes of both a participant and experienced facilitator and cofacilitator, I complete this applied text by underscoring some important lessons.

A continuous preoccupation of the participants of the weaker side, and to a large extent of the organizers themselves, is how to overcome imbalance in power relations. What real incentives does the strong side have to come into an egalitarian type of exercise? I have developed some rationale for "top dog" participation in conflict resolution in the introductory lecture. Clearly, we can make a point that in second track diplomacy there is nothing to lose, that the deliberations are confidential and that any agreed outcome is acceptable only by consensus of all participants. Often, the attraction of a "quality time" in Washington, D.C., or another interesting part of the world carries some weight. Once we manage to get both sides on board, it has been our repeated observation that the stronger feels more sensitive to the needs of the other and becomes more aware of the value of taking the other into account for a more permanent and stable solution.

Second, the expectation for tangible results is natural, especially with new experiments. Sometimes it happens that a single new idea or concept emerges from the workshop and is implemented by policy makers. We can also say that successful IPSWs replicated over time can assist in the formation of epistemic communities from contending parties in developing a shared understanding of their political realities and thus help them to come up eventually with innovative solutions to the conflict. If we see this as a continuous process, we do not need to push for shared ideas in the first round, let alone a joint statement. Beware of premature commitments and pressure for immediate results. The solutions have to click in the minds of the Partners, and we can only help by providing them with the conceptual and practical ability to open up to each other in new ways, and by generating an *esprit de corps* that allows them to transcend the conflict divide.

Third, many IPSW graduates appear to be dedicated privately or publicly to advancing a culture of conflict resolution in countries and regions where it is desperately needed. It also establishes personal ties among the Partners that can endure. One example from a workshop at College Park relates to a shared expression of concern for suicidal violence in the Israeli/Palestinian conflict. When a Jewish zealot machine-gunned a large group of Muslims praying in Hebron, perhaps it was to be expected that a long-standing Israeli "peacenik" would send a fax of condolences to his newly acquired friend, a young graduate and now administrator of an ardently nationalist Palestinian university. The fax was sent without actually imagining that it would be relayed over the phone to him while he was under curfew imposed by the Israeli authorities in his own city of Hebron and mourning a relative killed in the massacre. What was less expected a few weeks later, immediately after a bomb went off in Tel Aviv, was that the same Palestinian friend, a ten-time former detainee as a member of a radical group, would send a fax to several of his newly acquired Israeli friends, which contained the following:

> It was really a very hard moment not only for the Jewish people but for all peacemakers all over the world. I really know what the feeling is for the families and for normal people, and I felt shame for what some stupid peace killers have done, and how much pain they planted in the hearts of the families and the people of this region. I cannot find the words to express what I think about this terrible action. They did that just to kill the good things that we started together, and the best way to fight them is by going on in the peace process. So let's go on and hope that this will be the last episode of bloodshed and suffering in this century. On behalf of myself and my people I express my deep condolences to the families of the victims, to your people and yourself. I hope this will not stop the peace process: now I believe we should double our efforts to make peace.

Clearly, the learning about the reciprocal expression and acknowledgment of grief through the IPSW had had an impact. Reconciliation may remain a distant objective, but we can often achieve much in a properly conducted workshop. So it happened that one day, as I was working on a draft of this chapter, I was awakened with the news that back home in Jerusalem, eighteen of my people had been killed and fifty wounded in the Makhaneh Yehuda market by two Muslim fundamentalists. Calling home, we found out that our son-in-law had been there, at precisely the same time, and that our in-laws had been leaving for the market when they heard the news. In this atmosphere, writing about conflict resolution requires us to throw our memories back to the fax of our Arab friend, to remind ourselves that all Partners are together in a shared enterprise to stop the killing and move toward a lasting peace.

Focusing on process in itself is a necessary but insufficient condition for learning, and the IPSW is not a panacea. Historical knowledge of the region, issues and culture is a prerequisite. The workshop can meaningfully contribute to new ideas on conflict resolution, provided at least the facilitators take into account a current sociopolitical analysis by area specialists (see Gurr and Davies, this volume). Better again is to have cofacilitators from the contending parties, familiar with the problems, who have been previously trained in the conduct of IPSWs; but an adequate balance can be achieved by including in the facilitating team an expert from each of the Partners' nations. In retrospect, we feel confident that a well-selected menu of the exercises has invariably opened the appetite of participants coming from diverse parts of the globe. We have been able to adapt them to Partners as young as Palestinian and Israeli high-schoolers in the "Seeds for Peace" project, or as "established" as high-ranking officers from Peru.

There are many additional tools that we have used that have not been mentioned, such as training in conversational English for foreign participants through a conflict-resolution curriculum,[18] the early introduction of meditation or relaxation training and the use of psychodrama for the enacting of past traumatic events. We should not overburden a workshop with exercises at the expense of time for discussion of the substance of the problems. The delicate balance required for success means drawing selectively from an array of IPSW techniques and adapting them to the culture and situation. The IPSW should not become an occupational-therapy approach, displacing the unstructured space needed for substantive discussions. IPSWs are required in order to upgrade decision making in a conflict situation, and the best outcome is obtained when we leave sufficient space for constructive political exchange. The hosts or facilitators should not confuse hospitality with hospitalization but allow time both for substance and for breaks, where people have time to reflect and explore informally with their own team or other Partners their relationships and future activities.

We need to realize that often there are gaps between the IPSW concept and its actual implementation. Perfection is the enemy of good, and from our perspective, the workshops have undoubtedly promoted the learning curve and the motivation to do better. Whenever a crisis has erupted, it has strongly affected relations between Partners or those of one or more of them towards the facilitator. We can try to convert the moment of weakness into a source of strength. This is easier said than done, but possible. It has often been the case that the Partners realize that the initial investment of trust, energy and resources cannot be lost and that the momentum needs to continue. A frank discussion with the participants most likely will empower them to work hand in hand toward the successful completion of the workshop.

Budgetary and time considerations strongly constrain the nature of any second track program. It is important to plan the IPSW not as an isolated event but as one that at least has another IPSW or other joint activity built in for when the Partners reenter their communities. Our suggestion is to plan the original program for two weeks, plus two shorter workshops. At a minimum, a realistic model should include an initial workshop of seven days, followed by two follow-up sessions of three days each. Anything shorter than one week for the main workshop loses impact, although even a two-day IPSW can be run as a demonstration, whetting the appetite for further systematic use. In such cases, we should be very up-front with both the funders and the participants about the limited scope of such a presentation and training.

The importance of having at least some follow-up activities after reentry is not simply based on the difficulty of picking up momentum once it has been lost. We feel it is unfair to generate expectations (beyond personal enrichment of the participants during the workshop) and then, for all intents and purposes, drop them. The role of professional facilitators in initiating follow-up activities should be secondary to that of the Partners, but organizers and facilitators must undertake a responsibility to enhance possibilities for building on the second track process once it is begun, promising to continue with the project to the best of their abilities. This is the same responsibility that was required in the selection process and planning of the IPSW. At least one more activity with the Partners needs to be included initially. When funds first run out, it may simply mean that new and imaginative thinking is needed on how to move forward.

Paraphrasing Bernard Baroukh, we know that IPSW works in practice, and so we must hope that it works in theory as well. Yet, there is a need not only for further experimentation with the methods introduced in this book but also for research in new models. Development is needed of more sophisticated and theoretically grounded models that could be more appealing and relevant in promoting resolution of protracted conflict. For example, strategic choice problems played out as "games" among two or more parties have the potential for developing more cooperative behavior.[19] Cooperative games based on impartial reasoning tend to increase consensus for generating safety nets in which all sides to the conflict should have their minimal needs recognized and provided. Tools for a more objective and quantifiable evaluation are being developed for collaborative problem-solving settings and need to be adapted to the IPSW.

The original version of IPSW called for absolute respect for the "rules of the game." Over the years, we have learned to make better use of mixed models. Hence, having participants who are a mix of real Partners and locals in a third country in what for the latter is a simulation; bringing together several types of Partners as components of both groups; working on a small region with Partners of three comparable conflicts; and involving officials in reentry workshops, making them into "one and a half track" exercises—all these can improve and add new dimensions to the workshops. Once the basic principles are understood and applied, there is no reason not to explore jointly the construction of new formats.

Finally, to the best of my memory, I have thanked all those who inspired and helped us during the years of experimenting with IPSW. But many ideas have been transmitted anonymously, and I do not want to finish without acknowledging and apologizing to those whose names are omitted from the reference section. We have not sought to provide the reader with an extensive reference library. As mentioned, this section of the book is meant as a manual for action, and we trust that you will share with us the feeling that the main purposes of this type of work are to encourage the multiplication of this process and to support the development of a culture of conflict resolution among the nations that most need it.

As stated throughout, the purpose here is to provide a workable, effective and enlightening process of conflict transformation. It may not always work as planned, but the effort must be made. It is our hope that the facilitators and Partners who partake in these exercises will not only learn for their personal enrichment but also share methods that have worked best for them, and so add to the ongoing development, evolution and expansion of the general IPSW model.

It is also our hope that through the use of these procedures, second track conflict resolution can become a more powerful and practical aid to first track diplomatic efforts, as well as a viable alternative to the violent acts that are the plague of ethnopolitical and other disputes.

Notes

1. For a more systematic approach used in environmental conflicts, see Pritzker and Dalton's (1990: 19), "negotiated rulemaking."

2. I learned this exercise from a UNICEF facilitator.

3. For further discussion of self-determination and microstatehood options, see Duursma, 1996.

4. To illustrate how competitive norms result in confrontational attitudes, the "Robbers' Cave" experiment may be cited. This involved vacationing students who, after a fun week of camping, were separated into two contending groups through a series of competitive games. The organizers kept the score close to a tie and promised attractive rewards for the team that achieved the highest points. The students soon adopted escalatory, adversarial attitudes devaluing the other side, assuming that the objective was to prove their superiority. This can be compared to a declamatory forum such as the UN, where delegations often speak at cross-purposes (e.g., Cuban and American delegates) and where the main effort seems to be scoring points over other delegates rather than convincing them.

5. This is a tale developed from a story by Edward De Bono. A poor farmer with a beautiful daughter was indebted to a spiteful moneylender, who came to demand either repayment or the farmer's land. The farmer did not have the money and was preparing to give up his land when the moneylender saw the daughter and suggested another idea: "I will give you a chance to keep your land free of debt, if you allow me to marry your daughter." As the farmer hesitated, he added: "Even better, I will let you try your luck. I shall pick up two pebbles, one black and one white, and if your daughter can choose which hand has the white one, she is free and the land is yours without any bonds." The farmer felt miserable, but his daughter told him she was willing to take part, because they had no other choice. However, she noticed that the moneylender had picked up two black stones and put one in each hand. As she was looking around in dismay her lateral thinking process kicked in. She suddenly hit hard on one of the moneylender's hands, and a black stone fell to the ground. "So sorry," she told him. "But now I choose the other hand. If the stone in it is also black, we are both free."

6. In some countries the exercise is widely known. An alternative is: We have nine golden balls, eight solid and one hollow; how can we discover the hollow one in two weighings? The answer is not starting from one or nine, but weighing three on each side the first time, and then taking the less heavy three (the third set, if the first two were equal) and weighing a second time, one on each side. Either one of the two will weigh less (it is hollow), or if both the same, the remaining one is hollow.

7. There is a Chinese fable that illustrates creative win-win solutions. A man was given his wish to see the difference between heaven and hell before he died. When he visited hell, he saw tables covered with mouth-watering foods of all kinds, but all the people there were hungry and angry. They were forced to sit one meter from the table using chopsticks one meter long that made it impossible for them to get any food into their mouths. When he visited heaven, he was surprised to see exactly the same situation, except that the people were well fed and happy. What is the difference? In hell people were trying to feed themselves without success. In heaven they were feeding each other.

8. A Peruvian colleague has suggested another method in the event of a second brainstorming session. This involves giving each participant five large index cards and asking them to write in large characters (with different-colored markers) one idea on each card. After about ten minutes of separate idea creation, the participants read out one idea at a time and post them in different groupings on the wall. There is no need at this point to label their groupings. Only later, when the participants are to be divided into smaller working groups, are these lists divided according to clear criteria. This second method has the advantage that ideas are normally better drafted; the first method provides more of a creative stimulus, through the collective enthusiasm of generating ideas together.

9. Avoiding (when the relationship and goal attainment are not more important than confrontation); competing (when relationship is not important, but achieving the goal is); compromising (when both goals and relationships are moderately important); accommodating (when relationship is more important than goal attainment); and collaborating (when the relationship and goal are both important to all sides).

10. We draw the line for consensus at at least level 4.

11. Given the complexities in highly structured approaches such as IPSW, there has been some polarization of attitudes in the field of conflict-resolution training across cultures, between "prescriptive" and "elicitive" approaches (Lederach, 1995). On the one hand, the more anthropological "elicitive" approach considers that the best approaches to conflict can be found in the Partners' own cultures and traditions and that the facilitators need only to help local Partners bring out and refine techniques that may have been there for centuries, though perhaps only understood implicitly or subordinated to less appropriate practices which may have been imposed by foreign domination. Such a methodology implies a hands-off strategy confined to training "as an opportunity aimed primarily at discovery, creation, and solidification of models that emerge from the resources present in a particular setting, and responding to needs in that context" (Lederach, 1995).

On the other hand, the innovative methods developed mainly in the West by political and social psychologists and others can be powerful new tools for change in societies where conflicts have been brutal and protracted. Since traditional authorities may be providing mixed messages, third-party intervention may be needed to provide a fresh beginning, as exemplified in the previous days of this workshop. In the spectrum between the two approaches, I have tended to advocate this more hands-on approach as the more effective method, on the basis of my own background in a region of conflict. But we really need to go beyond this dichotomy in favor of an approach that aims pragmatically to incorporate "the best of each culture." Indeed, we have integrated into the IPSW ideas generated in non-Western cultures and incorporated the feedback of many workshops provided by Partners worldwide, producing a more global approach. We suggest discussing this issue openly with the participants, asking them to what extent current or traditional conflict-management processes are adversarial, accommodating (yielding to power), compromising or integrating (problem solving). Before recommending that they try the "old way" we suggest offering a "new way" and letting the Partners consider the advantages of each.

12. Another example of the need for translation of basic concepts is the term "second track" diplomacy. In the Latin American context, there is a need to clarify that this approach has nothing to do with the "track-two" operation that President Nixon's White House and the CIA conducted in Chile when attempting to overthrow the socialist president Salvador Allende through the use of "dirty tricks" and covert operations. Nor is this the "second track" which U.S. senator Torricelli used to try to destabilize Fidel Castro's Cuba by supporting antigovernmental activities. In Spanish, the term *segundo carril* is associated more with a negative connotation than *segunda via*, and one should be careful to clarify from the beginning differences such as these.

13. Study conducted for E. Kaufman and J. Davies (CIDCM) by Keiko Suzuno and Kana Fujii, "The Buraku and Korean-Japanese in Japan" (University of Maryland, 1999).

14. "Critical for the process of healing is the mutual acknowledgment of loss and hurt which make it possible to go on with a relationship" (Volkan, 1985).

15. For further information, contact the author, the WIAM Palestinian Center for Conflict Resolution, Bethlehem, or the Harry S. Truman Institute for the Advancement of Peace, Hebrew University, Jerusalem.

16. Monuments or shared public rituals can help the parties move on from their grieving process by linking it with external events. The mutual acknowledgment of loss and hurt clears the way for the communities to establish a new relationship (see also Borris, this volume).

17. For a development of this subject see Kaufman and Bisharat, 1998.

18. Based on a research project on English as a second language with a conflict-resolution curriculum conducted by Carrie Shaw at the College of Education, University of Maryland, College Park. This later resulted in an application involving a two-week "English for a Better Tomorrow" curriculum developed by her at CIDCM for the "Partners in Conflict in the Transcaucasus" program.

19. Fhrolich and Oppenheimer, 1996. This publication is one among the many relevant to the field produced over the years by the same authors, with whom I am currently working.

IV
Capacity Building and Action Evaluation

11

Building Capacity for JustPeace: Design, Implementation, and Evaluation of Training Programs[1]

Andrea L. Strimling

It was 1999, a year after the fall of the Suharto regime, and Indonesia was taking its first steps toward democracy. My U.S. and Indonesian partners and I were sitting in an NGO office in Jakarta, listening to several human rights leaders talk about the violence that was threatening to destroy Indonesia. They were looking for ways to stop the violence and build the foundations for lasting peace. "We need a training-of-trainers program," they concluded. "Can you provide one?"

Our answer was both yes and no. Yes, we had the organizational capacity to organize and lead a training-of-trainers program. The U.S. Agency for International Development (USAID), which had funded our trip, was eager to support such a program, and our senior Indonesian partner was enthusiastic about the idea. We were also convinced that our partners could convene an excellent group of NGO leaders to participate. But we did not believe that a training-of-trainers program, at that time, would achieve the desired results. Our partners wanted to build capacity for "justpeace"—the term John Paul Lederach (1999) developed to emphasize the link between justice and sustainable peace—and that would require sustained, strategic capacity building that supported and linked the efforts of many different actors. A training-of-trainers program would make sense only in this context, and only after prospective trainers had enough hands-on experience to train others.[2]

This story is repeated in variations all over the world. In communities traumatized by violence, people are appropriately impatient for conflict-transformation training, and trainers and funders are eager to provide meaningful assistance. However, it is essential that we design, implement, and evaluate training in ways that will maximize its long-term, positive impact.

This chapter is intended as a guide for organizers, facilitators, participants, funders, and evaluators involved in conflict-transformation training programs. It is organized around key questions of design, implementation, and evaluation. The emphasis, however, is on design, because that forms the basis for effective implementation and evaluation. The insights, examples, and suggestions are drawn from my experience designing and leading capacity-building programs, discussions with colleagues working in many parts of the world, and preliminary research in South Africa on the linkages between conflict-transformation training and long-term societal change. They are not intended as conclusive answers to these questions but as jumping-off points for reflection and dialogue.

Training as Capacity Building

Capacity Building

Capacity building, as used in this chapter, refers to a wide range of efforts intended to build local, regional, and global capacity for justpeace. Training is a tool for capacity building, not a strategy. As such, training should be linked to systems design and change processes in which stakeholders analyze the social, political, economic, and other systems in which they work and design and implement changes to those systems.[3]

The work generally associated with the conflict-transformation field takes place in a much broader context, in which organizations in human rights, sustainable development, humanitarian assistance, and other related fields play critical roles. Capacity building is strengthened when different initiatives from different fields interact synergistically, supporting and building off one another.[4] Far too often, organizations flock to areas of conflict without communicating with one another. While understandable, given lack of trust, competition for resources, and other factors, this is one of our most serious missed opportunities. Figure 11.1 shows training within its broader context. The arrows indicate some of the many opportunities for synergy.

Figure 11.1 Broader Capacity-Building Context: Synergistic Opportunities

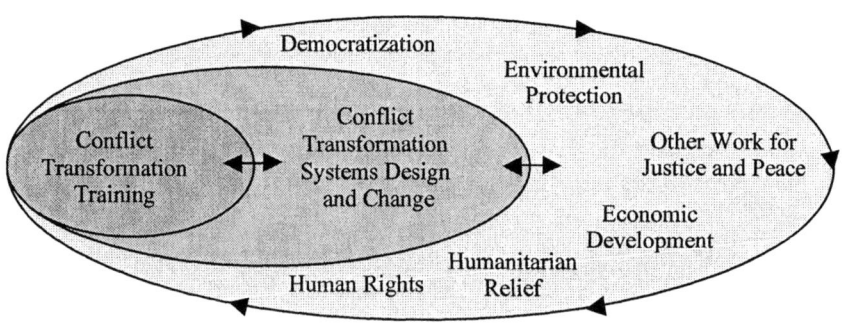

The recommendations for training design, implementation, and evaluation that follow are based on the following assumptions about capacity building:

1. Capacity building means building on a base of individual and community experiences, traditions, norms, and values, not starting "from scratch."
2. Individuals and communities must build their own capacity. Others can provide important, even critical, assistance, but true learning and growth come from within.
3. Capacity building should be a mutual, multidirectional learning process, in which "experts" are also learners and learners are also experts.

Training

The term "training" encompasses a wide range of different assumptions, values, activities, and actors. John Paul Lederach (1995) has suggested that training programs fall along a spectrum, from the most prescriptive at one end to the most elicitive at the other. "Prescriptive" programs can be characterized as those that emphasize transferring skills, models, and techniques from trainers to participants, and "elicitive" as those that emphasize drawing from and building on participants' values, experiences, and norms. Training programs differ along other dimensions, as well. Some emphasize individual learning and growth; others focus on the group experience and on building or improving relationships. Some are one-time events; others involve long-term commitments. Some are primarily analytical; others seek to connect with participants at emotional and/or spiritual levels.

There is no "right" approach to conflict-transformation training. What is right in one situation may be inappropriate or even counterproductive in another. However, there is no question that some programs are more effective in building long-term capacity than others. Their effectiveness is directly linked to the principles that underlie training design, implementation, and evaluation.

Principles

Professionals in many healing professions take oaths to follow the ethical codes of their professions. Since conflict transformation involves healing at individual and group levels, often in high-stakes situations, conflict-transformation professionals should also be guided by ethical commitments. While there is, as yet, no code of ethics for the field, there is broad consensus on several principles for ethical, effective conflict transformation:

1. *Self-awareness:* Trainers should understand clearly their own needs, goals, motivations, and intentions with respect to their work. While most trainers are driven by a desire to make a positive difference, they are also human beings, with their own interests and needs. Self-awareness and clarity of intention enable trainers to focus their energies on the needs of the group.

2. *Transparency:* Trainers should be transparent about their values, assumptions, and goals, which may or may not coincide with those of the participants. To create a learning environment in which differences are understood and respected, transparency is essential.

3. *Integrity:* Trainers should strive for consistency between their own behavior and the concepts and skills they teach. This applies both during training programs, in which effective modeling can play a key role in participants' learning, and in day-to-day life. The more clarity, skill, and commitment conflict-transformation professionals can bring to their own interpersonal, organizational, and community conflicts, the more effective their capacity-building work will be.[5]

4. *Commitment:* Trainers should engage in capacity building with sustained commitment to the individuals and communities with whom they work, to the values that drive their work, and to their shared purpose and goals. In addition, they should bring a commitment to life-long learning and growth, including learning from and with participants. This learning orientation enables trainers to lead from a base of "confident humility"—confident about what they have to offer and humble about all they have to learn.

While the focus here has been on trainers, it is equally important that participants, funders, and others involved in training programs engage with clarity, transparency, consistency, and commitment. Trainers can set positive examples, but participants must take responsibility for their individual and group learning experiences. Funders should ensure that their financial support is consistent with the purpose and goals that drive their funding, based on clear understanding of capacity-building processes and the needs of participants and their communities, and grounded in long-term commitment.

Design

Effective training depends on a design process that is simultaneously analytic and intuitive. At its best, design is done in partnership with the other stakeholders in the capacity-building process.

The key strategic questions are shown in figure 11.2. Although presented in a numbered sequence, the process should be iterative. This is particularly true of decisions about goals and participants, as those involved early in a design process may identify additional participants who, in turn, may have different goals. The arrows in the diagram show the ways in which preliminary answers to one question should inform answers to other questions.

Why? Purpose and Goals

Training design, implementation and evaluation should be grounded in clearly articulated, shared goals. These goals generally include some combination of the following:

Figure 11.2 Design Questions

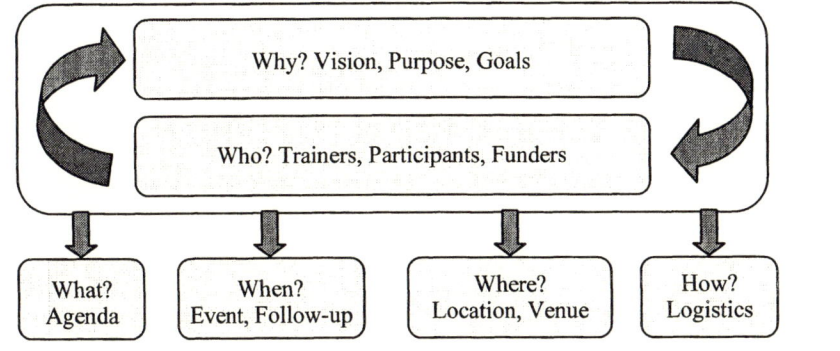

- *Developing skills* (e.g., communication, negotiation, mediation, facilitation, joint problem solving, consensus building);
- *Learning techniques, models, approaches* (e.g., step-by-step mediation processes; guidelines for brainstorming);
- *Improving relationships* (e.g., developing understanding of and empathy for others, breaking down stereotypes and "enemy images," improving communication, identifying shared needs and goals, building trust);
- *Building motivation* (e.g., commitment and energy to work for peace); and
- *Empowering* (e.g., building confidence, developing action plans).

Whenever possible, trainers, participants, and other stakeholders in the capacity-building program should work together prior to the training to identify and prioritize goals. This is important for practical, as well as ethical, reasons. To contribute to lasting, positive change, training must be relevant to the lives and needs of the participants. In many communities, for example, developing skills and/or building relationships must take place in the context of addressing concrete day-to-day issues, such as unemployment and violence.

Training should also connect with participants' deeper values and aspirations. To achieve this, trainers should encourage participants to explore the linkages between their specific training goals and the values and visions that drive those goals. In this way, we build into training programs explicit linkages to the changes people want in their lives and world.

While care must be taken to protect trainers' and participants' independence with respect to program design, the dialogue about goals should include funders and other sponsors. Many trainers keep interaction with funders to the bare minimum necessary to get financial support. Although understandable, this is often a strategic error. Funders are stakeholders in capacity-building processes and should be included as partners. Such partnership promotes stronger working relationships and more informed and consistent financial support.

Who? Participants, Trainers, and Funders

Participants

The decision about whom to involve in training is one of the most important decisions in capacity building. The central strategic question is: "What individuals and/or groups are in the best position to contribute, individually and collectively, to the transformation of conflict and the creation of justpeace?"

Whenever possible, trainers should work with community leaders and/or other appropriate stakeholders to develop criteria for participant selection, as well as a process that will be perceived as credible. Individual criteria may include commitment, interpersonal skills, and credibility. Group criteria may include institutional and/or political relationships, demographic and/or political diversity, as appropriate, and overall group credibility.

As in any conflict transformation convening process, it is important to think broadly about whom to involve. Young people, in particular, are an often-overlooked group that must be involved in long-term capacity-building programs. This need not always be done through separate "youth programs." Intergenerational training programs, if carefully and creatively designed, can be particularly effective. It is also easy to overlook the value of including perceived "enemies" and "opponents" in capacity-building processes.

Joint training programs involving conflicting groups, though requiring extra care in design and delivery, often offer significant conflict transformation opportunities. In addition to facilitating the development of personal relationships across conflict lines, they bring potential "spoilers" into the circle of stakeholders, thereby reducing the likelihood that they will disrupt the capacity-building process.

In many conflict situations, training becomes a form of intervention, in which the selection of training participants has implications that extend far beyond the training event.[6] Trainers and program organizers should, therefore, take great care to understand the political, social, cultural, and historical contexts in which participants are selected, and carefully monitor the short and long-term impacts of their decisions.

Trainers

Conflict transformation trainers come from a wide range of backgrounds and bring different values, approaches, and skills to their work. A trainer who would be highly effective in one situation may be much less so in another. Therefore, care must be taken to ensure that the trainers are well matched to the needs of the participants and their communities.

Selection of trainers should be based on a number of factors, including their knowledge of the situation, conflict-transformation experience, training skills, availability, and perceived credibility. Credibility is a particularly delicate issue. While program organizers and prospective trainers should be sensitive to community norms relating to religion, gender, age, and other factors, they should also recognize that preconceptions about credibility are sometimes inaccurate and that credibility often depends more on performance than on predetermined criteria.

Several years ago, a colleague with whom I worked closely was invited to design and lead a training program for an elite unit of the U.S. Army. Knowing of my interest in the program, he told me apologetically that he could not include me on the team because a female trainer would not be acceptable to the all-male unit. I objected, citing the potential benefits of a mixed-gender team, as well as the ethical implications of such a decision. We agreed that he would call his contact in the army to discuss the issue, and I heard back from him the following day: the commander of the unit preferred to have a mixed-gender team.

Training teams have several advantages over individual trainers. Trainers with different experiences and skills can complement one another, creating a richer learning environment than would be possible with a single trainer. Teams also provide key opportunities for trainers to model, in their team interactions, the communication and conflict transformation approaches and skills explored during the training. Teams that reflect the diversity (e.g., demographic, political, professional) of the participants can be particularly effective.

In assembling teams, local training resources should be considered seriously. Far too often, program organizers request assistance from external "experts," without first exploring local training capacity. While external trainers are necessary and appropriate in some situations, they always should support, not undermine, local resources. External trainers who are approached by program organizers should raise this issue before agreeing to provide training. Often it is useful to assemble teams that include both local and external trainers.

Funders

Program organizers and trainers usually have limited funding options. A relatively small number of foundations and government agencies in North America and Western Europe are responsible for funding the majority of conflict-transformation training programs around the world. Most have strict guidelines regarding the geographic locations and types of programs they will fund. In addition, few recognize, or are set up to respond to, the need for longer-term funding commitments and evaluation cycles. These are challenges that must be taken up, in partnership, by the field and its financial supporters.

Nevertheless, organizers' decisions about what funding sources to approach, and even whether to accept funding from available sources, can make or break a program. In making their decisions, program organizers, trainers, and funders should consider the following:

1. *Credibility:* If funding comes from one of several conflicting parties represented at the training or from a source considered suspect, the program's legitimacy may be compromised. Credibility problems often can be addressed by balancing suspect sources with more trusted sources.

2. *Flexibility:* Once a program is funded, trainers and participants must have the flexibility to revisit design decisions in the iterative process described above. Funders who require involvement in these decisions may compromise the integrity and effectiveness of the process.

3. *Transparency:* Trainers, program organizers, and funders should be transparent about funding, even in situations where this might raise concern. This is not only ethically but practically important, as the discovery of undisclosed information can derail the conflict transformation process.

4. *Commitment:* Funding decisions should reflect long-term commitments by organizers, trainers, participants, and funders. In addition, funders and conflict transformation professionals should work together to develop appropriate mechanisms for accountability that reflect the need for long-term commitments. Using multiple funding sources often increases the long-term financial security of capacity-building programs.

What? Program Agenda

Process

Whenever possible, trainers and program organizers should involve participants in setting the agenda. Encouraging participants to explore their goals prior to training begins the process of analysis and reflection on which training is based. However, participants' goals often change once they enter the training process, as they begin to understand more deeply what they need and why. This should be embraced as an essential part of the learning process.

Many trainers will develop a detailed agenda in advance and then ask participants to review the agenda and make recommendations about changes at the start of the program. Others prefer a more organic, consensus-based approach in which the participants themselves set the agenda during the program. The "open space" process is one example of an innovative, organic approach in which participants take full responsibility for setting the agenda.[7]

In engaging participants in decisions about the agenda, it is important to be sensitive to group dynamics and needs. A mistake during a program I led in Bulgaria in 1999 illustrates this point. My Bulgarian Department of Labor colleagues, our interpreter, and I were ready to begin a two-day introductory course for prospective labor mediators. This was the second phase in a systems design and training process that we hoped would lead to a new labor mediation agency. I had not been able to learn much about the participants, so the first item on my draft agenda, after introductions, was a dialogue about their experiences, goals, interests, concerns and desired modifications to the agenda. I did not understand how it would feed into participants' anxieties on a prior issue: whether labor and management would want to use mediators, and hence whether mediation training was of value. One of my Bulgarian partners, now functioning as both a cultural and linguistic interpreter, told me that the only way to cut through the mounting anxiety was to make an "executive decision" about the agenda and dive into the material. He was right. Within minutes, the anxiety had dissipated and participants were actively engaged in an initial role-play. By the end of the program, they had developed much more enthusiasm for mediation and greater confidence that labor and management could be persuaded to use it.

This story is not intended to undermine the value of engaging participants in setting or modifying agendas. Participant involvement usually results in stronger agendas and more energized participants. The point is that each situation is different, and therefore effective design and delivery require flexibility and sensitivity to the needs and experiences of all involved.

Product

In participatory agenda development, differences of opinion often emerge over perceived tradeoffs in the program. Several of these, as well as suggestions for dealing with them, are provided below:

1. *Structure/Flexibility:* Effective training programs balance structure and flexibility. The structure can be circular or linear, skeletal or highly detailed, as long as it conceptually links each training experience to the overall program and provides flexibility to adapt to group dynamics.
2. *Breadth/Depth:* Although some breadth is necessary to put training in context, in-depth training better equips participants to use what they have learned to address real-world problems. Programs that hold out the promise of conflict transformation but do not give people the knowledge, skills, confidence, and support to apply what they have learned can be counter-productive. Therefore, "survey" courses, which cover a lot of ground quickly, are often most useful when they are followed by in-depth training.
3. *Theory/Practice:* Theory should be grounded in real-world experiences and needs and linked to practical exercises. The participants should be able to answer the "so what" question: "How is this relevant to our goals for this program, our lives and our world?" They should also have opportunities to explore how the theory presented applies in their own cultural contexts.
4. *Heart/Mind:* Some training programs are highly analytical, others work more at the level of emotions and values. I am increasingly convinced that it is necessary to connect with people at both levels, and that sustained positive change in conflict situations depends on people being able to integrate their deepest values and aspirations with skillful, strategic action.

Two vital components of training agendas are often overlooked: establishing metrics and action planning. For training to contribute meaningfully to long-term capacity building, these must be integrated into the training program. Establishing metrics for evaluation promotes dialogue about the participants' visions of a changed future. It also encourages them to think concretely about how they will recognize whether they are on the right road, and what adaptations to the strategy may be necessary in the future. Action planning provides opportunities for participants to integrate what they have learned into their lives and work. In action planning, participants develop specific plans for who will do what, when, and how and determine when progress will be evaluated. Action plans should always include ways of addressing potential challenges, including lack of resources, breakdown in relationships, resumption or intensification of conflict, efforts by potential "spoilers" to disrupt the capacity-building efforts, and unexpected "openings" in the peace process.

In addition to agenda content, it is important to consider order and flow. The following guidelines highlight key issues to consider. Since each program has its own evolution and rhythm, these guidelines will not apply in every situation:

1. *Breadth and depth:* Start broad to set context, and go into more depth as training progresses.
2. *Complexity:* Increase conceptual and technical complexity as the program progresses, giving participants time to develop the knowledge, skills, and confidence to move to each new level.
3. *Emotional intensity:* Some programs are emotionally intense from the outset. If facilitated skillfully, emotional discussions can lay the foundation for mutual understanding. As far as possible, however, agendas should be designed to give participants time to develop trust in the trainers and the group before diving into highly charged areas.
4. *Connection to real-world issues:* Begin by linking training to real-world issues of concern to participants. As the training progresses, give participants space to step out of the conceptual, emotional, and behavioral patterns associated with specific conflicts by moving away from these issues. At the conclusion of training, provide opportunities for participants to reconnect with their real-world issues (e.g., through action planning).

When? Training Event and Training Relationships

Although one-time training programs can make a difference, training is much more likely to have lasting, positive impact with long-term follow-up. Therefore, training events should be designed within the context of ongoing training relationships. A training event may last for days or weeks. Training relationships should last for years.[8]

What does it mean to develop a long-term training relationship? It means a commitment to sustained capacity building, a strategy to deliver on that commitment, and the individual and organizational relationships necessary to support the ongoing work. Ambassador John McDonald (this volume) opened a training program for parliamentary leaders from Azad Kashmir by making a five-year commitment to support them in their conflict transformation efforts. The effect of this early commitment was visible during and after the program.

Commitment must be supported by the organizational and financial capacity to deliver. A long-term capacity-building plan may include some combination of preliminary training, follow-up training, technical and/or financial support for on-the-ground implementation, mentoring, training of trainers, systems design and change processes, and evaluation.

The relationships that develop among trainers and participants involved in long-term capacity building are not simply by-products of effective programs; they are essential components of long-term conflict transformation strategies. Capacity building often involves frustrations, disappointments, and perceived setbacks. Strong relationships hold and support individuals through the difficult times and enable them to focus their collective energies on shared goals. They also provide valuable opportunities to practice and reflect on conflict transformation, thereby extending the learning process.

The following example shows how training events can be integrated into a long-term capacity-building strategy that includes cycles of evaluation and reflection.

Figure 11.3 Example of Capacity-Building Strategy

EVALUATION

- Initial training event, concluding with action planning;
- Technical and/or financial support for implementation of action plans (may include mentoring);
- Follow-up training event(s) (may include debriefing and/or evaluation of prior training, review of action plan implementation, additional action planning, and/or training-of-trainers); and
- Ongoing technical and/or financial support for action plan implementation.

REFLECTION

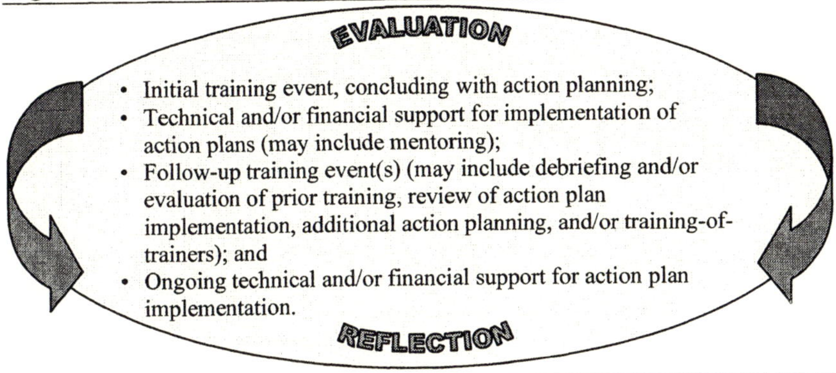

Where? Venue

The choice of venue is important for both practical and symbolic reasons. A training venue should meet as many of the following criteria as possible:

- Physically safe (geographic location, physical structures);
- Affordable;
- Accessible (safe, affordable transportation can be arranged);
- Private (with opportunities for undisturbed, confidential interaction);
- Legitimate (as perceived by participants and their communities);
- Flexible (in terms of room setup and use);
- Comfortable (accommodations, noise, temperature); and
- Inspirational (physical beauty, historical and/or spiritual symbolism).

How? Logistics

Early attention to the logistical aspects of training maximizes the chances of a smooth program in which trainers and participants can focus, uninterrupted, on what they are there to accomplish. The following checklist highlights key logistical issues and recommendations.

Figure 11.4 Logistics Checklist

Issue	Recommendations
Meeting space	Meeting rooms should be comfortable in terms of noise, temperature, lighting, and seating, and have moveable tables and chairs. Breakout rooms should be available for small group exercises and discussions.
Overnight accommodations	When participants will be staying overnight, accommodations should provide appropriate opportunities for informal interaction and relationship building.
Food and beverages	Meals should provide opportunities for informal interaction and should accommodate dietary needs of participants. Beverages and/or snacks should be available during training breaks.
Visual aids	Visual aids, including handouts, flip charts, overhead transparencies, and computerized presentations should be visible and understandable. This may require advance translation and/or the use of graphics.
Interpretation	Whenever possible, training should be conducted in the language(s) spoken by participants. When this is not possible, simultaneous and/or sequential interpretation is necessary. Interpreters should be selected based on fluency, interpretation experience, and familiarity with subject matter.
Technology	VCRs, computers, printers, photocopy machines, sound systems, equipment for simultaneous interpretation, and other technological systems should be tested in advance. Technical support should be available, if necessary.

Implementation

Although a solid design, developed in collaboration with participants and organizers, sets the stage for effective training, it must be followed by careful preparation, skillful facilitation, and committed follow-up.

Preparation

Trainer Preparation
In addition to preparing training materials and plans consistent with the agenda, trainers should carefully review the information they have gathered on the participants, their communities, and the relevant historical, political, and

cultural contexts in which the training will take place. In some cases, this information may be based on prior conversations with participants and/or organizers. Trainers should also prepare themselves emotionally and, if consistent with their own beliefs, spiritually. Just as mediators entering a conflict situation can contribute to positive outcomes through their own attitudes and energy (Bowling and Hoffman, 2000), trainers can set a tone of openness, respect, and commitment supportive of a positive learning experience.

If trainers will be working as a team, they should also prepare themselves for effective teamwork by discussing their expectations, hopes and concerns, and how they will work with one another and with the group. As in any cofacilitation process, however, all involved should understand clearly each other's needs and expectations regarding roles.

Several years ago, I was involved in a training program in Jakarta in which our Indonesian partners had agreed to work with the U.S.-based team as "cotrainers." They were highly accomplished professionals but had limited experience in several of the areas to be covered in the training. Our understanding was that they wanted us to lead most of the training but that they would select modules to lead corresponding with their areas of expertise. Most of our partners did, in fact, want to proceed in this way. One colleague, however, withdrew from the process. We learned later that she had expected to play a lead role throughout the program. Our lack of understanding of her needs and expectations had been interpreted as arrogance and disrespect. The experience highlighted the importance of taking the time to develop a shared understanding of training roles and relationships.

Participant Preparation

Different circumstances warrant different levels of participant preparation. At a minimum, participants should arrive at training ready to engage their fellow participants and the trainers openly and respectfully. At a minimum, participants should know who will be involved (particularly if participants come from contending groups) and be committed to working with them in the training. In addition, trainers may ask participants to prepare something in advance that will stimulate reflection about the issues to be addressed in training, their own goals and expectations, and/or those of others. Participants in some courses at Eastern Mennonite University's Summer Peacebuilding Institute, for example, are asked to bring objects and clothing that represent their cultural backgrounds and/or values.

Venue Preparation

Trainers should arrive at the training site in time to ensure that the space is set up correctly and that all necessary equipment is in place and working. Room setup is particularly important, as it significantly affects group dynamics. To maximize full group interaction, participants should sit in a circle or semicircle in which participants can see one another. For small group exercises and discussions, smaller circles are useful. The trainers should decide in advance where to sit, taking account of the signals they will be sending regarding their roles and the nature of the training relationship. In addition, they should discuss where individual participants might sit, how that will affect group dynamics, and whether and how to vary the seating arrangement.

Facilitation of the Training Event

Conflict transformation trainers should facilitate more than they "teach." Given that training goals usually include improving relationships, building motivation, and empowering participants, and given that participants often have significant experience dealing with conflict, trainers should facilitate processes in which participants learn from one another's experiences and insights, as well as from those of the trainers.

Effective facilitation involves skillful, creative, and purposeful improvisation. As in improvisational music, the leader may set the stage, but the music emerges from the group. Trainers should find appropriate balance between leading and responding, always keeping in sight the shared purpose and goals. In the face of unexpected challenges, especially those involving communication and relationships, trainers should help participants recognize and take advantage of opportunities for learning and growth. This requires experience, as well as the "confident humility" described above.

As in any facilitation process, trainers play a number of complementary roles, several of which are outlined below. The first four roles focus on participants' experiences; the fifth includes trainers' experiences as learners, an often-overlooked but essential leadership role.

1. *Inspiring:* Staying focused on the purpose and goals of the program, especially during difficult moments, and demonstrating practical idealism;
2. *Modeling:* Demonstrating, through interactions with participants and other trainers, the attitudes, skills, and approaches explored in the training;
3. *Challenging:* Challenging participants to stretch their minds in ways that may be difficult, and encouraging them to take responsibility for their individual and group experiences;
4. *Supporting:* Helping participants to deal constructively with challenges;
5. *Facilitating reflection and learning:* Creating an environment in which both participants and trainers reflect on their learning experiences.[9] This may include informal and/or formal mid-course assessment, self-assessment by trainers as individuals and as a team, and other approaches that promote individual and group reflection.[10]

Follow-Up

As explained above, follow-up should not be a one-time event but part of a long-term capacity-building strategy in the context of sustained relationships. In addition to evaluation and reflection, which are essential elements of capacity building, follow-up may include technical assistance, financial support, additional training, mentoring, advising, cofacilitating, and any other appropriate assistance that participants need to implement their action plans. If the trainers themselves are not able to provide the necessary assistance, they should help participants find appropriate resources.

Evaluation and Reflection

Evaluation and reflection enable us to learn from our experiences in order to work more effectively for justpeace. They are essential, interrelated components of capacity building that should be woven into design and implementation.

Evaluation

Evaluation is often seen as a necessary but unwelcome chore that must be tacked on to training programs to satisfy funders and/or generate support for future events. This is a mistake. While accountability and new support are essential, the ultimate purpose of evaluation should be to increase the effectiveness of future work. Understanding should, therefore, be given at least as much weight as measurement. Funders have pivotal roles to play in infusing a learning orientation into evaluation. They should promote the idea of learning from failures as well as successes and ensure that candor about the learning process enhances, rather than undermines, financial support.[11]

A key challenge we face is our limited knowledge of how to evaluate conflict transformation training processes. Jay Rothman's work on action evaluation is a significant contribution (see Rothman and Friedman, this volume), but we need many more people involved in developing, adapting, testing, and refining methodologies. This demand applies not only to the domain of academics; program organizers, conflict transformation organizations, trainers, funders, and participants also have key roles to play in developing evaluation tools. When possible, evaluation should be done in collaboration with experienced researchers. The following guidelines are offered to support innovation in this area.

What Should Be Evaluated?

Trainers, funders, and others often use the term "effectiveness" without defining it. At a minimum, effectiveness can be measured against the program's stated goals. But is that enough? If a program teaches mediation skills to educators but there are no opportunities for them to apply those skills, has the program succeeded? If a program supports community leaders in building relationships but those relationships so threaten members of their constituencies that they contribute to further violence, has that program succeeded?

Since the purpose of training is to build capacity for justpeace, the effectiveness of training programs must be evaluated in terms of both stakeholder goals and the program's broader intended and/or unintended impacts. This requires considerable thought and precision in the formulation of goals, the early establishment of metrics and evaluation processes, and the development of methodologies that will enable us to assess the impacts of programs and the ways in which participants diffuse their learning to broader communities.

Who Should Evaluate Training Programs?

Although it is valuable for all stakeholders (organizers, trainers, funders, participants, and communities) to conduct their own evaluations, their evaluations should supplement, not supplant, independent evaluation by professionals with no direct stake in the training. Independent evaluation, if done well, provides a broad, balanced and credible assessment of the impacts of training. Evaluators should focus primarily on participant and community experiences, while taking account of the experiences of other stakeholders.

How Should Programs Be Evaluated?

Evaluation should be multifaceted, stakeholder focused, and integrated into long-term capacity-building strategies. Evaluation strategies should emphasize qualitative methods that promote analysis and reflection.

Although much work needs to be done to develop appropriate methodologies, one approach deserves mention because of its emphasis on storytelling. It involves interviewing people individually and/or in small focus groups and asking two or three open-ended questions about the linkages between their visions for the future and their experiences during and after training.[12] By recording and transcribing a series of interviews, each based on the same questions, and identifying patterns and differences, it is possible to develop valuable insights about the connections between training and people's values, aspirations, and day-to-day experiences.[13] These insights, supported by concrete examples, can then be fed back into program design and implementation.

When Should Programs Be Evaluated?

Programs should be evaluated at intervals that enable all involved to (1) understand short and long-term impacts and (2) make mid-course changes consistent with program goals. The following chart provides an example of a multi-year evaluation plan within a long-term capacity-building program. Although the current funding environment does not support multi-year evaluation, conflict transformation professionals and funders should work together to make long-term, strategic evaluation the norm.

Training participants and communities should have access to the evaluation results. Findings, however preliminary, should be disseminated to participants and communities in ways supportive of capacity-building efforts.

Figure 11.5 Example of Multi-Year Evaluation Plan

When?	Who?	How?
Mid-training	Participants; trainers	Feedback mechanisms, facilitated dialogue, written questionnaires
End of training	Participants; trainers	Facilitated dialogue, written questionnaires
6 months after training	Participants; communities; trainers	Written questionnaires; individual interviews with participants during field-based follow-up
1 year after training	Participants; communities; trainers	Facilitated dialogue with participants during follow-up training; written questionnaires
3 years after training	Participants; communities; trainers	Individual and focus group interviews; written questionnaires
5-10 years after training	Participants; communities; trainers	Individual and focus group interviews; written questionnaires

Reflection

The purpose of reflection is to foster "cycles of learning" in which the training experience and the broader capacity-building activities within which training takes place are integrated into individual and group learning. Reflection should be built into evaluation processes, but there is also a role for reflection that is independent of evaluation. At its best, it should involve both analysis and creative expression. I recently taught in South Africa a university course in which I asked each student to bring to the final class a poem, song, painting, or other artistic creation that answered the question "What have you learned about yourself, your classmates, and/or the class material and how will you apply that learning in your life?" The session was an important integrating experience for all of us. Other ways in which reflection can be promoted include:

1. Facilitated dialogue, in which participants discuss what they have learned and how they plan to apply it;
2. Flip charting, in which participants move from one chart to another recording experiences and insights on different aspects of the training;
3. Training-team debriefings, in which trainers speak candidly about their performance as individuals and a team;
4. Journaling by participants and trainers during and after training.[14]

Regardless of what approaches are used, participants and trainers should have opportunities to reflect, individually and collectively, on their experiences in training and other capacity-building activities. In this way, training becomes one event in the ongoing process of learning and development called "capacity building," and we can just as easily speak of "capacity building as training" as speak of "training as capacity building."

Conclusion

If designed, implemented, and evaluated with clarity of purpose, skill, and commitment, conflict transformation training can empower participants to make lasting changes in their lives and communities that contribute to justpeace. Key points regarding training and capacity building are reviewed below.

1. Training should be focused on building long-term capacity for justpeace.
2. Training is a tool, not a strategy. As such, it should be integrated into capacity-building strategies that include systems design and change processes.
3. Training implementation and analysis should be based on informed, insightful, and strategic design.
4. Training design and implementation should flow from clearly articulated, shared goals.
5. Training should be relevant to the lives of the participants and their communities, and grounded in the issues about which they care the most.
6. Trainers should facilitate learning processes in which the participants' experiences, insights, and relationships are valued and integrated into the process.
7. Training should engage people's minds and hearts.
8. Stakeholders should explore the connections between their specific training goals, underlying values, and visions before, during and after training.
9. Training should be evaluated in terms of its long-term intended and unintended impacts, in addition to the achievement of specific training goals.
10. Evaluation and reflection should be oriented toward learning.
11. Capacity building should involve interorganizational and interdisciplinary collaboration.
12. All capacity-building processes should be grounded in the principles of self-awareness, transparency, integrity, and commitment.

Notes

1. This chapter is dedicated to Elise Boulding. I also gratefully acknowledge the Federal Mediation and Conciliation Service and the South Africa-U.S. Fulbright Commission for their support of the work that led to this chapter, as well as the many people in the United States, South Africa, and other parts of the world who generously shared their experiences and insights with me.
2. It is a common mistake to offer training-of-trainers programs prematurely. In the field of conflict transformation, where issues are complex and the stakes are high, people should not be trained to train others in skills they have never used themselves.
3. The National Peace Accord in South Africa, for example, established national, regional, and local peace structures that worked in interrelated ways to prevent violence and build peace. Training was only one component of the systems design and change process.

4. Justpeace requires both the transformation of individuals and relationships, and the transformation of social, political, and economic structures.

5. Many conflict-transformation organizations are themselves rife with conflict. Integrity requires addressing these conflicts in ways that are consistent with what is taught in training programs.

6. For example, selection of participants can shift the perceived balance within and/or among conflicting groups.

7. Additional information on open space processes can be found at the website www.openspaceworld.org.

8. Carl Stauffer first articulated this distinction for me.

9. Ideally, the learning process also includes program organizers, funders, and other stakeholders.

10. One approach suggested, by Peter Woodrow of CDR Associates, involves establishing a "listening committee," through which participants elicit feedback from their fellow participants and communicate regularly with the training team.

11. Most trainers and program organizers believe that funders' only interest in evaluation is as a mechanism for deciding whether to continue to support a project. Until funders articulate and commit to a learning orientation, trainers and organizers will continue to view evaluation in this way.

12. For example: "What is your vision of the future you want for your society?" "What will it take to achieve that vision?" "To what extent, and in what ways, has your participation in training enabled you to move toward this vision?"

13. Ethical issues, including those related to confidentiality and recording, must be addressed in advance.

14. I learned about this use of journaling from John Paul Lederach.

12

Action Evaluation for Conflict Management Organizations and Projects

Jay Rothman and Victor J. Friedman [1]

When staff and board members of the Dayton Mediation Center—a publicly funded agency that offers the services of trained volunteer mediators to people in the Dayton, Ohio community—wanted to define what a "successful" mediation would look like, they turned to a process called "action evaluation." By going through this process, the center hoped to assess the benefits it knew it had been providing to the community—and thus be able to further promote and expand the reach of its services.

After meeting with an action evaluator, however, the "stakeholders" decided to focus first on clarifying their own organizational goals and priorities. Thus, before addressing the question of a successful mediation, they needed first to take a look at the organization itself, to think about where it had been, and where it needed to go. To do this, they turned again to action evaluation.

Measuring the success of any process aimed at changing the way people relate to one another can be tricky business. Yet in fields such as conflict resolution and organizational development, those directly involved—as well as the funders and the general public—are more and more often asking for rich definitions of success and for valid and rigorous assessments of it, primarily as a means of accountability. At the same time, practitioners are trying to figure out how to inform the public, the funding community, and policy makers about the nature and long-term impact of their work. Researchers too are asking questions about assessment. How can it be more dynamic and integrated into practice? How can rigorous research contribute to the effectiveness of processes? Can it do so without violating issues of confidentiality or imposing control on real-life situations that rarely lend themselves to experimental conditions?

Since 1992, the Action Evaluation Research Initiative (now the Action Evaluation Project)[2] has addressed these complex and interrelated questions, resulting in a methodology that employs evaluation as a bridge between research and practice in ways that promote greater quality in both fields. At first focusing primarily on the field of conflict resolution, action evaluation has become an integrated research and intervention methodology for helping to define, promote, and assess success in conflict resolution processes, organizational and community development efforts, and the creation and enhancement of educational programs. The project focused on the development and application of a rigorous evaluation methodology, intended to help project organizers, facilitators, participants, and funders interactively define their shared goals as a project evolves, and effectively monitor and assess them.

The Action Evaluation Process

Relying in large part on a computer-assisted and Web-based instrument and database system for ongoing data analysis and program monitoring, action evaluation includes:

- A *baseline stage* that includes a systematic process for cooperative goal setting, team building, and participatory decision making within and between various project stakeholder groups.
- A *formative stage,* during which participants refine their goals, make them more "actionable," and begin working toward them.
- A *summative stage,* when participants take stock of their progress, using their evolved goals to establish criteria for retrospective assessment.

Baseline Stage

The action evaluation process is facilitated by a trained "action evaluator," who collects data on goals from the various stakeholders and summarizes the data in terms of what is shared, unique, and contrasting within (and later, across) stakeholder groups. In the case of the Dayton Mediation Center, there were two "stakeholder groups"—one including both staff and board members, the other consisting entirely of volunteer mediators.

Data Gathering
In the first phase of an action evaluation, all those involved with the project at hand articulate what are referred to as the "baseline," or initial and perhaps rather general, goals. These data are gathered via on-line questionnaires (designed for the project—see Website www.aepro.org), through interviews (which can also be used to supplement data gathered on-line), or through paper-and-pencil surveys. The preferred method is the on-line process, since it eliminates a data-entry step and makes the questionnaire both interactive and easily accessible from anywhere the Internet is available.

In addition to narrowing geographic gaps and aiding in data gathering and analysis, the computer-assisted goal-setting process is designed to be both user-friendly and self-referential. The Web technology allows respondents to refer back to their previous responses as they move through the questionnaire.

The data-gathering process begins with three basic questions: *What? Why?* and *How?*

- *What* goals do the stakeholders have for this initiative? Another way to think about this question is to compare visions of success with the current reality. The people involved may be asked to consider what they hope will change for participants—and in the larger social setting—due to the intervention and their involvement with it.
- *Why* do the various stakeholders care about their goals? What motivations are driving their outcome goals? More conceptually, and with respect to the conveners more than participants or funders, what are the theories of practice and domain assumptions that guide practice?
- *How* might the stated goals be met most effectively? What intervention processes should be used? Based on the goals and motivations articulated, stakeholders are asked to suggest what kinds of intervention strategies might best encourage movement from the present reality to the vision of success they have just articulated.

Data Analysis

Once everyone has responded to the baseline questions, the action evaluator organizes and analyzes the data of each stakeholder group on-line (using a password to protect confidentiality), synthesizing the questionnaire responses in a "prefeedback" page as follows:

- The *What* responses from everyone in a given stakeholder group are organized according to shared goals (of two or more respondents), unique goals (that only one respondent has articulated), and contrasting goals (between two or more respondents). For shared goals, the action evaluator may summarize, combine, or otherwise edit responses, as well as list each person's version of the overlapping goals, while preserving the original voice of the respondent.
- The *Why* responses are simply listed verbatim.
- The *How* data are listed and quantified according to each specific suggestion and the numbers of respondents who have proposed similar ideas, to be matched later with the shared *What* goals.

Feedback

Once the data are compiled, they are printed out and shared with respondents within each of the stakeholder groups during face-to-face meetings facilitated by the action evaluator. While the compiled data reflect the voice of the respondents, they preserve their anonymity. In addition to ensuring that the action evaluator gets his or her analysis "right," these feedback sessions help ensure that key project leaders, participants, and others are "on the same page" about their goals as they move ahead.

Feedback sessions begin with the participants' presenting their *Why* data. Not surprisingly, they often want to begin with the *What,* but the process begins with *Why* for a reason. It forces the stakeholders to go deeper, to look at their motivations, their values, as they begin to explore their own—and their group's—goals. The process also enables project members to learn more about each other and about their shared and differing motivations, in a safe and confidential environment.

Next, the action evaluator presents the compiled *What* data, inviting the group to check the re-articulation of the shared goals and determine whether those listed as unique and contrasting goals have been correctly interpreted.

While action evaluators regularly seek group consensus on goals, it is almost always lacking at the start of the feedback process. So following the presentations of *Why* and *What* data, the group negotiates until they arrive at a consensus on their shared goals and priorities. With a new understanding of the motivations, values and interests involved, the action evaluation process helps various interest groups define their shared project goals as well as employ creatively the diversity of their differences and divisions to enrich their efforts.

Ultimately each stakeholder group comes to a notion of a shared agenda, grounded in its common goals and values, for *What* should be accomplished and *Why* it is valuable for it to be accomplished.

After each stakeholder group completes this process, the action evaluator compares the shared goals of the different groups. Then the process is repeated with all stakeholder groups together, and they translate the *How* data into action steps related to the agreed-upon goals.

Box 12.1 Refining the Dayton Mediation Center's Goals

When the center's staff/board group, which included nine participants, convened for their feedback session, the evaluator began by asking each group member to present his or her own *Why* responses. While the written responses tended to be carefully considered explanations for what the participants felt needed to be done, the face-to-face presentation enabled them to go deeper, to share their gut-level feelings about what was most important. The time they spend articulating their *Why* responses also gives participants a chance to respond to and build on one another's concerns, in a manner that is impossible with the one-way responses entered into the project database. All shared the goal of financial security for the center, for example, but each came at the goal from a different place. Instead of focusing on their

Box 12.1—Continued

differences, they were able to focus on what they shared: a desire for the enter to thrive.

Once all participants had verbalized their *Why* responses and had a chance to respond to each other's concerns, the group turned to the *What* data. On flip charts, the action evaluator presented the compiled *What* data, which consisted of four shared goals, each initially proposed by four or more group members. As synthesized by the action evaluator, these goals were:

1. To establish financial stability/seek increased funding
2. To expand the number and variety of services, and to extend them both regionally and to other types of markets
3. To enhance staff training and opportunities
4. To increase referrals, visibility, and the usage of the center.

The evaluator also reported the following unique goals:

1. To increase and maintain an active, knowledgeable board
2. To establish and follow a focused mission policy
3. To research and publish Dayton's conflict-resolution needs.

Finally, the evaluator interpreted the following as contrasting goals:

1. To seek financial stability for existing services and programs versus seeking to expand and extend services (beyond the current budget)
2. To seek grant support versus city, corporate or citizen support
3. To undertake market research and marketing versus grant writing
4. Full-time staff versus part-time or volunteer.

Following the action evaluator's presentation, the group worked through the *What* goals together, refining and clarifying the evaluator's interpretations. During this give-and-take session, it became clear that some goals that the evaluator had interpreted as contrasting were not really so.

Once all goals were articulated to the group's satisfaction, they voted on them. For each goal, participants were asked to give a "thumb up" to indicate full support, as well as willingness to work toward that goal; a "thumb down" to indicate nonsupport; or a "thumb sideways" to indicate some ambivalence, perhaps recognition that a goal may be significant but not important enough to devote scarce resources to at the current time. Ultimately, the board/staff group reached consensus (no thumbs down) on the following six goals:

1. To establish financial stability/seek increased funding
2. To extend services regionally and to other types of markets
3. To enhance staff and volunteer training and opportunities
4. To increase referrals, visibility and usage of the center
5. To increase and maintain an active, knowledgeable board

Box 12.1—Continued

6.   To make research part of its practice.

The evolution of some of the goals illustrates the importance of bringing a group to the table, rather than having one or two people try to set goals for an entire organization. For example, "to enhance staff training and opportunities" became "to enhance staff and volunteer training and opportunities." Other goals, initially unique to only one stakeholder, are added to the list of shared goals as the group discusses them and comes to see them as essential to the long-term success of the organization. Such was the case with "to increase and maintain an active, knowledgeable board."

One aspect of action evaluation that makes it so appealing and so useful is its flexibility. Although there is an overall structure to the process, there is room for adaptation to the context and progress of a given project. The group took advantage of this flexibility in significant ways during their first feedback session. For example, the group began to consider whether a second stakeholder group, made up of volunteer mediators, should be consulted. The group worried about the appropriateness of involving the volunteers in policy-making activities, whether the volunteers would be interested in participating, if the volunteers had anything to contribute, the difficulty of assembling volunteers on short notice. They worried also about the loss of momentum that would come from stretching the process out over a longer period of time. Ultimately, the value of including the mediators' voices, and the further legitimacy those voices would give to the eventual outcome, overrode the staff and board's time concerns.

Within a couple of weeks, nine volunteer mediators entered their *What, Why,* and *How* responses into the database. They then gathered for their own feedback session and arrived at the following consensus goals for their group:

1.   Provide a variety of types and levels of education and training opportunities, as well as educational resources, for volunteers and staff
2.   Increase awareness of and referrals to the center through more publicity
3.   Continue to be a forum for resolving conflict in the community, especially among youth and neighbors
4.   Evaluate the impact of the center's services
5.   Seek ways to broaden revenue-producing opportunities
6.   Ensure personal safety for the staff, mediators, and clients in ways that are respectful to the clients and consistent with the center's mission
7.   Increase center involvement in providing services to the business community
8.   Offer mediation training and resources to community groups, youth leadership groups, and professional groups.

From Data Analysis to Action Planning

Once each stakeholder group has created a list of consensus goals, the action evaluator begins the next stage of data analysis by synthesizing the various groups' goals into a single list of shared goals, and matching them with stakeholders' *How* data. Then, bringing all stakeholders together, the action evaluator leads a process similar to that of the previous face-to-face meetings, in which all stakeholders agree to a single set of consensus goals.

At all stages of the action evaluation process, including this one, stakeholders have opportunities to learn not only about their own and each others' goals and motivations, but sometimes about the inaccuracy of their own preconceptions. This increased awareness can enable stakeholders to think more creatively about how best to address the organization's problems and work toward its goals.

Box 12.2 Meeting between the Center's Staff and Volunteer Groups

When the Dayton Mediation Center's board/staff group came together with the volunteer mediators' group, they came to consensus on five goals:

1. Promote financial stability
2. Extend services to new markets
3. Increase referrals, visibility, and usage of the center
4. Enhance variety of types and levels of education and training opportunities for staff and volunteers
5. Undertake research and evaluation as part of its practice.

After the group had articulated these goals, it divided into subgroups to begin work on an action plan. One board member (a businessman and past volunteer mediator), whose knowledge, especially of financial matters, had been of great value to the group, felt that the volunteer mediators would not be interested in working on the first goal—promoting financial stability. "But," one volunteer protested, "I'm interested." At that point, the action evaluator noted that when, earlier in the process, the participants had voted on each goal, all eight volunteer mediators present had given full support to that goal, while only five of six board/staff members had. Faced with the evidence, the businessman could not help but see a capacity—and a resource—he might previously have overlooked.

Once the subgroups were ready to work, then, each took one goal and prepared for it a list of "action items," based primarily on the two groups' combined *How* data. For example, the group responsible for the first goal—promote financial responsibility—produced a list of four action items:

1. Demonstrate to the city/management the value of mediation services
2. Formulate an ongoing grant writing strategy (local and national)

Box 12.2—Continued

3. Cultivate new revenue sources with other municipalities
4. Prepare a detailed revenue and line-item budget. Use to control on a monthly basis.

Each subgroup was also responsible for preparing a list of specific information to make the action items truly "actionable." The first action item was fleshed out with the following:

*   *What:* i. Quantify the value of our services; ii. Newsletter targeted to funders; iii. Presentation to key players
*   *Driving Forces:* Quality (and enthusiasm) of presentations
*   *Costs:* Minimal cost in time
*   *Who/When:* Tom lead person; George, Tim and Bill committee members—soon
    Restraining Forces: Lack of staff and time
*   *Benefits:* i. Continued commitment from city; ii. Basis to approach others for funding.

After an hour or so, when all subgroups had prepared their action plans, they reconvened, posting their results on flip charts around the room for everyone to view. Then, at the suggestion of the action evaluator, the group created a sixth goal—project management—"so we can maintain momentum and ensure we move from good ideas and energy to good implementation and action." Together the group articulated a plan to make this goal actionable.

Soon after the two groups worked out their action plan, a group made up of the center's staff members gathered to make plans for "follow through." One of their tasks was to get in touch with action plan committee heads, to ensure that all were committed to doing the work they had agreed to do and to encourage them to move forward.

Many projects have faltered at the very moment when a carefully crafted, eloquently articulated "action plan" was committed to paper. To avoid this all-too-common pitfall, the action evaluation process calls for individuals to be given specific responsibilities for each step of the plan, and it endeavors to make sure that all are truly committed to the goals they have created together.

Formative Stage

In the baseline stage, stakeholders articulate their goals and the motivations behind them in order to arrive at clear and consensual definitions of success. During the formative stage, participants refine their goals and develop strategies for overcoming obstacles to achieving them. The baseline ends with an action plan specifying what needs to be done (as well as by whom and when) in order to achieve these goals. The formative stage works back from action to a deeper understanding of project goals and of the obstacles that need to be overcome in order to achieve them.

One of the underlying assumptions of action evaluation is that goal setting is a process that continues throughout the life of a project. No matter how well project participants articulate and agree upon their goals at the baseline, they may discover new goals and opportunities as they go along. In addition participants frequently need to reconsider goals as they encounter resistance or other obstacles to implementation. Finally, project participants may discover that there is a gap between their espoused goals (what they said they wanted) and the goals implicit in what they are actually doing in their practice.

The formative stage actually overlaps with the baseline because the action plan, which is the output of the baseline stage, becomes important data in the formative stage. It provides project participants with an explicit basis for comparing intentions with what is actually happening in the project. The formative stage, however, is not simply a control mechanism for keeping the project on track. Rather, it uses the awareness of discoveries, gaps, and contradictions as opportunities for reshaping and fine-tuning a project design. Project stakeholders are asked to function as "reflective practitioners," by standing outside the situation, becoming more aware of their actual goals and strategies for action, and experimenting with new ones.

Data Collection

Since the formative stage of action evaluation focuses more on influencing processes than on assessing specific outcomes, the main objective of data collection is not to arrive at measurable outcomes but primarily to provide an account of what has occurred, or not occurred, in the project over time. While it is impossible to produce a factual account of everything that has happened, action evaluation strives to collect data that captures the most important processes and reflects the range of different perspectives. The role of the action evaluator is to analyze this "sample" and to put the pieces together into a relatively coherent and comprehensive picture.

Data at the formative stage are collected by and for project stakeholders to the greatest degree possible. Action evaluation provides a number of methods for collecting data that are minimally intrusive and demanding in terms of time. These methods include:

- *Project Log.* The log is located in the project area of the action evaluation web site. Project stakeholders can access the log at any time in order to report on important events, problems, thoughts, concerns, ideas, etc. The log provides not only an outlet for expression but also a sample of significant events recorded close to their occurrence. Other stakeholders can then read the entries, make comments or suggestions, and add entries of their own. In this sense the log represents an ongoing conversation among participants at all levels. The log is not a formal reporting device; there is no requirement for making entries or reading the log, and there is no standard format for making entries. Rather, it allows participants the freedom to enter data when and how they wish.

- *Diary.* Some events and thoughts may be too private for participants to share with all stakeholders. Therefore, each participant is provided with a confidential "diary," or area in the Website, accessible only to himself/herself and to the action evaluator (by password). The action evaluator may use data from the diaries only with the permission of the specific stakeholders.

- *Critical Incident.* Critical incident data focuses retrospectively on specific events that have been particularly important in the life of the project. Project participants are periodically asked to identify critical incidents and to tell their stories. In particular they are asked to think about events that reflect significant progress achieved and/or problems encountered in the project so far. Critical incident data may be entered directly into the Website by the participant or it may be told to the action evaluator, who later enters it into the database. The critical incidents recorded by different stakeholders represent an additional sample of what has happened in a project as well as different perspectives on, and interpretations of, these events.

- *Personal Case.* The personal case represents a particular kind of critical incident that focuses on an individual's attempts to deal with an important problem, conflict, etc. Personal cases include a brief account of the background of the incident, a reconstructed dialogue or description of what the case writer actually did to try to deal with the problem, a record of the writer's unspoken thoughts and feelings while trying to deal with the problem, and a brief description of the outcome. The action evaluation Website provides an easy set of directions/format for writing a personal case, entered by project participants directly into the general database or into the confidential diary area. They provide rich data for discovering implicit goals and action strategies of project participants. It is not only useful for individual learning but also provides important data about the interactions among stakeholders at all levels.

- *Interviews.* The action evaluator may choose to interview project stakeholders, individually or within their reference groups, at various times during the formative stage. An interview may be an extensive inquiry into participants' experiences, thoughts, and feelings, or it may be simply a way of filling gaps not accounted for in other data collection methods. Interview data is entered into the database by the action evaluator.

Data Analysis and Feedback

As at the baseline, the formative stage employs both data analysis by the action evaluator and feedback to project participants. The action evaluator reduces, sorts, and organizes data collected until she can put the pieces together into a relatively coherent and comprehensive picture of what has happened so far. This picture includes three components:

- *Time Line.* The time line is a brief sketch of the history of the project from the end of the baseline to the present time. It provides stakeholders with a quick, graphic look at the key events that have occurred over time.

- *Progress Report.* The progress report compares where the project was at the baseline and what was supposed to happen with what has actually happened over time. It compares the specific *What*, *Who*, and *When* data from the action plan of the baseline with the data collected so far. It also compares projected costs and benefits against what actually unfolds. The progress report addresses the following questions: Toward which goals has observable progress been made? Toward which goals has no observable, or negative, progress been made? In what ways are the goals implicit in project performance different from the declared goals at the baseline? What new goals have emerged over time? What existing goals have evolved or changed over time?

- *Mapping Key Problems.* As part of the formative stage analysis, the action evaluator attempts to identify and "map" the processes that account for the findings of the progress report. In general, problem maps graphically portray the causal connections between the problematic phenomenon, the conditions under which it occurs, the strategies stakeholders use to deal with it, the results of these strategies, and the long-term implications of the process itself. Problem mapping makes these processes visible to stakeholders so that they can be understood and changed, if desired.

Direct involvement of project participants is desirable, but not essential, for the initial data analysis of formative stage data. Direct participation in data analysis directly increases the validity of the discoveries and the extent of learning on the part of the participants. Many stakeholders, however, do not have the time or interest to take on this role.

On the other hand, it is essential that as many stakeholders as possible participate in the *feedback sessions* in which the formative stage analysis is presented and discussed. (It is also captured and presented in written form on the Website for project participants' review.) From the perspective of action evaluation, the feedback session is much more than just a presentation of results. The first objective of the feedback is to test the validity of the analysis—that is, whether it accurately reflects the experience of project participants themselves. The second objective is to provide participants with important insights into problems or uncertainties they may be experiencing. The third objective is to function as a springboard for deeper inquiry into the project and what has happened so far. The final objective is to provide a basis for revising the action plan both in terms of project goals and action strategies.

Experimentation at the Formative Stage

The formative stage in action evaluation is not intended to be a major, one-time event but rather an integrative as well as iterative process of experimentation, refinement, and learning. Each iteration involves a cycle of action planning, action, data collection, analysis, feedback, and redesign (cybernetic action planning). The timing and duration of a cycle depends very much on the specific nature and natural rhythms of a particular project. However, in order to be useful, this experimentation must be as close to real time as possible and take place not long after events occur.

Because uncertainty is generally highest at the early stages of a project, it may be important to have shorter and more frequent cycles. In this way action evaluation can function as a built-in learning mechanism for the project. In order to do so, however, action evaluation at the formative stage must be as user-friendly as possible.

Through the cycles of experimentation and fine-tuning, project participants gradually become clearer and more certain about actual project goals and what needs to be done to accomplish them. At that point, project participants should begin to define key indicators of success and ways of measuring them—setting the stage for the final, summative stage of action evaluation.

One of the goals of action evaluation is to integrate research with practice. Project participants, however, are always busy and rarely see themselves as researchers. Rather than trying to train practitioners to be researchers through formal up-front training, action evaluators attempt to achieve this integration gradually through collaboration, modeling, and guidance. Furthermore, action evaluators, like all action researchers or action scientists, negotiate a delicate balance between rigor and relevance, as practitioners become coresearchers and researchers become copractitioners.

Summative Stage

As a project reaches its conclusion, or a stock-taking point, participants use their evolved goals to establish criteria for retrospective assessment. Stakeholders will, for example, examine whether they have reached specified goals, and ask themselves "why?" or "why not?" They will ask themselves how and what they could have done differently or better.

It will be some time before the Dayton Mediation Center reaches this summative stage, but when it does, it will likely look back and see that some of its goals have evolved considerably. It may find that some of its goals remain the same, but also remain unmet. It will find that it has met some of the goals, but that the results were quite different from what it had anticipated. Most importantly, it will have established internally relevant standards to assess its own success or to have its success externally assessed based on its internally derived agreements about its goals.

Conclusion

Action evaluation is more than an effective process of goal articulation and data gathering that systematizes what is normally done in the design and implementation of most conflict-resolution and organizational development processes. The evaluation process and content enable participants to recognize the motivations, values, and interests necessary to negotiate consensus on shared goals and to promote reflexive evaluation among key stakeholders each step of the way as they move forward.

Action evaluation is by no means a completed methodology. For example, it is designed to culminate in a summative process. However, given the time and energy poured into development of the methodology, we have only had six of more than thirty projects reach that stage to date. Another gap between the aspirations and application of action evaluation so far is the limited input from foundations. We have been concerned with ensuring that those who fund conflict resolution become directly integrated into goal setting by making explicit what they seek to accomplish, and by participating in dialogue. The dialogue should address whether such goals are the most appropriate, and if so, how they may best be implemented, monitored, and directly assessed, rather than indirectly through funding choices. Yet to date only three foundation officers have provided data and participated in a feedback session (although several foundations have supported action evaluation projects). Finally, while action evaluation seeks to be useful and relevant across borders and has been applied on several continents, it is still primarily a U.S.-based practice. We look forward to close collaboration with, and critique from, non-U.S. and non-Western colleagues.

While action evaluation is still new, the methodology is evolving in use, and its application is undergoing further research and development, the need for such an integrated evaluation methodology is clearly an idea—and practice—whose time has come. We look forward to widening the circle of those who are using, and improving, action evaluation over the months and years ahead.

Notes

1. Substantial assistance in writing this paper was provided by Margie Loyacano. Useful comments and suggestions by Robin McLaughlin are gratefully acknowledged.

2. The project was initially funded by the Pew Charitable Trusts and since 1998 has been funded by the Hewlett Foundation.

References

Ackerman, P., and C. Kruegler (1994). *Strategic Nonviolent Conflict*. Westport, Conn.: Praeger.

Adler, E (1993). "Cognitive Evolution: A Dynamic Approach for the Study of International Relations and Their Progress." In *Progress in International Relations,* E. Adler and B. Crawford, eds. New York: Columbia University Press.

Alevy, D. I., B. Bunker, L. W. Doob, W. J. Foltz, N. French, E. B. Klein, and J. C. Miller (1974). "Rationale, Research, and Role Relations in the Stirling Workshop." *Journal of Conflict Resolution* 18: 276-284.

Alexander, C. N., J. L. Davies, et al. (1990). "Growth of Higher Stages of Consciousness." In *Higher Stages of Human Development: Perspectives on Adult Growth,* C. N. Alexander and E. J. Langer, eds. New York: Oxford University Press.

Alexander, C. N., S. M. Druker, and E. J. Langer (1990). "Introduction: Major Issues in the Exploration of Adult Growth." In *Higher Stages of Human Development: Perspectives on Adult Growth,* C. N. Alexander and E. J. Langer, eds. New York: Oxford University Press.

Alexander, C. N., M. V. Rainforth, and P. Gelderloos (1991). "Transcendental Meditation, Self-Actualization and Psychological Health: A Conceptual Overview and Statistical Meta-Analysis." *Journal of Social Behavior and Personality* 6(5): 189-247.

Almond, G. A., and S. Verba (1963). *The Civic Culture: Political Attitudes and Democracy in Five Nations*. Princeton, N.J.: Princeton University Press.

Alpher, J., and K. Shikaki, with participation of the additional members of the Joint Working Group on Israeli-Palestinian Relations (1999). "The Palestinian Refugee Problem and the Right of Return." *Middle East Policy* 6(3): 167-189 (Originally published as *Weatherhead Center for International Affairs Working Paper No. 98-7*. Cambridge, Mass.: Harvard University, 1998).

Apter, D. E. (1987). *Rethinking Development: Modernization, Dependency and Postmodern Politics*. Newbury Park, Calif.: Sage.

Auvine, B., B. Densmore, M. Extrom, S. Poole, and M. Shanklin (1978). *A Manual for Conflict Resolution*. Madison, Wisc.: Center for Conflict Resolution.

Ayers, R. W. (2000). "A World Flying Apart? Violent Nationalist Conflict and the End of the Cold War." *Journal of Peace Research* 37: 105-117.

Azar, E. E. (1970). "The Analysis of International Events." *Peace Research Reviews* 4 (1): 1-113.

——— (1978). "Protracted Social Conflict: Theory and Practice in the Middle East." *Journal of Palestine Studies* 8 (1).

——— (1979). "Peace amidst Development: A Conceptual Agenda for Conflict and Peace Research." *International Interactions* 6 (2): 123-143.

———— (1980). "The Conflict and Peace Data Bank (COPDAB) Project." *Journal of Conflict Resolution* 24: 143-152.

———— (1983). "The Theory of Protracted Social Conflict and the Challenge of Transforming Conflict Situations." *Monograph Series in World Affairs* 20 (M2): 81-99.

———— (1984). "The Theory of Protracted Social Conflicts and the Challenge of Transforming Conflict Situations." In *Conflict Processes and the Breakdown of International Systems*, D. A. Zinnes, ed. Denver, Colo.: Graduate School of International Studies, University of Denver.

———— (1985). "Protracted International Conflicts: Ten Propositions." *International Interactions* 12: 59-70.

———— (1986). "Management of Protracted Social Conflict in the Third World." *Ethnic Studies Report* 4 (2).

———— (1986). "Protracted Social Conflicts: Ten Propositions." In *International Conflict Resolution: Theory and Practice*, E. E. Azar and J. W. Burton, eds. Boulder, Colo.: Lynne Rienner.

———— (1988). "Protracted Social Conflicts in the International System: A Research Guide." CIDCM: Unpublished paper.

———— (1990). *The Management of Protracted Social Conflict: Theory and Cases.* Aldershot, U.K.: Dartmouth, Gower.

———— (1991). "The Analysis and Management of Protracted Conflict." In *The Psychodynamics of International Relationships, Vol. II: Unofficial Diplomacy at Work*, V. D. Volkan, D. A. Julius, and J. V. Montville, eds. Lexington, Mass.: Lexington, 93-120.

Azar, E. E., et al. (1984). *The Emergence of a New Lebanon: Fantasy or Reality?* New York: Praeger.

Azar, E. E., and J. W. Burton, eds. (1986). *International Conflict Resolution: Theory and Practice.* Brighton, U.K.: Wheatsheaf.

Azar, E. E., J. L. Davies, and H. Shahbazi (1990). "Track Two Diplomacy: Process and Critique." *The Annual Review of Conflict Knowledge and Conflict Resolution* 2: 269-304.

Azar, E. E., and N. Farah (1981). "The Structure of Inequalities and Protracted Social Conflict: A Theoretical Framework." *International Interactions* 7: 317-335.

Azar, E. E., P. Jureidini, and R. McLaurin (1978). "Protracted Social Conflict: Theory and Practice in the Middle East." *Journal of Palestine Studies* 8 (1): 41-60.

Azar, E. E., and C. I. Moon (1986). "Managing Protracted Social Conflicts in the Third World: Facilitation and Development Diplomacy." *Millennium: Journal of International Studies* 15: 393-406.

Azar, E. E., and C. I. Moon, eds. (1988). *National Security in the Third World: The Management of External and Internal Threats.* Aldershot, U.K.: Edward Elgar.

Bacow, L., and M. Wheeler (1983). *Environmental Dispute Resolution.* New York: Plenum.

Banks, M., ed. (1984). *Conflict in World Society: A New Perspective on International Relations.* New York: St. Martin's.

Bargal, D., and H. Bar (1990). *Lehyot im a Sijsuh* [Living with Conflict]. Jerusalem, Israel: The Jerusalem Institute for the Study of Israel.

Becker, D., et al. (1990). "Therapy with Victims of Political Repression in Chile: The Challenges of Social Reparation." *Journal of Social Issues* 40 (3): 133-149.

Bercovitch, J. (1984). *Social Conflicts and Third Parties: Strategies of Conflict Resolution.* Boulder, Colo.: Westview.

Berman, M. R., and J. E. Johnson, eds. (1977). *Unofficial Diplomats*. New York: Columbia University Press.

Blake, R. R., H. A. Shepard, and J. S. Mouton (1964). *Managing Intergroup Conflict in Industry*. Houston, Tex.: Gulf.

Bloomfield, D. (1995). "Towards Complementarity in Conflict-Management Resolution and Settlement in Northern Ireland." *Journal of Peace Research* 32 (2): 151-164.

Boardman, S. K., and S. V. Horowitz (1994). "Constructive Conflict Management and Social Problems: An Introduction." *Journal of Social Issues* 50: 1-12.

Boehringer, G. H., V. Zeruolis, J. Bayley, and K. Boehringer (1974). "Stirling: The Destructive Application of Group Techniques to a Conflict." *Journal of Conflict Resolution* 18: 257-275.

Boraine, A., and J. Levy, eds. (1995). *The Healing of a Nation?* Justice in Transition Project, Cape Town, South Africa: IDASA.

Bowling, D., and D. Hoffman (2000). "Bringing Peace into the Room: The Personal Qualities of the Mediator and Their Impact on the Mediation." *Negotiation Journal* 16 (1): 5-28.

Brams, S. J., and A. D. Taylor (1996). *Fair Division: From Cake-Cutting to Dispute Resolution*. New York, N.Y.: Cambridge University Press.

Bronfenbrenner, U. (1961). "The Mirror Image in Soviet-American Relations: A Social Psychologist's Report." *Journal of Social Issues* 17 (3): 45-56.

Bronkhorst, D. (1995). *Truth and Reconciliation: Obstacles and Opportunities in Human Rights*. Amsterdam: Amnesty International Dutch Section.

Burton, J. W. (1965). *International Relations: A General Theory*. London: Cambridge University Press.

———— (1969). *Conflict and Communication: The Use of Controlled Communication in International Relations*. London: Macmillan.

———— (1979). *Deviance, Terrorism and War: The Process of Solving Unsolved Social and Political Problems*. New York: St. Martin's.

———— (1984). *Global Conflict: The Domestic Sources of International Crisis*. Brighton, U.K.: Wheatsheaf.

———— (1987). *Resolving Deep-Rooted Conflict: A Handbook*. Lanham, Md.: University Press of America.

————, ed. (1990). *Conflict: Human Needs Theory*. New York: St. Martin's.

———— (1994). *Conflict Analysis: Its Past and Future-Changing Assumptions and Their Implications (An Introspective Account)*. Unpublished manuscript.

———— (1996). *Conflict Resolution: Its Language and Processes*. Lanham, Md.: Scarecrow.

Burton, J. W., and F. Dukes (1990). *Conflict: Practices in Management, Settlement and Resolution*. New York: St. Martin's.

Cahill, K. M., ed. (1996). *Preventive Diplomacy: Stopping Wars Before They Start*. New York: Basic Books.

Center for the Study of the Mind and Human Interaction (1995a). *Methodology for Reduction of Ethnic Tension, and Promotion of Democratization and Institution Building*. Charlottesville, Va.: University of Virginia.

———— (1995b). *A Psychopolitical Workshop. Parnu, Estonia, October 10-13, 1994*. Charlottesville, Va.: University of Virginia.

Chilton, S. (1988). *Defining Political Development*. Boulder, Colo.: Lynne Rienner.

Chufrin, G. I., and H. H. Saunders (1993). "A Public Peace Process." *Negotiation Journal* 9: 155-177.

Cohen, R. (1997a). *Apologies and International Conflict.* Unpublished manuscript, Hebrew University.

———— (1997b). *Negotiating Across Cultures.* Washington, D.C.: U.S. Institute of Peace.

Cohen, S. P. (1994). Personal communication with the author (Edy Kaufman).

Cohen, S. P., and E. E. Azar (1981). "From War to Peace: The Transition between Egypt and Israel." *Journal of Conflict Resolution* 25: 87-114.

Cohen, S. P., H. C. Kelman, F. D. Miller, and B. L. Smith (1977). "Evolving Inter-Group Techniques for Conflict Resolution: An Israeli-Palestinian Pilot Workshop." *Journal of Social Issues* 33 (1): 165-189.

Coleman, J. (1990). *Foundations of Social Theory.* Cambridge, Mass.: Harvard University Press.

Commons, M. L., F. A. Richards, and C. Armon, eds. (1984). *Beyond Formal Operations: Late Adolescent and Adult Cognitive Development.* New York: Praeger.

Cook-Greuter, S. (1990). "Maps for Living: Ego Development Stages from Symbiosis to Conscious Universal Embeddedness." In *Beyond Formal Operations: Late Adolescent and Adult Cognitive Development,* M. L. Commons, F. A. Richards, and C. Armon, eds. New York: Praeger.

Correa, J. S. (1992). "Dealing with Past Human Rights Violations: The Chilean Case After Dictatorship." *Notre Dame Law Review* 67 (5): 1464-1485.

Cousins, N. (1977) (Interview). "The Dartmouth Conferences." In *Unofficial Diplomats,* M. R. Berman and J. E. Johnson, eds. New York: Columbia University Press, 45-55.

Curle, A. (1986). *In the Middle: Non-Official Mediation in Violent Situations.* Oxford, U.K.: Berg.

———— (1990). *Tools for Change: A Personal Story.* London: Hawthorn.

Dalpino, C. E. (2000). *Deferring Democracy: Promoting Openness in Authoritarian Regimes.* Washington, D.C.: Brookings Institution Press.

Davidson, W. D., and J. V. Montville (1981-82). "Foreign Policy According to Freud." *Foreign Policy* 45 (Winter): 145-157.

Davies, J. L., and T. R. Gurr, eds. (1998). *Preventive Measures: Building Risk Assessment and Crisis Early Warning Systems.* Lanham, Md.: Rowman and Littlefield.

Davies, J. L., B. Harff, and A. Speca (1998). "Dynamic Data for Early Warning of Ethnopolitical Conflict." In *Preventive Measures: Building Risk Assessment and Crisis Early Warning Systems,* J. L. Davies and T. R. Gurr, eds. Lanham, Md.: Rowman and Littlefield.

De Reuck, A. V. S. (1974). "Controlled Communication: Rationale and Dynamics." *The Human Context* 6 (1): 64-80.

Deutsch, M. (1998). "Constructive Conflict Resolution: Principles, Training and Research" In *The Handbook of Interethnic Coexistence,* E. Weiner, ed. New York: Continuum, 199-216.

Diamond, L. (1994). *Political Culture and Democracy in Developing Countries.* New York: St. Martin's.

Diamond, L., and J. McDonald (1991). *Multi-track Diplomacy: A Systems Guide and Analysis.* Grinnell: Iowa Peace Institute.

Diamond, L., and J. McDonald (1996). *Multi-Track Diplomacy: A Systems Approach to Peace.* West Hartford, Conn.: Kumarian.

Doob, L.W., ed. (1970). *Resolving Conflict in Africa: The Fermeda Workshop.* New Haven, Conn.: Yale University Press.

———— (1974). "A Cyprus Workshop: An Exercise in Intervention Methodology." *Journal of Social Psychology* 94: 161-178.

——— (1975). "Unofficial Intervention in Destructive Social Conflicts." In *Cross-cultural Perspectives on Learning*, R. W. Brislin, et al., eds. New York: Wiley, 131-153.

——— (1981). *The Pursuit of Peace*. Westport, Conn.: Greenwood Press.

——— (1987). "Adieu to Private Intervention in Political Conflicts?" *International Journal of Group Tensions* 17: 15-27.

——— (1993). *Interventions: Guides and Perils*. New Haven, Conn.: Yale University Press.

Doob, L. W., and W. J. Foltz (1973). "The Belfast Workshop: An Application of Group Techniques to a Destructive Conflict." *Journal of Conflict Resolution* 17: 489-512.

——— (1974). "The Impact of a Workshop upon Grassroots Leaders in Belfast." *Journal of Conflict Resolution* 18: 237-256.

——— (1975). "Voices From a Belfast Workshop." *Social Change* 5 (3): 1-3, 6-8.

Dudley, R., and R. A. Miller (1998). "Group Rebellion in the 1980's." *Journal of Conflict Resolution* 42: 77-96.

Duursma, J. C. (1996). *Fragmentation and the International Relations of Micro-States: Self-Determination and Statehood*. Cambridge, U.K.: Cambridge University Press.

Eshelman and Standish (1996). *Transitions: Returning Home*. Baltimore, Md.: Crosslinks Monographs.

Estes, C. P. (1995). *Women Who Run with the Wolves*. New York: Ballantine.

Esty, D. C., J. Goldstone, T. R. Gurr, B. Harff, P. T. Surko, A. N. Unger, and R. S. Chen (1988) "The State Failure Project: Early Warning Research for U.S. Foreign Policy Planning." In *Preventive Measures: Building Risk Assessment and Crisis Early Warning Systems*, J. L. Davies and T. R. Gurr, eds. Lanham, Md.: Rowman and Littlefield.

European Centre for Conflict Prevention (1999). *People Building Peace: 35 Inspiring Stories from around the World*. Amsterdam: European Centre for Conflict Prevention.

Frolich, N., and J. A. Oppenheimer (1996). "Experiencing Impartiality to Invoke Fairness in the Ph.D.: Some Experimental Results." *Public Choice* 86: 117-135.

Finnemore, M., and K. Sikkink (1998). "International Norm Dynamics and Political Change." *International Organization* 52 (4): 887- 917.

Fisher, R., and W. Ury (1991). *Getting to Yes: Negotiating Agreement without Giving In*. New York: Penguin.

Fisher, R. J. (1972). "Third Party Consultation: A Method for the Study and Resolution of Conflict." *Journal of Conflict Resolution* 16: 67-94.

——— (1976). "Third Party Consultation: A Skill for Professional Psychologists in Community Practice." *Professional Psychology* 7: 344-351.

——— (1980). "A Third-Party Consultation Workshop on the India-Pakistan Conflict." *Journal of Social Psychology* 112: 191-206.

——— (1983). "Third Party Consultation as a Method of Conflict Resolution: A Review of Studies." *Journal of Conflict Resolution* 27: 301-334.

——— (1990). *The Social Psychology of Intergroup and International Conflict Resolution*. New York: Springer-Verlag.

——— (1991). *Conflict Analysis Workshop on Cyprus: Final Workshop Report*. Ottawa: Canadian Institute for International Peace and Security.

——— (1992). *Peacebuilding for Cyprus: Report on a Conflict Analysis Workshop, June 1991*. Ottawa: Canadian Institute for International Peace and Security.

——— (1993). "Developing the Field of Interactive Conflict Resolution: Issues in Training, Funding, and Institutionalization." *Political Psychology* 14: 123-138.

———— (1994a). *Education and Peacebuilding in Cyprus: A Report on Two Conflict Analysis Workshops.* Saskatoon: University of Saskatchewan.

———— (1994b). "Generic Principles for Resolving Intergroup Conflict." *Journal of Social Issues* 50 (1): 47-66.

———— (1997). *Interactive Conflict Resolution.* Syracuse, N.Y.: Syracuse University Press.

———— (In Press). "Third Party Consultation Applied to the Cyprus Conflict." In *Innovation in Unofficial Third Party Intervention in International Conflict*, N. Rouhana, ed. Syracuse, N.Y.: Syracuse University Press.

Fisher, R. J., and L. Keashly (1991). "The Potential Complementarity of Mediation and Consultation within a Contingency Model of Third Party Intervention." *Journal of Peace Research* 28 (1): 29-42.

Fisher, R. J., and J. H. White (1976). "Reducing Tensions between Neighborhood Housing Groups: A Pilot Study in Third Party Consultation." *International Journal of Group Tensions* 6: 41-52.

Fisher, S., et al. (2000). *Working with Conflict: Skills and Strategies for All.* New York: Zed.

Fowler, J. (1981). *Stages of Faith: The Psychology of Human Development and the Quest for Meaning.* New York: Harper and Row.

Freedman, S. C. (1981). "Threats, Promises and Coalitions: A Study of Compliance and Retaliation in a Simulated Organizational Setting." *Journal of Applied Social Psychology* 11: 114-136.

Fukuyama, F. (1992). *The End of History and the Last Man.* New York: Avon.

Galtung, J. (1969). "Violence, Peace and Peace Research." *Journal of Peace Research* 6: 167-191.

Galtung, J., and C. G. Jacobsen (2000). *Searching for Peace: The Road to Transcend.* London: Pluto.

Gilligan, C. (1982). *In a Different Voice: Psychological Theory and Women's Development.* Cambridge, Mass: Harvard University Press.

Graybill, L. (1996). "Remembrance of War in South Africa." *Peace Review* 8 (2): 255-260.

Gurr, T. R. (1970). *Why Men Rebel.* Princeton, N.J.: Princeton University Press.

———— (1993). *Minorities at Risk: A Global View of Ethnopolitical Conflicts.* Washington, D.C.: U.S. Institute of Peace Press.

———— (2000a). *Peoples versus States: Minorities at Risk in the New Century.* Washington, D.C.: U.S. Institute of Peace Press.

———— (2000b). "Non-Violence in Ethnopolitics: Strategies for Attainment of Group Rights and Autonomy. Symposium on A Force More Powerful: A Century of Non-Violent Conflict." *PS: Political Science and Politics* 33 (June).

Gurr, T. R., D. C. Esty, J. A. Goldstone, B. Harff, P. T. Surko and A. N. Unger (1999). "The State Failure Project: New Approaches, New Findings." In *Failed States*, M. Stohl, ed. London: Cambridge University Press.

Gurr, T. R., and B. Harff (1994). *Ethnic Conflict in World Politics.* Boulder, Colo: Westview.

Gurr, T. R., K. Jaggers, and W. Moore (1998). *Polity II Codebook.* Boulder, Colo.: Center of Comparative Politics.

Gurr, T. R., and M. Marshall (2000). "The Etiology of Ethnopolitical Conflict." In *Peoples versus States: Minorities at Risk in the New Century*, T. R. Gurr, ed. Washington, D.C.: U.S. Institute of Peace Press, 2000.

Gurr, T. R., M. Marshall, and D. Khosla (2000). *Peace and Conflict 2001: A Global Survey of Armed Conflicts, Self-Determination Movements and Democracy.* College

Park, Md.: Center for International Development and Conflict Management (also available at www.cidcm.org).

Hagelin, J. S., M. V. Rainforth, D. W. Orme-Johnson, K. L. Cavanaugh, C. N. Alexander, S. F. Shatkin, J. L. Davies, A. O. Hughes and D. Ross (1999). "Effects of Group Practice of the Transcendental Meditation Program on Violent Crime in Washington D.C. *Social Indicators Research* 47(2): 153-201.

Hamber, B., et al. (1998). "Survivors' Perceptions of the Truth and Reconciliation Commission and Suggestions for the Final Report." Compiled by Center for the Study of Violence and Reconciliation and Khulumani Support Group.

Hansard (1995). *Debates of the National Assembly, Second Session, First Parliament, 16-18 May.* Cape Town, South Africa: Government Printer.

Harff, B., and T. R. Gurr (1998). "Systematic Early Warning of Humanitarian Emergencies." *Journal of Peace Research* 35: 551-579.

Harff, B., with P. Surko, and A. Unger (2001). "Risk Assessment and Early Warning of Genocides and Political Mass Murder: Two Empirical Studies." Prepublication paper.

Harris, P., and B. Reilly, eds. (1998). *Democracy and Deep-Rooted Conflict: Options for Negotiators.* Stockholm: International Institute for Democracy and Electoral Assistance.

Hill, B. J (1982). "An Analysis of Conflict Resolution Techniques: From Problem Solving to Theory." *Journal of Conflict Resolution* 26: 109-138.

Hofstede, G. (1980). "Culture's Consequences: International Differences in Work-Related Values." *Cross-Cultural Research and Methodology Series,* Vol. 5. London: Sage.

Inglehart, R. (1990). *Culture Shift in Advanced Industrial Countries.* Princeton, N.J.: Princeton University Press.

Irani, G. E. (1997). "Islamic Mediation Techniques for Middle East Countries." *MERL4 Journal* 2: 1-10.

——— (1998). "Reconciliation and Peace: Rituals for the Middle East." *Middle East Insight* (September–October): 24-26.

Jacoby, S. (1985). *Wild Justice: The Evolution of Revenge.* New York: Harper and Row.

Jervis, R. (1976). *Perception and Misperception in International Politics.* Princeton, N.J.: Princeton University Press.

Joint Working Group on Israeli-Palestinian Relations (1999). "General Principles for the Final Israeli-Palestinian Agreement." *The Middle East Journal* 53(1): 170-175. (Originally published as *PICAR Working Paper.* Cambridge, Mass.: Program on International Conflict Analysis and Resolution, Weatherhead Center for International Affairs, Harvard University, 1998).

——— (2000). "The Future Israeli-Palestinian Relationship." *Middle East Policy* 7(2): 90-112. (Originally published as *Weatherhead Center for International Affairs Working Paper No. 99-12.* Cambridge, Mass.: Harvard University, 1999.)

Julius, D. A. (1991). "The Practice of Track Two Diplomacy in the Arab-Israeli Conferences." In *The Psychodynamics of International Relationships, Vol. II: Unofficial Diplomacy at Work,* V. D. Volkan, D. A. Julius, and J. V. Montville, eds. Lexington, Mass.: Lexington, 193-205.

Kahane, A. (1998). "Learning from Mont Fleur: Scenarios as a Tool for Discovering Common Ground." *Deeper News* 7 (1): 103-107.

Kaplan, M. (1984). "The Pugwash Conferences on Science and World Affairs." In *The Arms Race at a Time of Decision: Annals of Pugwash 1983,* J. Rotblat and A. Pascolini, eds. London: Macmillan, 281-283.

Kaufman, E. (1998). *Resoluciones innovadoras de problemas: un programa/taller modelo.* College Park, Md.: Latin American Studies Center.

Kaufman, E., and I. Bisharat (1998). "Human Rights and Conflict Resolution: Searching for Common Ground between Justice and Peace in the Israeli/Palestinian Conflict." *NIDR FORUM* 36: 16-23.

Kaufman, E., J. Oppenheimer, A. Wolf, and A. Dinar (1997). "Transboundary Fresh Water Dispute and Conflict Resolution: Planning an Integrated Approach." *Water International* 22 (1): 38-48.

Keen, S. (1986). *Faces of the Enemy: Reflections of the Hostile Imagination.* A PBS documentary film. San Francisco: Harper and Row.

Kegan, R. (1982). *The Evolving Self.* Cambridge, Mass.: Harvard University Press.

Kelman, H.C. (1972). "The Problem-Solving Workshop in Conflict Resolution." In *Communication in International Politics,* R. L. Merritt, ed. Urbana: University of Illinois Press, 168-204.

———— (1977). "The Problem Solving Workshop in Conflict Resolution." In *UnofficialDiplomats,* M. Berman and J. E. Johnson, eds. New York: Columbia University Press, 168-200.

———— (1978). "Israelis and Palestinians: Psychological Prerequisites for Mutual Acceptance." *International Security* 3: 162-186.

———— (1979). "An Interactional Approach to Conflict Resolution and Its Application to Israeli-Palestinian Relations." *International Interactions* 6 (2): 99-122.

———— (1982). "Creating the Condition for Israeli-Palestinian Negotiations." *Journal of Conflict Resolution* 26: 39-75.

———— (1986). "Interactive Problem Solving: A Social-Psychological Approach to Conflict Resolution." In *Dialogue Toward Inter-Faith Understanding,* W. Klassen, ed. Jerusalem: Ecumenical Institute for Theological Research, 293-314.

———— (1987). "The Political Psychology of the Israeli-Palestinian Conflict: How Can We Overcome the Barriers to a Negotiated Solution?" *Political Psychology* 8: 347-363.

———— (1990). "Applying a Human Needs Perspective to the Practice of Conflict Resolution: The Israeli-Palestinian Case." In *Conflict: Human Needs Theory,* J. W. Burton, ed. New York: St. Martin's, 283-297.

———— (1991a). "A Behavioral Science Perspective on the Study of War and Peace." In *Perspectives on Behavioral Science: The Colorado Lectures,* R. Jessor, ed. Boulder, Colo.: Westview, 245-275.

———— (1991b). "Interactive Problem Solving: The Uses and Limits of a Therapeutic Model for the Resolution of International Conflicts." In *The Psychodynamics of International Relationships, Vol. II: Unofficial Diplomacy at Work,* V. D. Volkan, D. A. Julius, and J. V. Montville, eds. Lexington, Mass.: Lexington, 145-160.

———— (1992). "Informal Mediation by the Scholar/Practitioner." In *Mediation in International Relations: Multiple Approaches to Conflict Management,* J. Bercovitch and J. Z. Rubin, eds. New York: St. Martin's, 64-96.

———— (1993). "Coalitions Across Conflict Lines: The Interplay of Conflicts Within and Between the Israeli and Palestinian Communities." In *Conflicts between People and Groups,* S. Worchel and J. Simpson, eds. Chicago: Nelson-Hall, 236-258.

———— (1995). "Contributions of an Unofficial Conflict Resolution Effort to the Israeli-Palestinian Breakthrough." *Negotiation Journal* 11: 19-27.

———— (1996a). "Negotiation as Interactive Problem Solving." *International Negotiation* 1: 99-123.

———— (1996b). "The Interactive Problem-Solving Approach." In *Managing Global Chaos: Sources of and Responses to International Conflict*, C. A. Crocker and F. O. Hampson with P. Aall, eds. Washington, D.C.: U.S. Institute of Peace, 501-519.

———— (1997a). "Group Processes in the Resolution of International Conflict: Experiences from the Israeli-Palestinian Case." *American Psychologist* 52: 212-220.

———— (1997b). "Social-Psychological Dimensions of International Conflict." In *Peacemaking in International Conflict: Methods and Techniques*, I. W. Zartman and J. L. Rasmussen, eds. Washington, D.C.: U.S. Institute of Peace, 191-237.

———— (1997c). "Some Determinants of the Oslo Breakthrough." *International Negotiation* 2: 183-194.

———— (1998). "Social-Psychological Contributions to Peacemaking and Peacebuilding in the Middle East." *Applied Psychology: An International Review* 47 (1): 5-28.

Kelman, H. C., and S. P. Cohen (1976). "The Problem-Solving Workshop: A Social-Psychological Contribution to the Resolution of International Conflict." *Journal of Peace Research* 13: 79-90.

Kelman, H. C., and S. P. Cohen (1986). "Resolution of International Conflict: An Interactional Approach." In *Psychology of Intergroup Relations*. 2nd ed. S. Worchel and W. G. Austin, eds. Chicago: Nelson-Hall, 323-342.

Keyton, J. (1993). "Group Termination: Completing the Study of Group Development." *Small Group Research* 24 (1): 84-100.

Klare, M. T., and Y. Chandrani (1998). *World Security: Challenges for a New Century*. 3rd ed. New York: St. Martin's.

Kohlberg, L. (1981). *Essays in Moral Development: The Philosophy of Moral Development*. New York: Harper and Row.

Kohlberg, L., F. A. Richards, T.A. Grotzer, and J. D. Sinnott, eds. (1990). *Adult Development, Vol. II: Models and Methods in the Study of Adolescent and Adult Thought*. New York: Praeger.

Kohlberg, L., and R. A. Ryncarz (1990). "Beyond Justice Reasoning: Moral Development and Consideration of a Seventh Stage." In *Higher Stages of Human Development: Perspectives on Adult Growth*, C. N. Alexander and E. J. Langer, eds. New York: Oxford University Press.

Kriesberg, L. (1996). "Coordinating Intermediate Peace Efforts." *Negotiation Journal* 12 (4): 341-352.

Kriesberg, L., and S. J. Thorson, eds. (1991). *Timing and the De-escalation of International Conflicts*. Syracuse, N.Y.: Syracuse University Press.

Lapidoth, R. (1997). *Autonomy*. Washington, D.C.: U.S. Institute of Peace.

Lederach, J. P. (1995). *Preparing for Peace: Conflict Transformation across Cultures*. Syracuse, N.Y.: Syracuse University Press.

———— (1997). *Building Peace: Sustainable Reconciliation in Divided Societies*. Washington, D.C.: U.S. Institute of Peace Press.

———— (1999). "Justpeace: The Challenges of the 21st Century." In *People Building Peace: 35 Inspiring Stories from Around the World*. European Center for Conflict Prevention, ed. Utrecht: European Center for Conflict Prevention, 27-36.

Lerner, M. J. (1980). *The Belief in a Just World*. New York: Plenum.

Lewicki, R. J. (1994). *Negotiations*. New York: Richard D. Irwin.

Lijphart, A. (1977). *Democracy in Plural Societies: A Comparative Exploration*. New Haven, Conn.: Yale University Press.

Lipset, S. M. (1981). "Economic Development and Democracy." In *Political Man: The Social Bases of Politics*. Baltimore, Md.: Johns Hopkins University Press.

Little, W., and C. Mitchell (1989). "The Maryland Workshops." In *In the Aftermath: Anglo-Argentine Relations since the War for the Falklands/Malvinas Islands*. W. Little and C. Mitchell, eds. College Park, Md.: Center for International Development and Conflict Management, University of Maryland, 3-11.

Lotter, H. P. P. (1993). *Justice for an Unjust Society*. Amsterdam: Rodopio.

Lund, M. S. (1996). *Preventing Violent Conflicts: A Strategy for Preventive Diplomacy*. Washington, D.C.: U.S. Institute of Peace Press.

Maoz, Z., and B. Russett (1993). "Normative and Structural Causes of Democratic Peace, 1946-1986." *American Political Science Review* 87 (3): 624-638.

Mason, L., C. N. Alexander, F. Travis, G. Marsh, D. W. Orme-Johnson, J. Gackenbach, D. Mason, M. Rainforth, and K. Walton (1997). "Electrophysiological Correlates of Higher States of Consciousness during Sleep." *Sleep* 20 (2): 102-110.

Mayer, B. (2000). *The Dynamics of Conflict Resolution: A Practitioner's Guide*. San Francisco: Jossey-Bass.

McDonald, J. W. (1991). "Further Exploration of Track Two Diplomacy." In *Timing and the De-escalation of International Conflicts*, L. Kriesberg and S. J. Thorson, eds. Syracuse, N.Y.: Syracuse University Press, 201-220.

McDonald, J. W., Jr., and D. B. Bendahmane, eds. (1987). *Conflict Resolution: Track Two Diplomacy*. Washington, D.C.: Foreign Service Institute.

Miller, A. *A Time to Remember*. Unpublished paper. Center for the Study of Violence and Reconciliation, South Africa.

Mitchell, C. R. (1966). *Cyprus Report*. London: Centre for the Analysis of Conflict.

────── (1973). "Conflict Resolution and Controlled Communication: Some Further Comments." *Journal of Peace Research* 10: 123-132.

────── (1981). *Peacemaking and the Consultant's Role*. Westmead, U.K.: Gower.

────── (2000). *Gestures of Conciliation: Factors Contributing to Successful Olive-Branches*. New York: St. Martin's.

Mitchell, C. R., and M. Banks (1996). *Handbook of Conflict Resolution: The Analytical Problem-Solving Approach*. London: Pinter-Cassell.

────── (1997). "Problem-Solving Exercises and Theories of Conflict Resolution." In *Conflict Resolution Theory and Practice: Integration and Applications*, D. J. Sandole and H. Van der Merwe, eds. New York: Manchester University Press, 78-94.

Montville, J. V. (1987). "The Arrow and the Olive Branch: A Case for Track Two Diplomacy." In *Conflict Resolution: Track Two Diplomacy*, J. W. McDonald, Jr. and D. B. Bendahmane, eds. Washington, D.C.: Foreign Service Institute, U.S. Department of State.

Montville, J. V. (1991). *Conflict and Peacemaking in Multiethnic Societies*. Lexington, Mass.: Lexington.

Moore, C. (2000). *The Mediation Process: Practical Strategies for Resolving Conflict*. San Francisco: Jossey-Bass.

Moses, R. (1996). "The Perception of the Enemy: A Psychological View." *Mind and Human Interaction* 7 (1): 37-43.

Niebuhr, H. R. (1941). *The Meaning of Revelation*. New York: Macmillan.

Notter, J., and L. Diamond (1996). *Building Peace and Transforming Conflict: Multi-Track Diplomacy in Practice*. Washington, D.C.: Institute for Multi-Track Diplomacy.

Offner, A. K., T. J. Kramer, and J. P. Winter (1996). "The Effects of Facilitation, Recording, and Pauses on Group Brainstorming." *Small Group Research* 27 (2): 283-298.

Orme-Johnson, D. W., C. N. Alexander, J. L. Davies, H. M. Chandler, and W. Larimore (1988). "Peace Project in the Middle East." *Journal of Conflict Resolution* 32: 776-812.

Piaget, J. (1971). "The Theory of Stages in Cognitive Development." In *Measurement and Piaget*. D. R. Green, M. P. Ford, and G. B. Flamer, eds. New York: McGraw-Hill.

Pearson, T. (1990). *The Role of "Symbolic Gestures" in Intergroup Conflict Resolution: Addressing Group Identity*. Unpublished Ph.D. dissertation, Harvard University.

Pettigrew, J. (1991). "Quaker Mediation." In *Peacemaking in a Troubled World*, T. Woodhouse, ed. Oxford, U.K.: Berg, 226-246.

Polzer, J. T. (1996). "Intergroup Negotiations: The Effects of Negotiating Teams." *Journal of Conflict Resolution* 40 (4): 678-699.

Powelson, J. P. (2001). *The Moral Economy*. Ann Arbor, Mich.: University of Michigan Press.

Preece, J. J. (1997). "National Minority Rights vs. State Sovereignty in Europe: Changing Norms in International Relations?" *Nations and Nationalism* 3 (3): 345-64.

Pritzker, D. S., and D. M. Dalton (1990). *Negotiated Rulemaking Sourcebook*. Washington, D.C.: U.S. Government Printing Office.

Pruitt, D. G., and P. J. Carnevale (1993). *Negotiation in Social Conflict*. Pacific Grove, Calif.: Brooks/Cole.

Putnam, R. D. (1993). *Making Democracy Work: Civic Traditions in Modern Italy*. Princeton, N.J.: Princeton University Press.

Regan, P. M. (1996). "Conditions of Successful Third-Party Intervention in Intrastate Conflict." *Journal of Conflict Resolution* 40 (2): 336-359.

Rest, J. R. (1986). *Moral Development: Advances in Research and Theory*. New York: Praeger.

Romer, P. (1986). "Increasing Returns and Long-Run Growth." *Journal of Political Economy* 94 (5): 1002-1037.

Rosenberg, M. B. (1983). *A Model for Nonviolent Communication*. Philadelphia: New Society Publishers–Mid-Atlantic MNS Network.

Ross, M. H., and J. Rothman, eds. (1999). *Theory and Practice in Ethnic Conflict Management: Theorizing Success and Failure*. New York: St. Martin's.

Rotblat, J. (1972). *Scientists in the Quest for Peace: A History of the Pugwash Conferences*. Cambridge, Mass: MIT Press.

Rothman, J. (1991). "Negotiation as Consolidation: Prenegotiation in the Israeli-Palestinian Conflict." *The Jerusalem Journal of International Relations* 13 (1): 22-44.

———— (1992). *Confrontation to Cooperation: Resolving Ethnic and Regional Conflict*. Newbury Park, Calif.: Sage.

———— (1997a). "Action Evaluation and Conflict Resolution in Theory and Practice." *Mediation Quarterly* 15 (2): 119-131.

———— (1997b). "Action Evaluation and Conflict Resolution Training: Theory, Method and Case Study." *International Negotiation* 2: 451-470.

———— (1997c). *Resolving Identity-Based Conflict*. San Francisco: Jossey-Bass.

Rouhana, N. N. (1995). "The Dynamics of Joint Thinking Between Adversaries in International Conflict—Phases of the Continuing Problem-Solving Workshop." *Political Psychology* 16 (2): 321-345.

Rouhana, N. N., and H. C. Kelman (1994). "Promoting Joint Thinking in International Conflicts—An Israeli-Palestinian Continuing Workshop." *Journal of Social Issues* 50 (1): 157-178.

Rubin, J. Z., D. G. Pruitt, and S. H. Kim (1994). *Social Conflict: Escalation, Stalemate, and Settlement*. 2nd ed. New York: McGraw-Hill.

Rwelamira, M. R., and G. Werle, eds. (1996). *Confronting Past Injustices*. Durban, South Africa: Butterworths.

Samovar, L., and R. Porter (1972). *Intercultural Communication: A Reader*. Belmont, Calif.: Wadsworth.

Sandole, D. J. D. (1991). "Institutionalizing Conflict Resolution: The First Decade." *ICAR Newsletter* 4 (2): 1, 3-5.

Saunders, H. H (1988). "The Arab-Israeli Conflict in a Global Perspective." In *Restructuring American Foreign Policy*, J. D. Steinbruner, ed. Washington, D.C.: Brookings Institution, 221-251.

———— (1991a). "An Historic Challenge to Rethink How Nations Relate." In *The Psychodynamics of International Relationships, Vol. I: Concepts and Theories*, V. D. Volkan, D. A. Julius, and J. V. Montville, eds. Lexington, Mass.: Lexington, 1-30.

———— (1991b). "Officials and Citizens in International Relationships: The Dartmouth Conference." In *The Psychodynamics of International Relationships, Vol. II: Unofficial Diplomacy at Work*, V. D. Volkan, D. A. Julius, and J. V. Montville, eds. Lexington, Mass.: Lexington, 41-69.

———— (1998). *A Public Peace Process*. New York: St. Martin's.

Saunders, H. H., and R. Slim (1994). "Dialogue to Change Conflictual Relationships." *Higher Education Exchange*: 43-56.

Schmookler, A. B. (1988). *Out of Weakness*. New York: Bantam.

Seagal, S., and D. Home (1990). *Individual and Team Empowerment*. Tel Aviv: Human Dynamics.

Sharp, G. (1973). *Politics of Nonviolent Action*. Boston: P. Sargent.

Sharp, G., and R. McCarthy (1997). *Nonviolent Action: A Research Guide*. New York: Garland.

Shriver, D. W., Jr. (1995). *An Ethics for Enemies*. New York: Oxford University Press.

Simpson, G., and P. van Zyl (1995). "South Africa's Truth and Reconciliation Commission." Johannesburg, South Africa: Centre for the Study of Violence and Reconciliation.

Singer, M., and A. Wildavsky (1993). *The Real World Order—Zones of Peace, Zones of Turmoil*. London: Chatham House.

Slim, R. M. (1995). "A Framework for Managing Conflict in Divided Societies: The Tajikistan Case Study." Paper presented at the Annual Scientific Meeting of the International Society of Political Psychology, July. Washington, D.C.

———— (1998). "The Nexus between Interactive Conflict Resolution and Building Civil Society: Implications for Training." Paper presented at the Annual Scientific Meeting of the International Society of Political Psychology, July. Montreal, Canada.

State Failure Task Force (1999). "State Failure Task Force Report: Phase II Findings." *Environmental Change and Security Project Report of the Woodrow Wilson Center* 5 (Summer): 49-72.

Stein, J. G. (1989). *Getting to the Table: The Processes of International Prenegotiation*. Baltimore: Johns Hopkins University Press.

Stewart, P. (1987). "The Dartmouth Conference: U.S.-U.S.S.R. Relations." In *Conflict Resolution: Track Two Diplomacy*, J. W. McDonald, Jr. and D. B. Bendahmane, eds. Washington, D.C.: Foreign Service Institute, U.S. Department of State, 21-26.

Susskind, L., and J. Cruikshank (1987). *Breaking the Impasse: Consensual Approaches to Resolving Public Disputes*. New York: Basic Books.

Tajfel, H., and J. C. Turner (1986). "The Social Identity Theory of Human Behavior." In *Psychology of Intergroup Relations,* S. Worchel and W. G. Austin, eds. Chicago: Nelson-Hall.

Triandis, H. C., and M. J. Gelfand (1998). "Converging Measurement of Horizontal and Vertical Individualism and Collectivism." *Journal of Personality and Social Psychology* 74 (1): 118-128.

Trompenaars, F. (1994). *Riding the Waves of Culture: Understanding Diversity in Global Business.* Burr Ridge, Ill.: Irwin.

Truth and Reconciliation Commission (1998). *Final Report.* Juta, Johannesburg.

Tutu, D. (1999). *No Future without Forgiveness.* New York: Doubleday.

UNICEF (1997). *Education for Conflict Resolution: A Training for Trainers Manual.* New York: Education for Development.

Ury, W. L. (1998). *Getting to Peace.* New York: St. Martin's.

Ury, W. L., J. M. Brett, and S. B. Goldberg (1988). *Getting Disputes Resolved.* San Francisco: Jossey-Bass.

Van der Merwe, H. W. (1999). *The Truth and Reconciliation Commission and Community Reconciliation: An Analysis of Competing Strategies and Conceptualizations.* Unpublished Ph.D. dissertation, George Mason University.

Verwoerd, W. (1997). *Justice after Apartheid? Reflections on the South African Truth and Reconciliation Commission.* A paper delivered at the Fifth International Conference on Ethics and Development, 2-9 January, Madras, India.

Volkan, V.D. (1985). *Depressive States and Their Treatment.* Northvale, N.J.: Jason Aronson

Volkan, V. D. (1988). *The Need to Have Enemies and Allies: From Clinical Practice to International Relationships.* Northvale, N.J.: Jason Aronson.

Volkan, V. D., and M. Harris (1992). "Negotiating a Peaceful Separation: A Psycho-political Analysis of Current Relationships between Russia and the Baltic Republics." *Mind and Human Interaction* 1 (1): 20-39.

———— (1993). "Vaccinating the Political Process: A Second Psychopolitical Analysis of Relationships Between Russia and the Baltic States." *Mind and Human Interaction* 4 (4): 169-190.

Volkan, V. D., D. A. Julius, and J. V. Montville, eds. (1991). *The Psychodynamics of International Relationships, Vol. II: Unofficial Diplomacy at Work.* Lexington, Mass.: Lexington.

Walton, R. E. (1969). *Interpersonal Peacemaking: Confrontations and Third Party Consultation.* Reading, Mass: Addison-Wesley.

Wedge, B. (1970). "A Psychiatric Model for Intercession in Intergroup Conflict." *Journal of Applied Behavioral Science* 6: 733-761.

———— (1983). "Peacemaking." *Psychiatric Annals* 13 (2): 135-137, 140-141, 144.

———— (1987). "Mediating Intergroup Conflict in the Dominican Republic." In *Conflict Resolution: Track Two Diplomacy,* J. W. McDonald, Jr. and D. B. Bendahmane, eds. Washington, D.C.: Foreign Service Institute, U.S. Department of State, 35-52.

White, R. K. (1965). "Images in the Context of International Conflict: Soviet Perceptions of the U.S. and the U.S.S.R." In *International Behavior: A Social-Psychological Analysis,* H. C. Kelman, ed. New York: Holt, Rinehart and Winston, 238-276.

Wilmer, F. (1993). *The Indigenous Voice in World Politics: Since Time Immemorial.* Newbury Park, Calif.: Sage.

Wimmer, A. M. (1994). "The Jolly Mediator: Some Serious Thoughts about Humor." *Negotiation Journal* 10 (3): 193-200.

Winslow, T. (1997). "Reconciliation: The Road to Healing." *Track Two: Constructive Approaches to Community and Political Conflict* 6 (3 and 4).

Yarrow, C. H. M. (1978). *Quaker Experiences in International Conciliation*. New Haven, Conn.: Yale University Press.

Zartman, W. I., ed. (1995). *Elusive Peace: Negotiating an End to Civil Wars*. Washington, D.C.: Brookings Institution.

Zartman, W. I., and S. Touval (1985). *International Mediation in Theory and Practice*. Boulder, Colo.: Westview.

Index

About the Contributors

Eileen R. Borris is founding President of Peace Initiatives, a non-profit organization that promotes peacemaking and conflict resolution. She is a trainer for the Institute for Multi-Track Diplomacy in Washington, D.C., and is on the Board of Directors of the Peace Psychology Division of the American Psychological Association.

John Davies is Co-Director of the Partners in Conflict Project and Senior Research Associate at the Center for International Development and Conflict Management, University of Maryland. He is a recent Board Member of the Forum on Early Warning and Early Response and consultant to the U.S. government's State Failure Task Force.

Ronald J. Fisher is a Professor of International Peace and Conflict Resolution in the School of International Service at American University, Washington, D.C. Previously he was Professor of Psychology and Founding Co-ordinator of the Applied Social Psychology Graduate Program at the University of Saskatchewan, Saskatoon, Canada.

Victor J. Friedman is Senior Lecturer in Organizational Behavior at the Ruppin Institute, Israel, and Senior Researcher with the Action Evaluation Research Institute Yellow Springs, Ohio.

Ted Robert Gurr is Distinguished University Professor at the University of Maryland, College Park, and directs the Minorities at Risk Project, which tracks the status and activities of over 300 communal groups world-wide, providing analytical data on the causes and management of ethnopolitical conflict. From 1994 to 2000 he was senior consultant to the U.S. government's State Failure Task Force.

Edward (Edy) Kaufman is the Executive Director of the Harry S. Truman Institute for the Advancement of Peace, the Hebrew University of Jerusalem, Senior Research Associate (and former Director) of the Center for International Development and Conflict Management, University of Maryland and Visiting Associate Professor of Government and Politics, University of Maryland.

Herbert C. Kelman is the Richard Clarke Cabot Research Professor of Social Ethics at Harvard University and Director of the Program on International Conflict Analysis and Resolution at Harvard's Weatherhead Center for International Affairs.

John W. McDonald, a U.S. diplomat for 40 years, wrote the first book on track two diplomacy in 1985, co-authored the first book on multi-track diplomacy with Louise Diamond in 1991, and co-founded the Institute for

Multi-Track Diplomacy in 1992. The Institute takes a systems approach to peace and has its focus on international ethnic conflict.

Christopher Moore is a Partner at CDR Associates, an international consulting firm in Boulder, Colorado, that provides professional decision-making, organizational consulting, public participation, and conflict management assistance to public, private, and non-governmental sectors.

Jay Rothman is President of the ARIA Group, Inc. a conflict resolution training and consulting company. He is also founder and Research Director of the Action Evaluation Research Institute, which provides research, training, and technical assistance in action research, and Scholar-in-Residence at the McGregor School of Antioch University.

Andrea Strimling is Commissioner for International and Dispute Resolution Services with the Federal Mediation and Conciliation Service, an independent agency of the U.S. government based in Washington, D.C.

Peter Woodrow is the Program Director for CDR Associates, an international consulting firm in Boulder, Colorado, that provides professional decision-making, organizational consulting, public participation, and conflict management assistance to public, private, and non-governmental sectors.